Barbarians, Gentlemen and Players, Second Edition

First published in 1979 this classic text was the first study of the development of Rugby and has a seminal place in the library of the history and sociology of sport. With a new foreword and a new afterword, Dunning and Sheard now provide a sociological analysis of the major developments that have taken place in Rugby since the 1980s, with particular attention to the professionalism that was predicted in the first edition of this text.

Rugby football is descended from a deeply rooted tradition of winter 'folk games' in pre-industrial Britain. Folk forms of the game were extremely violent and serious injuries – even death – were common features. The game was later refined in the public schools and with the spread of Rugby into the wider society the Rugby Football Union was founded to provide a national rule-making body. Class and regional tensions led to a split between 'Union' and 'League' and the text relates these important changes to developments in the wider structure of British society.

Barbarians, Gentlemen and Players, Second Edition will be an invaluable resource for sports lovers, rugby fans and students of the history and sociology of sport.

Eric Dunning was, until recently, a Senior Director of the Centre for Research Into Sport and Society (CRSS) at the University of Leicester, UK. Now retired, he remains Emeritus Professor at the University of Leicester and is also Visiting Professor at University College Dublin. A pioneer of the sociology of sport, he is also a founder of the Sir Norman Chester Centre for Football Research and the author of *Sport Matters*.

Kenneth Sheard is former Research Director at the Centre for Research Into Sport and Society (CRSS) at the University of Leicester, UK.

Barbarians, Gentlemen and Players, Second Edition

A sociological study of the development of rugby football

Eric Dunning and Kenneth Sheard

Routledge
Taylor & Francis Group

LONDON AND NEW YORK

First published 2005 by Routledge, an imprint of Taylor & Francis
2 Park Square, Milton Park, Abingdon, Oxon, OX14 4RN

Simultaneously published in the USA and Canada
by Taylor & Francis Inc
270 Madison Ave, New York, NY 10016

Routledge is an imprint of the Taylor & Francis Group

© 1979, 2005 Eric Dunning and Kenneth Sheard

Typeset in Goudy by RefineCatch Ltd, Bungay, Suffolk
Printed and bound in Great Britain by
TJ International Ltd, Padstow, Cornwall

British Library Cataloguing in Publication Data
A catalogue record for this book is available
from the British Library

Library of Congress Cataloging-in-Publication Data
Dunning, Eric.
    Barbarians, gentlemen, and players : a sociological study of the
development of rugby football/Eric Dunning and Kenneth Sheard.–
2nd ed.
        p. cm.—(Sport in the global society)
    Previous ed. : Oxford, England : M. Robertson, 1979.
    Includes bibliographical references and index.
    ISBN 0-7146-5353-5—ISBN 0-7146-8290-X (pbk.) 1. Rugby
football—Social aspects. I. Sheard, Kenneth. II. Title. III. Series.
    GV945.85.S65D86 2005
    796.333—dc22
                                                    2004050936

ISBN 0–714–65353–5 (hbk)
ISBN 0–714–68290–X (pbk)

Contents

PART III
The Development of Rugby Football as a Modern Sport   171

Series Editor's Foreword

Barbarians, Gentlemen and Players, as the authors gently remind us in their Afterword to this second edition, was a pioneering work. In 1979 Eric Dunning and Kenneth Sheard viewed the development of rugby football 'as a sociological problem'. While some academics, especially historians, might consider this approach to be a case of scholastic *lèse-majesté*, it resulted in an irradiant analysis of the game. In Sports Studies, Dunning and Sheard proved to be early sociological *maîtres à penser*.

In reality, their then innovative inquiry deals with an essentially English 'sociological problem'.

The actuality has been that, 'for over a thousand years, England has been the largest and most powerful state in the British Isles. It was always and to an increasing extent the most populous part. In 1801 England contributed over half the population of the United Kingdom: today the English make up more than four-fifths.'[1] In consequence, much of the earlier action on and off rugby pitches took place in England; the impetus that drove the development of the union game in its early years originated largely on late-Victorian public school playing fields and on the open spaces of their period 'finishing schools': Oxford and Cambridge. Today English rugby still sets the pace in Britain.

In *Barbarians*, in the face of the deafening volume of criticism over the years of the too frequent obtuseness, clumsiness and unreadability of the 'language' of sociology, Dunning and Sheard offer a defiant apologia for sociological 'jargon' as a linguistic instrument of professional precision. Many anguished academics and students will feelingly remark: 'If only!' Pretentious is not a synonym for precise. To his credit, however, Dunning is among the more accessible writers in his discipline. In this he sets an example; surely one reason for the sustained interest in *Barbarians*.

Dunning and Sheard consider in passing the growth of cricket and soccer. This should not be overlooked. Their interest has been responsible in part for at least one highly original investigation into the origins of association football.[2]

Barbarians, their alarum to the 1980s sociologists, also encouraged social anthropologists and historians to consider the then neglected subject of sport. If a personal comment may be permitted, I am one with feet in both disciplines who can assure the authors that their awakening call to academics was not ignored.[3] Thus, due to them *inter alios* (especially historians), sport is anything but neglected now in global academia. Happily too, historical studies of sport have long utilized judiciously the concepts of sociology and social anthropology. And did so hard on the heels of Dunning and Sheard.[4] Hence the emergence in Sports Studies, as elsewhere, of the New Historian.

To act briefly as an *amicus curiae*, in so large a canvas as *Barbarians*, understandably, the paint is more thickly applied in some places than others. It is helpful, therefore, to add the odd layer in the interests of even application. Rugby football was one of the means by which the public school house system was successfully utilized as a crucial instrument of control in the post-Cotton of Marlborough years. This revamped house system was a brilliant tool of social engineering; it helped ensure the survival and expansion of the schools at a time when they were assailed by middle-class critics; and it was a drag anchor against anarchy.[5] The fagging system came a distant second to the house system as a source of the game's expansion in the schools. Post 1851 the house system was a cornerstone, with its heavy reliance on team games, which ensured the structural stability of the public school edifice.

Barbarians is a confident and controversial work. It is a bold composition; more Beethoven than Bach. Arguably this is its greatest asset. It still challenges historians and sociologists; for them, in recent years, 'Boots and Saddles' has replaced 'Reveille'; it provokes their frontal and flanking attacks. As the authors' 2004 Afterword makes clear, it has stimulated extensive comment in the 'groves of academe'. In their Afterword also, the authors sound a note of measured optimism. They suggest with satisfaction that 'both figurational sociologists and hegemonic theorists', now advocate a historical approach among other things, lay stress on the importance of power in social relations and take the view that history is often made by those who inherit unacceptable pasts. Most importantly, the authors acknowledge that the marshalling of detailed historical evidence makes for meaningful sociological theory.

A final comment; Dunning and Sheard have unearthed a superb quotation from Anthony Trollope:

> (Sports) are being made too much of . . . All this comes from excess of enthusiasm on the matter; from a desire to follow too well a pursuit which, to be pleasurable, should be a pleasure and not a business . . . (This) is the rock against which our Sports may possibly be made shipwreck. Should it ever become unreasonable in its expenditure, arrogant in its demands, immoral and selfish in its tendencies or, worse of all, unclean and dishonest in its traffic, there will arise against it a public opinion against which it will be unable to hold its own.[6]

No sign of this yet; indeed things have got much worse since 1868! Norbert Elias has apparently anticipated, but surely would not be pleased with, this uncivilized turn of events.[7]

Barbarians is a work that should rightly endure; a rubric on which the authors' reputation should securely rest. I take pleasure in its republication in Sport in the Global Society.[8]

J. A. Mangan
Swanage, August 2004

Preface to the Second Edition

The original publication of *Barbarians, Gentlemen and Players* in 1979 was, for me, perfectly timed. It was the year in which I began my Ph.D. The thesis concerned the emergence of football hooliganism as a social problem. As such, *Barbarians, Gentlemen and Players* formed a template: it provided vital clues in understanding the making of modern sport; it made available a theoretical framework which could help in making sense of the evidence I began to gather; and, via the craft demonstrated throughout the book, it conveyed important messages about what constitutes good sociology. While its impact has remained with me throughout my own research career, I am not alone in recognizing that the work stands the test of time.

And yet, its impact could have been much greater. It was not marketed that well. Originally published by Martin Robertson [I have never asked why?], I am fortunate to have a copy of this and also the version released in North America by New York University Press. In the cover jacket of the latter, Dunning and Sheard note:

> Sociological analysis of these developments should, accordingly, reveal why it is difficult if not impossible under modern social conditions to retain forms of sport that are consistent with amateur ideals.

Within a decade, as Dunning and Sheard had concluded, amateur rugby union had indeed given way to the professional game. The book, contra some critics arguments about the lack of analysis of the commercialization of sport, was always as much about such developments as it was about tracing the civilizing processes associated with violence production and consumption. Yet, the detailed research in the book, and what Rick Gruneau (1983: p. 102) termed the 'masterful' reasoning could not prevent the inaugural Rugby Union World Cup in 1991 being named after William Webb Ellis, nor stop the RFU marketing people inviting the media to witness a staged re-enactment of the supposed first act in the making of rugby football. One of the many discoveries of *Barbarians, Gentlemen and Players* was that the story of the involvement of William Webb Ellis was a myth, constructed some 70 years after the alleged act of Webb Ellis. Such origin myths, we were later to write, 'are a kind of sports equivalent of the belief in the tooth fairy or Father Christmas' (Dunning *et al.* 1991).

Despite the poor marketing of the book, it has become well known, it is widely cited, and usually praised, even by critics of the sociological perspective that underpins the work. Taken up, as noted, by process sociologists such as myself, and others, *Barbarians, Gentlemen and Players* has also been used to support research done by Marxists, exponents of cultural studies, and feminists. Historians and anthropologists have also been drawn to the work – indeed, it was intended that that should be so. It is always odd, however, that they are drawn to the supposed historical aspects, when the full title of the book makes clear that it is a sociological study of the development of football.

A glance at Pierre Bourdieu's work on sport also reveals the impact that the book, and indeed the work of Norbert Elias more generally, had on his reasoning. *Barbarians, Gentlemen and Players* also stimulated specific case studies on rugby union in New Zealand by Rex Thompson and in South Africa by Gary Boshoff. Reflecting on his own significant contribution to sociology of sport, Rick Gruneau, while critical of aspects of figurational sociology, was also generous with his praise, noting how the book 'had influenced my thinking a great deal' (Gruneau, 1999: p. 121). I don't think Rick is alone, but perhaps others have been less public in acknowledging their debt.

Such comments are, in some small measure, testimony to the impact of *Barbarians, Gentlemen and Players*. Back in the early 1980s it was, I remember, a 'must read' book – hard perhaps to convey to younger scholars of this generation. Yet, to my mind, it remains, a 'must read' book. This is because *Barbarians, Gentlemen and Players* meets the hallmarks of what constitutes 'good sociology'. That is, as I note in *Theory, Sport & Society*, (Maguire & Young, 2002: p. 14), the concepts of precision, systematics, scope and relevance underpin the craft of doing good sociology. *Barbarians, Gentlemen and Players* expresses these qualities in an exemplary manner. The craft of sociological enquiry involves a set of tools for the production of knowledge. Researchers are confronted with several problems: of the blend between theory and evidence; of the issues associated with involvement and detachment; of the adequacy of evidence; and, of explaining and going public with their findings. Whichever sociological perspective a student follows, by reading books like *Barbarians, Gentlemen and Players*, she/he is better equipped to grasp the craft of doing good sociology. By conceiving of the book as a 'critical case-study' to test specific sociological concepts, *Barbarians, Gentlemen and Players* signals the shift away from sport sociology towards sociology of sport.

From an Eliasian perspective, the final word is never produced. The book could, and should, have spelt out the sociological perspective and concepts more fully. Further, perhaps a greater engagement with critics, seeking common ground, as well as seeing off the ill-informed, might have enhanced the appeal of the perspective that lies behind the book. Finally, it is a shame that developments since the book was originally published have not been fully explored in the same manner and depth as the earlier periods. That task still remains to be done. Perhaps, with the re-publication of this classic, a new generation of students will take up the challenge and be inspired as I was some 25 years ago.

Preface to the First Edition

As our subtitle says, *Barbarians, Gentlemen and Players* is a *sociological* study. We hope that it will appeal, not simply to professional sociologists and their students, but to a wider readership as well. However, since the aims and objects of sociology are not widely understood and since there is not even consensus among sociologists themselves on the nature of the subject, we shall say a few words in this preface about some of the basic assumptions that have guided us in our writing of the book.

A former President of the Rugby Football Union who helped us greatly at the beginning of our research, wrote to us that a sociological study of Rugby might 'deprive the game of some of its charm'. He even doubted whether it is any easier to analyse 'a game that has gradually evolved over 150 years' than it is 'to put Mozart and Monet into words'. We understand his feelings. We do not wish to minimize the difficulties posed by the sociological study of Rugby or to deny that, like the arts, sports have aspects that a poet, novelist or journalist would be better-equipped than a sociologist to express. Yet this is not to say that it is impossible to analyse Rugby sociologically for, like other institutions, sports are amenable to detached analysis. And that, put at its simplest, is what a sociological study consists of: it is an attempt to free oneself from the interests and values of particular groups and to study something dispassionately and objectively, i.e. in a frame of mind similar to that of the physicist when he studies atoms or of the biochemist when he studies DNA. And the object of a detached study of that sort is to present an unbiased picture, an account of the subject studied that portrays it 'as it really is', in that way hoping to add to knowledge.

It would be unnecessary to state this if sociology were not currently under attack. Yet, in Britain at least, the subject is not firmly rooted, and the critical chorus that was relatively silent during the expansion of the 1960s and early 1970s, seems to be rising again. The aspect of sociology that is most often singled out for attack is its technical language or, as most critics would put it, its 'barbarous jargon'. It will help to set the matter straight, therefore, if we explainsome of the technical language to be found in this book. Such a discussion may help to clarify why, as sociologists, we feel we need a special language and why some of the terms we use take the form that they do.

It is generally the case that specialized groups develop a language of their own. Doctors and lawyers do it and so, even though they seem unaware of it, do the 'literati' who figure prominently in the attack on 'sociological jargon'. The reason why is very simple: such language serves as a means of expressing common experiences and common goals and, especially in the case of groups whose task is scientific, of communicating ideas and findings more precisely than is possible using 'ordinary' language. At the same time, a specialized language can serve as a means of social control, e.g. of distinguishing between 'insiders' and 'outsiders' in order to facilitate the exclusion of the latter. In our view use of technical terms to facilitate precise communication is legitimate and valuable scientifically. Their use as a means of social exclusion is not.

The fact that sociologists are not the only group who use 'jargon', yet seem to be singled out for attack on this score more frequently than, e.g. doctors and lawyers, is at first glance rather puzzling. It could have something to do with the fact that sociologists attempt to study people and the societies they form, scientifically, i.e. in a detached, dispassionate or objective frame of mind. If that is so, it may be that we are attacked because we are perceived as equating human beings with molecules and atoms and, hence, at best, as using misplaced methods and, at worst, as posing a threat to human dignity. We do not wish to deny that there are sociologists who attempt to study human societies using methods more appropriate to physics, or others who attempt to invest their work with an aura of 'scientificity' by using abstruse jargon. But they are under attack within the subject and, in this book, we have applied the methods of Norbert Elias, a sociologist who, in our view, has done more than most to develop an approach to sociology that is both scientific and appropriate to the study of human beings. Let us, therefore, say a word or two about our use of Elias' approach.

Elias' approach to sociology is based on the twin observations that human societies are structured and that they change over time. Hence our technical language-our 'jargon' if you like-is attuned to these observations. As we use it, the term 'social configuration' refers to the structures or patterns formed by interdependent human beings, and our use of terms ending in the suffix 'ization', refers to the processual aspect of these configurations, to the fact that they, or aspects of them, change over time. Hence our frequent use of terms like 'industrialization', 'urbanization', 'modernization', 'civilization', 'professionalization', 'monetization', and 'democratization'. We realize that such terms are inelegant but can think of no more precise or economical way of conveying the idea of process, i.e. of something that is changing over time. Thus when we use, e.g. the term 'civilization', we are using it in its processual rather than its static sense to refer to a society or group that is not 'civilized' in an absolute sense but has grown 'more civilized' over time. In fact, we follow Elias' usage in this connection and refer to the 'civilizing process' rather than to 'civilization'. Similarly, when we use the term 'democratization', we are not trying to use a more complex and abstruse term than 'democracy' but referring to a process in which a society or group becomes 'more democratic' over time or, to express it more precisely, in which the balance of power within and among groups becomes less unequal. All the other terms in our book ending with the suffix, 'ization', are similarly used with a processual connotation.

'Configurational' and 'process' terms, then, are central to our sociological perspective. As a result, we have been unable to avoid then. In other respects, however, we have tried to write a book that will be readily understandable to a readership of non-sociologists. That is, we have tried not to make a complex subject seem more complex than it is by the use of unnecessarily complex language. We hope we have succeeded since it is our experience that a sociological understanding of the structure and development of Rugby has enhanced our enjoyment of it and we hope that our book may help others to share this experience. We also hope that our analysis may play a part in helping to resolve some of the tensions and conflicts by which Rugby is currently beset, more swiftly and more amicably than might otherwise be the case.

However, our book is not aimed simply at a readership of sociologists and Rugby devotees. We have dealt at some length with the development of cricket and soccer, and we believe that our analysis of amateurism and professionalism is relevant to the development of modern sport more generally, not just in Britain but in countries all over the world. Our analysis of the relationship between the development of Rugby and that of British society, particularly its class structure, may also be of wider interest. So, too, may our analysis of what we have called 'the crisis in modern sport'. We also hope that our study will encourage others, historians and anthropologists as well as sociologists, to undertake research in the neglected area of sport.

One does not need to be a sociologist in order to realize that a book is not only an individual but also a social product. That is the case with *Barbarians, Gentlemen and Players*, not simply because two of us have written it but also because our task would have been impossible without the help of numerous other people. Accordingly, we would like to take this opportunity to thank them. Academic help and stimulation have come so obviously from Norbert Elias that it would be superfluous to say more about it here. Our debt to him is immense and we should like to record our pleasure at the fact that his work is now beginning to be accorded the recognition that it should, in our view, have been granted years ago. Our colleagues in the Departments of Sociology at the University of Leicester and the Cambridgeshire College of Arts and Technology deserve thanks, too, but special mention must go to Al Wesson, our visiting fellow from Brown University in the USA, to David Mason, Joe and Olive Banks, Clive Ashworth and Tony Bilton. Earl Hopper of the London School of Economics and Derek Deadman of the Department of Economics at Leicester helped us greatly, too, and Judy Dunning and Janet Sheard, besides offering valuable comments on the text and providing moral, and emotional support, helped us throughout in ways that only we can know.

In the Rugby Union world, we should like to thank Dr T. A. Kemp and R. A. Kingswell for the help and support they gave us when we conducted our survey of present-day clubs and players. And, although they are too numerous to mention by name, we should also like to thank the players and club and Rugby Union officials who replied to our questionnaires. We are most grateful for their help. Thanks are also due to Bill Fallowfield, former Secretary of the Rugby League; to the editor and staff of the *Rugby Leaguer*; to the late A. N. Gaulton, editor of *The Rugby League Magazine*; and to Austin E. Birch and Miss K. lbbotson, Hon. Secretary of the Hull and District branch of the Rugby League Ex-Players' Association.

Finally, we must record our debt to the secretarial staff in the Department of Sociology at the University of Leicester. Doreen Butler, June Lee and Maureen Thompson were all involved in typing the manuscript at various times. But special thanks are due to Audrey Craig, on whom the onerous burden of typing the penultimate and final drafts fell. She helped on several occasions to prevent our footnotes from going astray and will one day, we are sure, be justly famous for the poem about Rugby that our study led her to compose.

For Julia, Michael, Rachel, Jenny,
Eleanor and Norma

Why do your young men behave like this, Solon? Some of them grappling and tripping each other, some throttling, struggling, intertwining in the mud like so many pigs wallowing . . . they put down their heads and begin to push, and crash their foreheads together like a pair of rival rams . . . Now I want to know what is the good of it all. To me it looks more like madness than anything else . . . I'm still more astonished at the spectators. You tell me the chief people from all over Greece attend. How can they leave their serious concerns and waste time on such things? How they can like it passes my comprehension—to look on people being struck and knocked about, dashed to the ground and pounded by one another.

Lucian of Samosata, *Anacharsis: On Physical Exercise* (second century AD)

[Sports] are being made too much of, and men who follow them have allowed themselves to be taught that ordinary success in them is not worth having . . . All this comes from excess of enthusiasm on the matter;—from a desire to follow too well a pursuit which, to be pleasurable, should be a pleasure and not a business . . . [This] is the rock against which our Sports may possibly be made shipwreck. Should it ever become unreasonable in its expenditure, arrogant in its demands, immoral and selfish in its tendencies, or, worse of all, unclean and dishonest in its traffic, there will arise against it a public opinion against which it will be unable to hold its own.

Anthony Trollope, *British Sports and Pastimes* (1868)

Introduction

The Development of Rugby Football as a Sociological Problem

1. The subject of this book is the development of Rugby football. We have attempted to explain this process by relating it to changes in the wider social structure. Our approach can be described as 'developmental'. Since such an approach does not slot neatly into the present division of academic labour, we shall start by saying a word or two about it. It differs from that of the conventional sociologist in the sense that we are concerned with a long-term social process. It also differs from that of the conventional historian in that we bring sociological concepts explicitly to bear on the task of explanation, and our concerns are theoretical and not simply empirical. It will probably help the reader to understand the specific character of this approach if we give a brief résumé of the stages through which Rugby passed in developing its modern forms. Such a discussion will enable us to clarify some of the conceptual problems that a 'developmental' approach entails and prepare the way for a consideration of the theoretical issues towards which our study is directed.

Along with 'soccer', Rugby is descended from the winter 'folk-games' which were a deeply-rooted tradition in pre-industrial Britain. Five main stages in the development of the two modern forms of football can be distinguished, each of them characterized by more elaborate behaviour and more complex, more formal rules and organization than its predecessor. Except in the case of the transition between stages one and two, each stage also involved the demand for behaviour which was more orderly and restrained than that of the one preceding it. And the transition between the first and second stages, and that between the third and fourth, involved changes in the social context of the game which proved significant for its further development.

A central aspect of this overall process was the gradual emergence of Rugby and soccer out of the general folk tradition as distinctive games. Both of them came subsequently to replace their folk-antecedents, spreading as they did so and undergoing processes of 'democratization'. That, in its turn, led them to experience pressure to develop as professional sports. More concretely, the stages in the development of modern football were:

(i)   a stage which lasted from at least the fourteenth into the twentieth century when 'football' was the name given to some among a whole class of folk-games. Such games were relatively simple, wild and unruly, and played according to unwritten rules. Considerable local variation existed within the overall pattern of the game at that stage. It represented, nevertheless, the 'common matrix' from which Rugby and soccer are descended;

(ii)   a stage which lasted from about 1750 to about 1840 when the folk-antecedents of modern football were taken up by boys in the public schools, elaborated in certain respects and adapted to their characteristic forms of social organization, in particular to the 'prefect-fagging' system, the peculiar system of authority relations which grew up in such schools. It was at that stage that Rugby began to emerge as a distinctive game;

(iii) a stage of rapid transition which lasted from about 1830 to about 1860 when the game in the public schools began to be subjected to more stringent and formal regulation, when the rules grew more elaborate and were, for the first time, written down—it was at Rugby School in 1845 where this first occurred—and when footballers were required to exercise greater self-control. It was at that stage—the stage of 'incipient modernization'—that soccer began to emerge as a distinctive game;

(iv)   a stage which lasted from about 1850 to about 1900 when football in its public-school forms spread into society at large and when independent clubs came to form its principal social setting. It was at this stage that national associations—the Rugby Football Union and the Football Association—were set up in order to organize football on a national level, in that way consolidating nationally the two distinct games which had begun to emerge in the public schools. Soon after the formation of these associations, Rugby and soccer began to attract paying spectators and the possibility emerged for men to 'work' as full-time players. Accordingly, it was also at this stage, the last in the pre-modern development of the game, that Rugby split into the amateur game of 'Rugby Union' and the professional game of 'Rugby League';

(v)   a stage which lasted from about 1900 to the present day. In Rugby League, it involved the gradual working out of rules, organizational forms and career patterns appropriate for a professional sport. Rugby League, however, has not met with conspicuous success in any of these regards. It remains confined to a few Northern counties and has never become capable of sustaining career opportunities for more than a handful. Most of its players are, and always have been, 'semi-' rather than 'full' professionals. By contrast, Rugby Union, after having to cope in the period immediately following the 'split' (after 1895) with diminished support and curtailed funds, has successfully expanded nationally as a sport ostensibly based on firm amateur principles. However, during the 1960s, largely in conjunction with the success of its expansion, it began to experience renewed pressure to transform itself, if not into a sport in which professionalism, i.e. the payment of money wages to players, is legitimate, then into one containing a syndrome of characteristics normally associated with professional rather than amateur sport, e.g. success-striving, formal competition and financial dependence on spectators. The growing crisis created by these pressures resembles in some respects that which led in the 1890s to the split between Union and League.

2. Our title, *Barbarians, Gentlemen and Players*, is meant to convey something of the flavour of these stages, more particularly of the growing demand for orderliness and the conflicts over amateurism and professionalism which Rugby experienced during the period covered by our study. A word about the concept of stages is probably in order at this point.

These stages in the development of Rugby were not stages in an 'evolutionary' process in the sense that each was 'immanent in' or grew 'automatically' out of the one preceding it. On the contrary, the transition from one to another was largely determined by the structure and dynamics of the overall social context within which, at any given time, the game was played. Nevertheless, they do represent a 'developmental' order in at least two senses: the first is that the later bear discernible traces of the earlier stages, i.e. they contain elements which show that they developed out of the antecedent forms; the second is that the order was necessary, not in the 'strong' sense of being inevitable but in the 'weaker' sense that fully-fledged modern forms of football could not have been born as such into the world but had to develop, as part of a long-term process, out of earlier and structurally more simple forms.

These stages were relatively distinct as far as ways of playing were concerned but, like stages in the development of society at large, they overlapped in a temporal sense. That is, there were no clear-cut dividing lines between them at specific dates. Hence our reference to them as lasting, e.g. 'from *about* 1830 to *about* 1860'. What we mean by this is that a particular form was *dominant* between those dates, not that it was the *only* form. We also mean that the game-form which was dominant at a given stage did not disappear immediately or entirely as soon as newer forms emerged: it merely ceased over time to be the dominant form. Thus the folk forms of football did not disappear when, in the course of the nineteenth century, newer forms emerged in the public schools. Nor did the forms characteristic of the third stage disappear when national rules were instituted. On the contrary, modified versions of most of these forms continue to be played in certain parts of Britain and among certain social groups. Ashbourne football and Hallaton 'bottle kicking' are, in that sense, 'survivals' of the folk stage, whilst the Eton 'wall' and 'field' games are, again in that sense, survivals of the types played in stages two and three.

It may help to make this development clearer if we represent it diagrammatically. Figure 0.1 depicts the overlapping character of the stages in this

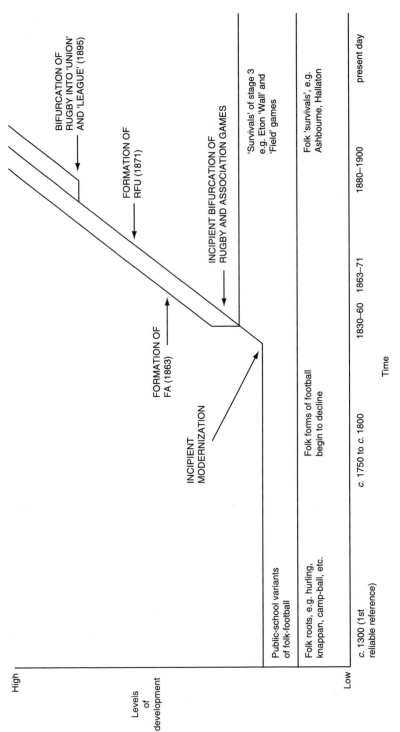

High

Levels
of
development

Low

BIFURCATION OF
RUGBY INTO 'UNION'
AND 'LEAGUE' (1895)

FORMATION OF
RFU (1871)

INCIPIENT BIFURCATION OF
RUGBY AND ASSOCIATION GAMES

FORMATION OF
FA (1863)

INCIPIENT
MODERNIZATION

Public-school variants
of folk-football

'Survivals' of stage 3
e.g. Eton 'Wall' and
'Field' games

Folk 'survivals', e.g.
Ashbourne, Hallaton

Folk forms of football
begin to decline

Folk roots, e.g. hurling,
knappan, camp-ball, etc.

c. 1300 (1st
reliable reference)

c. 1750 to c. 1800

1830–60   1863–71   1880–1900   present day

Time

Figure 0.1

long-term process. Levels of development—measured by degrees of structural differentiation, degrees of formalization of rules and organization, and levels of socially tolerated violence—are expressed on the vertical axis; the horizontal axis expresses time.

These stages are those through which football passed *in Britain*. No reference is implied in Figure 0.1 to early European forms such as the French, *la soule*, or the more advanced Florentine game of *calcio*.[1] Similarly, no reference is implied to offshoots of British football such as the American, Canadian and Australian games. In short, these stages are, in a direct sense, stages in the development of Rugby and soccer. To say this is not to discount the possibility that the folk-antecedents of these games may have been influenced by the game-traditions of other European societies. Indeed, since Britain became a colonial power early on, it is even possible that they may have been influenced by the game-traditions of non-European societies. The ball-games of the North American Indians could be a case in point. But whether such cross-societal influences played a part in the development of the antecedents of Rugby and soccer is a subject which will have to await further research.

3. Implicit in this discussion are the reasons why we believe a study of the development of Rugby can be of sociological value. In our view, such a study represents a useful vehicle for throwing light on four main problem areas:

(i)   the development of the British class structure and of related institutions such as the public schools;
(ii) the reasons why Britain was, so far as we can tell, the first country to develop modern forms of sport;
(iii) Norbert Elias' theory of the 'civilizing process';[2]
(iv) the worldwide trend towards growing competitiveness, seriousness of involvement and 'achievement-orientation' which, together with a trend towards growing cultural centrality, is evident in sport in most present-day societies.

At first glance, these problems may appear to be unrelated. As we hope to show, however, they reveal themselves on closer acquaintance to be interconnected in several ways. There is a difference between the first one and the others in that it relates to the 'independent variables' of our research. Accordingly, it is less central to our *theoretical* concerns. Nevertheless, it is worth pointing out that we have had to form our own picture of the development of the British class structure and that analysis of such occurrences as the split between Rugby Union and Rugby League, and of the dual, 'apartheid-like' pattern of rules, organization, values and social relations that Rugby football has retained ever since, may enable us to illuminate the developing structure of class relations in British society from a relatively novel angle. Similarly, analysis of the incipient modernization of Rugby may allow us to shed light on the early development of the public schools. However, our main concerns theoretically are with what the development of Rugby can tell us about why modern forms of sport began to develop in Britain first; with what, following Elias, one might call the 'civilization' of Rugby football; and with the development of Rugby as an exemplification of the worldwide trend outlined above. Accordingly, it is on these three issues that we shall elaborate in the discussion that follows.

(i) That Britain was not simply the first industrial nation but also the first 'sporting' one can be seen from the fact that cricket, horse-racing, tennis, boxing, athletics, Rugby and soccer were among the sports which began to achieve their modern forms in Britain, subsequently spreading, more or less widely, throughout the world. The major sports of the United States seem to be an obvious exception but it is worth pointing out that American football is an offshoot of Rugby[3] and that baseball is a development of the English game of 'rounders'.[4] Britain's crucial role in this regard was recognized by Huizinga when he pointed out that England formed the 'cradle and focus' for the development of modern sport.[5] It was Elias, however, who set forth the principal sociological questions which are posed in this connection. He wrote:

> What accounts for the fact that, mainly in the nineteenth and twentieth centuries, an English type of pastimes called 'sport' set the pattern for a world-wide leisure movement? Pastimes of this type evidently corresponded to specific leisure needs which made themselves felt in many countries during that period. Why did they emerge in England first? What characteristics in the development and structure of English society account for the development there of leisure activities with the specific characteristics which we designate as sport?[6]

Superficially, it may appear that the answer to these questions is a simple one, namely that Britain was the first country to industrialize and that the development of modern sport-forms was just a reflex of this economic transformation. We believe, however, that an answer based on such crude economic determinism is unsatisfactory. The development of modern sport was a complex process. In our view, it cannot be explained reductively in terms of determination by a single factor, however appealing such an explanation may at first appear to be. But to say this is not to imply that we espouse a multi-factor explanation. We have approached the task of explanation using the sociogenetic or [con]figurational methodology advocated by Norbert Elias.[7] We shall not give a lengthy outline of this method here, preferring to show the reader concretely what it entails in the main body of our study. It must be enough simply to say that it eschews the search for prime movers and causal factors and seeks instead, to attribute social processes to *structural* determination. Special attention is paid in this connection to the genesis within the developing social system of pressures and constraints which lead groups reciprocally to modify their behaviour. The structurally generated balance of power between groups is held to be of critical importance in this regard.

It is our belief that an examination of the development of Rugby using such a method may yield insights, not only into that process itself and the more general development of modern sport, but also into the structural characteristics which led Britain to become the first society to industrialize. It may, for example, help to show how and why it was that, up until about the middle of the nineteenth century, the British class system was structured in such a way as to be conducive to innovation in both the work and leisure spheres. However, in order to appreciate that fact and, indeed, the more general connections between industrialization and the development of modern sports, it is necessary to expunge from one's mind any tendency to assign causal primacy universally to a single social sphere. We shall now consider Elias' theory of the 'civilizing process', more specifically why we have chosen it as one of the main theoretical foci of our study.

(ii) For Elias, the concept of the 'civilizing process' is a non-evaluative term which describes an observable unplanned, unintended or blind long-term social process which, he holds, took place in West European societies between the Middle Ages and modern times. There is, he argues, no zero-point of civilization. Accordingly, he does not claim that this process was a development from an uncivilized to a civilized social condition but from a lower level to a higher one in terms of a constellation of determinable indices. The central elements of this process were: an elaboration and refinement of social standards regarding the control of 'natural' functions and the conduct of social relations generally; a concomitant increase in the social pressure on people to exercise self-control; and, at the level of personality, an increase in the importance of 'conscience' as a regulator of behaviour. In the course of this process, external restraints grew more subtle and all-pervasive, and the use of direct force was pushed increasingly behind the scenes. At the same time, social standards were more deeply and firmly internalized. According to Elias, these elements of the civilizing process were interrelated.

Implicit in this discussion is the fact that one strand in the civilizing process, as Elias conceives it, has been a long-term change in the pattern of violence-control. Crucial in that regard has been a change in social standards. That is, in the course of the civilizing process, standards developed in West European societies demanding that their members exercise stricter self-control over violence and aggression. Since sport is an area of social life in which problems of violence loom large, it follows that the development of Rugby represents a potentially fruitful vehicle for testing this aspect of the theory. Of course, the potential for violence is inherent in all sports and all social relations. However, since Rugby is an intensely competitive mock-fight based, to a large extent, on direct physical force—indeed, it is one of the roughest contemporary sports—this potential is ever-present and relatively close to the surface. Consequently, standards of violence-control are central and relatively easy to detect, although, as we shall show, they have not always taken the form of written rules and still exist today in part as unwritten conventions. Thus, if it can be shown that the standards of violence-control in this one sport in this one West European society underwent a correlative transformation during the period in which, according to Elias, the overall civilizing process occurred, this aspect of the theory can be held to have been given limited confirmation. Or at least, that is the case unless it can be demonstrated either that Rugby or British society is atypical or that there are reasons for believing that the social control of violence in sport and the wider society are unrelated or liable to develop in contrary directions. In our view, none of these possibilities can be supported on either theoretical or empirical grounds. We have now reached a point where we can discuss the third of our main theoretical concerns.

(iii) We suggested earlier that the development of Rugby is relevant to an understanding of what we take to be, worldwide, the dominant trend in modern sport, namely the growing competitiveness, seriousness of involvement and 'achievement-orientation' of sports-participation. Expressed differently, the trend we are referring to is the gradual but seemingly inexorable erosion of 'amateur' attitudes, values and structures, and their correlative replacement by attitudes, values and structures which are 'professional' in one sense or another of that term. Rugby is particularly well-suited for an investigation of this trend since the process which led to the split between Rugby Union and Rugby League is a clear-cut example of it. So, too, is the subsequent development of Rugby Union. The authorities in that game have fought this trend now for close on 100 years. Yet their efforts are seemingly to no avail for, whilst remaining nominally amateur, top-level Rugby Union has come to resemble a professional sport in all major respects. Therefore, if we can show why this has occurred, even in the face of strong official resistance, we should be able to shed light on the underlying causes of this trend.

Of course, we are not the first to draw attention to such a trend. It is an issue on which considerable work has been carried out already. However, the contributions of three authors—Johan Huizinga in his *Homo Ludens*,[8] Gregory P. Stone in an essay entitled 'American Sports: Play and Display',[9] and Bero Rigauer[10] in a book called *Sport und Arbeit* (Sport and Work)— merit detailed consideration because they postulate, at least implicitly, a number of testable propositions about this trend. They also introduce some concepts which will be useful in our own analysis. Accordingly, we shall now review their theories and subject them briefly to critical scrutiny.

Huizinga's *Homo Ludens*—'man the player'—is not a discussion of play as it is generally understood but an examination of his conviction 'that civilization arises and unfolds in and through play'. In earlier epochs, he suggests, Western societies maintained a balance between the polarities of 'seriousness' and 'play'. In the nineteenth century, however, with the acceleration of industrialization, the growth of science and the emergence of egalitarian movements, 'seriousness' began to gain the ascendancy. 'Never had an age taken itself with more portentous seriousness', he wrote: 'Culture ceased to be played.'

The relevance of this élitist critique of modern society for our analysis lies primarily in the devastating commentary which Huizinga offers on modern sports. The fact that the nineteenth century witnessed the large-scale growth of sports would seem, at first glance, to contradict his thesis but Huizinga contends that, on close inspection, it tends to confirm it since, in modern sports, 'the old play factor has undergone almost complete atrophy'. As part of the decline of the play-element in modern civilization generally, sports have experienced a 'fatal shift towards overseriousness'. The distinction between amateurs and professionals is the clearest indication of this trend. The latter lack 'spontaneity and carelessness' and no longer truly 'play'. However, their performance is superior, leading the former to feel inferior and engage in imitative action. Between them, according to Huizinga:

> . . . they push sport further and further away from the play-sphere proper until it becomes a thing *sui generis*: neither play nor earnest. In modern social life sport occupies a place alongside and apart from the cultural process . . . [it] has become profane, 'unholy' in every way and has no organic connection with the structure of society, least of all when prescribed by the government . . . However important it may be for the players or spectators, it remains sterile.[11]

Apart from descriptively relating it to a general trend and pointing to the 'detrimental' effects of the interaction between professional and amateur sport, Huizinga failed to address himself to the causes of the presumed trend towards 'sterility' and 'overseriousness'. This issue is tackled more satisfactorily by Stone, who modifies Huizinga's arguments, suggesting that modern sports are subject to a twofold dynamic: they change, he argues, because they are caught up in the 'contests, tensions, ambivalences and anomalies' of the wider society, and because of certain features inherent in their structure.

Unlike Huizinga, Stone does not speak of a trend towards 'overseriousness' in sports but points, instead, to the ambivalence of contemporary Americans towards them. In the United States, he suggests, especially among the 'middle mass' of the large cities and suburbs, 'play is often conceived in archaic restraint and carried on in frenzies of unrestraint. Americans are uneasy with play, sometimes inept'. This has arisen, Stone maintains, because the old play-norms have broken down. Until the beginning of the present century, the dominant value system in the United States was a Protestant Ethic which dictated a polarization of social categories, among them, work and play. The two were kept strictly apart and not allowed to intermingle. However, with continuing industrialization, this polarization has begun to erode. As Stone expresses it:

> ... with the loss of the social frame that once ensured their separation, work and play have spilled over their former bounds and mingled together in American life. However, the amalgam is new, untested, strange. Traces of the old distance remain and are expressed in vital anomalies.[12]

A manifestation in sport is the amateur–professional dichotomy: for amateurs sport is 'play', for professionals it is 'work'. According to Stone, the severe conflicts which accompanied the professionalization of sports in the United States are symptomatic of the 'vital anomalies' inherent in the transitional situation.

He goes on to suggest that industrialization leads to 'democratization' and that this leads, in turn, to the development of 'mass societies'. In sport, 'massification' produces spectator participation *en masse* and the interaction between players and spectators leads to further transformations. 'All sport', Stone contends, 'is affected by the antinomial principles of play and display', i.e. it is oriented towards producing satisfaction either for players or spectators. But, he continues, 'display' for spectators is '*dis*-play', destructive of the play-character of sport. Whenever large numbers of spectators attend a sports event, it is transformed into a spectacle, played for the spectators and not the participants. The interests of the former take precedence over those of the latter. Enjoyment from playing becomes subordinate to the production of crowd-pleasing moves. The sport begins to lose its spontaneity, uncertainty and character of playful innovation. It becomes a type of ritual, predictable, even predetermined in its outcome. As we shall see, this argument is reminiscent of a central tenet in the official Rugby Union ethos.

Rigauer's analysis depends heavily on Marxist assumptions about the exploitative character of work in capitalist societies. It thus starts from ideological premises different from those of Huizinga and Stone. Nevertheless, it reaches similar conclusions about trends in modern sport. According to Rigauer, modern sport is a 'bourgeois' product. It was initially a type of recreation pursued by members of the ruling class for their own enjoyment. For them, it functioned as a counter to work. But, with increasing industrialization and its spread down the social hierarchy, sport has come to take on characteristics which resemble those of work:

> Division of labour, mechanization, automation, bureaucratization—in short, rationalization and the 'technicization' of the production of goods

and services have exerted pressure on ways of behaving and making decisions even in those areas which do not appear to be directly related to the world of industrial work. More and more, sport is coming to incorporate these general tendencies towards rationalization within its own framework of action. The increasing dehumanization of work has helped to determine the form, the content and the organization of sports activities.[13]

Rigauer adduces a range of evidence to support these contentions. Like forms of work in industrial societies, he maintains, sport is coming to be characterized by achievement-striving. This is seen in the drive to break records, in the hours of gruelling training which are employed towards that end, and in the application of scientific methods to the goal of improving performance. Training techniques such as 'interval' and 'circuit' training, he suggests, replicate the 'alienating' and 'dehumanizing' character of assembly-line production. Even in the 'individual' sports, the role of sportsman is being reduced to just one in a whole constellation which includes trainers, coaches, managers, doctors and masseurs. This tendency is doubly apparent in team sports. There, the modern sportsman is compelled to fit into a fixed division of labour and to comply with the demands of a prescribed tactical plan. He plays little part himself in working out this plan. His scope for the exercise of initiative is reduced to a minimum. That is even more true of sports administration. Increasingly, it is full-time officials and not sportsmen themselves who decide matters of policy. The result, says Rigauer, is a steady constriction of the scope for private decision-making and dominance over the majority by a bureaucratic élite.

The growing structural similarity between sport and work, Rigauer contends, is mainly apparent at the top levels of sport, both amateur and professional. However, it is not restricted to those levels, since top-level sportsmen set standards which others tend to emulate. He admits that the scope for exercising initiative remains larger in sport than in most forms of work but maintains that the gap between sport and work in this respect is getting narrower all the time. If his diagnosis is correct, it follows that sport must increasingly be unable to function as a means of providing relief from the strains of work. It has become, he contends, demanding, achievement-oriented and alienating. The belief that it functions as a counter to work remains widespread but it is a 'masking ideology'. That is, it hides from the participants the 'real' function of sport, namely that of reinforcing in the leisure-sphere an ethic of hard work, achievement and group loyalty which is necessary for the operation of an advanced industrial society. According to Rigauer, it helps to maintain the *status quo* and bolster the dominance of the ruling class.

4. These three ideas—that sport is growing more 'serious'; that 'display' is coming to predominate over, and destroy, 'play'; and that sport is becoming

indistinguishable from work—seem, at first glance, to be apposite as descriptions of a central trend in modern Rugby. However, elements of value-bias enter each of these critiques, casting doubts on their adequacy. Huizinga, for example, is a romantic who yearns for an 'organic' society. Moreover, it is implicit in his analysis that the 'democratization' of sports is the main reason for their 'decay'. In short, he implies that creativity and high moral standards are restricted to élites. Nevertheless, his critique of modern sports strikes home, especially his contention that a 'shift towards overseriousness' has occurred. Yet it is difficult to believe that sports could have managed to sustain their popularity if the play-element within them had atrophied to the extent that he asserts, or if they had become, in his sense of the term, 'profane'. Indeed, if anything, the opposite seems to be the case, namely that they have become more 'sacred'. That is, the cultural centrality of sport has grown to such an extent that it now appears to be a social phenomenon of quasi-religious proportions.

Similar considerations apply to Rigauer's critique. He is right to suggest that sport has come in some ways to assume a work-like character. He has also provided a powerful critique of the ruling sports ideology of modern times. Yet it is doubtful whether his analysis is entirely adequate since if, as he contends, sport has become as 'alienating' and 'repressive' as work, then surely—unless participation is dictated by some equally powerful individual or social compulsion—one would expect a decline in its popularity to have occurred. Rigauer fails, that is, to consider adequately the combination of internal and external constraints which form the pressure to participate in sport. Nor does he concern himself with the reasons why sport occupies a high place in the value-scale of modern societies. Instead, he remains content with the assertion that the growing structural correspondence between sport and work is functionally necessary in advanced societies and serves the interests of the ruling class.

More importantly, he makes no attempt to analyse empirically the manner in which this structural correspondence has been brought about. Nor does he distinguish between forms of work, forms of sport and different countries in this respect, or attempt to locate socially the different values which have grown up in this area. In other words, he makes no attempt to determine whether different groups are proponents, on the one hand, of achievement-oriented values or, on the other, of values which stress the pleasure-giving, leisure character of sport. Nor does he attempt to document empirically the changes which, he maintains, have occurred over time in the balance between these values. Instead, he simply paints a blanket picture which asserts that all sports in all industrial countries have developed work-like characteristics and hence serve ruling interests to the same extent.

Sociologically, Stone's analysis is more satisfactory. Nevertheless, there is reason to believe that his analysis of the balance between 'play' and 'display' may not reach to the heart of the matter. This, it seems to us, is not simply a question of the presence or absence of spectators or, where the latter are present, of the interaction between them and the players, but, more importantly, of the values of the participating groups and, more importantly still, of the patterns of *interdependence* among them.[14] Thus the presence of spectators at a sports event may *induce* players to engage in display but it cannot *constrain* or *compel* them to do so. The play-element is more likely to be threatened when players become *dependent* on spectators—or on agencies external to the game, such as commercial interest groups and the state—for financial and other rewards. Under such conditions, whether the players are openly professional or nominally amateur, the pressures to allow the interests of spectators to assume an important role, for the 'game' to become a 'spectacle', are likely to be formidable.

5. Implicit in this discussion is our belief that, in examining the development of modern sport, Huizinga, Rigauer and Stone have not dealt satisfactorily with the dynamics of that process. Their analyses are, in a sense, curiously impersonal. They postulate a trend connected with industrialization but pay little attention to clashes of group interest and ideology. It almost appears in their analyses as if the old values and forms of sport were fading away without conflict.[15] That such a conceptualization, whatever its merits as a first approximation to a sociological theory of sport, is oversimplified, can be seen if we repeat a few facts about the structure and development of Rugby.

There are, as we have seen, two varieties of this game. Rugby Union is, nominally at least, an amateur game, played and run throughout Britain principally by members of the middle and upper middle classes. The only major exception is provided by Wales where a considerable proportion of the personnel are working-class. By contrast, Rugby League is restricted almost solely to the North of England. It supports a number of professional clubs and caters to an almost exclusively working-class clientele. This pattern of class and regional differentiation, with its differences of Rugby organization and ethos, arose, as we have seen, in conjunction with conflicts at the end of the nineteenth century. However, its development is of more than simple historical interest. It offers an opportunity for examining within the framework of a single sport, issues such as the growth of professionalism, the correlative decline of amateurism, and the clashes of group interest and ideology which occurred in that connection. Other sports could have served this purpose, too. However, so far as we know, none of them has Rugby's complex relation to and pattern of spread through the class structure. Thus, Rugby Union is generally middle-class, but working-class in Wales. On the other hand, Rugby League is almost entirely working-class. The only permutation which is lacking is middle-class Rugby League.[16] We are thus presented with an almost ideal, 'natural experiment', a situation well-suited for separating the effects of class from those of factors which are 'sport-specific'.

However, our choice of subject does not stem simply from the sociological interest of the problems posed by, and the analytical possibilities inherent in, the emergence of this configuration in the nineteenth century, but also from the fact that, in the final quarter of the twentieth, a broadly similar social configuration seems to be re-emerging in Rugby Union. We noted earlier that, virtually since its foundation, the RFU has fought the tendency which is leading Rugby, along with other modern sports, to be transformed into a serious and achievement-oriented pursuit. It has developed an ethos which embodies antagonism to professionalism, and distrust of spectators, and which insists on maintaining Rugby Union as an enjoyable, 'character-forming' leisure activity for players. However, a struggle is currently occurring between the game's 'establishment' who wish to preserve Rugby as a player-centred, amateur sport, and the leading clubs who wish to see it made more seriously competitive and attractive for spectators. It is similar in many ways to the struggle which led to the split between Union and League. The fact that another schism may be imminent or that Rugby Union may, in essentials, be becoming indistinguishable from Rugby League, is one of the reasons why the current struggle is viewed with urgency by the RFU. Sociologically, however, it is principally of interest because it shows the strength of the pressures in modern society which are leading to the transformation of sports into serious, intensely competitive, achievement-oriented and, at least in that sense, 'professional' pursuits. So strong are these pressures that even an organization such as the RFU which has striven for more than eighty years to defend the 'amateur ideal' is unable, under modern conditions, to maintain a game-structure consistent with that ideal. That is why Rugby is a valuable, even unique, vehicle for testing the theories of Huizinga, Rigauer and Stone, and, therefore, for advancing our understanding of the structure and dynamics of modern sport and, with it, of modern society.

6. To sum up: apart from the fact that it is intrinsically interesting as a sociological problem, we have chosen to study the development of Rugby because it seems to us that no other sport could help in the same way to realize our four main theoretical objectives: namely, to throw light on our 'independent variable', the development of the British class structure and of related institutions such as the public schools; to illuminate the structural sources of Britain's emergence as the world's first 'sporting nation'; to test Elias' hypothesis that a long-term change in patterns of violence-control has occurred in West European societies; and to test the theories of Huizinga, Rigauer and Stone regarding the trend towards greater seriousness in modern sport. As we have said, the first of these objectives is incidental to our main concerns. Our principal explicit theoretical focus is on the other three. Although there is considerable overlap in this respect, consideration of the second and third issues occupies the first part of our book; consideration of the fourth is undertaken in the second.

We suggested earlier that these theoretical objectives are not as disparate and disconnected as may seem at first to be the case. We shall explore their connections explicitly in the conclusion. In that context, we shall also concern ourselves with wider issues, e.g. with the alleged trend towards greater violence in modern sport and, as part of it, with the vexed British problem of 'football hooliganism'. At this juncture, it is sufficient just to note that the increasing violence and growing seriousness and competitiveness of sport would appear, on *a priori* grounds, to be connected. Furthermore, the mounting violence would appear, again on *a priori* grounds, to constitute a refutation of Elias' theory. But whether it does or not is another issue that we shall return to in the conclusion.

Just one more subject needs to be broached in this introduction. Implicit in the discussion so far is our belief that the development of Rugby represents what Durkheim would have called a 'decisive' or 'crucial' case.[17] As he expressed it:

> . . . the value of . . . facts . . . is much more important than their number. . . . to establish relations it is neither necessary nor always useful to heap up numerous experiences upon each other; it is much more important to have a few that are well studied and really significant. One single fact may make a law appear, where a multitude of imprecise and vague observations would only produce confusion.[18]

We agree with him. That is why we have chosen to achieve our theoretical objectives through the medium of examining a single sport. By studying this one case intensively and in detail we hope that it may be possible, not to formulate a 'law'—in our view, 'law-like' generalizations are neither a necessary nor a feasible sociological objective[19]—but to penetrate to and illuminate the 'deep structure', the fundamental basis, of the development of modern sport. We realize that our results may not be generalizable beyond this one case. Thus it is possible that the example we have chosen as representative of a worldwide trend may be so contaminated by features which are specific either to Rugby or to Britain that we shall be led to single out as central features which are specific to one or both of these contexts. We have tried to eliminate the first of these dangers by comparing the 'professionalization' of Rugby with that of cricket and soccer. But, of course, that does nothing to obviate the second. All that we can say in that regard is that we have tried to guard against the more obvious dangers of ethnocentric bias but that, in the last analysis, it must be up to others to say how far we have succeeded.

Part I

Folk-Antecedents and Transitional Forms of Football in the Public Schools

1 The folk-antecedents of modern Rugby and their decline

1. Our first empirical task in this study is to examine the available data on the folk-games from which Rugby and soccer are descended. That is necessary in order to build up a picture of these folk-games and their differences from modern sports. It is also necessary because of a simple methodological point: namely, that if one wishes to establish the occurrence of a trend or the 'direction' of a social process, it is necessary to have firm knowledge of its 'starting point' or 'base'. And that, in the case of Rugby and soccer, means the folk-games of pre-industrial Britain, even though they were, themselves, stages in an ongoing process.

There is no firm evidence that a game called 'football' was played in Britain before the fourteenth century. However, lack of data has not deterred writers from speculating about the pre-fourteenth-century origins of the modern games. Some have seen them as descended from the Greek game, *episkyros*.[1] Others regard the Roman game, *harpastum*, as the ancestral form.[2] Still others see Rugby and soccer as having developed from a Celtic game, from games imported by our Anglo-Saxon and Norman forebears, and from a ritual first established by the native inhabitants of the British Isles in order to celebrate the defeat of an invading army.[3] Yet another historical conjecture attempts to establish links between modern football and an ancient fertility rite.[4]

Because reliable evidence is lacking, there is no way of determining which, if any, of these theories is correct. All that can be said with certainty is that Rugby and soccer are descended from a type of medieval folk-games. However, the origins of these folk-games remain obscure. They may have been brought here by an early 'immigrant' or invading group or borrowed by native Britons from abroad. Alternatively, they may have been an entirely indigenous development or have contained a mixture of 'native' and 'foreign' traditions. One simply cannot tell.

Starting in the fourteenth century, however, references to 'football' become fairly common, firstly in the developing literature of Britain, and secondly in the records of prohibitions by kings and civic authorities.[5] The literary references establish that the name was part of English usage by that time but tell us nothing about the structure of this type of games. The court records are, by contrast, more revealing. They often contain the rationale which lay behind the prohibition and thus, assuming them to be reliable as a source of evidence, suggest how wild these folk-games were and how the authorities regarded them as a threat to life, property and public order. We shall discuss the adequacy and reliability of these records later. It is necessary, first, to look at a few examples in order to extract the picture they contain.

2. Between 1314 and 1667, 'football' and other popular games were banned on more than thirty occasions. The following list gives an idea of the frequency with which it was felt necessary to re-enact such prohibitions (Table 1.1).

The list is indicative of the inability of the authorities in pre-industrial Britain to suppress activities of which they disapproved. Had the prohibitions been successful, it would have been superfluous to repeat them. It will shed light on the structure of these games and the circumstances in which they were played if we examine a few examples in greater detail.

The order issued in Manchester in 1608 was reissued almost verbatim a year later and it shows that people played 'with the "ffotebale" ' in the streets and not simply in open spaces where they claimed the customary right to engage in pastimes of this type. There 'hath beene great disorder in our

Table 1.1 Selected List of Prohibitions by State and Local Authorities of the Folk-Antecedents of Rugby and Soccer

1314	Edward II	London	1474	Edward IV	London
1331	Edward III	London	1477	Edward IV	London
1349	Edward III	London	1478		London
1365	Edward III	London	1488		Leicester
1388	Richard II	London	1491	James III of	
1401	Henry IV	London		Scotland	Perth
1409	Henry IV	London	1496	Henry VII	London
1410	Henry IV	London	1570		Peebles
1414	Henry V	London	1572		London
1424	James I of		1581		London
	Scotland	Perth	1594		Shrewsbury
1450		Halifax	1608		Manchester
1454		Halifax	1609		Manchester
1457	James II of		1615		London
	Scotland	Perth	1655		Manchester
1467		Leicester	1666		Manchester
1471	James III of		1667		Manchester
	Scotland	Perth			

Sources: Marples, *op. cit.*, Young, *op. cit.*, and Magoun, *op. cit.* Local rather than state authorities were responsible for those prohibitions where the name of the reigning monarch is not included.

towne of Manchester', we are told, and 'glasse windowes broken yearlye and spoyled by a Companie of lewd and disordered persons usinge that unlawful exercise of playing with the ffotebale in ye streets of the said towne, breaking many men's windowes and glasse at their pleasure and other great inormyties'.[6]

A set of documents from Chester provides a further idea of the reasons why such games gave the authorities cause for alarm. It had, apparently, been a Shrove Tuesday custom in that city, 'time out of man's remembrance', for a football worth 3s.4d. to be presented by the Shoemakers' to the Drapers' Company. We are told, however, that by 1533 'evil disposed persons' had come to take part in the ensuing match with the result that '. . . much harme was done, some in the greate thronge falling into a trance, some having their bodies brused and crushed; some their arms, heades or legges broken, and some otherwise maimed or in peril of their lives'.[7]

These folk games were often *ad hoc* affairs, played by an unspecified number. They provided the players with an opportunity to pay off old scores as can be seen from the description of a match which took place in 1579 between some Cambridge students and villagers from Chesterton. The students had apparently turned up unarmed but:

> . . . the sayd townsmen of Chesterton had layd divers staves secretely in the church porch, and in playing did pike quarrels agenst the schollers and did bringe owte there staves wherewith they did so beat the sayd schollers that diveres had there heads broken, divers being otherwise greatly beaten, wear driven to runne through the river, divers did crye to Parise the constable to keep the Queen's peace, who then being a player at the footeball with the rest did turne to the schollers, willing them to keep the Queene's peace.[8]

Eruptions of violence which broke out because of tensions generated outside the game were, it seems, fairly common in the folk-antecedents of modern football, adding to their intrinsic wildness. There were no referees or relatively impersonal rules to keep the players in check. In this respect, these folk-games reflected what Huizinga has called 'the violent tenor of life' in Europe during the 'autumn' of the middle ages.[9] The capacity of the people, especially the 'common people', to exercise emotional restraint was comparatively small. This was reflected in their sudden swings of mood and relatively weak 'armour' of internalized restraints. At the same time, the authorities found it difficult to establish an effective monopoly on the right to use physical force. Under such conditions, inter-group and inter-personal friction was more liable to lead to open fighting than is the case in societies such as modern Britain.

The folk forms of football were a channel into which these violent tendencies could be directed, a kind of ritualized fight in which groups could pit their strength against local rivals and secure release of the tensions generated by the inevitable frustrations of day-to-day life. In many parts of the country, it was common to have a 'match at football' annually on a Saint's day or 'holy day'. Shrovetide, it seems, was the favourite occasion for engaging in such pastimes. Something of the ritual flavour is brought out in the description of a match which, from at least the sixteenth century until fairly recently, was played annually by members of the 'Company of Freemen Marblers' of Corfe Castle, Dorset.

Football formed part of a series of Shrovetide ceremonies held by the company. On Shrove Tuesday itself, officers were elected, apprentices initiated and each member married in the previous year had to pay a 'marriage shilling'. This was a form of insurance paid in acknowledgement of his widow's right to have an apprentice work for her when he died. However, the last married was excused payment and had to provide a football instead. On Ash Wednesday, this was carried to the lord of the manor and presented, together with a pound of pepper, as payment for an ancient right of way. Finally, a football match was played over the ground for which the Company claimed this right.[10]

It would be wrong to assume from the ritual aspect of these combat-games that they were solemn and disciplined in the manner of modern ceremonies. On the contrary, they were wild and, according to modern notions, savage brawls. Their violence probably constituted one of the sources of enjoyment. This is not to suggest that players simply took sadistic pleasure in the opportunities afforded for inflicting pain but that may have played a part in their motivation. After all, the people of pre-industrial Britain enjoyed all sorts of pastimes—e.g. cock-fighting, bull- and bear-baiting, burning cats alive in baskets, watching public executions[11]—which appear uncivilized in terms of present-day values. But a combat-game such as football was different for, in taking part, one ran the risk of receiving and not simply inflicting injury. By adding the spice of fear, such a risk may have heightened the enjoyment, but it is reasonable to suppose that a central function of these folk-games lay in the opportunity they provided for generating, in a pleasurable form, excitement akin to that aroused in battle. But the folk-antecedents of modern football were closer to 'real' or 'serious' fighting than their twentieth-century offspring. That this was so will emerge from a discussion of two seventeenth-century accounts, one by Carew of a Cornish game called 'hurling',[12] the other by Owen of a Welsh game called 'knappan'.[13]

3. Some authorities have been reluctant to use these accounts as evidence regarding the antecedents of modern football. That is understandable but based, we believe, on a failure to comprehend the nature of this type of games. They were, for example, based on local custom, not on common national rules; hence the chances of variation between localities were great. That is, there were neither written rules nor central organizations to unify the manner of playing. Therefore, references to, for example, 'football'

in pre-industrial sources do not imply, as similar references in modern documents would, a game played always and everywhere according to a single set of rules. That is, identity of name is no guarantee of identity of the game itself. By the same token, the differences between folk-games which were locally given different names were not necessarily drawn so sharply as is the case with modern sports; e.g. the differences between 'hurling', 'knappan' and 'football' were not so clear-cut as those between Rugby, soccer and hockey.

It is possible that one reason why the historical sources refer by different names to what appear, to modern eyes, to be similar games is the fact that they were played with different implements. Thus references to football in some early accounts seem to refer to a type of ball and to a type of game only in so far as the type of ball might have been one factor which helped to determine the manner of playing. For example, the Manchester prohibition of 1608 referred to playing '*with* the ffotebale' and not to 'playing ffotebale'. As far as we can tell, the type of ball to which this name was given was an inflated animal bladder, sometimes, but not always, encased in leather.

Balls of this type probably lent themselves better than smaller, solid balls to kicking, which could explain their name. Alternatively, such a name could signify a game that was played *on* foot as opposed to horseback. We shall probably never know. However, it would still be wrong to assume that in folk-games called 'football' the ball was only propelled by foot, and conversely that in games such as 'hurling' and 'handball' it was only propelled by hand. That is because prohibitions in these folk-games were less clearly defined and less rigidly enforced than is the case in modern sports. They were, as we have seen, spontaneous, often *ad hoc* affairs, characterized by traditions of physical fighting. Such restraints as they contained were imposed by custom rather than elaborate formal regulations which have to be learned from an early age and which require players to exercise a high degree of self-control. As a result, the basic game-pattern—their character as struggles between groups, the open enjoyment of excitement akin to that aroused in battle, the riotousness and relatively high level of socially tolerated physical violence – was everywhere the same. In short, these games were cast in a common mould which transcended local differences in names and playing traditions. That is why a vivid impression of the folk-antecedents of modern football can be gained from reports of 'folk-games' such as 'hurling' and 'knappan', even though they were not played 'with a football' but with balls of a different kind.

According to Carew, 'hurling' matches were usually organized by gentlemen. The 'goals', were either those gentlemen's houses or two towns or villages some three or four miles apart. There was he said "nether comparing of numbers nor matching of men". The game was played with a silver ball and the object was to carry it "by force or sleight" to the goal of one's side. He described the game itself in the following terms:

Whosoever getteth seizure of this ball, findeth himself generally pursued by the adverse party; neither will they leave, til . . . he be layd flat on Gods deare earth; which fall once received, disableth him from . . . detayning the ball: hee therefore, throweth the same . . . to some one of his fellowes, fardest before him, who maketh away withall in like manner . . .

The Hurlers take their next way over hilles, dales, hedges, ditches; yea, and thorow bushes, briers, mires, plashes and rivers whatsoever; so as you shall sometimes see 20 or 30 lie tugging together in the water, scrambling and scratching for the ball. A play (verily) both rude and rough, and yet such, as is not destitute of policies, in some sort resembling the feats of warre: . . . there are horsemen placed . . . on either party . . . and ready to ride away with the ball if they can catch it . . . But . . . gallop any one of them never so fast, yet he shall be surely met at some hedge corner, crosselane, bridge, or deep water, which . . . they know he must needs touch at: and if his good fortune gard him not . . ., hee is like to pay the price of his theft, with his owne and his horses overthrowe . . .

The ball in this play may be compared to an infernall spirit: for whosoever catcheth it, fareth straightwayes like a madde man, strugling and fighting with those that goe about to holde him: and no sooner is the ball gone from him, but hee resigneth this fury to the next receyver, and himselfe becommeth peaceable as before. I cannot well resolve, whether I should more commend this game, for the manhood and exercise, or condemne it for the boysterousness and harmes which it begetteth: for as . . . it makes their bodies strong, hard, and nimble, and puts a courage into their hearts, to meete an enemie in the face: so . . . it is accompanied by many dangers, some of which do ever fall to the players share. For proofe whereof, when the hurling is ended, you shall see them retyring home, as from a pitched battaile, with bloody pates, bones broken, and out of joynt, and such bruses as serve to shorten their daies; yet al is good play, and never Attourney nor Crowner troubled for the matter.

This account gives a good idea of the loose overall structure of this type of games. There was, for example, no limitation on numbers of participants, no customary stipulation of numerical equality between sides, and no restriction on the size of the playing area. Cornish 'hurling' was above all rough and wild but it was not totally unregulated. One of the customary rules emerges clearly from Carew's account: when tackled, a player was obliged to pass the ball to a team-mate. There was also a rudimentary division of labour within each team into what Carew, using a contemporary military analogy, called a 'fore-ward', a 'rere-ward' and two 'wings'. He also mentioned a division into players on horseback and players on foot. That is interesting sociologically since it suggests that, in these folk-games, elements of what were later to become separate games – in this case, hurling and polo—were rolled together in a single whole. Welsh 'knappan' was similar in most respects.

According to Owen, 'knappan' matches could take one of two organizational forms. On the one hand, there were 'standing knappans' played annually on 'holy days' and, on the other, scratch matches made by local gentlemen. Sometimes, whatever the organizational form, the number who took part exceeded 2,000 and, just as in Cornish 'hurling', some of the participants played on horse-back. The horsemen, said Owen, 'have monstrouse cudgells, of iii foote and halfe longe, as bigge as the partie is well able to wild (wield) . . .' In the past, rules had existed to temper the wildness but now they were no longer observed. As one can see from the following extract, 'knappan' was a rough affair:

> . . . at this playe privatt grudges are revendged, soe that for everye small occasion they fall by the eares, wch beinge but once kindled betweene two, all persons on both sides become parties, soe that sometymes you shall see fyve or vi hundred naked men, beatinge in a clusture together, . . . and there parte most be taken everyeman with his companie, so that you shall see two brothers the on beateinge the other, the man the maister, and frinde against frinde, they nowe alsoe will not sticke to take upp stones and there with in theire fistes beate theire fellowes, the horsemen will intrude and ryde into the footemens troupes, the horseman choseth the greatest cudgell he can gett, and the same of oke, ashe, blackthorne or crab-tree and soe huge as it were able to strike downe an oxe or horse, he will alsoe assault anye for privatt grudge, that hath not the *Knappan*, or cudgell him after he hath delt the same from him, and when on blowe is geven, all falleth by the eares, eche assaultinge other with their unreasonable cudgells sparinge neyther heade, face, nor anye part of the bodie, the footemen fall soe close to it, beinge once kindled with furie as they wholey forgett the playe, and fall to beatinge, till they be out of breathe, and then some nomber hold theire hands upp over theire heades and crye, . . . peace, peace, and often times this parteth them, and to theire playe they goe a newe. Neyther maye there be anye looker on at this game, but all must be actours, for soe is the custome and curtesye of the playe, for if one that cometh with a purpose onlye to see the game, . . . beinge in the middest of the troupe is made a player, by giveinge him a *Bastonado* or two, if he be on a horse, and by lending him halffe a dozen cuffs if he be on foote, this much maye a stranger have of curtesye, althoughe he expecte noethinge at their handes.

It is difficult to believe Owen's suggestion that 'knappan' had regressed from an earlier stage of agreed-on rules for the roughness which emerges so vividly from his account is confirmed by other surviving descriptions of these folk-games. It is what one would expect in games played by such large numbers, according to loosely defined oral rules, and in which there was no outside body which could be appealed to in cases of dispute. However, his mention of the fact that, if they happened to get in the players' way, onlookers were not allowed to retain a spectator role, is of particular interest sociologically. It suggests that a loose distinction between players and spectators may have been a general feature of the folk tradition. Thus, players probably came and went as they pleased; i.e. sides would have had a fluctuating membership, not the fixed number characteristic of sports today. Moreover, whatever their initial intentions, spectators must often have become directly involved in the struggle. If this is correct, it points to a crucial difference between folk-games and modern sports: namely, the absence in the former of a clearly defined and strictly maintained distinction between players' and spectators' roles. That, coupled with the failure to maintain equality of numbers between sides, ties in with what we know about the informal character and low level of role differentiation in folk-games generally.

None of the examples we have quoted so far dates from later than the seventeenth century. It must be enough if we cite just one example to show that folk-games continued to be played in this form until the nineteenth century. The following account of a type of 'football' played in South Cardiganshire in the early 1800s appeared in the *Oswestry Observer* in 1887:

> At Llanwennog, an extensive parish below Lampeter, the inhabitants for football purposes were divided into the Bros and Blaenaus . . . The Bros . . . occupied the high ground of the parish. They were nick-named 'Paddy Bros' from a tradition that they were descendants from Irish people . . . The Blaenaus occupied the lowlands and, it may be pre- sumed, were pure-bred Brythons . . . the match did not begin until about midday . . . Then the whole of the Bros and Blaenaus, rich and poor, male and female, assembled on the turnpike road which divided the highlands from the lowlands. The ball . . . was thrown high in the air by a strong man, and when it fell Bros and Blaenaus scrambled for its posses- sion, and a quarter of an hour frequently elapsed before the ball was got out from the struggling heap . . . Then if the Bros . . . could succeed in taking the ball up the mountain to . . . Rhyddlan they won the day; while the Blaenaus were successful if they got the ball to their end of the parish . . . The whole parish was the field of operations, and sometimes it would be dark before either party secured a victory. In the meantime, many kicks would be given and taken, so that on the following day the competitors would be unable to walk, and sometimes a kick on the shins would lead the two men concerned to abandon the game until they had decided which was the better pugilist. There do not appear to have been any rules . . .; and the art of football playing in the olden time seems to have been to reach the goal. When once the goal was reached, the victory was celebrated by loud hurrahs and the firing of guns, and was not disturbed until the following Christmas Day.[14]

The whole community took part in this play-fight, women as well as men, rich as well as poor. It served as a vehicle for the release of tension, and for the establishment of superiority between members of what perhaps were 'real', or possibly only presumed, ethnic groups. According to the author, the game was unregulated. However, two customary rules emerge from his account: that relating to the commencement of matches, which required a strong man to throw the ball into the air; and that relating to goals and, therefore, the determination of victory and defeat.

4. This discussion can be summarized as follows. The folk-antecedents of modern football were loosely organized, often *ad hoc* affairs which could be played at any time when work and other obligations were not pressing. However, it was common in many parts of the country for a 'standing' match between rival groups to take place annually on a Saint's day or 'holy day'. In such cases, matches were often highly ritualized but, as was the case with pre-industrial rituals generally, they were more spontaneous than modern ceremonies tend to be. These ritualized annual folk-contests—this did not apply in quite the same way to the 'scratch' matches of an *ad hoc* kind—were not an individually chosen recreation as is the case with amateur sports today, but a type of game in which strong pressure to participate was exerted. The principal participants were members of local community, occupational and status groups but, at least in rural areas, members of the aristocracy and gentry also took part.

These folk games were rough and wild, closer to 'real' fighting than modern sports. The latter, as Riesman and Denney have pointed out, are 'abstract', removed from 'serious' combat. Football's folk-antecedents may have been 'mock battles' in the sense that the life chances of contending groups were not directly at risk and that the infliction of injury was not their central aim. Nevertheless, injury was frequent, built into the structure of a type of games which reflected, on the one hand, the violent tenor of life in society at large and, on the other, the comparatively low 'threshold of repugnance' with regard to witnessing and engaging in violent acts which, as Elias has suggested, is characteristic of people in a society which stands at an earlier stage in a 'civilizing process' than our own.

The rules of these games were oral and not very elaborate. Some means of starting matches which did not confer advantage on one side or the other, and some means of determining victory and defeat—what the 'goals' of the match were to be—were usually agreed upon. However, no attempt was made to establish precise territorial limits. That is, matches were not played on a pitch with specifically demarcated boundaries but across country and through the streets of towns. The length and width of the playing area could, therefore, vary between a few score yards and two to three miles. Nor was any attempt made to establish rules to limit numbers of participants or the duration of matches. Sometimes as many as 2,000 took part and no attempt was made to secure equality of numbers. Matches commenced about noon and continued until one side had scored or it was too dark to play any longer.

They were more symbolic struggles for territory than ball games as we know them today. The whole identity of the contending groups was at stake and not simply their ability as players. If one group was able to enlist stronger support or could call upon superior facilities, that was evidently accepted, as a matter of course, as proof of its 'natural superiority'. As Ashworth has suggested, norms of equality and 'fairness' were not applied. Indeed, they probably would not have struck the majority of players as a possibility.

The ball in these games could be carried and thrown if kicking was the norm, or kicked and hit with sticks if carrying and throwing were the norm. However, absolute taboos were rare. Even if the attempt was made to introduce them, little could be done to ensure compliance. Practices were accepted as 'the rules' which had the support of locally powerful groups. They probably claimed legitimacy by invoking tradition. Such direct control as there was, was accomplished by the players within the context of the game. There were no outside bodies to determine relatively impersonal rules or agents appointed by such bodies to secure compliance. As a result, control was probably characterized by that mixture of rigidity and arbitrariness which Max Weber has shown to be characteristic of traditional authority generally.[15]

The available data tell us little about changes in these folk-games. It is reasonable to suppose, however, that they would have exhibited the mixture of fixity and fluidity characteristic of oral traditions. If this is correct, their 'game-patterns' would have tended to drift imperceptibly over time or to fluctuate, sometimes markedly, from generation to generation. However, despite such tendencies to change and despite their regional variability, over the six centuries of their duration (c.1300 to c.1900) these folk-games retained a distinct family likeness determined by the fact that they were loosely organized local games played according to oral rules but, above all, by the fact that, correlative with the stages in a 'civilizing process' through which pre-industrial Britain passed, they were rough and wild.

In addition, these games were relatively undifferentiated in three respects: (i) elements of what later became highly specialized games such as Rugby, soccer, hockey, boxing, wrestling and polo, were often contained in a single game; (ii) there was little division of labour among players; and (iii) no attempt was made to draw a hard and fast distinction between playing and spectating roles. And finally, since the games were rough and wild, the authorities regarded them, especially when played in an urban context, as a danger to life, limb, property and public order. They attempted, accordingly, to suppress them but, given the level of state formation reached and the means of social control available, their efforts were to no avail. Custom was stronger than the law and the popular pastime of playing 'with a football' which, as we shall see, received a degree of support from the aristocracy and gentry, continued to be played, along with many comparable folk-games, into modern times.

This account of the folk-antecedents of Rugby and soccer can be represented in the form of a typology which contrasts them with modern sports (see Table 1.2). Our task in the chapters which follow is to explain the development of Rugby as a modern sport, i.e. to show how a game which approximates closely to the constellation of structural properties listed in the right-hand column of Table 1.2 emerged from a matrix of folk-games with characteristics corresponding to those listed in the left-hand column. Two principal sets of problems present themselves in this connection: we shall have to explore, firstly, the decline of the folk-antecedents of modern football and, secondly, the development of the newer forms which came to replace them. The remainder of this chapter is devoted to the first set of problems.

5. In his *Survey of Cornwall*, Carew described two types of hurling: 'hurling to the countrie', which we discussed earlier, and a second type, 'hurling to goales', which as one can see from the following account, was more orderly and controlled:

> For hurling to goales, there are 15, 20, or 30, players, more or less, chosen out on each side, who. . . joyne hands in ranke one against another. Out of these ranks they match themselves by payres . . . every of which couples, are specially to watch one another during the play.
>
> After this, they pitch two bushes in the ground, some eight or ten foote asunder; and directly against them ten or twelve score off, another twayne in like distance, which they terme their Goales. One of these is appoynted by lots, to the one side, and the other to his adverse party . . . some indifferent person throweth up a ball, the which whosoever can catch, & cary through his adversaries goales, hath wonne the game. But therein consisteth one of *Hercules* his labours: for he that is once possessed of the ball, hath his contrary mate waiting at inches, and assaying to lay hold upon him. The other thrusteth him in the breast, with his closed fist, to keepe him off; which they call Butting, and place in weldoing the same, no small poynt of manhood.
>
> If he escape the first, another taketh him in hand, and so a third, neyther is hee left, untill having met . . . hee eyther touch the ground with some part of his bodie, in wrastling, or cry, Hold; which is the word of yeelding.
>
> Then must he cast the ball (named Dealing) to some one of his fellowes, who catching the same in his hand, maketh away withall as before.
>
> The Hurlers are bound to the observation of many lawes, as, that they must hurle man to man, and not two set upon one man at once: that the Hurler against the ball, must not *but*, nor hand-fast under the girdle: that hee who hath the ball, must but onely in the others brest: that he must deale no Fore-ball, *viz.* he may not throw it to any of his mates, standing neerer the goale, than himselfe. Lastly, in dealing the ball, if any of the other part can catch it flying between, or e're the other have it fast, he

Table 1.2 The Structural Properties of Folk-Games and Modern Sports

Folk-Games	*Modern Sports*
1. Diffuse, informal organization implicit in the local social structure.	Highly specific, formal organization, institutionally differentiated at the local, regional, national and international levels.
2. Simple and unwritten customary rules, legitimated by tradition.	Formal and elaborate written rules, worked out pragmatically and legitim-ated by rational-bureaucratic means.
3. Fluctuating game-pattern; tendency to change through long-term and, from the view-point of the participants, imperceptible 'drift'.	Change institutionalized through rational-bureaucratic channels.
4. Regional variation of rules, size and shape of balls, etc.	National and international standardiza-tion of rules, size and shape of balls, etc.
5. No fixed limits on territory, duration or numbers of participants.	Played on a spatially limited pitch with clearly defined boundaries, within fixed time-limits, and with a fixed number of participants, equalized between the contending sides.
6. Strong influence of natural and social differences on the game-pattern.	Minimization, principally by means of formal rules, of the influence of natural and social differences on the game-pattern: norms of equality and 'fairness'.
7. Low role differentiation (division of labour) among the players.	High role differentiation (division of labour) among the players.
8. Loose distinction between playing and 'spectating' roles.	Strict distinction between playing and 'spectating' roles.
9. Low structural differentiation; several 'game-elements' rolled into one.	High structural differentiation; special-ization around kicking, carrying and throwing, the use of sticks, etc.
10. Informal social control by the players themselves within the context of the ongoing game.	Formal social control by officials who stand, as it were, 'outside' the game and who are appointed and certificated by central legislative bodies and empowered, when a breach of the rules occurs, to stop play and impose penal-ties graded according to the seriousness of the offence.
11. High level of socially tolerated physical violence; emotional spontaneity; low restraint.	Low level of socially tolerated physical violence; high emotional control; high restraint.
12. Generation in a relatively open and spontaneous form of pleasurable 'battle-excitement'.	Generation in a more controlled and 'sublimated' form of pleasurable 'battle-excitement'.
13. Emphasis on physical force as opposed to skill.	Emphasis on skill as opposed to physical force.

14. Strong communal pressure to participate; individual identity subordinate to group identity; test of identity in general.	Individually chosen as a recreation; individual identity of greater importance relative to group identity; test of identity in relation to a specific skill or set of skills.
15. Locally meaningful contests only; relative equality of playing skills among sides; no chances for national reputations or money payment.	National and international superimposed on local contests; emergence of élite players and teams; chance to establish national and international reputations; tendency to 'monetization' of sports.

thereby winneth the same for his side, which straightway of defendant becommeth assailant, as the other, of assailant falls to be defendant. The least breach of these lawes, the Hurlers take for a just cause of going together by the eares, but with their fists onely; neither doth any among them seek revenge for such wrongs or hurts, but at the like play again.

'Hurling to goales' was thus a fairly advanced type of folk-game. Its rules, although oral, were explicitly defined. It was also, relatively speaking, orderly and controlled. It involved the institutionalization of a rudimentary sense of 'fairness', that is of a tendency to equalize chances between contending sides. Thus, although the size of teams was not fixed, custom decreed equality of numbers. The rules, furthermore, stipulated that 'ends' should be determined by drawing lots, that is, in terms of an impersonal chance criterion rather than particularistic social criteria such as the residential locations of the contending parties or their power and social status. The game had to be started by an impartial outsider who threw the ball into the air. There was also a form of 'marking' and two or more players were not allowed to wrest the ball from an opponent simultaneously. Another rule decreed that players should not hit or grasp one another 'below the belt'; the chest was the only legitimate target. And there was also an 'offside' rule and a rudimentary division of labour between attackers and defenders.

With its fairly elaborate rules, requirement that the players exercise a relatively high degree of self-control and rudimentary division of labour, 'hurling to goales' was, as we have said, more advanced than the majority of folk-games. Nevertheless, it was relatively undifferentiated in that its game-pattern contained elements of wrestling. Moreover, since punching on the chest ('butting') was a central tactic, it remained fairly violent. There was no referee and no linesmen, i.e. representatives of an outside agency whose task was to ensure that players conformed to the rules. 'Foul play' was simply dealt with by the players within the context of the game. That is, orderliness was primarily maintained, in Carew's apt expression, by 'going together by the eares'. In that way, self-regulation by the players added to the relatively high level of violence which remained inherent in the game.

Despite the existence of similarities between 'hurling to goales' and modern Rugby—both, for example, involve an emphasis on handling and a taboo on forward passing – there is no evidence to suggest a direct link between them. Indeed, as far as we can tell, 'hurling to goales' remained of local significance only. There is, however, limited evidence that the more complex division of labour, greater orderliness and embryonic tradition of 'fairness' it embodied may not have been an isolated development. Thus, in a book published in 1561, Richard Mulcaster advocated a reduction in the numbers who took part in football, elimination of some of the game's rougher features and the introduction of an 'outside' authority. Here is the relevant extract:

> . . . Football . . . be neither civil, neither worthy the name of any traine to health. Wherein any man may evidently see the use of the trayning maister, . . . (ie. a man), which can judge of the play, and is judge over the parties, and hath authoritie to commande . . .
>
> Some smaller numbers with such overlooking, sorted into sides and standings, not meeting with their bodies so boisterously, . . . may use footeball for as much good to the body, by the chiefe use of the legges, as the arme ball, for the same, by the use of the armes.[16]

We shall take up later the implications of the fact that Mulcaster appears to have described a mainly kicking game. Other evidence which points to the gradual emergence—and, we suspect, over time predominance—of such a game comes from the eighteenth century when the Frenchman, Saussure, wrote from London to his family that, for football, 'a leather ball filled with air is used, and is kicked about with the feet'.[17] If we are right, the development and spread of such a game played an important part in the emergence of the Rugby way of playing. For the moment, however, what we want principally to note is the fact that Mulcaster advocated the transformation of football into a game which, at least formally, would have closely resembled 'hurling to goales'. We do not know whether his recommendations were adopted. However, what he wrote does suggest that the sort of modified folk-game described by Carew may not have been an isolated phenomenon. If nothing else, these two examples show that some elements of the modern concepts of 'fairness' and control in sport had begun to develop as early as the sixteenth century. To say this, however, is immediately to raise the question of the structural preconditions which made possible limited developments of that kind.

6. A distinctive feature in Britain's pre-industrial development was the fact that a rural population living in varying degrees of serfdom was transformed into a class of comparatively free peasants. At the same time there emerged, together with a class of landowning noblemen, a class of untitled landowners

who were only 'gentlemen'. It is reasonable to suppose that this configuration, i.e. of noblemen, gentlemen and a formally free peasant class, formed the structural base which made possible the emergence of the modified type of folk-game described by Carew. Thus, in Cornwall, members of the landed classes made it their business to organize and perhaps also to participate in 'hurling' matches alongside lower-status people. This meant that the game was not played among groups of villagers autonomously, without reference to people with authority who could check what, according to the élite social standards of the time, appeared excessive violence. It was, one can suggest, members of the higher classes who were primarily responsible for the introduction into 'hurling to goales' of elements of 'fairness' such as numerical equality between sides, restrictions on numbers of participants, and rules to limit the use of physical force.

'Hurling' was not alone among the folk-games of pre-industrial Britain in drawing participants from the higher strata. They also took part in the Scone ball game, South Cardiganshire football, 'knappan' and the Haxey 'hood game'. Other accounts show that it was not just members of the gentry but members of the aristocracy, too, who took part. Thus, on 5 March 1600 John Chamberlain wrote to Dudley Carleton, later Viscount Dorchester, inviting him to 'come and see our matches at football, for that and bowling will be our best entertainment'.[18] Archibald Campbell, Seventh Earl of Argyll, Lord Willoughby of Eresby, and Emanuel Scrope, Earl of Sunderland, are three more seventeenth-century noblemen, all known to have taken part in football.[19] And Charles II attended a match between his own servants and those of the Duke of Albemarle.[20] Thus, at least during the restoration monarchy, the seal of royal approval was set on the aristocratic patronage of these folk-games.

If participation by the landed classes was regular, one would have expected the sort of modifications described by Carew to be common. Unfortunately, none of the surviving accounts contains detailed information about the nature and frequency of upper-class participation. We are forced, therefore, to speculate. It could, for example, have been merely occasional, a form of 'slumming', or even a social phenomenon in some ways equivalent to the attendance of the 'boss' at the modern office party. There is, however, reason for believing that it was regular. In that case, the fact that the level of violence was not reduced and that norms of 'fairness' and other, related changes were not widely introduced is probably to be explained by the fact that, in the sixteenth and seventeenth centuries, many members of the landowning classes would themselves have stood at a relatively low level of 'civilization'. Only leading families, especially those connected with the court, would have had a 'threshold of repugnance' sufficiently refined to condemn and wish to eradicate the rougher features of folk-games such as football. Dennis Brailsford provides support for this hypothesis with his description of the 'civilizing' function of the 'courtly movement'.[21] However, the English court never achieved the significance of its French equivalent as a 'civilizing agent'.[22] English kings were unable to establish themselves as 'absolute monarchs' and this meant that the aristocracy and gentry were able to retain greater independence than their counterparts in France. This goes some way towards explaining why many managed to escape the 'civilizing' influence of the court and, hence, were able to derive enjoyment from rowdy folk-games. It also helps to explain why the authorities found it difficult to eradicate these games, for, if our analysis is correct, they had among their protagonists people who, if not perhaps the most powerful in the land, were nevertheless locally influential.

These data on participation in the folk-antecedents of modern football by the landed classes suggest that barriers to interaction between class and status groups were in some respects lower in sixteenth- and seventeenth-century Britain than was the case at the time in continental countries such as France and than later became the case in Britain itself, especially from the early nineteenth century with the gathering momentum of industrialization. They support Laslett's contention that, during the sixteenth and seventeenth centuries, 'hierarchy was notoriously less rigid in England than elsewhere in Western Europe'.[23] In fact, prior to the nineteenth century, with the exception of the extremes of the class and status hierarchies in an urban context, the daily lives of the different classes were intertwined in a closer, more direct and personal manner than later became the case.

To say this is not to deny that inequality existed. On the contrary, class mixing in sport probably went hand in hand with the maintenance of great social distance and the demand for deference from subordinates. Indeed, the power discrepancy between the landowning and landless classes probably helps to explain this pattern. It meant that the former were secure in their status and not threatened by participation in the games of 'common' people. Precisely because their status and self-image as 'gentlemen' were secure, they could expose themselves to the possibility of defeat by 'social inferiors' and being made to look ridiculous in their eyes. However, such a state of affairs did not survive long into the nineteenth century for industrialization led to the erection of status barriers more rigid than those in existence hitherto. This increase in the rigidity of status in English society, as we shall show, played an important part in the decline of folk-football.

7. In 1801, Joseph Strutt wrote that the game of football was 'formerly much in vogue among the common people . . ., though of late years it seems to have fallen into disrepute and is but little practised'.[24] This was an exaggeration. We could cite several examples to show that football and similar folk-games were still widely played at the beginning of the nineteenth century. Yet there are reasons for believing that Strutt was not entirely wrong for folk-football was virtually extinct by the end of the nineteenth century and it is reasonable to suppose that its decline was already under way at the time he wrote.

This decline was a complex process. One of its aspects probably lay in the effects of industrialization on the time available to 'ordinary' people for participating in this kind of pastimes. According to Malcolmson, the tightening of labour discipline had a similar effect. So, too, he argues, did the declining availability of open space.[25] We do not disagree but believe that more deeply-rooted 'social forces' were at work. Thus, although there were undoubtedly class differences in this respect, Englishmen during the early stages of industrialization underwent a 'civilizing' change. According to Perkin: 'Between 1780 and 1850 the English ceased to be one of the most aggressive, brutal, rowdy, outspoken, riotous, cruel and blood-thirsty nations in the world and became one of the most inhibited, polite, orderly, tender-minded, prudish and hypocritical.'[26]

This change was not confined within the seventy-year period identified by Perkin but formed part of a long-term process which started before 1780 and continued after 1850. It is clear, nevertheless, that this period formed a watershed, a stage of rapid transition in which there occurred a 'civilizing spurt', an advance in people's 'threshold of repugnance' with regard to engaging in and witnessing violent acts. Evidence that this change may have contributed to the decline of folk-football is provided by Edward Moor in his discussion, written in 1823, of East Anglian 'camp ball'. He describes how, according to a friend, the game had fallen into disuse in Suffolk 'in consequence of two men having been killed at Easton about 40 or 50 years ago, in their struggles at a grand match'.[27] To our knowledge, no pre-nineteenth-century account mentions fear of death as a reason for giving up the game or invokes it as a motive to explain the action of others. It was simply accepted as a matter of course.

Marples mentions an account of a camp-ball match between Norfolk and Suffolk in the early 1800s in which, it seems, nine men lost their lives.[28] Apart from this, however, we are unable to provide support for our hypothesis. Nor can we describe in detail the ways in which the decline of folk-football was affected by regional and class variations in the speed, depth and firmness of these 'civilizing' changes. Such issues will have to await further research. One variation, however, does require discussion. During the early stages of industrialization, sections of the working class were 'brutalized' rather than 'civilized'. They were probably, in the main, first-generation urban dwellers, recent migrants from the country. If they could find secure employment, such people were forced to work long hours in dangerous factories and mines. Moreover, in the urban-industrial context, they encountered forms of discipline more impersonal than those to which they were accustomed. They had been uprooted from a relatively stable, rural setting and herded together in squalid, overcrowded slums. Their experiences were such that they no longer had the energy or will to maintain their rural traditions. In short, it is reasonable to suppose that the impoverished and degrading conditions under which such men were forced to live would have contributed to the decline of folk-games such as football. Paradoxical as it may seem, therefore, if our analysis is correct, both the 'civilizing process' and the 'contra-civilizing' or 'brutalizing process' that occurred among different sections of the British population in the eighteenth and nineteenth centuries played a part in the decline of the folk-antecedents of modern football.

8. However, this decline did not occur simply because people chose to abandon folk-football or were constrained to give it up by circumstances which arose in conjunction with the balance reached in the early nineteenth century between advance and regression in social standards. In part, it was forcibly suppressed. We showed earlier how the authorities had tried for centuries to abolish folk-games. During the nineteenth century, they began to meet with success for two principal reasons. Firstly because members of the aristocracy and gentry withdrew their support; and secondly because an improvement occurred in means of social control. More or less simultaneously, that is, those who wished to continue playing lost a powerful ally and were faced with an enemy whose effective power had grown.

It is reasonable to suppose that members of the aristocracy and gentry stopped mingling on the sports field with their status inferiors largely as a consequence of the changing balance of power between classes which occurred with industrialization. As this process gathered momentum, so the power of bourgeois groups increased. At the same time, members of the lower classes grew restive. Faced with a two-pronged threat to their dominance, members of the aristocracy and gentry began to abandon their paternalism towards the 'lower orders' and became increasingly status-exclusive in their social relations. Carlyle described the resultant process as an 'abdication on the part of the governors'.[29] In 1820, an anonymous contributor to *Blackwood's Edinburgh Magazine* outlined what he thought was happening as follows:

> Everywhere . . . it is too evident that the upper orders of Society have been tending . . . to a separation . . . from those whom nature, providence and the law have placed beneath them . . . The rich and the high have been indolently . . . allowing the barriers that separate them from their inferiors to increase . . . Men have come to deride . . . a thousand of those means of communication that in former days knit all orders of the people together.[30]

One of these 'means of communication' had been provided by folk-games. However, in the early nineteenth century, it became regarded as socially 'contaminating' for a 'gentleman' to take part. Thus, an anonymous Old Etonian wrote in 1831 that:

> I cannot consider the game of football . . . gentlemanly. It is a game which the common people of Yorkshire are particularly partial to, the

tips of their shoes being heavily shod with iron; and frequently death has been known to ensue from the severity of the blows inflicted . . .[31]

Faced with growing bourgeois power, members of the landed classes withdrew into their own exclusive circles, partly as a means of coping with the bourgeois attack and partly because they no longer had the security which had previously enabled them to mix freely with social inferiors. At the same time, they viewed members of the lower classes increasingly as a threat. Events in France probably intensified their fears. In that way, together with their willingness to countenance overt repression, their tendency to status-exclusiveness was reinforced.

As the aristocracy and gentry withdrew their patronage, the folk forms of football lost a prop which had enabled them to survive official attacks. After 1829, moreover, the authorities had at their disposal an instrument of social control more effective than any previously available: Sir Robert Peel's police force. The result was that, by the early twentieth century, the old forms of football which had not died out already had been effectively suppressed, save in one or two areas where they were allowed to survive in a modified, less violent and destructive form.

One or two examples must suffice to illustrate this process. At Kingston upon Thames the authorities had been trying for years to stop the local game without success. Then, in 1866, the Mayor refused to comply with the old custom of kicking off at the start of the Shrovetide match, issuing a notice pointing out that a public recreation ground had been made available and that the police had orders to stop football in the streets. This combination of measures—the provision of alternative facilities, the threat to use the police and, perhaps, the increasingly 'civilized' climate of public opinion and, hence, of opposition to such games—seems to have proved enough. At any rate, after 1866, the Kingston game is not heard of again.[32]

Elsewhere, the authorities did not meet with success so easily. For example, at Nuneaton in 1881, pitched battles broke out between footballers and the police but, even then, the game appears to have continued for several years.[33] At Ashbourne in 1860, the police prosecuted players under the Highways Act but they refused to give up what they believed to be their customary right. Finally, in 1862, after a number of further arrests, they signed an agreement, which is still in force, to play outside the town in future.[34] Such was the strength of footballers' attachment to their Shrove Tuesday game in Derby, that the Riot Act had to be read and troops called out to suppress them.[35]

Similar conflicts are reported elsewhere. There were probably more which went unrecorded and still more for which the evidence has been destroyed or remains to be collated.

Whenever in the nineteenth century a community was drawn into the mainstream of social development, the local variant of football was gradually but effectively suppressed. This process took the form of numerous separate struggles, fought in different places by different people. In each village and town, they probably experienced their struggles as unique but, in fact, they formed part of a compelling social process. As we have seen, where these folk-games did not die out spontaneously with the advance of social standards, the authorities, particularly after the 1830s, were able to back the legislation they had been enacting for centuries with the use of specialized armed organizations. The result was that, by the end of the nineteenth century, the folk forms of football were virtually extinct. However, by that time, Rugby and soccer had arisen to take their place. It is reasonable to suppose that the spread of these newer forms would itself have contributed to the decline of the folk-games from which they had originally sprung. People who found the roughness of the old forms distasteful or who were prevented from playing by the new-found power of the authorities, were presented with alternative models, more consistent with the demand for greater orderliness and more 'civilized' behaviour characteristic of an advanced industrial society.

We shall turn to these developments in Chapter 2. First of all it is necessary to address a crucial methodological issue: that of the adequacy of the evidence on which our analysis of the folk-antecedents of modern football is based.

9. The types of data on which this analysis rests—legal records, extracts from newspapers and books—have one feature in common: all are descriptions by members of the upper and middle classes of an activity in which the principal participants were lower-class. That immediately raises the question of bias, i.e. how can one be sure that these descriptions of folk-football as a rowdy affair are reflections of the game *as it really was* and not of middle- and upper-class prejudices about the lower orders? Walvin articulated this problem when he wrote:

> ... beneath the accident of surviving evidence there run a number of basic assumptions and attitudes ..., on the part of the governing class towards the game ... and ... the people who played it. The pre-industrial game of football reveals as much about the frame of mind of the governing orders, as it does about the distinctive qualities of lower-class life.[36]

Walvin does not completely doubt the validity of the sources but his book is peppered with erroneous contentions to the effect that 'open tolerance' of folk-football 'was rare among men of property and influence'.[37] Such contentions derive from his failure to grasp certain key features of the British aristocracy and gentry, and of the class structure over which they ruled. Thus, not only was the support of the landed classes crucial to the survival of folk-football in the face of centuries of opposition; it is also a fairly reliable guarantee of the adequacy of the data. This requires elaboration.

The regular participation of aristocrats and gentlemen in folk-football is indicative of a central aspect of the social structure of pre-industrial Britain: namely of a class structure which despite—or, more probably, because of—the existence of massive inequalities, permitted non-status-exclusive patterns of association to develop in the leisure-sphere. This means that the writings of gentlemen such as Carew, Owen and Moor were based on direct observation and, very often, participation in the games they were describing. Unlike the evidence from official prohibitions and the writings of Puritans such as Stubbes[38]—which they tend anyway, by and large, to confirm—they are in no way censorious even when they document what the modern observer would regard as the 'barbarous' and 'uncivilized' character of these games. Since their authors had no axe to grind, it follows that such accounts can be taken as reliable descriptions of folk-football 'as it really was', a wild and disorderly affair.

Other factors point in the same direction. Sources from different parts of the country and over several centuries combine to produce a picture of folk-football as rough and violent. Their authors were all members of the upper and middle classes but their motives and interests differed. State and local authorities and Puritans, were concerned with abolishing the game; Carew, Owen and other members of the gentry wished to produce accurate descriptions of the folk-culture of particular regions. And yet, despite these differences of motive, interest and, indeed, familiarity with the game, the same overall picture emerges. Therefore, we believe, the picture we have presented can be accepted as reliable.

2 Football in the early nineteenth-century public schools

1. Although, starting around 1800, the folk forms of football began gradually to decline, in the public schools they survived intact. As we shall show, they enjoyed immunity in that context partly because, there, they were not perceived as a threat to property and public order, and partly because, even when public school masters tried to suppress them, e.g. because they believed them to be a threat to property and order *in the schools*, they lacked the power to put their wishes into effect. The reasons why will emerge from a brief discussion.

In the late eighteenth and early nineteenth centuries, the types of football played by public schoolboys were local adaptations of the folk tradition. There was, however, a central difference between public school football and the forms played in society at large. In each case, the game was bound up with the 'prefect-fagging' system, the system of 'self-rule' which had grown up in these schools. It was the fact that football in the public schools was integrated into this authority system and not any intrinsic factors which made the public schools the setting for the earliest modernizing developments. It follows that, in order to illuminate the structure and development of football at this stage, we shall have to examine its relationship to the structure and development of authority relations in the public schools.

The schools in question were: Charterhouse, Eton, Harrow, Rugby, Shrewsbury, Westminster and Winchester. It was symptomatic of authority relations in these schools between about 1750 and 1840, that football was adopted and run by the boys themselves, sometimes in defiance of the masters. It was not, that is, an activity introduced by the staff as a matter of deliberate policy but, on the contrary, a leisure activity of the boys for which they alone were responsibile. Newsome has suggested that the educational ideology of public school masters in that period was based on 'the deeply respected tradition' that boys should be allowed the freedom to use their leisure as they wished.[1] That may have been the case but our evidence suggests that such an ideology was less a chosen educational value than a reflection of the inability of public school masters in the late eighteenth and early nineteenth centuries to control the leisure activities of their pupils.

Some public school masters in that period echoed in their attitudes to football the growing status-consciousness of the landed classes, the social strata from whose ranks their pupils were increasingly recruited. For example, Samuel Butler, headmaster of Shrewsbury from 1798 to 1836, described it as 'fit only for butcher boys ... more fit for farm boys and labourers than young gentlemen'.[2] He prohibited the game but the boys continued to play in defiance of his ruling.[3] Butler's inability to suppress an activity of which he strongly disapproved is indicative of the marked discrepancy between the *formal* authority system and the *factual* balance of power between masters and pupils at Shrewsbury School. As we shall show, such a 'power-gap' was general in the public schools at that stage. Thus, just as the authorities in society at large had, for centuries, lacked the power to suppress football and comparable activities, so, despite the authority conferred on them by statute, masters in the public schools were insufficiently powerful to prevent their pupils from playing football and engaging in other leisure pursuits of which they, the masters, disapproved. In order to explain why that was so, it is necessary to examine the structure and early development of the public schools, especially the structure and development of the prefect–fagging system. Such a discussion will shed light on the social setting in which football was played at this crucial stage in its development. It will also illuminate the social characteristics of the people involved.

2. The earliest public schools were foundations endowed by wealthy benefactors for the education of 'poor boys'. The foundation deed of Winchester, for example, states that free instruction was to be provided for 'seventy poor and needy scholars clerks living college-wise'.[4] Statutory provision was likewise made at Eton for the free education of seventy 'poor scholars' and at Westminster for forty. Charterhouse, Harrow, Rugby and Shrewsbury were also at first open, nominally at least, to the poor of their respective communities. Some have suggested that pupils at the earliest public schools were not poor but from the local middle classes. That may have been the case. It is clear, nevertheless, that the boys who attended them tended to be of *relatively* low social status.

Central among the reasons for founding educational establishments of this type was the wish to provide a training in Latin and Greek for future clerics, either so they could act as priests or administrative servants to the crown. They became known as 'public' principally because their headmasters, unlike those of 'private' schools, did not own the establishments but were salaried employees appointed by boards of trustees. More germane to the present analysis, however, is the fact that the foundation charters of the first public schools provided for the admission of fee-paying pupils. The Winchester statutes, for example, stated that, whilst the college was intended primarily for the free instruction of poor scholars, the masters were allowed to admit a limited number of pupils from wealthy and influential families provided their tuition, board and lodgings were paid for.[5]

Fee-paying pupils were called at the various schools 'oppidans', 'town-boys', 'commoners', 'boarders' and 'foreigners'. 'Poor scholars' went by names such as 'collegers', 'gownboys' and 'foundationers'. At first, the latter formed the majority and fee-payers were merely a marginal minority. During the eighteenth century, however, members of the aristocracy and gentry began to send their sons to public schools in growing numbers. As a result, the schools grew rapidly in size and the proportions and order of importance in them of 'collegers' and 'oppidans' were reversed.

The factors underlying this 'takeover' by the landed classes need not detain us. It is enough to note that central among them was a growing belief that the system of private tutors on which they had hitherto relied was now out-moded. One of the main disadvantages they perceived in it was the fact that boys educated at home lacked contact with peers and early training in independence, i.e. kinds of experience which could only be gained by mix-ing, away from home, with youngsters from the same class. The point is to explain why such a perception began to grow from about 1700 onwards.

It is, we think, reasonable to suppose that this change occurred mainly in connection with transformations then occurring in the overall structure of British society, especially in the position, composition and values of the landed élite. Central in this respect was the fact that, during the eighteenth century, the landed classes gradually consolidated, on the one hand, their power as the country's ruling class and, on the other, their independence from the king. They were divided into conflicting factions, but, in contrast to the violent upheavals of the seventeenth century, they slowly worked out rules for non-violent, above all, parliamentary struggles. These were intensi-fied by the fact that boundaries within the élite—e.g. that between the aris-tocracy and gentry—were not defined in a hard and fast manner. At the same time, partly in an attempt to bolster its waning power, the crown created new peerages, in that way changing the social composition of the aristocracy and adding to the haziness of status-group boundaries within it. The result was an increase—within the ruling class though not with respect to people below it—in status uncertainty and status striving. The emphasis on social life in what became, for the first time in that period, primarily upper-class schools was evidently connected with this pacification of the political life of the ruling élite, with the gradual consolidation of their power, and with the intensification of the status struggle that took place within their ranks. Parents who sent their sons to public schools, it is reasonable to suppose, wanted them to learn at an early age how to cope with the nepotism and peculiar mixture of 'refinement' and competition which life in 'Society' involved.

The takeover of the public schools by the aristocracy and gentry thus led to a change of emphasis in their educational pattern. The acquisition of classical knowledge—the most important requirement for a commoner who wished to be upwardly mobile through the channels offered by the church—lost weight. At the same time, the lessons to be learned from the social life of a school, from the relations which young noblemen and gentlemen formed among themselves, gained in importance. That is, the public schools came to serve as training grounds for the social life which young gentlemen and nobles would have to lead as adults, e.g. during the London 'Season', in their clubs and parliament. During the nineteenth century, this aspect of public school education was justified as 'character training' but, initially, practical considerations seem to have played a larger part in its development than educational theory.

As long as pupils in the public schools were largely 'poor scholars', the masters appear to have retained command. When, however, pupils from the ruling classes flocked to them, their position deteriorated. Central among the developments which reduced the masters' power was the changed dependency pattern which resulted from the upper-class takeover. When 'poor scholars' had formed the majority, most pupils had wanted from the schools what the masters could offer, namely a classical education. The boys, in that respect, depended on the masters. As the social composition of the schools began to change, however, so the masters grew financially dependent on the fees paid by the families of their wealthy pupils. Their power was reduced accordingly. It was limited, too, by their growing career dependency on the patronage of upper-class families, for example, if they wanted to move from teaching into the church. In short, the emergent pattern of inter-dependencies was asymmetrical. The masters' power was accordingly reduced.

The fact that upper-class boys were not dependent on the formal education which the schools could offer worked in the same direction. That is, their parents sent them to public schools primarily for the experience of independence to be obtained from living away from home and for the informal education they could gain from relations with their peers. The struggles which the boys engaged in, both among themselves and with the masters, were considered crucial in this respect. So were their rough and disorderly sports. Upper-class parents came, as we have seen, to believe that such aspects of the informal life of public schools offered a useful training in 'manly independence'. They valued them, on that account, more highly than Latin and Greek.

However, asymmetrical interdependence was only one aspect of a wider configuration which limited the masters' power. For example, as the composition of the schools began to change, so the position of the masters became reminiscent of that of the private tutors employed in noble and gentry households. That is, they became paid servants, inferior in status to the families of their pupils.[6] This reduced their power because it meant they were caught in a mesh of conflicting expectations. They were accustomed to acting deferentially towards members of the aristocracy and gentry but, at the same time, used to being treated deferentially by their pupils. Confronted with pupils who were aristocrats and gentlemen, they became hesitant and uncertain in the execution of their role. As a result, still more of their authority was eroded. It was diminished even further by the deterioration in the staff–student ratio which accompanied the upper-class takeover.

3. In such a situation, conflict and tension were bound to be endemic. The boys, particularly the older oppidans, resented being given orders by men they considered socially inferior. And since in most cases the boys lacked either the motivation or the parental pressure to take anything other than superficial advantage of the opportunities for formal education offered by the schools, the classical learning of the teaching staff did not compensate, in their eyes, for the more general social inferiority of the latter. For their part, the masters resented being looked down upon by boys who, whatever the social status of their families, were only young and who refused to treat them with the respect they thought their status as school-masters, classical scholars and adults made due. Not surprisingly, this combination of class resentment, status tension and conflicting educational objectives frequently became manifest in direct clashes. Sometimes they escalated into open rebellion. Our list of rebellions (see Table 2.1) in the eighteenth and early nineteenth-century public schools gives an idea of the powerlessness of the school authorities relative to their pupils in that period.

These rebellions were sparked off in a variety of ways. A few examples will show, however, that, recurrent among their causes, was the fight waged by generations of public schoolboys for autonomy and the rights and privileges later accorded to them formally. Thus at Eton in 1768, the prefects rebelled because the headmaster, Dr Foster, would not recognize what they regarded as their right to punish junior boys for breaking bounds. It is significant that his father was a tradesman and that he was despised by the aristocratic boys. They forced him to resign.[7] The two revolts at Harrow occurred because the boys attempted to gain a say in the election of headmasters and were not consulted over the appointments of Drs Heath and Butler.[8] The 1808 Winchester rebellion broke out because the headmaster, Dr Goddard, tried to make a Saint's day a schoolday without consulting the prefects.[9] In 1818,

Table 2.1 Selected List of Public School Rebellions (1728–1832)

1728	Eton	1797	Rugby
1768	Eton	1798	Eton
1770	Winchester	1808	Charterhouse, Harrow, Winchester
1771	Harrow	1810	Eton
1774	Winchester	1818	Eton, Shrewsbury, Winchester
1778	Winchester	1820	Rugby
1783	Eton	1822	Rugby
1786	Rugby	1828	Winchester
1793	Winchester	1832	Eton

his successor, Dr Gabell, faced a revolt directed in the name of 'liberty' against his use of 'spying methods'.[10] And the Winchester 'commoners' rebelled in 1828 because the headmaster, Dr Williams, appointed as prefects boys of whom they disapproved.[11]

It is no misnomer to describe these disturbances as 'rebellions'. The 1818 Winchester revolt could only be quelled by the militia using bayonets and, in 1793, the boys there 'victualled the College for a regular siege, ransacking the shops for provisions; they . . . provided themselves with swords, guns and bludgeons and . . . mounted the red cap of liberty and equality'.[12] An account of the revolt at Rugby in 1797 sheds more detailed light on these rebellions and describes a key aspect of the circumstances at the school immediately prior to a formative period in the development of the game which bears its name. It began when the headmaster, Dr Ingles, heard the sound of pistol shots from a boarding house. He apprehended the culprit, demanding where he had obtained the gunpowder. The boy named a local tradesman but the latter denied the offence. The boy was flogged and, with a group of friends, sought revenge by smashing the tradesman's windows. Learning of this, the headmaster demanded that the damage be paid for by the whole fifth and sixth forms. The boys then drew up a 'round robin' declaring that they would do no such thing and events moved to a climax. The headmaster's classroom door was blown off its hinges with explosives and its windows were smashed. A fire was started in the Close out of desks, benches and wainscoting from the walls, and the headmaster's books were thrown on top. Order was only finally restored by reading the Riot Act and with the help of a party of soldiers, drawn swords in hand, who happened to be in Rugby at the time.[13]

This account illustrates the difficulties which late-eighteenth- and early-nineteenth-century public school masters faced with respect to control of their schools. There took place a struggle between masters and boys in which neither party was able to establish permanent and effective dominance. As a result, there gradually emerged a customary system of dual control in which the rule of masters was regarded as legitimate in the classroom in return for their recognition of the prefects' right to exercise dominance as far as extra-curricular activities were concerned. This system was unstable, however, and open conflict was constantly liable to recur.

4. 'Fagging' emerged as part of the same process. The fact that masters were no longer able to control the oldest boys meant they were unable to control them in relation to their younger and weaker fellows. As a result, there emerged a dominance hierarchy determined mainly by relativities of age and physical strength; i.e. the boys who were older and/or physically stronger 'lorded it' over those who were younger and/or physically weaker. The juniors were forced into the role of 'fags', i.e. to perform menial services for their seniors. The strongest held sway and, as one would expect of teenagers

untrammelled by effective adult control, they often exercised their power cruelly. Bullying was the order of the day in the late-eighteenth- and early-nineteenth-century public schools. It was often physically severe as the following examples show. The Earl of Albemarle records that, when he revolted against the system, his fag-master made him stand to attention and repeatedly knocked him down.[14] Moody, a boy at Winchester, was told by a prefect to take off his gown and then beaten, in the words of the victim, 'with a great whip, I believe as big as my wrist, and as long as he was able'.[15] Charles Milnes Gaskell, a boy at Eton, wrote in 1824 that: 'Rolles got spurs and rode some of us over a leap positively impossible to be leapt over with a person on your back, and every time (which is every time) we cannot accomplish it, he spurs us violently, and my thigh is now quite sore with the inroads made by that dreadful spur.'[16]

Of course, these examples show only one side of the coin. The prefect–fagging system was not conducive simply to cruel treatment of the younger by the older boys. There were, for example, some kind fag-masters and relations of mutual affection sometimes grew up between prefects and fags. More importantly, the system came to be accorded customary status and, as that occurred, fags were able to obtain from their fag-masters a degree of protection from the tyrannical propensities of other boys. In short, the system came to involve an element of reciprocity: protection was exchanged for performance of the services of a fag. It is nevertheless correct to describe the system as one of customary dominance of the younger by the older boys since, given the absence of effective adult control, the prefects and, more generally, the older and physically stronger boys, were able to act in relation to their younger and weaker fellows in accordance with their whims, unchecked by anything other than the customary restraints which they forged among themselves. These were based on the standards of masculinity characteristic of the period and class from which they came and received support from the majority of parents. By present-day standards, fagging may seem to have been a brutalizing institution. However, from the standpoint of upper-class parents in the eighteenth and nineteenth centuries, at least of those who sent their sons to public schools, it was a crucial means of training boys in 'manliness' and 'independence'.

5. The leisure activities of public schoolboys corresponded to these power relations. At each school, football was one means by which older asserted their dominance over younger boys. Accordingly, one of the customary duties which developed for fags was that of 'fagging out' at football. This meant they were forced to play and restricted, for the most part, to the role of 'keeping goal', i.e. ranged *en masse* along the base lines. At Winchester, lines of fags were even used to demarcate the pitch!

A few examples will give an idea of the way in which public school football at that stage depended organizationally on the prefect–fagging system and reflected the roughness of older in relation to younger boys. Since the accounts from which these examples are taken were written by 'old boys' reminiscing in the middle and later parts of the nineteenth century about their school-days, it is possible that they may have been coloured by memory-lapses and the tendency to romanticize youth often found in the writings of older men. There is, however, a remarkable consistency in what they wrote. Indeed, regarding the organizational dependency of public school football at that stage on the prefect–fagging system and its character as a rough, wild game, there is total unanimity. It is not unreasonable, accordingly, to suppose that their accounts approximate closely to public school football 'as it really was'.

An account by Bloxam of the football played at Rugby during Dr Wooll's headmastership (1806–28) brings out the dependency of the game at that stage on the prefect–fagging system:

> All fags were stopped on going out after three o'clock calling over . . . and compelled to go into the Close . . . When . . . all had assembled . . ., two of the best players . . . commenced choosing in about a score on each side. A somewhat rude division was made of the remaining fags, half of whom were sent to keep goal on the one side, the other half to the opposite goal for the same purpose. Any fag, though not specially chosen in, might follow up on that side to the goal of which he was attached . . .[17]

An account by Captain Markham shows that a similar type of football was played at Westminster in the early nineteenth century:

> The small boys, the duffers and the funk-sticks were the goalkeepers, twelve or fifteen at each end, . . . if any fellow who was playing out showed any sign of 'funk', he was packed off into goals . . ., not only for that day, but as a lasting degradation. But . . . if any goal-keeper made a good save . . . or made a plucky attempt to tackle . . ., he was called for immediately to play out, and thenceforth played out always . . .
>
> A bully was formed in the middle . . . and the ball was thrown in between the lines; then there was a general shinning match till it worked out. No off-side play was allowed . . . Handling . . . was allowed, but only to this extent: you might not pick a ball up from the ground, or after first bound was over, but you might catch it before or after first bound if fairly in the air; and you might then, if . . . not previously charged, and knocked head-over-heels, take two or three paces . . ., sufficient for a half-volley kick off the hand. You might not 'punt' it from the hand— that is, kick it full volley—or drive it with your fist . . . there were perpetual rough-and-tumble bullies. . . . In these . . . shinning was allowed, and many a hack one got. Shin-guards were unknown. . . . The boys in goals had a cold time of it . . . jackets on, but no caps, and hands deep in

their pockets. There was no 'time' or changing of ends, and the only break in the game was at a goal or before a kick-out.

> ...when I first came running with the ball (Rugby fashion) was allowed, and 'fist-punting' when you had the ball in hand ... when running like this, the enemy tripped, shinned, charged with the shoulder, got you down and sat upon you—in fact, might do anything short of murder to get the ball from you. I think that this running and 'fist punting' was stopped in 1851 or 1852.[18]

Charterhouse boys played a similar game when the school occupied premises in London (1611–1873). It was called 'football in cloisters'. The cloister in question was seventy yards long, twelve feet wide, paved with smooth flagstones and surrounded by walls made of sharp, jagged flints. A number of buttresses protruded into it, providing hazards for the players and helping to shape the tactics. The doors at each end served as goals. Its form in the early nineteenth century is described by Eardley-Wilmot and Streatfield:

> ...the ball very soon got into one of the buttresses, when a terrific squash would be the result, some fifty or sixty boys huddled together vigorously 'rouging', kicking and shoving to extricate the ball. A skilful player, feeling that he had the ball in front of his legs, would patiently bide his time, until, perceiving an opportunity, he would dexterously work out the ball and rush wildly with it down the Cloisters towards the coveted goal. The squash would then dissolve and go in pursuit. Now was the time for the pluck and judgement of the Fags to be tried. To prevent the ball getting in amongst them at the goal, one of the foremost Fags would rush out and engage the onset of the dribbling foe, generally to be sent spinning head over heels for five yards along the stones. It served a purpose, however, for it not only gave his side time to come up, but also his fellow Fags encouragement to show a close and firm front. If the boy with the ball happened to be well backed up by his own House, they would launch themselves right into the middle of the Fags, when a terrific scrimmage would ensue. The Fags would strive their utmost to prevent the ball being driven through, and hammer away with fists at hands grasping the corners of the wall to obtain a better purchase for shoving. One of these scrimmages sometimes lasted for three quarters of an hour. Shins would be kicked black and blue; jackets and other articles of clothing almost torn into shreds; and Fags trampled underfoot. At the end nearly the whole contending mass would collapse upon the ground, when the ball would be discovered under a heap of prostrate antagonists, all more or less the worse for the fray.[19]

G. S. Davies corroborates this account and illuminates the organizational variability of Charterhouse football at that stage:

When the game was played by a limited number . . . —say, nine a side, or even better still, six a side—it was a really fine game. But when a big game was ordered, such as Gownboys versus School, in which all the fags had to block the respective goals, it was, in my opinion, a very poor game indeed, consisting in a series of 'squashes' or dead blocks, in which the ball was entirely lost to sight, and a mass of humanity surged and heaved senselessly, often for as much as half an hour at a time. But whether played by many or by few the game was unavoidably rough. Hard knocks had to be taken cheerfully. A fierce charge was apt to send a player with his head against the wall and much skin was lost at times. But it was a fine training for keeping the temper under very trying circumstances.[20]

Writing of Charterhouse football during his schooldays in the 1820s, the Rev. T. Mozley shed further light onto its danger. 'There were', he wrote, 'a good many broken shins, for most of the fellows had iron tips to their very strong shoes, and some freely boasted of giving more than they took.'[21] Iron-tipped shoes were also used at Rugby where they had a special name for them—'navvies'. According to an Old Rugbeian reminiscing in the 1920s, navvies had 'a thick sole, the profile of which at the toe much resembled the ram of an ironclad'.[22]

The fags at Winchester were used as 'boundary markers' and 'goal posts'. This aspect of the game there is described by H. C. Adams thus:

An oblong space was marked out . . . fenced . . . by a row of juniors, who stood side by side for the entire distance, and whose business it was to prevent the ball from escaping. At either end, in the centre of the open space, a boy was placed who stood with outstretched legs, and a gown rolled up at either foot: he was called the 'goal'.[23]

6. The main characteristics of public school football at that stage emerge clearly from these accounts. It was a loose, informally organized affair in which 'scratch' matches were the norm. Teams had neither names nor permanence and were not related to structural features other than the prefect–fagging system. As a result, membership had to be determined entirely on a match-by-match basis. Yet, despite its informal character, the game was not structureless. It had a firm structure which derived, in part, from its folk roots and, in part, from its dependency on the prefect–fagging system. It is the latter source of structure which concerns us here.

Football was a means by which older boys and prefects asserted their dominance over younger boys and fags. For the former, it was a recreation but also a means of symbolizing their power and prestige. For the latter, it was partly a recreation but also partly a duty which expressed, often painfully, their subordinate position. 'Douling', the name given to football at Shrewsbury and reputedly derived from the Greek for 'slave', was the same as they used for 'fagging',[24] a double meaning which gives clear expression to the close relationship which existed between public school football in the eighteenth and early nineteenth centuries and the prefect–fagging system in its then-existing form.

In order to express their dominance, the prefects made football compulsory. Each boy had to attend but fags were subject to double compulsion: during the season, one of their customary duties was 'fagging out' at football. That is, the status and role of the individual in the game were largely dependent on his status and role in the authority system of the boys. The older boys and prefects were the main participants: their power and status gave them the right to determine who should perform an attacking role. It was a privilege they reserved almost entirely for themselves. Most fags were relegated to a defensive role, that of 'keeping goal'. This meant, as we remarked before, that they were ranged *en masse*, either along the base-lines or, as at Winchester, along the sides of the pitch. Their task was to prevent the ball being driven across. Whether any escaped this role depended on whether, in the judgment of the prefects, they were 'plucky', i.e. 'manly' players. Apart from this status-linked division between attackers and defenders, there was, as far as we can tell, no permanent or formalized division of labour in these games.

The boys alone were responsible for running their football at this stage. In no case was it controlled by masters. In fact, the official attitude towards it, largely on account of its lower-class associations, was one of outright hostility and contempt. However, the attitudes and values of the masters were, at best, a marginal factor in the situation. Their power in the schools was insufficient to enable them to stamp their imprint on the leisure activities of the boys. One might have expected upper-class boys, many of them sons of noblemen and gentlemen, to have exercised greater self-control in their football. However, they were young and, whilst in residence at school, free from direct parental influence. The masters, as we have seen, lacked the power to function effectively *in loco parentis*. Hence, there was no effective restraint on the boys who controlled the game. Those who were older and/or physically stronger were able to exercise virtually unrestrained dominance over their younger and weaker fellows. They played roughly with each other and do not appear to have tempered the violence of their play in relation to younger boys. In short, the relatively 'uncivilized' character of social relations at that stage in the development of the public schools was reflected in the types of football they played.

These games were essentially local variants of the folk tradition. In the public schools, however, the roughness inherent in folk-football was reinforced. Thus at Charterhouse and Rugby the boys wore iron-capped boots to make their 'hacking' more effective. Since football was rough and physically dangerous, it expressed the virtues of 'manliness' and physical courage prized by the English ruling classes. It was able, therefore, to serve as a means whereby the boys could test each other and single out promising candidates for future power and prestige. One can detect here in embryo the system of choosing leading pupils—the prefects or praepostors—principally from among the boys who were good at games. It was not until the 1840s, however, that this system began to be run with the approval of masters as well as senior boys.

Like the folk-games to which they were related, the ancestral forms of football in the public schools stood at a stage of variable local customs rather than of unified national rules. However, despite the existence of local differences, an underlying similarity can be detected in the games of all the schools. For example, the 'scrummage', although called a variety of names such as the 'squash', the 'hot' and, at Westminster and Eton, the 'bully',[25] was everywhere a central feature. At all the schools, moreover, both kicking and, under certain circumstances, catching and handling were permissible. The Westminster and Rugby customs governing use of hands are described in the accounts by Markham and Bloxam but there were similar customs at the other schools. Thus at Winchester, players who 'caught the ball in the air were allowed a run of three yards and then a kick . . .'[26] At Shrewsbury, 'a player who caught the ball direct from a kick could take a "hoist" [i.e. a drop-kick]; otherwise the ball might not be handled'.[27] And in the 'field' variant of Charterhouse football, 'handling . . . was allowed, and the ball, if caught or stopped at first bound, might be used in a drop-kick'.[28]

However, recognition of the underlying similarities in public school football at that stage should not divert attention from the differences that existed. The structure of British society in the late eighteenth and early nineteenth centuries did not lend itself to unification of the type that came later. Means of transport and communication were still in a relatively undeveloped state. The game at each school was, therefore, played in relative isolation and there were no inter-school competitions. Consequently, there was ample room within the general model for the occurrence of local innovation. Since the rules exhibited the mixture of fixity and fluidity characteristic of oral traditions, new playing practices must have cropped up again and again and congealed into custom. At Rugby some time during the 1820s or 1830s, carrying the ball or 'running in', the practice which has since become the most distinctive feature of Rugby football, emerged and gradually hardened. It can initially have been no more than one of those fluid local customs often found at such a stage in the development of rules. It received its wider significance only when local customs began to be replaced by unified national rules for, only then, did the question arise as to which local rules were to be incorporated into the national model. For the moment, it remained just one local custom among many. This downgrading of the significance of the initial emergence of this distinctive feature of Rugby football differs so widely from the currently dominant idea that it is necessary to conclude this chapter with a brief discussion of the reasons why we find the traditional ideology unacceptable.

7. It is widely believed that Rugby acquired its distinctive form as a result of a single deviant act. The 'actor' in question was William Webb Ellis and the act is held to have taken place in 1823. A stone inset in a wall at Rugby commemorates it. Despite the authority apparently thus conferred, there is reason to believe that the Webb Ellis story is a myth. It was first put forward by Bloxam in 1880,[29] but he had left the school in 1820, i.e. three years prior to the supposed event. His account, therefore, was based on hearsay recalled at a distance of over fifty years. It would probably have faded into obscurity had it not been for circumstances which affected the development of Rugby football in the 1890s. By that decade, the game had spread to the North where it had begun to emerge as a commercial spectacle with players and spectators drawn principally from the working class. This process of commercialization and 'proletarianization' was conducive to conflict and led, in 1895, to the split between Union and League. It cannot have been accidental that 1895 also witnessed the publication of a report by the Old Rugbeian Society in which Bloxam's story was resurrected.[30] It was also in that year and also at the instigation of Old Rugbeians that the commemorative stone was erected.

There is no need to go into the details of the Old Rugbeian report. It is enough simply to note that it was basically occasioned by what Rugbeians perceived as the threat posed to their game by its spread to groups they considered 'alien' and 'inferior'. They were increasingly being beaten, quite literally 'at their own game', by these groups. It was beginning to escape from their control and to change in directions which ran counter to their values. By giving pride of place in their report to the Webb Ellis story, an origin myth which correctly locates the beginnings of Rugby football in their school, they were, it is reasonable to suggest, attempting to consolidate their ranks and reassert their proprietorship in the face of a powerful 'alien' threat.

Simply to put forward this hypothesis and an account of the circumstances surrounding the introduction of the Webb Ellis story is not, of course, to disprove it. However, there are further grounds for doubt. It is just not sociologically plausible that a deeply-entrenched traditional game could have been changed fundamentally by a single act, particularly that of a low-status individual such as Webb Ellis is reputed to have been.[31] In any case, the story is incomplete. It fails to consider how, in the social circumstances which prevailed at Rugby in the early nineteenth century, the practice of 'running in' became institutionalized; i.e. it fails to show what it was that led the boys to accept his innovation, not as a punishable misdemeanour, but as a desirable modification, worthy of incorporation into their football as a permanent and legitimate feature. Furthermore, it was also in the second quarter of the nineteenth century that Rugby acquired such distinctive features as an oval ball, 'H-shaped' goals, scoring above the cross-bar, and points for 'tries' as well as 'goals'. Thus, in focusing solely on the development of carrying, the Webb Ellis story fails to explain all aspects of the emergent uniqueness of the game.

In the chapters which follow, we shall propose a sociologically more adequate explanation, more specifically that the emergence of Rugby as a distinctive game occurred in conjunction with its modernization and that this was connected, in its turn, with Britain's industrialization. However, before we explore these links in greater detail, it is necessary to touch briefly upon a theoretical issue which the Webb Ellis story raises, namely the scientific status of attempts to explain social developments in terms of the actions of single individuals.

Reductionist origin myths of this kind are common in our society. They reflect the currently predominant atomistic image of social structure and the notion of the historical process as a structureless sequence of events. In terms of the prevailing ideology, social developments result from the ideas and actions, either of 'great men' or identifiable individuals who, even if they were not recognized as 'great' in their own time, have a kind of charisma posthumously thrust upon them. Such ideas are indicative of the way in which our individualistic values tend to blur the perception of social structure and social process, for it is clear that a complex game such as Rugby could not have developed simply as a result of a single deviant act by a specific individual. It must have been, as Norbert Elias would express it, '*men*-made' rather than 'man-made', a collective invention and not the invention of a single individual, an institution which emerged over several decades as part of an unintended social process involving the interactions of numerous interdependent individuals. It is our task in the chapters which follow to unravel the manner in which this unplanned long-term process took place.

Part II

The Modernization of Rugby Football

3 The preconditions for modernization: *embourgeoisement* and public school reform

1. Social changes more fundamental than any which occurred in pre-industrial Britain were required to free football from its traditional mould and transform it into a modern sport. It was in the public schools in conjunction with industrialization that such changes took place. In these schools, starting in the 1830s the game began to change fundamentally and in a specific direction. More particularly, it began to be organized more formally, to become more complex and the rules began to be written down. It also grew more 'civilized' in at least two senses: players began to be required to exercise greater self-control and some of the wilder features began to be eradicated or subjected to more stringent control. As we shall show, Rugby was the first school at which football began to undergo this transformation, i.e. Rugby was the first variant of the game to begin to acquire its modern form.

In all the schools, the incipient modernization of football was a *collective* process. In no case did a single individual or single group sit down and deliberately produce a blueprint for a type of football which it was hoped would be more appropriate for the new form of social relations which industrialization was bringing into being. It was, that is, an unplanned process, an unintended consequence of the social changes wrought by industrialization. It took the form of step-by-step adjustments to contingencies as and when they arose; i.e. fully-fledged modern forms did not spring into existence suddenly. Thus, when written rules were produced for the first time in the 1840s, no attempt was made to legislate for the game as a whole; several aspects continued to be subject to customary controls. Similarly although the organization of football began in this period to grow more formal, it remained for some time a purely local game; i.e. national rules were still some distance in the future. Finally, although the game began in about 1830 to change in the direction of greater 'civilization', it remained by present standards rough and 'uncivilized'. In short, one is dealing here with a transitional stage. That is what we mean by referring to the *incipient* modernization of the game.

The part played by industrialization in this process was complex and indirect. That is, modern game-forms were not brought into being mechanically, as an automatic reflex of this economic transformation, but developed as a result of a sequence of interwoven changes which took place on separate though interconnected levels of social integration. Since, however, it was industrialization which set these interwoven changes in motion, one could say that it formed the 'prime mover'. Thus, at the 'societal' level, industrialization led to a change in the balance of power between classes, more specifically to an increase in the power of the bourgeoisie—the urban-industrial middle classes—relative to the aristocracy and gentry. Since its central feature was a growth in bourgeois power, we have referred to this change as a process of *embourgeoisement*.[1] In its turn, *embourgeoisement* led at the 'intermediate' level to a struggle for control of major institutions, among them the public schools. This produced a crisis which was resolved by reform of the prefect–fagging system, a process first successfully accomplished at Rugby under Thomas Arnold. The reforms he undertook led to the emergence at the school, i.e. at the 'microsocial' level, of a social structure conducive to modernizing innovation. It was in that context that incipient modernization began to take place.

However, such a structure formed a 'necessary', not a 'sufficient' condition for the occurrence of this process. In order to explain why the boys at Rugby acted in ways which unintentionally led to the transformation of their game in a modernizing direction, reference has to be made to another causal sequence. As we shall show, it, too, was initially set in motion by industrialization and *embourgeoisement*. Important among the links in this second causal chain were an intensification of status-competition within and between the upper and middle classes and, as part of it, an increase of status-rivalry among the public schools. Also significant was the transformation in the ideal of 'gentlemanly' behaviour which occurred in that connection.

It will probably help the reader if we set forth diagrammatically the manner in which these processes were related. Figure 3.1 portrays schematically the links in the chain by which industrialization led the 'modernizing agents', the boys at Rugby School, to act in ways which, even though they did not set out with such an aim in mind, resulted in the production of a more distinct, more complex and what, in retrospect, one can call more 'modern' form of football. This representation of the interwoven processes involved in the incipient modernization of Rugby is complex. We have decided, therefore, to split our treatment of the evidence from which it was constructed into two separate chapters. The remainder of the present chapter is devoted to a brief discussion of industrialization, *embourgeoisement* and their role in producing public school reform. We then look more intensively at the reforms effected by Arnold and at his attitudes and policies in respect of sport. Then in Chapter 4 we trace the different causal chains which link industrialization and the incipient modernization of Rugby, concluding with a brief discussion of the bifurcation between it and soccer.

It may seem strange that a whole chapter in a book about Rugby should be devoted to the social context within which it developed and hardly mention the game itself. Such an approach is necessary, however, because our analysis

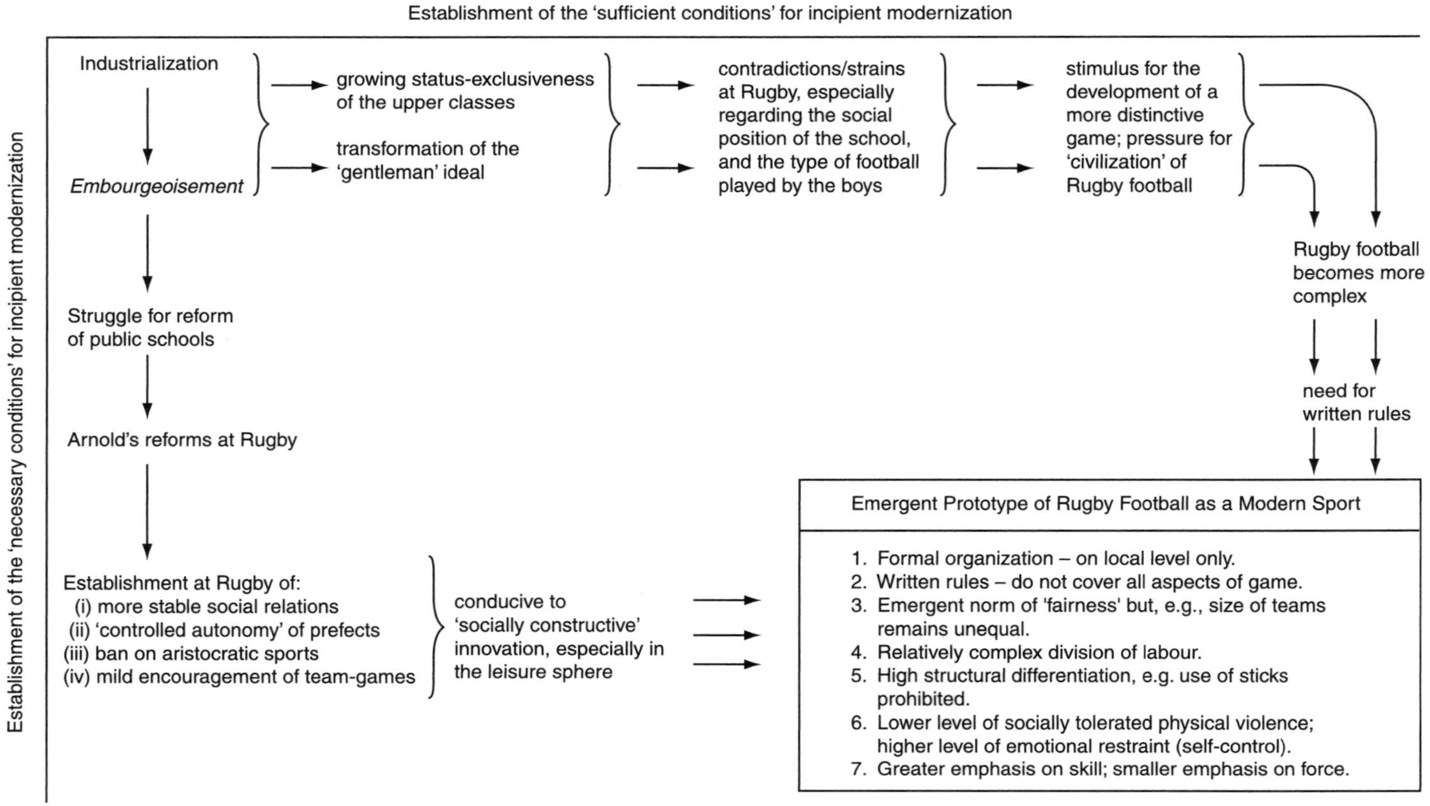

Establishment of the 'sufficient conditions' for incipient modernization

Industrialization → growing status-exclusiveness of the upper classes

Embourgeoisement → transformation of the 'gentleman' ideal

} → contradictions/strains at Rugby, especially regarding the social position of the school, and the type of football played by the boys

→ stimulus for the development of a more distinctive game; pressure for 'civilization' of Rugby football

} → Rugby football becomes more complex → need for written rules →

Struggle for reform of public schools →

Arnold's reforms at Rugby →

Establishment at Rugby of:
(i) more stable social relations
(ii) 'controlled autonomy' of prefects
(iii) ban on aristocratic sports
(iv) mild encouragement of team-games

} → conducive to 'socially constructive' innovation, especially in the leisure sphere

Emergent Prototype of Rugby Football as a Modern Sport

1. Formal organization – on local level only.
2. Written rules – do not cover all aspects of game.
3. Emergent norm of 'fairness' but, e.g., size of teams remains unequal.
4. Relatively complex division of labour.
5. High structural differentiation, e.g. use of sticks prohibited.
6. Lower level of socially tolerated physical violence; higher level of emotional restraint (self-control).
7. Greater emphasis on skill; smaller emphasis on force.

Establishment of the 'necessary conditions' for incipient modernization

Figure 3.1

does not tally in all respects with the 'received wisdom'. Therefore we have to spell out the intricate ways in which we believe industrialization, *embour-geoisement* and the development of the public schools were interwoven and how, together with the normative changes referred to in Figure 3.1, they contributed to incipient modernization. If you like, the remainder of the present chapter is concerned with the emergence of the *preconditions* for that process, with the creation of a social structure at Rugby School which was conductive to innovation by the boys. As we have said, these preconditions were formed as a result of interwoven developments at different levels of social integration. Our analytical strategy involves us in starting at the 'macro-' and working down to the 'microsocial' level. It is to developments at the 'macrosocial' level that our attention will now be turned, in the first instance to *embourgeoisement* and its part in producing public school reform.

2. The dominant long-term process in nineteenth-century Britain was a process of *embourgeoisement*. By this, we mean that, as the nineteenth century progressed and industrialization gathered momentum, the power of the bourgeoisie grew with the result that institutions which had previously been adapted to the interests of the aristocracy and gentry began to reflect bourgeois interests and bourgeois values. The public schools were no exception.

In the 1830s and 40s, *embourgeoisement* was still in its early stages. That is hardly surprising when one remembers that the British economy remained largely agricultural until about 1850. In fact, the bourgeoisie never became powerful enough during the nineteenth century to dislodge the aristocracy and gentry entirely from their position as the country's ruling class. As a result, many bourgeois, even the most radical, were forced to pare their aspirations down to a level commensurate with their power as members of an ascendant class. Others were constrained to adopt aristocratic and gentry values, i.e. to use the landed classes as a 'reference group'.

For their part, the landed classes were not sufficiently powerful to smash the bourgeois challenge. That was partly because they had begun to grow dependent on the latter for the performance of essential functions. Thus, as warfare grew dependent on industrial production, so the state, which was then controlled by the landed classes, grew dependent on the bourgeoisie for the conduct of international affairs. The growth of the state domestically worked in the same direction. The expansion of the civil service, the creation of a factory inspectorate, the establishment of the police force, and many other aspects of state-formation, all served to make the ruling more depen-dent on the middle class. That was true, not only in 'affairs of state', but in social life more generally.

At the same time, the growth of bourgeois wealth and power led to an increase of status-inconsistency within the upper classes. That is, the wealth and power of some members of the bourgeoisie began to surpass that of some members of the aristocracy and gentry. As a result, gentry and aristocratic status no longer uniquely signalled a dominant position on all dimensions of social stratification. Hence, in order to defend their interests, members of the aristocracy and gentry were forced to adopt economic strategems inconsistent with the dominant values of their class. For example, some began to profit from the sale or leasing of mineral rights, others to obtain a financial stake in commercial and industrial enterprises. Others still became businessmen in their own right.[2] At the same time, they were forced as a class to accommodate, to change some of their ideas and values, and to permit reform in areas of social structure which, hitherto, had been organized to serve their interests almost solely.

Despite this mutual accommodation and value-convergence in which sections of the landed classes underwent 'partial bourgeoisification' and sections of the bourgeoisie, 'partial aristocratization', it remains correct to conceptualize the dominant social process in nineteenth-century Britain as *embourgeoisement*. At the beginning of the century, the bourgeoisie were a subordinate, 'middle' class. However, their power-base lay principally in the relatively dynamic sphere of industrial production. Therefore, in the long term, they were destined to triumph over the aristocracy and gentry whose power derived primarily from the ownership and control of land, a relatively 'static' resource. In short, the bourgeoisie were the future ruling class. Mutual accommodation and value-fusion occurred at a stage of *embourgeoisement* when the power of the established and ascendant classes was approximately equal. That stage is described by historians as the 'mid-Victorian compromise'.[3] In the long term it was unstable but, while it lasted, there began to occur, in addition to the accommodation and value-fusion mentioned above, a partial unification and amalgamation of the established and rising classes. It was in that context that reform of the public schools and, with it, the modernization of football, began to occur.

3. Public school reform did not come about as a result of a growing bourgeois demand for entry to the schools for their sons. In the medium term, that was one of its *consequences* but the reform itself was achieved as part of the struggle for national supremacy which accompanied industrialization and *embourgeoisement*. A struggle over the public schools formed part of that contest because, as élite-training institutions, they were considered socially and politically important.[4] And, in its turn, the prefect–fagging system formed a major focus of that struggle because it was widely regarded as the fulcrum on which the overall system rested.

By the 1830s, the pressure for public school reform had grown sufficiently to force the authorities to respond. Fuel was added to the fire by the fact that, largely as a result of the adverse publicity which resulted from the struggle for reform, all schools except Eton and Rugby experienced a substantial decline in numbers.[5] However, as was generally the case in Britain in that period, no class or party was in a position to impose its will. In short, the situation was conducive to compromise, to moderate rather than radical reform. Conservatives who wished to retain the *status quo* were out-numbered and outflanked. So were radicals who wished to abolish public schools. In fact, faced with bourgeois pressure and that from reactionary groups who wanted change in order, as they saw it, to resurrect a vanished 'golden age', more and more conservatives were led to espouse the doctrines of 'liberal Toryism'. As a result, they became politically indistinguishable from the majority of liberals. The latter, too, demanded only moderate reform. Their adherence to *laissez-faire* principles prevented them from contemplating state education. At the same time, even though the prefect–fagging system in its existing form offended against the universalistic, humanitarian sentiments which many of them, as members of a rising class, adhered to, their *laissez-faire* ideas led them to favour a degree of self-rule by the boys. Thus, circumstances conspired to make a majority among the interested parties favour moderate reform. They wanted the schools kept free from state interference. At the same time, they wanted the hand of the masters strengthened yet autonomy preserved for the boys. Faced with such diffuse yet mounting pressure, the schools were forced to undertake reform. They had to in order to survive.

Reform was attempted in several public schools in the early nineteenth century. However, lasting reform of a type capable of being adopted elsewhere was achieved for the first time at Rugby under Thomas Arnold (1828–42). He succeeded where others failed largely because his reforms were consistent with the stage of *embourgeoisement* reached by the 1830s. They were, that is, of a compromise character. They managed to restore staff authority yet retain a measure of pupil freedom. A few words about Arnold's personal history and social situation will show why and how he was able to institute reforms of that type. We shall then explore aspects of the structure and composition of Rugby School in order to show why it, rather than some other school, was the first to undergo reform. Finally, we shall examine Arnold's attitudes and policies in respect of sport. Such an analysis will not only enable us to establish in detail what, at a 'microsocial' level, the structural preconditions for the incipient modernization of Rugby football were and how they came to be established. It will also shed light on the social characteristics of the boys involved in what was a crucial, innovative period in the development of the game.

4. Arnold was born in 1795, the son of a collector of customs. He was educated at Winchester and Oxford, and became, in 1814, a fellow of Oriel College. Before obtaining the Rugby headship, he spent nine years working as a private tutor at Laleham. In 1841, the year before his death, he was appointed to the Regius Chair of Modern History at Oxford. He became deeply committed at an early age to an ascetic brand of Christianity but his

religious commitment was 'this-worldly'. He wanted to assist in solving the crisis which had arisen in British society in conjunction with industrialization by transforming Rugby into a school for training 'Christian gentlemen'. He wanted the boys to act as 'disciples', for example, in the universities, and in that way to contribute to the nation as a whole by producing an enlightened ruling class, sensitive to modern conditions. In the words of Harold Perkin:

> [Arnold's] concept of the Christian gentleman was not that of the old chevalier, jealous of his paramilitary honour but otherwise indifferent to morality, but that of the new 'gentle' gentlemen competing not in duels but in consideration for others.[6]

Since it embraced aspects of the old, aristocratic and new, bourgeois ideals, it is not unreasonable to suppose that the 'civilizing' transformation in the ideal of gentlemanly behaviour subscribed to by Arnold occurred in conjunction with *embourgeoisement*. Nor is it surprising that Arnold should have adhered to such a concept. As a public schoolmaster at that stage in Britain's social development, there were four realistic choices open to him as far as patterns of social allegiance and belief were concerned: he could have opted out and become an 'ivory tower' academic; identified with the established classes and attempted to benefit from their patronage; aligned himself with the rising middle class; or adopted a compromise, middle-of-the-road position.

   Arnold's social situation pushed him towards the latter choice. Thus, for his appointment and tenure as head of a public school, he depended mainly on the established classes. In terms of social origins, occupation and income, however, he was middle-class. He was subject as a result to contradictory pressures and seems, at first, to have wavered between extremes. Finally, however, partly because the balance of opinion in society at large was moving in that direction, he settled on a compromise position, coming to support extension of the franchise, to fight for middle-class education, and to favour a paternalistic stance towards the 'lower orders'. Above all, he developed an intense dislike for the aristocracy, feeling, along with his friend Carlyle, that they had abdicated from their responsibilities as rulers and that their recalcitrance on reform could lead to revolution.[7] As we shall show, Arnold's opposition to the aristocracy led him to exclude their sons from Rugby. The fact that he had few reservations about expressing his anti-aristocratic sentiments, whether verbally or in his educational policies, provides, we think, a measure of *embourgeoisement*. More significantly, the fact that Arnold could express such sentiments and retain the headship of a public school, is indicative of the occurrence of that process and his dependency on it. We shall now examine the structural modifications introduced by Arnold, paying special attention, once again, to their connections with *embourgeoisement*.

5. Arnold's main instrument in his attempt to transform Rugby into a school for training 'Christian gentlemen' was the prefect–fagging system. He realized that it was symptomatic in its existing form of the disorderliness endemic in public schools, i.e. that it reflected the power imbalance between staff and pupils. Nevertheless, he was constrained by the balance of forces in society at large to attempt to modify and not abolish it. Accordingly, he transformed the old system into a regularized system of indirect rule in which, while considerable autonomy was preserved for the boys, the rights and duties of prefects and fags were defined more clearly, more formally, to some extent written down and, above all, subject to ultimate control by the headmaster.

Arnold met with considerable success. During his earliest years in office there was a discrepancy between the formal system that he wanted to establish and authority relations in actual operation. Thus, not all boys immediately accepted the new type of prefectorial authority as legitimate.[8] Prefects had previously been selected by virtually autonomous competition among the boys and many of those chosen by Arnold, e.g. on moral and academic grounds, failed to measure up to the norms of masculinity dominant in the pupil subculture and supported by the majority of parents. Furthermore, bullying remained rife throughout Arnold's regime.[9] However, it was probably confined mainly to the middle and lower sections of the school since there is little doubt that, under Arnold, the possibility and inclination towards prefectorial tyranny were reduced.

Without completely doubting the image of Arnold as a successful reformer, Newsome suggests that his success in attracting pupils may have led discipline problems to increase.[10] That is not unlikely. Larger numbers are more difficult to control and, hence, as the pupil population at Rugby grew, there probably occurred a parallel increase in infractions of the rules. Indeed, in the context of an early nineteenth-century public school, one would expect a reforming headmaster to have provoked resistance. To say that, however, does not mean that Arnold failed to implement reforms. The main measure of his success is the fact that, under his rule, the refractoriness of the pupils never reached the heights of rebelliousness endemic under his predecessors.[11] By the time of his death in 1842 he had succeeded in placing the new system on firm foundations and Carlyle could describe Rugby as 'one of the rarest sights in the world, a temple of industrious peace'.[12]

The tendency to cast doubt on Arnold's achievement is not the only fallacy in this field. It is, we think, equally wrong to follow the popular belief and attribute his success solely to his individual qualities. He was forceful and creative, even possessed of a measure of 'charisma' but did not live in a social vacuum. We have discussed his dependency on *embourgeoisement* already. However, he was also dependent on less central aspects of social structure. Thus, as Bamford has shown, the British intelligentsia in the early nineteenth century consisted of a series of interlocking networks united by marital, kinship and friendship ties.[13] Members of the same networks as Arnold such as Longley and Moberly, the headmasters of Harrow and Winchester, tried at the same time to institute similar reforms. Indeed, Arnold corresponded with them on such matters and, according to his biographer, looked on Longley and Moberly 'as models for himself'.[14]

More importantly, Rugby seems to have been more amenable to reform than any other school. It only became a public school at the end of the eighteenth century and was, therefore, not 'burdened' to the same extent by public school traditions. That was also true of Harrow but, at Rugby, social composition interacted with recent acquisition of public school status to render the structure pliable. Thus, between 1801 and 1850, the proportion of boys from titled families at Rugby never exceeded seven per cent in any decade and sometimes fell as low as five per cent. By contrast, the proportions at Eton and Harrow ranged between eighteen per cent and twenty-two per cent, and eighteen per cent and twenty per cent.[15] That is, young aristocrats formed only a small proportion—about one-twentieth—of the boys at Rugby. Their social influence in the school cannot have been as great as it was at Eton and Harrow where about one-fifth of the boys came from titled families. It is also reasonable to suppose that the low proportion of aristocratic boys at Rugby would have meant that the sort of discipline problems which stemmed from 'asymmetrical interdependence' and a status discrepancy between boys and masters were, if not entirely absent, at least less marked than at other public schools. In short, Arnold is more likely than the heads of schools such as Eton and Harrow to have been the status-equal of his pupils. Moreover, the latter are more likely to have been dependent on an academic education for their careers.

Indeed, as we suggested, there is reason to believe that Arnold realized the sort of problems which could result from a high proportion of aristocratic boys in a school and sought, on that account, to exclude them. Alicia Percival, for example, notes that the proportion of aristocrats was lower at Rugby under Arnold than under Thomas James (1778–94), the man under whom it became a public school.[16] That this resulted from deliberate exclusion is suggested by Anna Merivale who wrote that: 'Rugby was flourishing in numbers and reputation and aristocrats tried, and tried in vain, to make him open its door for the admission of pupils from the higher classes.'[17] And in a letter written in 1839, Arnold's wife related her husband's response to a request from the Duchess of Sutherland that her son be allowed to enter the school:

> . . . He very earnestly advised *not*, and that he should rather go to Eton, where he would meet with others of his own rank, while here he would certainly be considered as being of a rank so different from the sons of gentlemen of moderate fortune, who formed the mass of our boys.[18]

It is reasonable to suppose that such a policy would only have suggested itself and could only have worked in a society undergoing *embourgeoisement*, for only under such conditions would a public school headmaster have been able to gain the necessary independence from the aristocracy.

6. Arnold's opposition to the aristocracy did not only lead him to exclude their sons from Rugby, thus helping to give the school a comparatively tractable social composition. It caused him, in addition, to wage war on hunting, shooting, fishing and other aspects of the traditional aristocratic–gentry life-style which had hitherto been firmly embedded in the leisure life of the school. This, in its turn, provided an indirect stimulus to the incipient modernization of football. However, before we follow through this link in the causal chain between *embourgeoisement* and the incipient modernization of Rugby, it is necessary to examine another myth.

The belief that it was his charismatic personality alone which enabled him to reform the prefect–fagging system is not the only misconception to have grown up regarding Arnold's achievements. He is supposed, in addition, to have introduced a 'games cult' to the public schools,[19] in that way, it is occasionally added, providing an unintentional spur to the development of modern sport.[20]

There is, however, no evidence to support contentions of this kind. As we showed in Chapter 2, games were important in the public schools long before Arnold's reign. They were introduced by the boys, supported by the parents and maintained in the face of the indifference—sometimes the hostility—of the school authorities. It would seem, therefore, that we have encountered here an individualistic origin myth similar in some respects to that which developed about William Webb Ellis. However, we are not entirely ignorant concerning Arnold's ideas and policies in respect of sport. Therefore, it is a myth based on a more solid factual core. What we know can be summarized as follows.

One of Arnold's first acts on taking up the Rugby appointment was to interview local farmers in order to ascertain their complaints about the boys under his predecessor, Dr Wooll. On learning that many hired cottages from local countrymen as hideouts for guns and dogs, he drew up a list of such cottages and placed them out of bounds.[21] He also ordered the destruction of the pack of hounds kept by the boys for hare-hunting.[22] By acting in this manner, Arnold was attempting to remove a source of friction which had hitherto soured relations between the school and its neighbours. However, it is reasonable to suppose that his actions were also connected with his general opposition to the aristocracy and that he banned 'field sports' because they involved the arbitrary treatment of social subordinates and the wanton destruction of property and animal life. They were, that is, relics of the old, chivalric ideal, incompatible with the 'civilizing' concept of the 'Christian gentleman' that Arnold wished to instil.

It is unlikely that Rugby boys who were committed to the field sports would have abandoned them without a fight. Gradually, however, as

Arnold's effective power grew, he was able to translate his formal prohibition into factual abolition. He was helped by the fact that, from the standpoint of the majority, sports such as cricket and football were satisfactory substitutes for those which had been banned. That is, they were mock-fights in which strong pleasurable excitement could be generated. They also served as vehicles through which boys could test one another in terms of values such as 'manliness'. We cannot say definitely that Arnold believed modern sports to be effective 'functional substitutes' for field sports. It is clear, however, that he was opposed to the latter and adhered to an emergent educational ideology which laid stress on the 'character-forming' properties of team-games.

Unlike headmasters such as Samuel Butler who were opposed in principle to the educational use of sports and games, Arnold espoused a philosophy of education which stressed the need to balance the 'physical' and 'intellectual'.[23] That he put this ideology into practice is suggested by what Theodore Walrond, head boy at Rugby in 1842, wrote about his headmaster in *The Dictionary of National Biography*:

> . . . the manliness, the independence, the buoyant cheerfulness of his own temperament, his hearty interest in the school games, which he looked upon as an integral part of education, put him in sympathy with all that was good, even in the least intellectual of his scholars.[24]

We also know that Arnold played ' "divers little matches at cricket" with his family on the ground reserved for the Eleven'.[25] However, even though cricket was more highly developed than football in that period, there is no evidence to suggest that Arnold followed the practice of later public school masters and played with his pupils. Nor, apart from helping to secure the appointment of the school's first professional coach, does he seem to have concerned himself with the organization and administration of that game.[26]

A similar picture holds for football. Apart from 'Old Brooke's' mention in *Tom Brown's Schooldays* that 'the Doctor watched the Schoolhouse match for half an hour',[27] one of the few pieces of evidence to link Arnold with the game is contained in a description of the visit paid to the school in 1839 by the Dowager Queen Adelaide, wife of William IV, who, it seems, 'expressed a desire to see . . . football'.[28] Thus, by 1839, Arnold's work had received the accolade of a royal visit. Moreover, along with that of the headmaster and the school, the fame of Rugby football had spread, even reaching the circles of the court. However, there is no evidence that Arnold played a direct part in the playing and organization of the game. He may, as Walrond put it, have regarded games as an 'integral part of education', but they remained for him one part among others, subordinate to the achievement of moral and religio-political goals. In that, he was typical of his period. It was not until later that public schoolmasters came to espouse a fully-fledged 'games ideology' in terms of which team-games were seen as indispensable instruments of moral education and, in some cases, as 'ends in themselves'.

Arnold's ideas on physical education were representative of an early stage in this ideological development. His principal *direct* contribution to the development of football lay in his prohibition of field sports and mild encouragement of team-games. This policy meant that, for the first time, football was accorded official legitimacy in the school. Moreover, the fact that it began to be perceived as performing important, if as yet vaguely defined, educational functions, meant that the boys were constrained to play by the staff and no longer simply by their fellows. However, despite this, under Arnold, football remained, along with sports in general, a virtually independent activity of the boys. That this should have been the case was in accordance with the system of indirect rule which he established and which was emerging more generally at that time as the typical mode of organizing authority relations in a public school. It was control of this type which Arnold established over games and bequeathed to his successors. As we shall show in the next chapter, it played an important part in the incipient modernization of Rugby football.

4 The incipient modernization of Rugby football

1. In the present chapter, we shall analyse the way in which industrialization, *embourgeoisement* and public school reform led to the emergence at Rugby School of a social structure conducive to the incipient modernization of their football. We shall first discuss the 'necessary' then the 'sufficient', i.e. motivational, conditions for this process. We shall then review the evidence which shows the occurrence of modernizing changes in the game. And finally, in a short postscript, we shall return to the emergent division of football into Rugby and soccer. Our first task, however, is to examine the connections between Arnold's reforms and the incipient modernization of Rugby football.

2. Norbert Elias has shown how state centralization, in particular the establishment of an effective monopoly on the use of physical force, was a necessary precondition for pacification in the societies of Western Europe, for reducing within them the potential for and actual frequency of violent outbreaks. Similarly, the more stable and effective control established by Arnold at Rugby, i.e. the fact that he was able to concentrate power into his own hands and reduce prefects to the role of 'lieutenants', led to a reduction in the school of violent confrontations, both between masters and boys and among the boys themselves. This concentration of effective power was a necessary precondition for the incipient modernization of their football. Let us elaborate on this.

In the late eighteenth and early nineteenth centuries, Rugby shared the recurrent disorderliness endemic in public schools. It would be wrong to suggest that an unstable situation of that type was inimical to development. The evolution of the prefect–fagging system shows that was not the case. It was, however, a conflictful process, taking place through a power struggle between the masters and oldest boys. Arnold's transformation of this system into an effective instrument of indirect rule established at Rugby, for the first time in the context of a public school, a social structure within which non-conflictual innovation could occur, i.e. innovation which was not regarded by the masters as a threat and which, consequently, they did not resist. The social structure established in this manner was also conducive to development in the leisure-sphere. Previously, much of the time and energy of the older boys had been channelled into securing or defending what they regarded as their rights. But once these had been formally granted, they no longer had to fight. Therefore, in the stabler climate established by Arnold's reforms, they could devote more time and attention to matters such as football.

However, it was not simply the greater stability of this structure that was conducive to innovation. In addition, the system of indirect rule fashioned by Arnold was characterized by what one might term 'controlled autonomy'. That is, the reformed prefect–fagging system was one in which the prefects retained much of the scope for initiative and power over younger boys they had fought for in the past. That was especially the case as far as leisure was concerned. Even there, however, they were subject to more effective staff control and it is reasonable to suppose that a social structure of that type would have been more conducive to innovation than one which was more authoritarian or more anarchic. A brief discussion will show why.

In an important sense, the leisure activities of Rugby boys were voluntary affairs. Or rather, they were activities in which the only direct compulsion came from other boys. This meant they could regard football as 'private property', as their own affair which should not be interfered with by masters. Since they were not subject to direct or continuous official interference, their interest tended to be aroused and sustained at a high level. That is, there was no extraneous interference with their enjoyment of the game *per se*, with its function of arousing pleasurable excitement and permitting the inculcation and expression of 'manly' norms. On the other hand, since the level of interest generated in this manner was coupled with the use of compulsion on younger boys and those who did not wish to play, and since, in the last resort, the prefects could call on support from the headmaster, the game was free from the constraints of *laissez-faire*, i.e. of a social situation in which individuals were free to follow their own inclinations, with a consequent loss of continuity and sustained collective focus. However, simply to say that the 'controlled autonomy' institutionalized by Arnold, the balance struck at Rugby between freedom and control, was more conducive to innovation than a social structure of a more authoritarian or more anarchic type, does not explain why the innovative tendencies of the boys were actualized and channelled into football. In order to see why that was the case it is necessary to probe deeper.

Up until the 1830s, Rugby boys enjoyed a varied leisure life. Football was just one among a number of sports traditionally engaged in, less central in their value-hierarchy than hunting and other favoured pursuits of the aristocracy and gentry which, in the eighteenth and early nineteenth centuries, were the principal activities to which the name 'sport' was attached. However, as we showed in the last chapter, Arnold was hostile to and banned 'field' sports. He was able to make his prohibition stick because industrialization and *embourgeoisement* were reducing the power of the aristocracy and gentry, and because Rugby was primarily a gentry school, i.e. one in which there were relatively few aristocratic boys. As a result, the boys were deprived of what had served hitherto as an important source of leisure-excitement and means of expressing 'manly' standards. However, they were not totally deprived for, as we also saw in the last chapter, Arnold adhered to an emergent educational ideology which laid stress on the character-forming properties of team-games. As a result, he began to encourage his pupils to play sports such as cricket and football which became their only legitimate channel for arousing leisure-excitement and expressing masculine norms.

This helps to account for the greater centrality of football among the leisure activities of Rugby boys but still does not explain why they began to innovate. After all, they might simply have devoted more time to the game and nothing else. Had that been the case, their skills as footballers would undoubtedly have improved but they would not necessarily have acted in ways which altered *the structure of the game*. In short, the greater stability established by Arnold, the 'controlled autonomy' of the prefects, the pro-hibition of field sports and official encouragement of team-games were not, by themselves, sufficient to spark off incipient modernization. They were facilitating changes, 'necessary' rather than 'sufficient' conditions. They led to the emergence of a social structure which was conducive to innovation and in which time and energy were canalized into football. However, they do not explain why the boys were motivated to engage in innovation. Once again, therefore, it is necessary to probe more deeply.

The case of cricket provides an instructive contrast. It began to develop in a modernizing direction in the eighteenth century. Members of the aris-tocracy and gentry were the chief modernizing agents.[1] Together with their hired retainers—the first professional cricketers—they established, in broad outline, the main features of the modern game. They also founded the MCC which, by the early nineteenth century, had emerged as a rule-making body with enough authority to ensure more or less uniform adherence to its rules throughout the country. At Rugby under Arnold, the boys were encouraged to devote more time to the game. This meant they were able to improve their ability as cricketers but there was neither stimulus nor opportunity for them to alter its basic structure. The case of football differed markedly. It was still a crude folk-game played according to locally determined rules. There was no prestigious body to act as legislator on a national level. Therefore, the boys at Rugby were in a position, should the need arise, to act independently and change their rules of football in whatever ways they thought fit.

Of course, local determination of football rules was nothing new. What happened at Rugby in this period was that there emerged, for the first time, a social configuration which was not simply conducive to innovation in the leisure-sphere but in which the necessary stimuli existed to motivate the boys deliberately to change the structure of their football. The 'catalytic agents' in this process were a complex of interrelated tensions which arose due to contradictions inherent in the structure, composition and position of Rugby School in the early nineteenth century. Class tensions and tensions associated with status rivalry between public schools were important in this respect. So, too, were tensions which arose due to the attempt of Arnold and his successors to instil more 'civilized' values into the boys.

It was this complex of tensions which led Rugby boys to embark on a process of changing and differentiating their football. It began, as a result, to develop into a more complex, restrained and 'civilized', i.e. more modern type of game. As it got under way, moreover, this process achieved its own momentum; i.e. the rules became so numerous and complex that they had to be written down. In that way, incipient modernization became, in part, a self-propelling process.

It follows from this discussion that, in order to account for the sufficient as well as the necessary conditions for incipient modernization, we shall have to return to the relationship between Rugby School and its wider social setting. In particular, we shall have to look at the school's standing in the rank-hierarchy of public schools and examine the effects of *embourgeoisement* on its clientele. We shall also have to enquire more closely into the internal structural consequences of Arnold's reforms.

3. We suggested that the stimuli which led Rugby boys to develop a more elaborate and distinctive form of football were produced by a complex of interrelated tensions. More specifically, these tensions arose due to contradictions between the values and ambitions of the personnel at Rugby and specific aspects of the structure, culture, composition and social position of the school in the early nineteenth century. Basically, there were three such contradictions:

(i)   that between the status-ambitions of the personnel and the relatively low social standing within the upper classes both of themselves and the school;

(ii) that inherent in the desire of parents that their sons should receive at Rugby a 'manly' education which trained them simultaneously as 'gentlemen'; and

(iii) that which stemmed from the incompatibility between the form of football inherited by the boys and the more 'civilized' values that Arnold and his successors wished to instil.

This requires elaboration. At the beginning of the nineteenth century Rugby occupied a low position in the rank-order of public schools. Even as late as about 1850, i.e. at a time when the school had begun to acquire a national reputation, the captain of cricket wrote to his Eton counterpart requesting a match. He is said to have received as his reply: 'Rugby, Rugby . . . well, we'll think about it if you can tell me where it is.'[2] This deliberate snub is indicative of the status-exclusiveness which was rife among nineteenth-century public schools. It shows how difficult it must have been for Rugby to gain acceptance from the more established schools. A prosperous foundation, new buildings and a new constitution were not enough to offset the disadvantages which stemmed from the comparatively low standing of its personnel and its recent elevation from grammar school status.

However, the majority of Rugby personnel were anxious that it should gain acceptance, not simply as a public school but as a *leading* one. Such an ambition was symptomatic of the growing competitiveness among the higher strata of British society as the processes of industrialization and *embour-geoisement* got under way. In such a situation, the benefits to be derived from raising the school's standing were clear. For parents, attendance at a school accepted in élite circles as a leading public school would help their sons to maintain and perhaps improve the family's position. For teachers, movement of the school up the ladder of public school prestige would be financially and socially beneficial. It was as part of this attempt to raise Rugby's position that Arnold was appointed to the headship.[3] As we have seen, his efforts were directed principally into an attempt to raise the moral and intellectual standards of the school, to transform it into a school for training 'Christian gentlemen'. However, the boys were recruited principally from a class in which a physical concept of 'manliness' prevailed. More of them were dependent on an academic education than was the case, for example, at Eton but, nevertheless, their parents did not simply require for their sons a training oriented towards performance in a future career. On the contrary, they wanted an education which would help to make them, in terms of current standards, 'men', i.e. give them a stable and secure identity which would enable them to hold their own in a class which was the principal reservoir from which the country's military leadership was recruited and whose values, correspondingly, stressed virtues such as strength, courage and physical prowess.

Since it was a vehicle through which 'manly' virtues could be expressed, football was an activity common to all the public schools. Therefore, given the desire of Rugby's personnel to get it accepted as a leading school, it is reasonable to suppose that one of the motives which led the boys to start developing a form of football peculiarly their own was a desire to draw attention to the school by developing a distinctive variant of an activity which permitted expression of a central upper-class value. That their efforts were successful is suggested by Queen Adelaide's request to watch a match and by the fact that aspects of the Rugby game were adopted at more established schools such as Westminster.

It is reasonable to assume that it was principally in order thus to attract attention that Rugby boys developed a form of football played with an oval ball and 'H-shaped' goals. However, this hypothesis does not explain why, in their attempt to create a distinctive variant, they hit upon these rather than some other features. Perhaps a minutely detailed explanation of the causes of their innovative endeavour is beyond the reach of sociological interpretation? However, it is possible to go one step further. Since an oval ball lends itself better than a round one to carrying, it is plausible to suppose that the adoption of such a ball may have been connected with the emergence of a game-pattern in which handling and carrying began to be emphasized at the expense of kicking. In order to see why such a game may have begun to develop, it is necessary to look more closely at the tensions generated at Rugby School in the early nineteenth century.

We have stressed repeatedly that, due mainly to industrialization, *embourgeoisement* and the associated rise in class tensions, the beginning of the nineteenth century was a period in which status-exclusiveness—a desire to separate and distance themselves from the mass of ordinary people—grew among the British upper classes. Under such conditions, it was not enough for public schools to provide, whether formally or informally, a 'manly' education. Parents who sent their sons to such schools wanted them to be trained as 'gentlemen' as well. That is, they wanted a 'manly' education tempered by 'civilizing' restraints and, therefore, denotative of high social status. This meant that public schools were constrained to divest themselves of socially 'contaminating' attributes, to abandon activities with a lower-class connotation.

In its folk form, football fell into that category. As we saw in Chapter 2, Samuel Butler and the anonymous Etonian regarded it as 'ungentlemanly' and 'uncivilized', thus giving expression to the fact that a distinct status-hierarchy of sports had emerged in Britain and that football stood on the lowest rungs of the ladder; i.e. one could not play it in its existing form and remain a 'gentleman'. Given that, Rugby boys were faced with a dilemma. Field sports had been banned by Arnold. Therefore, they could not during term-time realize their own and their parents' status-aspirations by taking part in them. They could, however, refine and elaborate their football, transform it into an activity which was 'manly' and 'gentlemanly' at the same time, i.e. they were constrained to produce a form of football which was not simply distinctively their own but also clearly different from the forms played in society at large.

We suggested in Chapter 1 that, by the beginning of the nineteenth century, folk-football was beginning to become a mainly kicking game. It is plausible, therefore, to suppose that Rugby boys evolved a game in which handling and carrying were central in direct opposition to this wider trend; i.e. an oval ball, running in and other forms of handling were incorporated into Rugby football as part of an attempt to develop a game-form radically different from that played by the lower classes; that is, a type of football devoid of socially 'contaminating' lower-class associations and, therefore, appropriate as a game for 'gentlemen'.

However, in order to realize that aim, a type of football was needed which was not simply different from the folk forms but also, whilst retaining the quality of 'manliness', more 'gentle'. The anonymous Etonian put his finger on this issue when he singled out violence as one of football's 'ungentle-manly' characteristics. It is not unreasonable to suppose that such a judgment reflected a more widespread upper-class sentiment at that time; i.e. Arnold's concept of the 'Christian gentleman' was probably not idiosyncratic and, if we are right, it means that Rugby boys were subject to both specific and diffuse pressure to 'civilize' their football, to reduce the violence of the game.

So far, we have discussed this issue only in general terms. It is now appropriate to examine the evidence for our contention that, following Arnold's reforms, the game of Rugby football began to become more complex, distinct and 'civilized', i.e. that it began to undergo a process of modernization.

4. Light on the differentiation of Rugby football at this stage, both from the game at other public schools and with respect to its own internal structure, is shed by two fictional accounts by Old Rugbeians, both published in the 1850s. The first, by Thomas Hughes, appeared in *Tom Brown's Schooldays*. The second, by W. D. Arnold, one of the headmaster's sons, appeared in an essay entitled, 'Football: the First Day of the Sixth Match'.[4] Since they corroborate one another in most respects, we shall confine our discussion to Hughes' account. The developments which took place during Arnold's regime emerge clearly from the contrast between what he wrote and the account by Bloxam of the game as played before the 1820s. Bloxam summarized the character of Rugby football when he had been at the school in these words:

> Few and simple were the rules of the game; touch on the sides of the ground was marked out, and no one was allowed to run with the ball in his grasp towards the opposite goal. It was football not handball, plenty of hacking but little struggling. As to costume, there were neither flannels nor caps; the players simply doffed their hats and coats or jackets which were heaped together on one side near the goal till the game was over. All were scratch matches: one boarding house was never pitted against another and there was no Cock House. There were no Old Rugbeian matches.[5]

Bloxham's account suggests that, in the first two decades of the nineteenth century, Rugby football was not markedly different from the forms of other schools. Like them, it was a variant of the folk tradition and practices such as 'running in' had not emerged. The rules were still unwritten and there was neither formal organization nor regular competition. Moreover, as one can see from the fact that players wore everyday clothes, football was not yet set apart from and given special emphasis among the leisure activities of the boys.

Hughes was a pupil at Rugby from 1834 to 1842. His account shows how the game had become more complex by the period of Arnold's headship. For example, he describes the goals and the scoring-system thus:

> [The goals are] a sort of gigantic gallows of two poles eighteen feet high, fixed upright in the ground some fourteen feet apart, with a cross bar running from one to the other at the height of ten feet or thereabouts . . . the match is for the best of three goals . . . it won't do . . . just to kick the ball through these posts—it must go over the cross bar; any height'll do, so long as it's between the posts.[6]

To our knowledge, this is the first recorded mention of 'H-shaped' goals and scoring above the cross-bar. After describing the division of labour in the Schoolhouse team and the disposition of players on the field, Hughes goes on to describe a scrummage:

> The ball has just fallen . . . and they close rapidly around it in a scrummage. It must be driven through now by force or skill . . . Look how differently the boys face it. Here come two of the bull-dogs, bursting through the outsiders: in they go, straight to the heart of the scrummage, bent on driving the ball out on the opposite side.[7]

Then, as now, the scrummage was a central feature. Rugby remained, in that respect, similar to the forms of football played at other public schools. However, not every player entered the scrum. This emerges from Hughes' description of a further aspect of the role differentiation which had, by then, become customary:

> . . . the boys who are bending and watching on the outside, mark them—they are most useful players, the dodgers; who seize on the ball the moment it rolls out from amongst the chargers, and away with it across to the opposite goal; they seldom go into the scrummage, but must have more coolness than the chargers.[8]

Although Hughes saw no reason to stress this point, it would seem from this passage that the 'dodgers' were allowed to carry the ball. Later, however, in an ambiguous passage depicting a 'line-out' and a 'touch-down', it appears possible that he was describing a game in which 'dribbling'—controlling the ball by foot—was more prominent than in present-day Rugby:

> . . . old Brooke kicks out . . . Away goes the ball, and the bull-dogs after it, and in another minute there is a shout of 'In touch', 'Our ball' . . . Old Brooke . . . stands with the ball in his hand, while the two sides form in deep lines opposite one another . . . Old Brooke strikes it out straight and strong, and it falls opposite his brother. Hurra! That rush has taken

it right through the School line . . . and young Brooke and the bull-dogs are close upon it. The School leaders rush back . . . and strain every nerve to catch him . . . There they go straight for the School goal-posts, bull-dogs go down, *but young Brooke holds on*. 'He is down'. No! a long stagger, but the danger is past. That was the shock of Crew, the most dangerous of dodgers. And now he is close to the School goal, *the ball not three yards before him*. There is a hurried rush of the School fags to the spot, but no one throws himself on the ball, the only chance, and young Brooke has touched it right under the School goal-posts.[9]

It seems from this passage that the ball was kicked, not thrown in from the line-out. That is consistent with Marples' view. He takes the second italicized phrase as evidence that Hughes may have been describing a mainly kicking game.[10] Thus it is clear that 'young Brooke' was not carrying the ball immediately prior to touching down. However, the first italicized phrase suggests that he may have been carrying it when he started and that it was knocked from his grasp by an opponent. Fortunately, we are not solely dependent on this passage for an idea of the balance between kicking and carrying in Rugby football at that stage. In his submission to the Old Rugbeian sub-committee of 1895, Hughes said that 'running in', though rare when he entered the school in 1834, was granted formal recognition in 1841–2, and, later, a more central place. This, he suggested, was due, not to Webb Ellis as the sub-committee emphasized—according to Hughes, the Webb Ellis story was unknown during his schooldays—but largely to the prowess of a boy called Mackie. This individualistic explanation was based on personal, not second-hand, reminiscence. It may, therefore, contain a germ of truth. However, that, for present purposes, is not the central point. More important is the fact that Hughes' account establishes that Rugby football grew more complex during Arnold's reign and that, at the same time, handling began to be emphasized at the expense of kicking. As we suggested earlier, the socio-logically most plausible explanation for the occurrence of that process links it to Rugby's position in a social configuration which led the boys to want to differentiate their football from the forms played in other public schools and society at large. The social structure established at Rugby by Arnold's reforms encouraged innovation and, hence, favoured the occurrence of a process of that kind.

5. The consequences of Arnold's reforms for the development of Rugby football were not restricted solely to its role structure and tactics. At the same time, it began to be given greater emphasis among the leisure activities of the boys, to be organized more formally, and to grow more 'civilized'. An Old Rugbeian writing in the 1840s had this to say:

Considerable improvement has taken place within the last few years, in the appearance of a match, not only from the great increase in the number of boys, but also in the use of a peculiar dress, consisting of velvet caps and jerseys. The latter are of various colours and patterns, and wrought with many curious devices, which on their first introduction were accompanied by mottoes . . . as, for instance, 'Cave Adsum'.[11]

The use of special dress is indicative of the fact that football was beginning to be marked out by the boys as an activity high up in their value-scheme. However, at that stage, as one can see, there was still no standardized football 'uniform'. Costume depended on individual choice and parental capacity to pay. Moreover, competition took place in terms of appearance as well as ability at the game. In about 1843, these two levels of status-rivalry were formally related and the practice began of restricting the use of velvet caps, inlaid with gold or silver braid, only to the most skilful players.[12]

In 1839 or 40, Rugby boys began, for the first time, to play matches between sides of limited, equal numbers, fifteen or twenty a side.[13] However, the main matches continued to be between numerically unequal sides such as 'Schoolhouse' or 'Sixth Form v School'. These were regular, annual confrontations. In addition, more occasional matches were arranged between strange-sounding combinations such as 'Disyllables v School', 'Patriarchs v School', 'Anomalies v School', and, more understandably, 'A to K v School' and 'North v South'.[14] It was not until the 1870s, some time after it had become standard in society at large, that matches between numerically equal sides became the regular practice.[15] Thus, Rugby football came only slowly to incorporate a central constituent of modern sport. In this slow adoption of the principle of numerical equality, it probably reflected a society in which inequalities were being taken less for granted. However, most important for present purposes about this aspect of the process of modernization is the fact that it, too, was set in motion during Arnold's reign.

Hughes' account shows another respect in which the modern concept of equality began to be incorporated into Rugby football.[16] Apparently, the teams did not defend territories assigned by custom but 'ends' chosen on the basis of the toss of a coin, an impersonal, chance criterion. This meant that the chances of making the crucial choice of ends were distributed randomly between the rival captains. In addition, sides had to change ends each time a goal was scored, thus ensuring that advantages conferred by irregularities of the pitch and vagaries of the weather were to some extent equalized.

Changes also began to occur in that period in the way in which the boys administered their football. A means of running leisure activities by a system of informal assemblies called 'levées' had begun to develop earlier. Initially, these had been rather rowdy but, according to Rouse, the boys learned under Arnold 'the necessity for order and decent procedure'[17] and they began to become more orderly and democratic. W. D. Arnold may have reflected his father's opinion when, in 1856, he wrote as follows of an imaginary levée called to fix the start of the football season: '. . . this law and legislating in all its degrees, this constitutional settling of these excited questions by a recognized authority, is very good and humanizing ... All orderly and proper now: plenty of excitement, but under decorous restraint.'[18]

Levées could be of four types: School levées, Bigside levées of the Upper School, Sixth Form levées, and House levées.[19] It was a Sixth Form levée in 1845, not, as most authorities have it, a Bigside levée in 1846[20] which set the rules of Rugby down on paper, thus producing the first ever written football rules. They appeared in a pamphlet called *The Laws of Football as Played at Rugby School* and it seems that W. D. Arnold was one of the three drafters.[21] These 'laws' are sociologically important, not simply because they are the earliest surviving written rules of football, but also because of what they tell us about the way in which the structure of the game and, correlatively, of authority relations at Rugby School, were changing at that time. This codification took place under Arnold's successor, A. C. Tait (1842–52). It is clear, nevertheless, that the preconditions for its occurrence were laid down under Arnold's regime.

The 1845 rules were divided into two sections. The first dealt with discipline and general organization; the second was a detailed working out of the main rules governing the playing of the game itself. Through the rules of Section I, the administrative role of prefects, particularly their right to punish non-attenders, was legitimized. Under the old system, boys had often evaded 'football fagging' in order to engage in field sports or simply to do nothing at all, but now football had risen in the school's value-hierarchy and been given official blessing. Hence it was stipulated in writing that the game could henceforth be avoided only on medical grounds or because a boy had a more compelling engagement with a master. In this and similar ways, the meshes of compulsion were tightened and loopholes through which escape had been possible began to be filled in.

Thirty-seven rules were included in Section II but their status was experimental. That emerges from the fact that, on 7 September 1846, they were, with one or two minor additions and alterations, ratified by a Bigside levée and so accorded wider legitimacy. Thus, the older boys and prefects were no longer able to dictate the rules of football at their pleasure but had to submit them for approval to an assembly of boys in the upper school. This suggests that a process of democratization was attendant on Arnold's reforms. That is, under the impact of the more effective control 'from above' to which members of the Sixth Form were henceforth subject, they were, whilst continuing to be the main initiators of changes, now subjected to the constraints of institutional pressure 'from below'.

No rules regarding administration were included among those published in 1846. That remained a preserve of the Sixth Form and was not felt to be a matter of concern to the rest of the school. The 1846 rules were, however, preceded by a short preamble:

> The following set of rules is to be regarded rather as a set of decisions on certain disputed points, than as containing all the Laws of the Game,

which are too well known to render any explanation necessary to Rugbeians.

These rules were thus intended for local consumption and did not cover the game as a whole. Custom was still regarded as satisfactory for dealing with such basic aspects as size of teams, the dimensions of the pitch and ball. However, disputes had arisen around certain points and it was this which made codification necessary. Since thirty-seven written rules were needed, the amount of controversy was apparently considerable. Close inspection reveals that it had occurred mainly over practices such as 'offside', the legitimacy of different types of physical force, and 'fair', i.e. legitimate means of controlling and propelling the ball. Thus six rules were needed in order to clarify the circumstances which constituted 'offside' and determine the penalties and restrictions to be imposed on players 'off their side'. Seven were needed to regulate the use of physical force, e.g. 'hacking' and 'holding', and distinctions were drawn between four legitimate ways of using hands—catching direct from a kick, 'knocking on', throwing and 'running in'—and three legitimate ways of kicking—'place' kicking, 'drop' kicking and 'punting'. Finally, it was stipulated that players were to use only their persons for controlling and propelling the ball. This suggests that, prior to 1845, bats and sticks had sometimes been used. Now, however, a firm rule was laid down prohibiting the use of such devices and Rugby was clearly distinguished from emergent games such as hockey which stemmed from the same roots but in which the use of sticks became the central distinguishing feature.

We have seen how the division of labour in Rugby football had grown more complex. The present discussion shows that the rules had grown more complex, too. In the past, when the game had been relatively simple, oral rules had sufficed to ensure a relatively harmonious and smooth-flowing game. However, oral rules are 'dysfunctional', conducive to disruptive tensions, once a given level of complexity has been passed. Such tensions do not necessarily give rise to open conflict. They do, however, when, as was the case at Rugby following Arnold's reforms, the balance of power between groups begins to change so that formerly subordinate groups are able openly to challenge their erstwhile superiors. One can imagine how, once the complexity of Rugby football had reached the critical point, and once the boys who were not prefects, especially those immediately below the Sixth, realized that the reformed social structure gave them the chance to express opinions openly, the frequency of disputes would have begun to mount regarding whether this or that practice was 'fair' and consistent with the football traditions of the school. As one can see from the 1846 preamble, this point was reached in the 1840s. By that time, Rugby football had become sufficiently complex and the balance of power among the boys had changed in an equalizing direction enough for a set of clear and unambiguous written rules to be necessary to preserve the 'mock-fight' character of the game, i.e. to reduce the possibility of disruption and minimize the chances that matches which started out as playful competition would be transformed into 'serious' fighting. The intensity of the conflict attested to by the 1845/46 rules is such that, had the disputed points not been resolved in writing, the further development of the game would have been jeopardized. In short, given the level of development reached by the 1840s, written rules were a precondition for further modernization.

6. That the game had begun to grow more 'civilized' as well as more complex can be seen from the seven 1845 rules which dealt with physical force. They were:

(ix)   Charging is fair in the case of a place kick as soon as the ball has touched the ground; in the case of a kick from a catch, as soon as the player's foot has left the ground and not before.
(xi)   No player being off his side shall hack, charge, run in, touch the ball in goal or interrupt a catch.
(xvi)   A player standing up to another may hold one arm only, but may hack him or knock the ball out of his hand if he attempts to kick it or go beyond the line of touch.
(xxv)   No hacking with the heel or above the knee is fair.
(xxvii)   No player but the first on his side may be hacked except in a scrummage.
(xxviii) No player may wear projecting nails or iron plates on the soles or heels of his shoes or boots.
(xxxvii) No player may be held unless he himself is holding the ball.

Thus, practices such as 'hacking', holding and charging became subject to more stringent regulation. For example, hacking—kicking a player on the legs—was restricted to the area below the knee and players were forbidden to hack with their heels. Indiscriminate hacking was still allowed in the scrummage but, otherwise, it was decreed legitimate to hack only the player who was 'first on his side', i.e. nearest to or in possession of the ball. Holding and charging, too, were subject to stricter controls. Henceforward, a player was allowed to hold only the opponent in possession and, even then, by only one arm. Charging was defined as 'fair', in the case of a 'place-kick' as soon as the ball had touched the ground, and in the case of a 'drop', as soon as the kicker's foot had left it. It was also restricted to players 'on their side'. At the same time, permissible footwear was subject to stricter regulation. In the past, cuts and bruises inflicted and received through the use of 'navvies' had been a source of pride. Such boots were regarded as vital to the 'manliness' of the game. Now, however, iron-tipped boots had been identified by an Etonian as characteristic of a violent and 'ungentlemanly' game, popular with the 'common people' of

Yorkshire. Hence, the attempt was made through rule xviii to eliminate their use.

Of course, there had been standards governing physical contact in the stage of oral rules. At that stage, however, a level of violence was customarily tolerated which was incompatible with the more 'civilized' values now coming to prevail. Hence, from the 1840s onwards, the types of physical force regarded as legitimate in Rugby football began to be hedged in with written conditions and prohibitions. Some of the more brutal practices of earlier times were rooted out and, to the extent that players could be persuaded or compelled to adhere to the new rules, the game began to resemble 'serious' fighting less. To say that, however, is not to imply that the chances of obtaining satisfaction from taking part in a 'manly' physical struggle were eliminated. The social pressures outlined earlier may have been leading Rugby to become more 'gentlemanly' and, hence, more 'civilized' and restrained, but the then prevailing upper-class norms of masculinity still permitted a level of violence greater than that socially tolerated in the game today. This can be seen from an account by an Old Rugbeian, published in 1860, in which he contrasts the current game with that of his schooldays, two or three years earlier. It is reasonable to assume that what he wrote provides a reasonably accurate assessment of the game's continued roughness, even after the introduction of the 'civilizing' rules of 1845 and 1846:

> You should just have seen the scrummages in the Sixth Match two years ago . . . Fellows did not care a fig for the ball then except inasmuch as it gave them a decent pretext for hacking. I remember a scrummage! . . . we'd been hacking for five minutes already, and hadn't had half enough, in fact, the swells had only just begun to warm to their work, when a bystander . . . kindly . . . informed us that the ball was waiting our convenience on top of the island . . . And then there was Hookey Walker, the swell hack on the Sixth side; my eye! didn't he walk into the School! only shut up ten fellows for the season, and sent half a dozen home for the rest of the half . . . merely to see him come through a scrummage was the signal for all the ladies to shriek and faint. Bless you, my dear fellow, they enjoy looking on at a scrummage of all things now—more shame to us. And there was none of that underhand shuffling play with the ball then that there is now; no passing it along from one to the other; all was manly and straightforward. Why, to let the ball go after you had once got into a scrummage was considered to be as flagrant a transgression of the rules of football as to take it up when you were off your side. Nor did you see any of that shirking outside scrummages that's always going on nowadays. No one thought you worth your salt if you weren't the colour of your mother earth from head to toe ten minutes after the match had begun. But, dash my buttons! you haven't a chance of getting a decent fall in the

present day; and no wonder either when you see young dandies 'got up regardless of expense', mincing across Big Side, and looking just as if their delicate frames wouldn't survive any violent contact with the ball. Hang the young puppies! We shall have fellows playing in dress boots and lavender-coloured kid gloves before long ... My maxim is hack the ball on when you see it near you, and when you don't, why then hack the fellow next you.[22]

This account gives a good idea of the norm of 'manliness' which continued to govern Rugby football even after the establishment of the first written rules. It also provides further evidence for our contention that the game was gradually being transformed in the direction of greater 'civilization'. Thus the Old Rugbeian recommended a return to the 'glories' of his schooldays when, he claimed, hacking had occupied a more central place. At the same time, he deplored the advent of 'passing' since, in his opinion, it was leading to 'emasculation'. The earlier standard he described is reminiscent of Ancient Greek boxing and wrestling which, as Elias has shown, were based on a warrior ethos which decreed it to be cowardly to dodge or retreat from an opponent's blows. Since the Old Rugbeian considered it 'underhand' and 'unmanly' to feint or pass to a team-mate to avoid being hacked, it seems that Rugby football was at first based on a similar ethos. The ball was relatively unimportant to the game at that stage. Scrummages were indiscriminate kicking matches in which the 'manly' thing to do was to stand up to an opponent and engage in toe-to-toe hacking. It followed that strength and courage as a 'hack' were the main criteria for establishing a reputation at the game.

However, despite opposition from players of the 'old school', the 'passing' game caught on. It did so as part of the transformation of Rugby into a 'mock fight' at a higher level of 'civilization' which began in the 1840s. That is, in that period, the game began noticeably to become a type of group contest which provided the pleasures of 'real' fighting but which was regulated in such a way that the attendant dangers were reduced, a kind of group struggle which the players could enjoy but in which they had less chance than formerly to inflict serious injury. Pleasure in playing began to be derived less from brute force and more from force transformed by the use of complex skills, e.g. in passing, kicking and running with the ball. Rugby had taken a small step towards its modern form, towards, that is, a game-pattern involving an intricate balance between force and skill, spontaneity and control, individuality and team-work. Ample room was left for individual 'flair' and 'manly' physical contact but barriers—in the form of written rules—began to be set up to ensure that, in the excitement of the struggle, the players did not get 'carried away' and transgress the emergent, more 'civilized' standards that were coming to prevail. In that way, the game was brought into line with the more 'refined' standards which, in conjunction with industrialization and *embourgeoisement*, were developing in British society at large. In short,

Rugby was beginning to emerge as a game considered suitable for 'English gentlemen'.

7. Even though it was beginning to develop towards stricter control, the primary emphasis in Rugby continued to be laid on internalization of the rules, on self-imposed rather than external restraint. This can be seen clearly in rule xxiv which enjoined that 'the heads of sides, or two deputies appointed by them, are the sole arbiters of all disputes'. That is, it was felt that, as future 'gentlemen', the captains could be relied upon to settle controversies by discussion. Behind this lay the assumption that no player would deliberately contravene the rules and that, in cases of dispute, all would abide by their captains' decisions. Of course, these expectations were backed up by the diffuse pressure of public opinion and, in the last resort, the newly won authority of the headmaster. It is significant, nevertheless, that the need was not yet felt for formally appointed officials who are not themselves participants in the game.

In this emphasis on self-control, Rugby depended partly on the social homogeneity of the players. As future 'gentlemen', most could be expected, most of the time at least, to play 'fairly', i.e. to comply voluntarily with the rules. There were few extraneous sources of tension in their matches such as arise when teams from different class, regional, national, ethnic and even public school backgrounds compete. However, the stress on self-control was also partly dependent on the recently established system of indirect rule. One of the central aims of this system was to teach boys at an early age to exercise self-control. Hence the attempt was made in all spheres to reduce external, especially adult, control to a minimum. It was possible to do this because of the stable social climate established by Arnold's reforms.

The structure and ethos of the reformed prefect–fagging system were thus reflected in the emergent Rugby game. That is, in its emphasis on self-restraint, its finely struck balance between force and skill, spontaneity and control, the individual and the group, Rugby football in the 1840s was a microcosm of its wider social setting. Such a game could only have developed within a social structure of that type. That is, it could not have developed given a more anarchic or more authoritarian system. Thus, the relative anarchy of Rugby and other public schools in the late eighteenth and early nineteenth centuries was not conducive to the emergence of regulated games. The most powerful boys had to be subjected to strict rules and firm, albeit indirect, control by adults before they could work out among themselves rules to reduce the arbitrariness and wildness of their football. It is a measure of the balance struck in the reformed prefect-fagging system, that they could accomplish this without, at the same time, destroying the character of football as an enjoyable pastime.

If the pre-Arnoldian public schools are examples of a more anarchic system, the schools of nineteenth-century Prussia provide an authoritarian contrast. There, the main parallel of football and organized games was 'drill', a regimented activity in which masters barked orders which were mechanically obeyed. Drill reflected the authoritarian, militaristic character of Prussian society and the submission of the individual to the group. Duelling in the German universities provides another illuminating contrast. It was a more open outlet for aggression. Injury, disfigurement, even death, were frequent. Indeed, since they signified membership of a duelling fraternity, attendance at university and, hence, élite social status, duelling scars were positively desired. By contrast, as it developed at Rugby and the other English public schools, football was a relatively constructive means of satisfying the needs for aggression and excitement. It is, we think paradigmatic for the contrast between the nineteenth-century English upper classes and their German counter-parts, that the former came to participate in leisure activities such as cricket and football which involved a fine balance between freedom and control, the individual and the group. It is also paradigmatic that they obtained their social cachet, not from physical disfigurement, but from demonstrating a capacity to behave in accordance with 'gentlemanly' standards.

Postscript

At the end of Chapter 2, we discussed the belief that Rugby acquired its distinctive form as a result of a single deviant act by a single individual. Although it is more complex and less temporally precise, the hypothetical explanation advanced in the present chapter is based on firmer and more detailed evidence. It is also sociologically more plausible and more comprehensive. That is, its explanatory import is not restricted to a single feature of Rugby football but covers the whole emergent constellation. Moreover, it is, we think strengthened by the fact that the incipient bifurcation of football into Rugby and soccer can be explained by reference to the same social facts. It is to that issue that we shall now, very briefly, address ourselves.

We have shown how Rugby was the first school to commit its football rules to writing. We did not discuss, however, the fact that all the other public schools embarked on processes of codification shortly afterwards. Thus, written rules were produced at Eton in 1849,[23] Shrewsbury in about 1855,[24] Westminster in about 1860,[25] and Charterhouse in 1862.[26] In each case, the conditions for the occurrence of this process were laid down by reform of the prefect–fagging system more or less along Arnoldian lines. However, for present purposes, that is less significant than the fact that it seems unlikely that it can have been either accidental or unconnected with the earlier occurrence of codification at Rugby, that Eton was the second school to commit its football rules to writing. This suspicion is reinforced by close inspection of the Eton rules which reveals that they were, in crucial respects, diametrically opposite to their Rugby counterparts. It must be enough in this context to cite just two of the 1849 Eton rules:

(i)   The ball may not be caught, carried, thrown, nor struck by the hand.

(ii) The goal sticks are to be seven feet out of the ground and the space between eleven feet. A goal is gained when the ball is kicked between them, provided it be not above them.[27]

We showed earlier how the fame of Rugby football had begun to spread, reaching even to the court. We also showed how aspects of it were incorporated into the game at other public schools. Given the intense status rivalry between schools in that period, it must have incensed the boys at Eton to have their thunder stolen by an obscure, Midlands establishment which had only recently become a public school. They considered their own to be the leading public school in *all* respects. By placing an absolute taboo on the use of hands in their version of football and decreeing that goals could only be scored below the height of the 'goal sticks', they were, one can suggest, attempting to assert their leadership of public schools and put the 'upstart' Rugbeians in their place.

If this is correct, it means that what later became an important driving force in the early development of football, namely a struggle between public schoolboys to be 'model makers' for the game on a national level, made its initial appearance in the 1840s. The emergence of distinguishing marks in the game at Rugby and the imposition of an absolute taboo on the use of hands at Eton are probable examples of how the game developed under the impetus of such competitive pressure. However, for the moment, these newly evolving models remained of local importance only. They received their wider significance only later when the game in its newly-fashioned public school forms spread into society at large and when, as a result, the struggles for national dominance between the exponents of rival models increased in intensity. It is to that process that we shall turn in the next chapter.

5 The 'civilizing process' and the formation of the RFU

1. Starting in the 1850s, Rugby football spread into the wider society. The newer forms of football developed at the other public schools underwent similar processes of diffusion almost simultaneously. Two wider developments underpinned this general process: the continued expansion of the middle classes and an educational transformation usually referred to as the 'public school games cult'.[1] There is no need for us to analyse these wider developments here. It is enough simply to note that the games cult reflected and, at the same time, helped to establish social conditions conducive to the spread of modern football in its embryonic forms, above all playing a part in transforming Rugby and what was to become soccer into status-enhancing activities for adult 'gentlemen'. It is also relevant to note that the games cult was connected with an upgrading of ball-games relative to field sports in the leisure-preferences of the upper classes and that it is, accordingly, best conceptualized as, in part, a 'civilizing' change. As we shall show, 'civilizing' changes were also involved in the formation of the FA and the RFU, the national associations formed as a result of the spread of the new forms of football into the wider society.

This process of diffusion led to pressure for unified rules to replace the existing plethora of local codes. An attempt was made to form a single national game but there was no basis for consensus among the participating groups. Or more precisely, there were two, i.e. they polarized around support for the embryo Rugby and soccer models but neither party was able to establish unequivocal dominance. Consequently, the bifurcation into Rugby and soccer set in motion by Rugby–Eton rivalry in the 1840s was perpetuated on a national level and marked by the formation of separate ruling bodies, the Football Association in 1863, and the Rugby Football Union in 1871.

The data available at present suggest that most leading proponents of the embryo soccer game were Old Etonians, Old Harrovians and old boys of other established public schools, whilst most protagonists of Rugby were Old Rugbeians and former pupils of the newer schools formed to accommodate the educational aspirations of the expanding middle class. Wherever members of these groups came into contact in a football context—for example, when they played together in the universities and when the attempt was made in London to establish unified rules—the conflict, especially between Etonians and Rugbeians, was intense. It is, we shall suggest, reasonable to suppose that this conflict was not simply over divergent forms of football but symptomatic of the deeper struggle within the upper classes which accompanied *embourgeoisement*. It is also reasonable to suppose that the inability of either party to establish undisputed dominance was connected with the relatively equal balance of power between the established and ascendant classes at the stage of *embourgeoisement* reached by the second half of the nineteenth century.

However, a complete explanation of the bifurcation cannot be attained by reference to *embourgeoisement* alone. The 'civilizing process', more specifically the gradual emergence within the upper and middle classes of norms demanding stricter control of aggression, was equally important. Thus, one of the central issues on which the Rugby and soccer parties were divided was that of the types of physical violence henceforth to be permitted in football. The former adhered to a traditional concept of 'manliness' which stressed courage and physical strength; the latter advocated 'manliness' of a more restrained and 'civilized' kind. We shall return to this issue later. Our first task is to examine the spread of the new forms of football. We shall look at the diffusion of Rugby first.

2. From about 1850, according to Morris Marples, the new public schools 'with one accord adopted the Rugby way of playing football'.[2] That this is exaggerated is suggested by the fact that Ardingly, Bradfield, Brighton, Felsted, Hurstpierpoint, Lancing, Malvern, Radley, Repton and Rossall played soccer as late as 1902.[3] However, Marples' point is generally correct since the majority of new schools, especially those established on Arnoldian lines and staffed by Old Rugbeians and former Rugby masters, did adopt the Rugby game.

The diffusion of Rugby was facilitated by its written rules. However, since unwritten custom continued to cover many aspects and some rules were adapted to physical peculiarities of 'the Close', local differences, often influenced by topographical aspects of the playing area in particular schools, began to spring up from the beginning. As a result, inter-school matches were difficult to arrange. In fact, for three principal reasons, such matches did not become the norm in England until the 1890s.[4] These reasons were: (i) the intense pride which led schools to cling tenaciously to their own football traditions; (ii) the fact that, at least in moderate and large-sized schools, the house system provided scope for organizing meaningful contests; and (iii) the high status-barriers which led schools to play regularly only against others which they recognized unequivocally as public schools. The last was most decisive. A few examples will show how deep-rooted such status-barriers were.

As early as 1818, Charterhouse challenged Westminister to a cricket match but were 'refused not only on account of their being such inferior players, but also because it was thought beneath Westminster to accept the challenge from a private school . . .'[5] Harrow boys in the 1840s are reported as recognizing 'only Eton, Harrow, Winchester, Westminster and Charterhouse as public schools'.[6] And when in 1866 the Shrewsbury football captain wrote to his Westminster counterpart requesting a match, he received the following dismissive reply:

> The Captain of the Westminster Eleven is sorry to disappoint Shrewsbury, but Westminster plays no schools except Public Schools, and the general feeling in the school quite coincides with that of the Committee of the Public Schools' Club, who issue this list of Public Schools—Charterhouse, Eton, Harrow, Rugby, Westminster and Winchester.[7]

The Shrewsbury captain responded angrily:

> I regret to find from your letter that the Captain of the Westminster Eleven has yet to learn the first lesson of a true public school education, the behaviour due from one gentleman to another.[8]

Thus Rugby by this time was an accepted public school but Shrewsbury, even though defined as such by the Clarendon Commission, was not. The even greater status-exclusiveness which typified relations between old and new public schools is brought out by the terse reply received by Mill Hill in 1870 when they challenged Harrow to a football match. It was written on a postcard and read: 'Eton we know, and Rugby we know, but who are ye?'[9]

Games assumed importance in the relations between public schools because they had become, in connection with the 'games cult', a central medium for expressing 'gentlemanly' values. Given the widening compass of that concept and the uncertainties, anxieties and tensions roused by *embourgeoisement*, it is hardly surprising that this was a matter on which schools were touchy. However, for present purposes the most important aspect of this status-exclusiveness of the English schools is its consequences for the development of football. More specifically, since it was central in preventing the early organization of regular inter-school matches, it meant that, even though they had formed the setting in which incipient modernization took place, these schools were not destined to play a part in the formation of unified rules. Accordingly, it is to football at Oxford and Cambridge, especially the latter, and the formation of the first independent clubs that our attention will now be turned.

3. The significance of Oxford and Cambridge for the development of football lies partly in the fact that it was at those institutions that young upper- and middle-class adults began, for the first time, regularly to play the more

'civilized' forms of football which were emerging in the public schools. These forms were adopted by undergraduates in the 1840s in conjunction with the spread of the games cult to the universities, a process which is hardly surprising if only because the majority of students came from public schools. Sport was, of course, already established as a university leisure-institution. What happened in conjunction with the games cult was that ballgames, together with rowing and 'track and field' athletics, began to replace field sports at the top of the prestige hierarchy of university sports. Cricket and rowing were the first to be established but, from about 1850, football began to vie for a position on the ladder of university sporting prestige. As it gained acceptance, men from different schools, brought up according to different football traditions, were thrown together. Since only small numbers from particular schools found themselves in the same university or college at the same time, in order to secure meaningful and exciting contests it was necessary for old boys of different schools to play together. However, the absence of common rules meant that such matches were fraught with tension. It was the desire to avoid this which led to attempts to construct unified rules.

Common rules were produced at Cambridge between about 1837 and 1842,[10] in 1846,[11] 1848,[12] about 1856[13] and 1863[14] but only those of 1863 were of lasting significance. That was because they played a part, when the independent clubs tried to lay down unified rules, in perpetuating the emergent bifurcation of Rugby and soccer. However, the 1863 Cambridge rules were themselves the product of a 'split'. Signs of the impending conflict can be traced back to 1848. Thus, in an account of a meeting to determine common rules held at Trinity College in that year, the author, H. C. Malden, noted how 'the Eton men howled at the Rugby men for handling the ball'.[15] This suggests that the main axis of tension in Cambridge football at that stage was between Old Etonian and Old Rugbeian undergraduates. The school rules of these groups had developed in almost diametrically opposed directions. The chances of conflict were, therefore, greatest when they played together. It must have been exacerbated by the more general rivalry between their schools which, as we hypothesized earlier, seems to have been occasioned by *embourgeoisement*, and to have been in large part responsible for the divergent development of their football in the first place. In short, the conflict between Etonians and Rugbeians over football is best seen as just one aspect of the more general conflict between their schools and, hence, between the established and ascendant classes.

According to Malden, the 1848 rules worked satisfactorily. However, that seems unlikely since it was necessary to construct a new set some eight years later. These rules were produced by a committee consisting of Eton, Harrow, Rugby, Shrewsbury and University representatives. They were compromise rules, based on elements from the Eton, Harrow, and Shrewsbury games. Only Rugby rules were totally excluded. The willingness of Rugbeians to accede to such a compromise was probably conditioned by the fact they were then isolated exponents of Rugby football at the University, i.e. Old

Marlburians and former pupils of other schools to which their game spread were not yet attending university in significant numbers. That this situation had begun to change by 1863 is shown by the fact that an Old Marlburian added his signature to the rules of that year. Six schools were represented on the committee which produced them: Eton, Harrow and Rugby each contributed two representatives; Marlborough, Shrewsbury and Westminster, only one.[16] The Rugbeians could count on three votes in case of disagreement but, should the others choose to combine, they outnumbered supporters of the Rugby model by two to one. Combination between them was facilitated by the fact that their rules differed more from Rugby football than from one another. That they did, in fact, combine is suggested by the following rules:

13. The ball, when in play, may be stopped by any part of the body, but NOT be held or hit by the hands, arms or shoulders.
14. ALL charging is fair, but holding, pushing with the hands, tripping up and shinning (i.e. hacking) are forbidden.[17]

The Rugbeians and Marlburians added their signatures to these rules but the Rugby-playing group at Cambridge had grown and was no longer forced to put up with a game from which central features of their model were excluded. Accordingly, they severed relations with old boys of the non-Rugby schools and began to play in isolation. As we shall see, this action heralded the similar breakaway that was to occur some three months later at the inaugural meetings of the Football Association. Before we consider this, however, it is necessary to examine the formation of independent clubs.

4. Clubs specifically for playing football were first formed in the 1850s. The data available on this process are at present rather scanty but show clearly enough that members of the upper and middle classes were the founders. That is not surprising, firstly because the embryonic forms of modern football were still restricted almost entirely to the clientele of public schools, and secondly because, even today, the formation and membership of voluntary associations tends to be characteristic of the higher social strata.

Most early clubs were founded in the South, particularly in London and the Home Counties. Nevertheless, the first reliable record comes from Sheffield where occasional matches were recorded as early as 1855 and where Sheffield FC issued a constitution and set of rules on 24 October 1857.[18] Another club is recorded in the Sheffield suburb of Hallam in that year and, by 1862, there were sixteen in the district. Since more is known about the formation of Sheffield FC than its contemporaries, we shall discuss it at some length. Most members were old boys of Sheffield Collegiate School. Among the members of the first committee were: President, Frederick Ward

(1827–1908), sometime chairman of the Sheffield Forge and Rolling Mills Company; Vice-President, T. A. Sorley (1825–85), partner in his family's firm; committee member, T. E. Vickers (1883–1915), son of Edward Vickers of Tapton Hall, sometime head of Vickers and Co., JP., and Honorary Colonel of the 1st Volunteer Battalion of the Yorkshire and Lancashire Regiment. Numbers 5 and 8 of the rules formulated by this committee in 1857 show that Sheffield football was based on one or more of the embryo soccer games. They were:

5. Pushing with the hands is allowed but no hacking or tripping up is fair under any circumstances whatever.
8. The ball may be pushed on or hit with the hand, but holding the ball except in the case of a free kick is altogether disallowed.[19]

Data on other early clubs are even scantier. We know, for example, that Forest, a club which played at Snaresbrook in the Epping Forest, was founded in 1859 by a group of Old Harrovians and that C. W. and J. F. Alcock, the sons of a Sunderland JP, were among the founders.[20] We also know that Stoke-on-Trent FC was founded in 1867 by a group of Old Carthusians employed as managers at the North Staffordshire Railway Works,[21] and that the War Office and Civil Service Clubs were founded in 1862, presumably by government servants employed in an administrative or executive capacity.[22] Other clubs known to have been formed before 1863 are: Blackheath (1858), Richmond (1859), Harlequins (1859), Crystal Palace (1861), Notts County (1862), Barnes (1862), and Leeds Athletic. And, since they sent representatives to the inaugural meetings of the Football Association, the following clubs must also have been formed in, or prior to, that year: Kensington School, Blackheath School, Perceval House School (Blackheath), and 'No Names', Kilburn.

For the upper- and middle-class adults who formed these clubs, football was a chosen recreation and not, as with folk-football and football in the public schools, an activity where the social pressure to participate was strong. Folk and public school football were playforms adjusted to the life of close-knit communities. Participation was less a matter of choice than the accompaniment of a particular status. Now, for the first time, the game became a matter of individual choice: or more correctly, the balance between choice and compulsion swung in favour of the former. At the same time, the game achieved an organization of its own and, hence, greater autonomy from the wider social structure. It was thus one of the earliest leisure activities not to be organized commercially or at least partly as a spectacle or for other extraneous purposes such as gambling but by and for the participating individuals themselves, largely for the pleasure it afforded and because it was a vehicle for expressing currently important values.

Because they were small and unable to sustain meaningful intra-club contests over periods as long as a season, the independent clubs had a built-in tendency to seek outside competition. At the same time, wider developments made inter-club matches more feasible and desirable. Important in this regard was the improvement of transport and communications which took place in Britain from the mid nineteenth century onwards. This facilitated more effective central control and thus paved the way for greater national unification. As part of this development, a more homogeneous national upper- and middle-class culture began to emerge. At the same time, individual and group identities (i.e. those of organizations such as schools and clubs, and collectivities such as local communities) began to be perceived within a wider, national framework and, in a growing number of fields, of which sport was just one, it became possible to establish more than a local reputation. The expansion of the national press, the reporting of sport in newspapers and the emergence of a specialized sporting press, all contributed to this widening of the field within which sporting identities and reputations could be established.

The new forms of football were included in this development because they had become acceptable as media for expressing 'gentlemanly' values. More positively, skill at football had become a socially desirable accomplishment, an asset indicative with a high degree of probability of public school or university attendance. In short, it was growing more feasible and desirable for teams and individuals to establish national rather than simply local reputations at the game. Hence, their status as footballers and gentlemen could be accorded wider recognition. At the same time, the improved means of transport and communication enabled school, university and, subsequently, class and regional rivalries to be subjected to a test of strength and skill on the football field.

Between them, these developments led to a demand for interschool and inter-club matches, and, hence, for unified rules. In response, a series of meetings—six in all—was held in London towards the end of 1863 in order to establish a definite code of rules 'for the regulation of the game of football'.[23] These inaugural meetings of what was to become the Football Association were held at the Freemason's Tavern, Lincoln's Inn Fields, a venue possibly indicating that many prominent players in that period worked in the City, perhaps in the legal, financial and accountancy fields. At the first meeting, on 26 October, eleven London clubs were represented but none from outside the metropolis. Some unattached players also came but Charterhouse was the only public school. In fact, no public school, not even Charterhouse, joined the Association for many years. The reason why was suggested by an Oxford undergraduate in a letter published that November in *The Sporting Life* in which he wrote that the London meetings were not 'attended by people or clubs of sufficient influence to cause their suggestions to be generally acted upon'.[24] From our twentieth-century vantage point, we know that events proved him wrong. The FA was able within a short time to establish the legitimacy of its claim to construct binding rules. Nevertheless, the status-consciousness of the late-nineteenth-century upper and middle classes, of which this letter provides an example, was one of the major obstacles in its path.

The first three meetings of the embryo Association proceeded smoothly. At the fourth, however, on 24 November, the hitherto dormant conflict inherent in the incipient bifurcation into Rugby and soccer broke into the open. The occasion was provided when the draft rules agreed at earlier meetings were read out. 'Running in' and 'hacking', the distinguishing marks of Rugby, had been included, which suggests either that adherents of the Rugby model had been represented at the early meetings in numbers sufficient to force their adoption or that its opponents did not, at that stage, feel united and strong enough to demand their exclusion. What is certainly the case is that, as time wore on, supporters of the embryo soccer game gradually gained the upper hand. Between the third and fourth meetings, it came to their notice that the rules drawn up at Cambridge in October prohibited 'running in' and 'hacking'. Support from such a prestigious quarter gave them encouragement. Further support came from W. Chesterman of Sheffield FC[25] and Lieutenant H. C. Moore of the Royal Engineers Club, Chatham,[26] who both wrote deploring the inclusion of these elements of the Rugby game. As the former put it, the Association's proposed rules were 'directly opposed to football and . . . more suggestive of wrestling'. As one can see, the tide was running in favour of the embryo soccer model. It was, however, over the Cambridge rules that the two sides split.

At the beginning of the fourth meeting, the Old Harrovian, J. F. Alcock proposed 'that the Cambridge rules appear to be the most desirable for the Association to adopt'. His motion was defeated. So was one by F. W. Campbell of Blackheath to the effect that the Cambridge rules were merely 'worthy of consideration'. According to the minutes, Campbell's proposal only 'appeared to have a majority against it', a fact which led subsequently to accusations of 'ungentlemanly' conduct. Eventually an amendment by E. C. Morley passed. It stipulated that '. . . a committee be appointed to enter into communication with the committee of the University to endeavour to induce them to modify some of their rules . . .'[27] Before the close, however, a motion was carried by a majority of one instructing this committee 'to insist on hacking' in its negotiations, indicating that neither party enjoyed a clear advantage at that stage.

It was thus the fourth meeting of the embryo Football Association which witnessed the first open clash between supporters of what were shortly to become the rival national games. At the fifth meeting, on 1 December, this conflict came completely into the open. Discussion centred, yet again, on the contentious draft rules regarding 'running in' and 'hacking'. The Secretary-elect, E. C. Morley, said that he did not personally object too strongly to 'hacking' but felt that to retain these rules would seriously hinder the development of football as an adult game. Campbell of Blackheath replied that, in his opinion, 'hacking' was essential if an element of pluck was to be retained and threatened that, if 'running in' and 'hacking' were abolished, his club would withdraw. In due course, the contentious rules were struck out and, just as the meeting was about to close, Campbell rose to say that, although his club approved of the Association and its aims, the rules adopted would 'emasculate' football, rob it of all interest and excitement. Blackheath was unwilling to be party to a game of that kind and wished, accordingly, for its name to be withdrawn. By this action, the Black-heath Club paved the way for the formation, in 1871, of the separate Rugby Football Union and the final and irrevocable parting of the ways between 'soccer' and 'rugger'.

5. The inaugural meetings of the Football Association are not only signifi-cant for what they tell us about the development of football but also, we believe, because they provide further confirmation of Elias' theory of the 'civilizing process'. More specifically, the controversy over 'hacking' shows that sections of the British upper and middle classes grew more 'civilized' in the late nineteenth century in the sense of developing standards demanding stricter violence-control. For example, E. C. Morley clearly believed such 'civilizing' standards to be widespread, for he said:

> . . . if we carry these two rules it will be seriously detrimental to the great majority of the football clubs. . . . Mr. Campbell himself knows well that the Blackheath clubs cannot get any three clubs in London to play with them whose members are for the most part men in business, and to whom it is of importance to take care of themselves.
> . . . If we have 'hacking' no one who has arrived at the years of dis-cretion will play at football and it will be entirely relinquished to schoolboys.[28]

However, that the new standards were not adhered to uniformly—i.e. that one is dealing with a long-term process, not a sudden, total transformation— is suggested by the response elicited in F. W. Campbell. He gloried in the violence of the game, predicting, as we have seen, that abolition of 'hacking' would lead football to be 'emasculated':

> 'Hacking' is the true football game and if you look into the Winchester records you will find that in former years men were so wounded that two . . . were actually carried off the field . . . Lately, however, the game has become more civilized than that state of things which certainly was, to a certain extent, brutal.
> As to not liking 'hacking' . . . it savours of those who like their pipes and grog or schnapps more than the manly game of football. I think . . . the reason they object . . . is because too many . . . began late in life, and were too old for that spirit of the game . . . so fully entered into at the public schools and by the public school men in after life.[29]

Thus, Campbell implied that the opponents of 'hacking' had not attended public schools and were, as a result, socially inferior 'outsiders' who had no right to object. A. C. Pember, the President-elect, had not attended public school and was stung into responding:

> Perhaps you will allow me to say that I took down 'Fifteen' the other day to play a match and I was the only one who had not been at a public school and we were all dead against 'hacking'.[30]

Campbell, however, was unimpressed and replied in nationalistic vein:

> Be that as it may, Sir, I think that if you do away with it you will do away with all the courage and pluck of the game, and I will be bound to bring over a lot of Frenchmen who would beat you with a week's practice.[31]

Campbell made no attempt to deny the violence of 'hacking'. An element of physical danger, he thought, is necessary if football is to be a test of, and medium for developing, courage. In this respect, he was a spokesman for the old order, for values more appropriate to a stage when state control had been less effective, when the level of violence had been greater and when, correspondingly, norms of masculinity had laid stress on physical courage and stength. In his mind, 'civilization' equalled 'emasculation' but he and those who argued like him were swimming against the tide. 'Hacking' was tabooed in both soccer and Rugby, and the most distinctive feature of the latter game, even though it remained in most respects rougher and more dependent on physical contact than its counterpart, became the practice of 'running in'. Indeed, as we shall show, the spread and intensification of the controversy over 'hacking' was one of the reasons why Rugby clubs were forced to unite. It is to that issue, the formation of the RFU, that our attention will now be turned.

6. For eight years after the foundation of the FA, Rugby players continued without a central body invested with the authority to enact binding rules. In 1871, however, the discrepancy which had thus existed between the two embryo national codes for practically a decade was brought to an end by the formation of the RFU. Three factors led Rugby players to emulate their Association counterparts in this crucial respect: (i) the fact that, following the formation of the FA, soccer began to outstrip Rugby in the competition for popular support; (ii) the fact that, in the absence of a central-ruling making body, different forms of Rugby began to appear; and (iii) the growing body of opinion, inside and outside Rugby circles, that 'hacking' was a 'barbarous' practice which ought to be abolished or at least severely curtailed. The need for an organized response to the controversy over 'hacking' was causally most important. Accordingly, it is to that issue that we shall

devote the remainder of this chapter. First of all, however, it is necessary to examine the rivalry between soccer and Rugby, and the occurrence of local differentiation within the latter game.

To say that the formation of the Football Association conferred on soccer an advantage in the competition for popular support is not to imply that the FA and its rules were accorded legitimacy immediately. Its early difficulties were legion but, nevertheless, it was able as early as 1867 to inaugurate representative soccer, starting with a match between London and Sheffield, and following with county matches between Middlesex and Surrey–Kent, and Surrey and Kent. The county matches attracted large crowds and were the subject of reports in *Bell's Life*. 'Football', said the first report, 'has lately increased to such gigantic dimensions that it needs something more than ordinary club matches to bring out the rising talent.'[32]

However, it was the playing in November 1870 of an 'international' between English and Scottish members of the London soccer clubs which spurred Rugby players into action.[33] At that time, soccer had hardly spread north of the Tweed. Rugby men regarded Scotland as their preserve and, accordingly, Scottish Rugby players issued a challenge to their English counterparts for a bona fide international. One was arranged for 27 March 1871. However, if such matches were to be a regular occurrence and help promote Rugby in opposition to the rival code, a central body with the authority to pick representative sides and the capacity to organize internationals was needed in each country.

The need for central control was further increased by the occurrence of local differentiation. Such processes took place largely because Rugby had only been partly codified in 1845. That is, custom continued to regulate many aspects. Moreover, some rules had grown up in relation to geographically specific features of the Close, whilst others were so complex or obscure that initiation at the school was a prerequisite for understanding. In short, the 1845 rules were not sufficiently clear or explicit on their own but needed supplementation by reference to the body of oral tradition which had grown up at Rugby School. Given that, it is not surprising that, wherever the game was not played by Rugbeians or in a context where constant recourse to Rugbeians could be made, the gaps in the rules were filled in an *ad hoc* manner by new rules and customs. But whichever it was, the game began to take on a different form.

The existence of gaps in the written rules due to incomplete codification was not, however, the only reason for the occurrence of local differentiation for, in the absence of a central legislative body, particular clubs were able to introduce such changes as they thought fit. It was apparently in this manner that Leeds Athletic, although nominally clinging to the Rugby code, abolished 'running in' and introduced goals without a crossbar.[34] Similarly, Blackheath started to use short flag-posts instead of the tall Rugby goals and to play a goalkeeper behind the full-backs.[35] And it seems that Richmond were virtually alone among London Rugby clubs in the 1860s in adhering to the school rule which prohibited players from picking up a rolling as distinct from a bouncing ball. Others, including Blackheath, Woolwich and Sandhurst, allowed the ball to be picked up in the open as long as it was moving.[36] Blackheath School even went so far as to abolish 'offside' with the result that their forwards would charge 'down the ground as an advance guard to ward off opponents from the back who was in full run with the ball behind them'.[37]

As had been the case prior to the formation of the FA, such differences were a serious obstacle to inter-school and club matches. Rugby boys overcame it by limiting matches to clubs composed solely of Old Rugbeians, of which there were two, Richmond and Ravenscourt Park, by 1872.[38] This refusal to play 'outsiders' was probably motivated as much by status-exclusiveness as concern about the dangers of such matches. But, whatever motives lay behind it, it did nothing to meet the needs of the growing number of non-Rugbeians who wished to play Rugby or of those Rugbeians who wished to test their ability in a wider context.

7. We suggested earlier that the dispute over 'hacking' at the inaugural meetings of the FA was only the precursor of a more heated controversy which erupted some eight years later and played a crucial part in the formation of the RFU. On both occasions, Rugby supporters were the most persistent advocates of a rougher and, as they saw it, more 'manly' game. However, a growing body of opinion, inside as well as outside Rugby circles, regarded practices such as 'hacking' as barbaric. In the emergent social climate, Rugby traditionalists were unable to retain the older, more violent form and there gradually emerged a type of Rugby which could be considered both 'manly' and 'civilized' according to the emergent standards of the late-nineteenth-century upper and middle classes.

The most public aspects of this struggle took place in the press. A warning shot was fired in November 1869 when an accident in a 'house match' at Rugby School was reported in *The Rugby Advertiser*. In itself, that was unexceptional but evidence of mounting public concern is provided by the fact that the editor of *The Times* regarded the accident as sufficiently important to merit reprinting the report. Here is the relevant extract:

> . . . in the course of a severe scrimmage a young gentleman named Lomax got down, with his head bent under his chest, and in this position was trampled on by many of the players. He was picked up insensible, and, with the exception of short intervals of consciousness, he has remained so until the present time . . . If he survives, (which is still doubtful!), it is feared he will be a cripple for life.[39]

This prompted an immediate response from a participant in the match, casting doubt on the objectivity of reports in *The Rugby Advertiser* and their suitability for inclusion in a national paper:

A statement in *The Rugby Advertiser* is scarcely worthy either of explanation or contradiction: but since you have copied the advertised account of Mr. Lomax's accident, which must of necessity prejudice many against Rugby football, it is advisable you should hear the truth. Mr. Lomax's accident—the worst within recollection—is due in great measure to himself. A few weeks ago an attempt was made to change the part of the game, technically called 'mauling', from which Mr. Lomax received his hurt. The attempt was unsuccessful, chiefly owing to the vigorous opposition of Mr. Lomax. During the match Mr. Lomax endeavoured to pull over one of the School House side, who was pressing forward with the ball, and in so doing he fell down, drawing some half-dozen upon himself.

My object in writing is that you should know the truth, that it was pure accident, and that it would not have happened if that change had been made in the game which we soon hope to see.[40]

It is difficult in retrospect to establish just how violent Rugby football in that period was. Nevertheless, it is interesting to note that, despite his desire to present the game in a favourable light, the author of this letter denied neither the seriousness of the accident nor the dangers of 'mauling'. Indeed, he admitted the existence of internal opposition to that practice. It probably formed part of a more general campaign in the school to reduce football violence. Thus, Frederick Temple, who retired from the headship in 1869, launched an attack on 'hacking'.[41] However, the evidence regarding his success is ambiguous. Writing in 1892, A. J. Guillemard argued that 'hacking over' was nothing more than a form of 'tripping', less dangerous than the name implies. However, he contradicted himself when he observed how Temple, '. . . noticing a much-dreaded "hack" hewing his way through a Bigside scrummage with unnecessary violence, threatened to make him take off his "navvies" and play in slippers for the rest of the afternoon'.[42] This suggests that the 1845 prohibition had failed to eliminate the use of 'navvies'. However, some lines from a poem published in *The New Rugbeian* in 1858 suggest the opposite:

This is the Football bigside: but where are the navvies that through it
Hackt like the woodsman that fells in the forest the oak with his
    hatchet?
Gone are those well known forms, and their navvies forever
    departed . . .[43]

Such ambiguity may be indicative of the fact that one is dealing with a process involving 'civilizing' waves and counter-waves, i.e. in which the use of 'navvies' declined for a while only to be taken up later. That would be consistent with Elias' model but the available evidence is insufficient to enable one to determine whether that is what, in fact, occurred. However, even if there were fluctuations in the level of violence, it remains the case that, by present-day standards, mid-nineteenth-century Rugby was pretty rough. Thus Guillemard went on to describe how it was not uncommon at that stage 'to see a couple of players vigorously engaged in kicking each other's shins long after the scrummage had broken up', thus seemingly contradicting his initial testimony yet again.[44]

Less ambiguous evidence comes from the anonymous Old Rugbeian quoted earlier. He describes how, after the 'tight scrummage' had unravelled, there

> . . . began the loose scrummage with its indiscriminate hacking, though always an interesting moment for those actually on the ball. But the latter had to be driven fairly through the opposing ranks; it was not the thing to wriggle it out at the side. Only a few, however, could be on the ball, and what could the rest do but hack one another?[45]

From this it emerges, firstly, that the 'loose scrummage' was characterized by 'indiscriminate hacking' and, secondly, that the latter practice was not restricted to players challenging for or in possession of the ball. On the contrary, it was engaged in by all when the 'tight scrummage' broke up. The Old Rugbeian went on to enumerate the types of injury most frequent in Rugby football at that stage:

> There were a great many accidents, as might be expected with such numbers playing, such prolonged scrummages and indiscriminate hacking. They were taken as a matter of course—arms, legs, collar-bones, knees, ankles were constantly broken, dislocated or fractured, while I recall one tragic case of a boy well known to me whose back was broken at the bottom of a scrummage. I wonder there were not more.[46]

Not surprisingly, it was the accident rate which formed the central issue in the public controversy over Rugby. We have seen how, in 1869, a small-scale skirmish took place in the columns of *The Times*. Battle was joined again a year later but, this time, the struggle was more protracted and, in its consequences for the game's development, deeper and more lasting. It began with a letter to *The Times*, signed, 'A Surgeon', and headed, 'Rugby and its Football'. It read:

> I . . . have within the last few weeks been consulted in different cases of injury resulting from . . . 'hacking' . . . One boy with his collar bone broken, another with a severe injury to his groin, a third with a severe injury to his ankle, a fourth with a severe injury to his knee, and two others sent home on crutches, . . . hacking . . . has nothing to do with the game, but . . . frequently injures for life, and is a licence for a malignant grudge. I am not a milk-sop . . ., but I do protest against a system which

results in injury more or less felt for life, because it is a practice easily remedied, and for which the Headmaster is solely responsible.[47]

Despite the fact that his competence was called into question, the head-master, Dr. Hayman (1870–4), did not reply. However, an angry response was sparked off among boys and old boys. Three letters appeared in *The Times* on 26 November 1870. The first is worth quoting in full:

['A Surgeon'] gives a list of six accidents which he says have occurred here this year. Of these two never happened at all, one I have never heard of, and the other three, I can show were not the results of 'hacking'. He says that a collar-bone was broken and that two boys went home on crutches. Well, no collar-bone has been broken and only one boy has gone home on crutches, and he with an injury to his knee, which he obtained nearly two years ago when out brook-jumping and which he twisted again when running and not from a hack, as he was playing 'little-side' at the time—a game in which there is absolutely no hacking. The fellow who was hurt in the groin got accidentally hurt by another fellow's knee, and not by his foot, and that might happen in any game. The other with the 'severe injury to his knee' also obtained his in 'little-side', where, as I said before, there is no 'hacking', and this was caused to his knee when trying to dodge a fellow; he is nearly well now, and will play again very soon. The one with the bad ankle I have not heard of, so it is evidently not very bad. On 'bigside' where the proper Rugby game is played, there has not been an accident this term. I really think people should make enquiries before making such statements as those of 'A Surgeon' as it is not pleasant to see such things in the paper about us, especially when untrue.[48]

The second and third letters corroborated the first, insisting that 'hacking' was harmless and not the cause of the accidents listed. They show how anxious the majority of Rugby personnel were to preserve the game in its existing form. However, the surgeon was quick to notice that, whilst indi-vidually the three letters denied the accuracy of his allegations, collectively they corroborated them. In reply, he asked:

Is 'hacking' a legitimate part of football? Is it practised at any other public school? Is it not fraught with great danger? May it not be a means of paying off an old grudge? And was not the death of a boy recorded in the public papers as the result of 'hacking' played in accordance with Rugby rules quite sufficient to justify its being discontinued? Football is a manly game, and accidents will occur even when played fairly, but 'hacking' forms no part of the game, and is to my mind a brutal and unnecessary addition.[49]

By this time, the surgeon was gathering support. As the following letter shows, the question of 'hacking' was now replaced by a wider and, from the standpoint of the existing form of Rugby, more threatening issue: the dangers of the game *per se*:

> Your correspondent is . . . right . . . when he says that the question . . . is not whether . . . accidents have arisen from 'hacking'. The question for the public is whether the game . . . at Rugby is attended with serious accidents which do not occur elsewhere . . . the accidents themselves . . . are beyond question . . . I challenge the Rugbeians to show that such serious accidents occur so frequently elsewhere, and if this cannot be done, is it not natural to conclude that they arise from the style of play adopted at Rugby. But it is well known by those interested in . . . public school games, that Rugby football is rougher and more dangerous than the same game at Eton and Harrow. This need not be; . . . it is high time that public opinion should be brought to bear upon it. The Rugbeians cannot be allowed to be their own judges . . .[50]

Rugbeians were forced onto the defensive. An Old Rugbeian Oxford undergraduate, for example, felt compelled to write:

> Sir, . . . 'A Surgeon' asks four questions, which I should like to . . . answer.
>
> 1. 'Is hacking a legitimate part of the game?' It is. Rugby football differs from other football in the prevalence of what are technically known as 'tight scrummages' to force the ball through which a certain amount of kicking is necessary. There are, however, certain rules to prevent the abuse of 'hacking' such as that it must be below the knee etc., and 'hacking', therefore, when carried on in accordance with the rules, is entirely 'legitimate'.
> 2. 'Does the practice exist at any other public schools?' Yes: at all playing Rugby rules, though, of course, in a greater or less degree.
> 3. 'Is it not a source of great danger?' No. Accidents sometimes arise from a kick aimed at the ball taking effect on a player, but this has nothing to do with 'hacking'.
> 4. 'Does it not give opportunities of paying off old scores?' Yes: and no system of football could be devized in which it would not be possible for a player, so minded, to kick another while pretending to aim at the ball . . .
>
>   It is undoubtedly true that football is the cause of a great many accidents. It is, perhaps, true that the Rugby game, as being played with greater numbers, is the more dangerous game. That 'hacking' is the cause of many accidents all those who have ever played the game know to be absolutely false. During five years stay at Rugby, and four years as a Cap, I can remember but one serious

accident to be directly attributed to 'hacking'. Since my time—that is to say, in the last two years—'hacking' has gone out so much at Rugby that a new evil has arisen, and to prevent this evil, known as that of 'mauling', a certain amount of hacking is absolutely necessary . . .[51]

This letter is chiefly remarkable for its inconsistencies. The author admitted that the larger number of players probably made Rugby football more dangerous than the game at other schools. But he claimed, on the one hand, that 'hacking' was tactically necessary as a means of forcing the ball through 'tight scrummages' and, on the other, that it was dying out, a doubtful proposition unless the 'tight scrummage' was also disappearing. It is possible, of course, that an alternative means of forcing the ball through in such a game situation was being evolved but the Old Rugbeian made no reference to such a tactic. Moreover, he mentioned the practice of 'mauling', describing it as an 'evil' and claiming that it, too, had to be countered by 'hacking'. He also admitted that accidents could occur when a player missed the ball and unintentionally kicked an opponent or when, in order to pay off a grudge, he pretended to kick the ball but aimed deliberately for an opponent's legs.

The last word as far as *The Times* was concerned was had by Robert Farquharson, Medical Officer to Rugby School. After denying the accuracy of the surgeon's information, he wrote:

It is impossible that 500 boys can engage two or three times a week in rather a rough game without accidents . . . but it seems quite arbitrary to assume that a greater proportion . . . are met with here than elsewhere. One of the worst fractured legs I ever saw occurred . . . in Dublin, under the Eton rules, and it would be most satisfactory if Medical Officers connected with other public schools would supply statistical data for an inquiry of this sort. Such an investigation if conducted in a calm judicial spirit with a due regard for facts on the one hand and an avoidance of sensational padding on the other, could not fail to be of the deepest interest.[52]

To our knowledge, Farquharson's proposal for a comparative study of accident rates was not taken up. Perhaps the other schools were frightened of the findings which might have emerged? However, most important for present purposes is the fact that, despite his close identification with the school and desire to clear its reputation, he was forced to admit the roughness of Rugby football.

Punch also joined the struggle. In an article entitled, 'Fighting at Football', the author recounted the injuries listed by the surgeon, arguing that the Rugby rules

. . . render a player liable . . . to be kicked when down on the ground, and . . . in any part of the body. His opponents are allowed to force the ball out of his clutch by any means other than fisticuffs. Is it not advisable to amend this rule . . . directing that it be allowable to get the ball away by no greater violence than that of blows with the fist, and those only when the ball holder is on his legs? Then will the manly game of football be so far humanized as not to exceed in brutality the noble art of self-defence as normally practised in the prize-ring. If there is to be fighting at football, let it be fair.[53]

Punch later retracted this indictment. The editor accepted the argument, apparently put forward by a Rugby pupil, that the frequency of injuries in Rugby football was low given the large numbers involved and the amount of time spent playing.[54] However, if *Punch* was satisfied, other journals were not. One described Rugby as 'brutal and unmanly' and called for 'instant reformation if not total abolition'. Another characterized it as 'a mixture of hacking, scragging, gouging and biting'. It was even recommended that Parliament should abolish the game.[55] However, state intervention was unnecessary for, in 1871, Rugby's own 'parliament', the RFU, was formed and one of its first acts was to construct rules for a game in which 'hacking' had no legitimate place. It is to the formation of the RFU and its abolition of 'hacking' that our attention will now be turned.

8. The close-knit character of the school community served to insulate Rugby boys from the pressure of those who sought to force them to 'civilize' their football. It formed a protective shell which enabled them to resist outside pressure and hence to retain, at least for longer than was possible elsewhere, the traditional structure of their game. Old Rugbeians, however, and other adult players were situated differently. They were geographically dispersed and, hence, more vulnerable to the influence of those who regarded Rugby as 'barbaric'. It is not, therefore, surprising that the next step in the 'civilization' of the game should have taken place, not in the school, but in the wider society.

It did not matter in this connection whether Rugby was as dangerous as opponents alleged: it was enough for a sufficient body of people to *believe* it to be excessively rough. As we suggested earlier, the predominant upper- and middle-class conscience was coming at that time to involve internalized standards based on a relatively low tolerance for overt violence. Entailing, as it did, the deliberate kicking of an opponent's shins and sometimes the use of iron-tipped boots, 'hacking' was a practice that a decreasing number could tolerate. And, pushing in the same direction, were the occupational requirements of a society increasingly dominated by a work ethic.

Some, such as F. W. Campbell, fought hard against this trend. The violence characteristic of football in its earlier stages was, they felt, the essence of its

'manliness'. They were willing to forgo membership of the Football Association in order to preserve the *status quo*, but even they could not withstand
the 'civilizing forces' then at work for very long. As early as 1862, the Blackheath Club found it necessary to introduce a rule designed to limit the
violence of their football. It read:

> Though it is lawful to hold a player in a scrummage, this does not include
> attempts to throttle or strangle, which are totally opposed to the
> principles of the game.[56]

And in 1866, acting under the influence of the same 'civilizing pressures', a
meeting of the Richmond Club passed three resolutions. Copies were sent to
all the London clubs, together with the declaration that Richmond would
not play in matches where they were not observed:

1. That in the opinion of this meeting all unnecessary hacking should be
    put a stop to.
2. That all hacking in scrummages, except by those immediately on the ball,
    is contrary to the spirit of the Rugby game and is forbidden.
3. That no player be hacked over except he has the ball in his hands.[57]

Richmond RFC may have called here merely for the imposition of restrictions on 'hacking'. Nevertheless, their action is indicative of the effects
which 'civilizing' pressures were having on Rugby players. They were constrained—and to some extent came to desire—to limit the violence of their
football. However, there was no body to act collectively in these matters.
Therefore, particular clubs had, by and large, to act independently. It
is hardly surprising in such a situation that local differences regarding
the control of violence were added to those already emerging among the
Rugby-playing schools and clubs.

   On 4 December 1870, the Old Rugbeians, E. H. Ash and B. H. Burns,
secretaries respectively of the Richmond and Blackheath clubs, wrote to
The Times, suggesting 'that some code of rules should be adopted by
all clubs who profess to play the Rugby game'. The fact that their letter
appeared only two days after the last contribution to the 'hacking' controversy is, we think, indicative of the part played by that controversy in the
formation of the RFU. But, whether this is correct or not, the letter soon
produced the desired response, namely a meeting of Rugby clubs with the
express purpose of forming a central body with the authority to enact
binding rules. Such a meeting was held in London on 26 January 1871,
at the now non-existent Pall Mall Restaurant at the corner of Pall Mall
East and Cockspur Street. Thirty-two men representing twenty-one clubs
attended. We have been unable to obtain detailed information on the membership of these clubs. However, most played in London and its immediate
environs, and it is pretty clear that the majority of their members were

upper-middle- or middle-class. Thus four public schools were directly represented and occupationally-named clubs such as Civil Service, Guy's Hospital and Law were presumably composed of professional men. There were no divisions among those present comparable to that which led to rupture at the formative meetings of the FA. Moreover, virtually everyone was willing to bow to the authority of Old Rugbeians. Thus a 'working consensus' was soon established. E. C. Holmes was appointed to the chair and the election of A. E. Rutter as President and E. H. Ash as Honorary Secretary-Treasurer of the 'Rugby Football Union' soon followed. All three were Old Rugbeians. So were four more members of the first committee. This is shown in Table 5.1 which sets forth the names of this committee, together with such educational and occupational data on its members as we have been able to obtain.

At this first meeting, a constitution was drawn up and a subcommittee of three Old Rugbeians, A. E. Rutter, E. C. Holmes and L.J. Maton, all solicitors, was appointed to draft the rules which were henceforth to govern the playing of the game. Maton, it seems, was the principal drafter. After one or two amendments had been incorporated, his proposals were accepted by a special general meeting convened on 24 June 1871. There is no need for us to reprint the first RFU rules here.[58] It is enough to note that the chief points of difference with the rules then in operation at Rugby School were: (i) 'hacking', 'hacking over' and 'tripping' were abolished; (ii) a player in an offside position was placed onside if one of his own side ran in front of him either with the ball or having kicked it when behind him; the offside rules in general were more fully explained; (iii) in case of a 'knock on' or forward throw, if no fair catch had been made, a scrummage on the spot might be claimed; and (iv) the ball was to be returned into play from the spot where it crossed the line of touch.[59]

9. The formation of the RFU was a significant step in Rugby's modernization. There now existed a central body which claimed the authority to enact binding, universal rules, a 'third party' which could be called upon to mediate in cases of dispute. It could also coordinate the affairs of the game nationally and develop long-term policies. In this way, more effective competition with Association football became possible and, at the same time, the stage was set for the emergence of Rugby as a fully-fledged modern sport. However, it was still not completely modernized for, even though the 1871 rules laid down a framework distinctly recognizable as a less developed variant of the modern game, it remained dependent on custom in several respects. Thus, although a 'Plan of the Field' was included with the first rules, no mention was made of the allowable pitch dimensions. Consequently, these depended on available space and varied considerably from ground to ground. For example, the ground for the first England–Scotland match, played at Raeburn Place, Edinburgh in 1871, was 120 by 55 yards, whilst

Table 5.1 Social characteristics of the first RFU committee*

Name	School	Occupation	Name	School	Occupation
A. E. Rutter	Rugby	Solicitor	F. I. Currey	Marlborough	Solicitor
E. H. Ash	Rugby	Lecturer, Military College, Richmond.	F. Luscombe	Tonbridge	Businessman
F. Stokes	Rugby	Solicitor, Proctor to the Lords	R. Leigh	–	–
		Commissioners of the Admiralty	P. Hartley	–	–
			A. J. English	Wellington	–
E. C. Holmes	Rugby	Solicitor	I. H. Ewart	–	Doctor
E. Rutter	Rugby	–	R. H. Birkett	Haileybury	–
A. G. Guillemard	Rugby	Solicitor			
W. F. Eaton	–	Civil Servant			
L. J. Maton	Rugby	Solicitor			

* Data on the Old Rugbeians were obtained from the *Rugby School Register, 1675–1874*, Rugby, London, Oxford and Cambridge, 1886. The occupations of Eaton, Luscombe and Ewart were inferred from the addresses given in Owen, *op. cit.*, p. 65.

that for the return match at the Oval in 1872 was 120 by 70 yards.[60] Among the other items not dealt with by the 1871 rules were size of teams, duration of matches, and size and shape of the ball. No penalties were stipulated for the punishment of infringements and no provision made for non-playing officials. The captains remained solely responsible for the legitimate exercise of control, and heavy reliance continued to be placed on the fact that, as 'gentlemen', players were expected to exercise self-control and abide voluntarily by the rules.

Despite the existence of a hiatus in these respects, the 1871 rules did represent a more complete codification. Moreover, the total prohibition of 'hacking', 'hacking over' and 'tripping' was a further move in a 'civilizing' direction. However, the authority of the newly-founded RFU to enforce the abolition of such practices was not immediately accepted. They did not die out at Rugby School, for example, until the demise of twenty-a-side games in 1881.[61] Moreover, many players shared the belief, articulated by F. W. Campbell in 1863, that abolition of the rougher parts of Rugby would lead to its 'emasculation'. Thus it is recorded that some clubs commemorated the 'good old days' until late in the 1870s with five minutes of 'glorious hacking' at the end of a match known as a 'Hallelujah'.[62]

The England–Scotland match in 1871 was one of the first played according to the new rules. What we hear about it is instructive regarding the adjustment-difficulties of players:

> It was among the first no-hacking matches for many of the players . . . Now hacking becomes an instinctive action . . . you hack at a man running past . . . as surely as you blink when a man puts his finger in your eye. There were a good many hacks-over going on, and, as blood got up, it began to be muttered, 'Hang it! why not have hacking allowed?' 'It can't be prevented – far better have it.' The question hung in the balance. The teams seemed nothing loth. The Captains . . . both looked as if they ought to say 'no' and would rather say 'yes', . . . when Almond, who was umpire, vowed he would throw up his job if it were agreed on, so it was forbidden, and hackers were ordered to be more cautious.[63]

10. Writing in 1899, Montague Shearman claimed that, in the 1860s, Rugby began to outstrip soccer in the struggle for popular support.[64] At first glance, he appears to be supported by information in *The Football Annual*, a publication edited by C. W. Alcock which appeared yearly between 1867 and 1887. For example, the 1873 edition reports the existence of 230 clubs in England. In seven cases, they are listed as playing both Rugby and Association, as adhering to the Cambridge or Uppingham rules, or the type of game they played was not included. Of the remaining 223, 132 are reported as playing Rugby and only 91 Association football. Of the latter, moreover, 22 are listed as playing the distinctive Sheffield game. This leaves only 69 clubs as

unambiguous adherents to the soccer code. However, close inspection of the data reveals that by 1873, whilst Rugby was becoming more popular in London and its environs, soccer was outstripping its rival in the provinces. Thus, 105 Rugby but only 35 Association clubs are listed from the metropolitan area. By contrast, only 27 Rugby but 56 provincial soccer clubs are listed. Even if one subtracts the 22 Sheffield clubs from the soccer total, the latter game appears, if only slightly, to have been gaining more in popularity in the provinces.

Besides listing the names of active clubs, the 1873 *Football Annual* includes the numbers of affiliated players in 189 cases. The total number registered was 16,313. Of these, 6,767 were affiliated to soccer and 7,638 to Rugby clubs. This appears to provide further support for Shearman's contention, but these figures mask a significant characteristic of many Rugby players: the number who were schoolboys. Thus, 28 of the Rugby clubs listed were connected with schools but only nine of the soccer clubs. None were Old Boy clubs, moreover; i.e. they all consisted of pupils still at school. The nine school soccer clubs contributed only 691 to the 6,767 listed players of that game. The 28 school Rugby clubs, however, contributed between them no fewer than 3,836 to the 7,638 listed Rugby players. In other words, while 6,076 adult soccer players were listed in 1873, the corresponding number of adult Rugby players was only 3,702 – just over half as many. Thus it seems that soccer was increasing more in popularity in this period as an adult game. That is what one would expect given the length and complexity of the Rugby rules—59 were laid down in 1871 as opposed to the 14 laid down by the FA in 1863—and the growth of opposition to the roughness of the game they were supposed to regulate. However, a further reason for Rugby's slower growth as an adult game may have been connected with the changes introduced by the RFU, particularly, as it became successful, the abolition of 'hacking' and 'hacking over'. This requires elaboration.

Apart from reducing the violence of Rugby, one of the principal effects of this rule-change was to make the scrummage more central. Previously, 'hacking' had been the central tactic for breaking up the scrum. As such, it had helped to make the game relatively fast and open. Its abolition, however, made Rugby slower and more closed, transforming it into little more than a succession of tight scrums in which the ball was lost to sight and the sides pushed each other, their heads up in the air,[65] in an attempt to gain territorial advantage. Sometimes, scrummages lasted for minutes and connoisseurs judged playing standards by their duration. 'I have often in the old days heard spectators cheer vociferously over the prolonged equipoise of a well-balanced scrummage', wrote Arthur Budd, President of the RFU in 1888–9.[66] The relatively static game of that stage was evidently not totally lacking in spectator appeal. However, it cannot have had much immediate appeal to people not socialized into its mysteries at school.

A further consequence of the abolition of 'hacking' and the increased centrality of the scrum, was the fact that there occurred a re-emphasis on strength as opposed to skill. Heavy forwards became the norm, the greatest assets of a side. Thus, in bowing to public pressure and abolishing 'hacking', the RFU upset the balance of their game. They did not, it seems, perceive the need for compensatory measures to preserve its relative openness. In that way, whilst introducing changes which made the game in one way more consistent with the advancing standards of 'civilization', in another they reduced its level of 'civilization' whilst, at the same time, hindering its chances of competing effectively with the structurally more open and, hence, potentially more exciting, Association game.

With its earlier, more comprehensive reduction of physical violence, soccer was a game better suited to Britain's temper in the third quarter of the nineteenth century. Rugby was less compatible with the dominant trends in a society where the most powerful and prestigious groups were coming to regard as odious and distasteful forms of violence accepted by earlier gener-ations as normal. Even the abolition of 'hacking' was insufficient, by itself, to placate their conscience, for scrummaging, tackling and other aspects of Rugby which involved close physical contact were experienced as repulsive. However, factors other than its greater 'civilization' were probably as, if not more, important in the faster growth of soccer as an adult game. Among them was the fact that it did not have to contend with the sort of tactical difficulties which followed in Rugby from the abolition of 'hacking'. It was, therefore, from the outset, more open, mobile and exciting. Its rules were also simpler and could be learned more easily by men who had not played at school. And finally, in 1871, its excitement-generating potential was augmented by the establishment of the FA Challenge Cup, an event which may not have been unconnected with the formation of the RFU in that year.

11. A question posed by this discussion is why, in a society undergoing a 'civilizing process', Rugby should have remained more violent than soccer. This raises a number of difficult issues to which, at present, only tentative solutions can be proposed. The first thing to note is that Rugby was the first variant of football to advance to more 'civilized' standards. We are thinking mainly of the written rules of 1845. However, the pride Rugbeians took in that achievement led the game for a while to become 'frozen'. That is, the innovative adaptations made in the fluid social situation at Rugby School in the 1830s and 40s, became, in the more stable situation which followed, a relatively fixed structure which tended to preclude the possibility of further endogenous change. In addition, the game in that form was a balanced whole. Its structure permitted the arousal of pleasurable excitement and it served as a means for inculcating and expressing the values of masters and boys. Further changes could easily have upset that balance. Indeed, as we have seen, that is precisely what happened in 1871 when, acting under the impetus of external pressure, the RFU abolished 'hacking', 'hacking over' and 'tripping'.

We appear to be dealing here with an example of the dilemma described by Veblen as 'the penalty of taking the lead'.[67] Thus, just as Britain was the first country to industrialize and, for a time, socioeconomically more advanced than other nations, so Rugby in the 1840s was more advanced than rival forms. Subsequently, however, Britain's ability to compete industrially was hampered by an outdated technology and by structures and values adapted to the 'first industrial revolution' if not, in some respects, to a pre-industrial stage. Similarly, Rugbeians became committed to a form of football which, although initially more advanced, was later overtaken by the forms of other groups. In the 1840s, these forms were less advanced than Rugby but their 'developmental potential' and, hence, capacity for adaptation to the more advanced stage of 'civilization' reached in late nineteenth-century Britain, was correspondingly greater.

As one can see, a 'civilizing process' is complex. It does not occur in a simple linear or 'progressive' manner with all groups in a society growing at the same rate and to the same extent more 'civilized' over time. In Europe in the period studied by Elias, the dominant strata at each stage usually stood at the most advanced level. They were the standard-setting groups, i.e. 'civilizing' standards tended to percolate from the top to the bottom of the social scale. However, the process was complicated by the occurrence of conflict. The longer chains of interdependence which developed in connection with 'state-formation' and especially with the emergence of an urban-industrial division of labour, increased the power of lower groups and led to intensified pressure 'from below'. In order to maintain their distinctiveness and, hence, their privilege and power, the higher strata were forced, as a means of distinguishing between 'insiders' and 'outsiders', to elaborate still further their already differentiated standards, and these new, more elaborate and differentiated standards, necessitated the exercise of greater self-control.

The development of a more 'civilized' form of football at Rugby and—if our earlier hypothesis is correct—the counter-imposition of an absolute taboo on the use of hands at Eton, are examples of the way in which the 'civilization' of football took place under the impetus of the competitive pressure generated by growing interdependence and the changing balance of power between classes. Thus, the boys at Eton were led to impose a taboo on the use of hands due to the competitive pressure exerted by Rugby, the public school most representative of the ascendant middle classes. Since it prohibited the use of the human being's chief bodily implement, such a taboo, especially in the context of an emotionally arousing game, required the exercise of a high order of self-restraint.

As we have seen, most Rugby players in that period were middle- and upper-middle-class. By contrast, most leading soccer players came from the older public schools, i.e. schools which retained strong establishment links. Although they were first to develop a more 'civilized' version, Rugby players had a strong, deeply emotional attachment to standards of masculinity reminiscent in their stress on courage and strength of an earlier stage. Thus, members of the rising stratum clung to earlier standards, regarding them as compatible with their new status, even though the established groups had moved to a higher level of restraint. Perhaps their insecurity as members of an ascendant class helps to explain the tenacity with which Rugby players clung to standards of masculinity more appropriate to an earlier stage? But whether that was so or not, they were, as we have seen, forced by external pressure to modify their game and bring it into line with the more 'civilized' standards which became the norm as industrialization, *embourgeoisement* and state-formation continued.

6 The democratization of Rugby football

1. During the 1870s, spurred on partly by competition between the new associations, soccer and Rugby spread throughout the country, ceasing to be monopolized by the upper and middle classes. In short, they began to undergo 'democratization'. We have used this term rather than 'popularization' because, as we shall show, diffusion led to a shift in the balance of power within, and hence, to a change in the structure and dynamics of, both games.

Hitherto, conflict between the landed classes and the bourgeoisie had provided the main impetus to their development. Now, however, members of less prestigious bourgeois groups, e.g. middle-class men who had not been to public school, began to play. So did members of the working class. The consequences of this change of social composition were decisive. It meant, for example, that a purer type of bourgeois values, unsullied by direct contact in the public schools or elsewhere with aristocrat and gentry values, was added to those of the public school élite. Working-class values were added, too. Not surprisingly, such a situation was conducive to new sources of tension and to a challenge to the dominance of the upper- and upper-middle-class groups who had been the central agents in the development of football for the previous forty or fifty years. Subsequently, these tensions escalated into a full-blown crisis over amateurism and professionalism, leading in Rugby to the split between 'Union' and 'League'. We shall analyse that process later. For the present, our central task is to lay the foundations through an examination of the processes of diffusion and democratization which led the split to occur. It will help if we begin by considering a conceptual issue which, in our view, has not been properly understood in the past.

2. The majority of football's historians base their analyses on a gross concept of class, seeing the diffusion of Rugby and soccer as a direct transfer from the middle to the working class. A crude 'dichotomic' model of that kind, however, is inadequate. It involves, for example, no reference to the ruling and upper classes. It is also static and takes no account of the changes which took place in class relations in the nineteenth century. Moreover, it ignores the fact that the middle class was internally differentiated,

for example in terms of property ownership into the 'grand' and 'petit' bourgeoisie; occupationally, into business, professional and clerical sections; and in prestige terms, into 'upper middle', 'middle middle' and 'lower middle strata'. It also ignores what has served in Britain as a major status mark since the eighteenth century, namely, public school attendance. And finally, it ignores the existence of differentiation in the nineteenth-century working class, e.g. that between the 'rough' and 'respectable' sections.

Those who subscribe to a dichotomic model are unable properly to explain the manner in which the diffusion of football took place for, as we shall show, the new forms did not spread simply from the middle to the working class, but from the upper to the middle classes, and from one level of the middle class to another. The differences between our approach and that based on a static, crude dichotomic model will emerge if we start by discussing the diffusion of Rugby beyond the ranks of the public school élite. As we shall show, the sort of conceptual distinction just introduced, especially that based on public school attendance, is crucial in order to gain an understanding of what actually occurred.

In the early 1870s, Rugby was played by a relatively homogeneous upper-middle-class clientele and confined mainly to schools and clubs in the South. As we showed in the last chapter, the data in the 1873 *Football Annual* give an indication of the social characteristics of football players at that time. Thus, thirty-seven of the listed clubs were school clubs, mostly connected with public and grammar schools. Of these, twenty-seven adhered to Rugby, nineteen playing in the metropolitan area and eight in the provinces. Thus, schoolboy Rugby in that period was centred on London and was a domain of upper-middle-class boys. Adult sides came from similar backgrounds. Thus, six of the known Rugby clubs in 1873 were connected with hospitals. It is safe to assume that, in the main, the players were medical students and doctors. The hospitals were: Guy's, London, St Bartholomew's, St George's, St Thomas' and University College. Two other clubs, Civil Service and Law, evidently drew their membership from the 'professional classes', too.

A further indication of the social status of Rugby players in the 1870s is given by what we know about the social composition of early international sides. Thus nineteen of the 1872–3 England 'XX' had been to public school. Five were Old Rugbeians, five Old Marlburians, three Old Cliftonians, three Old Wellingtonians, two Old Tonbridgians and two Old Haileyburians. Similarly, fifty-two of the ninety-nine 'chief' English players listed in the 1873 *Football Annual* were public school old boys. The schools in question and the number of players they contributed were: Rugby, twenty-two; Marlborough, thirteen; Wellington, five; Clifton, four; Cheltenham, three; Tonbridge, three; Eton, one; and Haileybury, one.

However, this picture had begun to change by 1900. That is, Rugby had ceased to be a socially exclusive, upper-middle-class game and was even played, although on a national level not extensively, by members of the working class. Some idea of the extent to which it had begun to percolate down the class hierarchy by the 1890s is given in Table 6.1 which reports the types of schools attended by members of England sides in each of the last three decades of the nineteenth century. Thus, we see that, public school old boys formed sixty-seven per cent of the membership of England sides in the first decade after the formation of the RFU but, in the two remaining decades of the nineteenth century, the proportion had fallen, respectively, to thirty-seven and thirty-eight per cent.

Further light on the downwards diffusion of Rugby is shed by Table 6.2 which reports the approximate class composition of teams selected to represent England in the same three decades. It was constructed from the limited data currently available on the occupations of these players and uses the Registrar General's classification of occupations for 1966. It thus rests on the rather crude assumption that relativities of occupational status at the end of the nineteenth century were the same as those held by the Registrar General to have prevailed in the mid-1960s. For that reason, it cannot provide anything more than a gross approximation to the class composition of late-nineteenth-century England sides.

Thus, whilst all English internationals in the first two decades after the foundation of the RFU were employed in non-manual occupations, nine, or seven per cent, of those who played for their country in the subsequent decade were manual workers. More specifically, they comprised an

Table 6.1 Types of school attended by England players, 1871–1901

Type of school	1871–81	1882–92	1892–1901
Public	91 (67%)	32 (37%)	53 (38%)
Grammar and other	22 (16%)	24 (27%)	20 (14%)
Not known	23 (17%)	34 (38%)	67 (48%)
TOTALS	136	90	140

These figures were worked up from the data given in Part II of the biographical section in Titley and McWhirter, *op. cit.*, np.

Table 6.2 Class composition of England sides, 1871–1901

Social class	1871–81	1881–92	1892–1901
I	54 (40%)	26 (29%)	33 (24%)
II	38 (28%)	30 (33%)	33 (24%)
III (non-manual)	–	–	2 (1%)
III (manual)	–	–	8 (6%)
IV	–	–	1 (1%)
V	–	–	–
Not known	44 (32%)	34 (37%)	62 (45%)
TOTALS	136	90	139

ironmoulder, a tailor, a metal worker, three masons, a deputy foreman in a coal mine, a coal miner, and a public works contractor. However, there is reason to believe that non-sports criteria played a part in the selection of England Rugby sides in the late nineteenth century and that, accordingly, the figures in these tables underrepresent the number of working-class men who came in that period to take part. They also mask the regional disparities which existed in that respect for it was in the North that the game percolated furthest down the social ladder. In particular, they do not accurately reflect the number of Northern working-class players in the decade 1892–1901, for after the split between Union and League in 1895, Rugby League players, many of whom were working-class and all of whom, whether justly or not, were defined by the RFU as 'professionals', were no longer eligible for selection for Rugby Union international sides. The manner in which working men in the North became involved in Rugby will emerge from a closer examination of the game's spread to that region, particularly to Lancashire and Yorkshire.

3. Rugby was played in Lancashire and Yorkshire to a limited extent even prior to the formation of the RFU. As was generally the case, it was monopolized at first by the upper middle class. For example, Manchester, the oldest Lancashire club, was formed in 1860 by Old Rugbeians who aroused local interest by playing an 'experimental' match with some Old Rugbeians from Liverpool.[1] Liverpool RFC was formed shortly afterwards by Old Rugbeians who worked in that city. Old boys of other public schools were obviously soon welcomed, however, for during the 1880s and 90s, Liverpool could count among its members, E. Kewley of Marlborough and H. H. Springman of Craigmont School, Edinburgh. Grammar school old boys were also allowed to join, for A. T. Kemble, a solicitor and later president of the club, had been educated at Appleby Grammar School.[2]

More is known about the club founded at Rochdale in November 1867 and given its present name, 'Rochdale Hornets', in April 1871. Founder members of the original club included Lt. Col. C. M. Royds, JP, DL, and H. Butterworth, a watchmaker. Among the early members of 'the Hornets' were, S. V. Milne, Lord of the Manor at Thornham, and R. Collinge, the son of a clergyman and senior partner in the firm of Richard Yates & Co., flannel manufacturers. Collinge was, in addition, managing director of two firms, Charles Clegg & Co., and Ashworth and Butterworth, both of Rochdale. He was also a director of the Eclipse Spinning Co. Other early members of the Hornets were: W. Brierley, a clerk; A. Bamford, a tobacconist and athletics outfitter; A. Irving, a travelling draper; W. Butterworth, a smallware dealer; H. Healey, a yarn agent; R. R. Osborne, a solicitor; R. Butterworth, a publican; J. W. Baron, a cotton merchant; A. Taylor, a shopkeeper; J. Davies, a tailor; W. Peters, a builder; and G. Fountain, a cotton merchant.[3]

Other Rugby clubs formed in Lancashire in this period included Broughton, Manchester Rangers, Free Wanderers and Swinton.[4] We have singled these out for special mention because, in 1881, they achieved a degree of prominence by leading a movement which successfully broke the stranglehold which, until then, Manchester RFC had exercised over the organization of Lancashire Rugby. Broughton was formed by ex-pupils of Broughton College and later absorbed the Wellington and Withington clubs. It included among its early members two solicitors, J. H. Payne and A. R. Rogerson. The former received his education at Manchester Grammar School and St John's College, Cambridge; the latter was the son of J. R. Rogerson of the Salford firm, Langworthy Bros & Co., cotton spinners and manufacturers.

Manchester Rangers RFC was formed in 1870 by members of St Michael's Church, Hulme. It was at first called 'Moss Side Rangers', obtaining the name 'Manchester Rangers' in 1873. Among its earliest members were A. H. Pownall, an accountant and partner in the firm of Butcher, Litton and Pownall, and E. T. Markendale, a hide and skin dealer and butcher. Free Wanderers was also a Manchester side. It was formed largely by old boys of the Charlton and Victoria Park High Schools but included among its members E. H. Inckle, an Old Rugbeian, and J. M. Yates, an Old Westminster. Yates went to Trinity College, Cambridge, and was later called to the Bar. Other members were E. J. Deardon, a surgeon educated at King William's College, Isle of Man, and Owen's College, Manchester, and J. W. Hulse, a draper. Swinton RFC included among its early members, F. C. Hignett, a grey cloth agent, J. Mills, chairman of the Worsley Brewery at Pendlebury, and J. Marsh who obtained an Edinburgh degree.

The diffusion of Rugby to Yorkshire followed a similar pattern, for the game there was, again, at first monopolized by the upper middle class. However, fewer public school old boys seem to have been involved, with the result that Yorkshire clubs were, from the outset, less socially exclusive than their counterparts in Lancashire and other parts of the country. One of the first to be formed was Leeds Athletic. It began with an advertisement placed by 'K.99' in *The Leeds Mercury* on 7 March 1864. Responding, a Mr J. G. Hudson found that 'K.99' was Henry Irwin Jenkinson, a clerk at the Northeastern Railway Goods Depot. Hudson and Jenkinson, together with R. O. Berry—who later became a carting agent in Leeds—and W. Dickenson—later the manager of a savings bank in Sheffield—were among the founder members.[5] Halifax RFC was also formed as the result of an advertisement. It was placed in *The Halifax Guardian* on 1 November 1873, by S. Duckitt, a member of the firm, William Duckitt & Co., brass-founders and finishers. Other early members included: E. Buckley, another brassfounder; M. Brown, a wool and waste dealer; J. Pearson, a boot and shoe manufacturer; G. T. Thomson, a stuff merchant and manufacturer of sheeting; and J. Dodd, a victualler.[6]

The first Hull club was formed in the autumn of 1865. W. H. H. Hutchinson, C. B. Lambert, F. A. Scott, E. Waltham and H. J. Wade were among the founding members.[7] Hutchinson was head of the Scarborough firm,

W. H. H. Hutchinson & Son, steamship owners and shipping commission and forwarding agents; Lambert belonged to the firm of J. B. Lambert & Sons, wine and spirit merchants; while Scott was a solicitor and partner in the firm of F. A. Scott and Cooper.[8] Soon after its foundation, the club was joined by three public school old boys, E. A. Hollingbery and F. O. Moss of Rugby, and E. W. Harrison of Cheltenham.[9] However, it seems that Hull was an 'open' club from fairly early on for, in 1871, three artisans, William, Richard and Edward Hodgson, were accepted as members.[10] William and Richard worked as plumbers, glaziers and gas fitters, while Edward was described as 'a foreman'.[11]

4. It is clear, then, that the initial impetus to the playing of Rugby in the North came from men who considered themselves 'gentlemen'. However, they were, in many cases, 'gentlemen' of lower social status than those responsible for the formation of clubs in the South. This can be seen from the higher proportion of club founders and early players who worked in industry and trade, and the lower proportion employed in the professions or who had attended public schools.

Exactly how Northern working men came to play Rugby, often like the Hodgsons of Hull, in the same teams as 'gentlemen', is not at present clear. Nicholson assumes that the process took the form of a gradual infiltration with working men being pressed into service to make up the numbers in predominantly middle-class teams.[12] Brook argues similarly, writing that, in the North prior to the formation of the Northern Union, 'Rugby had been played by all classes of men; all had been equal on the field whether the sons of mill-owners or factory hands'.[13] In short, these authors presume the existence in the North of a social structure characterized by low barriers to class interaction, a relatively low degree of status-exclusiveness in patterns of inter-class association similar to that which had prevailed in the eighteenth century. Although neither author produces evidence to support this supposition, there is reason to believe it to be partly valid. It is, however, an oversimplification for it fails to treat as problematic the structural and motivational preconditions necessary for the growth of working-class support for Rugby. This process is best considered in relation to the parallel process which occurred in soccer.

It was in the 1870s in the industrializing North and Midlands that working men first began to play Rugby and soccer in significant numbers. Even more were attracted as spectators. Soccer and Rugby teams came to serve as foci of community identification and to be seen as symbolic of working-class values. At the same time, both games provided an injection of excitement into the work-dominated existence of people compelled to live in dingy industrial towns. Yet, although the general pattern is clear, it is difficult to explain why Rugby was adopted in some areas and soccer in others. It is, however, possible to hazard one or two guesses. The first thing to note is that the prior establishment of the FA and the 'evangelizing' policy of its officials—e.g. in promoting the game via media such as the FA Cup—meant that soccer had a head start over its rival. That is, it started to diffuse beyond the public school élite both earlier and more rapidly than Rugby. The latter was also more complex and this hindered its adoption by groups who had not learned it at school. Moreover, as we saw in the last chapter, following the abolition of 'hacking', Rugby tended to become closed and relatively static. This decreased even further its chances of competing effectively with the faster and more open Association game for the playing and spectator support of groups who had not been brought up to play it at school.

There is, however, one respect in which Rugby may have enjoyed an advantage. That is, its greater roughness may have made it more appealing to groups among whom traditional concepts of masculinity continued to prevail. If that is correct, it helps to explain why Rugby became firmly rooted in mining towns and other areas where the occupational base encouraged the retention of standards of masculinity in which physical toughness, strength and courage were emphasized. It would be wrong to lay too great store by this hypothesis, however, if only because soccer at that stage, while it involved less stress on physical contact than Rugby, was considerably rougher than it is today. At the same time, Rugby's greater roughness may have served to some extent as a disadvantage. It seems, for example, to have been one of the reasons why 'Muscular Christian' clergymen who saw soccer as a potentially useful weapon for helping the urban poor, did not, to anything like the same extent, view Rugby in that light. We shall explore this issue further in a moment. It is necessary first to examine some of the underlying conditions which facilitated the growth of working-class participation in, and support for, the new forms of football.

At least two preconditions were necessary for the occurrence of this process: the availability of spare time and a financial surplus which could be used to purchase equipment, rent grounds and, as soon became necessary for spectators, to pay for admission to matches. The necessary spare time was provided by the shortening of working hours which followed as a consequence of the Factory Act of 1847[14] and the gradual institutionalization of the Saturday halfday.[15] It is important to recognize, however, that this reduction of working time was not evenly distributed for, as Walvin has pointed out, '. . . on the whole, it was granted only to industrial workers and did not apply to the armies of clerks, shopkeepers and agricultural workers whose working hours continued to be almost as oppressive as ever'. The result was that 'those sports, notably football, which came to dominate the Saturday afternoons of working men, tended to be watched by workers in the heavier industries—textiles, metals, engineering, mining, shipping and port industries'.[16]

The financial surplus which formed the second precondition for the expansion of working-class support became available in the 1850s because that decade marked an upturn in the business cycle, the beginning of a period of mounting prosperity in which working men, especially those in skilled occupations or expanding industries with a labour shortage, could share. In addition, the practice developed in the North and Midlands for middle-class players and officials to subsidize working-class players, either from their own pockets or from money taken 'at the gate'. In that way, the expansion of working-class participation was to some extent contingent upon middle-class wealth, and to some extent upon a redistribution of resources from other members of their own class, i.e. those who were able and willing to exchange money for the thrill of watching what they hoped would be a skilful, exciting and, in the sense that it was played by teams representative of communities with which they could identify, socially meaningful football match. It goes without saying that both preconditions rested on a normatively buttressed power structure in marital and family relations which permitted husbands to keep for themselves the bulk of any financial surplus and which did not demand that time free from occupational constraints should be spent on household tasks or in the company of families.

5. As far as we can tell, there was, initially, little middle- and upper-class opposition to the participation of working men in soccer and Rugby. On the contrary, they often encouraged them to play. In fact, the limited evidence available at present strongly suggests that the growth of working-class participation was not an autonomously working-class affair. Rather, the impetus seems to have come, in a structural sense, 'from above'; i.e. although participation evidently satisfied strong needs in those sections of the working class who were presented with the opportunity and capable of responding, they were, in most cases, taught to play by upper- and middle-class men. It was, moreover, in the first instance, almost always the latter who shouldered the organizational 'burden'. However, the pattern by which soccer and Rugby were transmitted to the working class differed in some respects in different parts of the country and between the two games. We shall look briefly at the case of Association football first.

The main sources of institutional contact between the upper and middle and the working classes in late-nineteenth-century England were the church, industry and, after 1870, the schools established under the Education Act of that year. It is not, therefore, surprising that these institutions were the principal setting of soccer's downwards diffusion. Much of the initial impetus came from 'Muscular Christians' and others who professed similar beliefs. The fresh air and exercise provided by participation in outdoor sports formed, they felt, a means of promoting health and combatting physical degeneracy among the urban poor. However, the 'games ideology' of these groups was not based solely on a belief in the physical functions of games for, just as in the context of the public schools, they were rationalized as a vehicle of 'moral' education; i.e. it was believed that games could help to spark off a 'moral revolution' among the poor.

Attempts to control the working class through paternalistic policies of this kind were common in the third quarter of the nineteenth century. They contrast markedly with the frequent use of openly repressive measures characteristic of earlier in the century and correspond to the fact that the years between 1850 and 1880 were lacking in the more overt forms of class conflict[17] and accompanied accordingly by a relatively harmonistic perception of class relations. That meant that the dominant classes could view their subordinates, not as a threat to be smashed but as 'poor unfortunates' who needed help. It also meant they were able fearlessly to enter working-class communities to perform the social-work functions by which they set such store.

A measure of Muscular Christian success is provided by the fact that, in Liverpool in 1878, when 'local teams began to form, they sprang in the first instance almost exclusively from churches . . . As late as 1885, 25 of the 112 football clubs in Liverpool had religious connections . . . [and] in Birmingham in 1880, 83 of the 344 clubs (some 24 per cent) were connected to churches'.[18] Among today's professional clubs, Aston Villa, Birmingham City, Bolton Wanderers, Burnley, Fulham, Liverpool, Queens Park Rangers, Southampton, Swindon and Wolverhampton Wanderers can trace their origins to church teams of that period or to teams founded by clergymen in connection with Sunday schools and schools. Industrial connections can be traced in the cases of Coventry City, Manchester United, Millwall, Stoke City and West Ham.[19] The latter can serve as an example. It originated with a team founded in 1895 at the Thames Ironworks and, as Korr has recently shown, the driving force behind it was Arnold Hills, an Old Harrovian and Oxford graduate who inherited the firm from his father.[20]

6. We suggested earlier that the manner in which Rugby was transmitted to the working class was different in some respects from the pattern of transmission of the sister game. For one thing, the 'missionary' zeal of Muscular Christians does not seem to have played a strong part. Perhaps, as we suggested earlier, its greater roughness represented too great a contradiction of the morality they wished to transmit? However, it is certainly the case that Rugby clubs all over the country tended to be more status-exclusive than their counterparts in soccer, refusing even to contemplate matches against working-class teams. Perhaps because they had attended lower-status schools, they were socially less secure than Association players, many of whom had been to schools such as Eton and Harrow? We shall return to that issue later. For the present, it is enough to note that the RFU was opposed from the outset to the introduction of cups as means of popularizing the game. In Lancashire and Yorkshire, however, matters were somewhat different. In those two counties, as we have seen, the first Rugby clubs tended to be as

socially exclusive as their counterparts elsewhere but, from an early stage, some began to allow working men to become playing members. Moreover, as early as 1876, taking their cue from the FA, the leading Yorkshire clubs introduced a county challenge cup. Cup competitions were introduced on an experimental basis in other counties, too, but in Yorkshire, as we shall show, this innovation proved decisive.

Marples writes of the existence of 'working class clubs' in the North in that period.[21] However, when one probes the matter, one finds that, in all cases, Northern Rugby clubs were either, like Manchester and Liverpool, socially exclusive or, like Hull, 'open' in the sense of recruiting their membership from different levels in the class hierarchy. It is reasonable to hypothesize that Rugby was transmitted to the Northern working class principally through the medium of the 'mixed' or 'open' clubs. This points to the existence in that region of a social configuration in some respects different from that which existed in the South. We alluded earlier to one aspect of this different configuration, namely an occupational structure which contained, on the one hand, a greater proportion of businessmen and manufacturers, and on the other of working men employed in industry, mining and the like. Such an occupational structure had arisen because industrialization had started in the North and because, with the obvious exception of the West Midlands, industry in that period was still largely confined to that region. At that stage, moreover, given the level of industrialization reached, the majority of firms were, in comparison with their modern counterparts, relatively small. Their owners were often 'self-made' men who kept in direct touch with the manufacturing process, supervising production on a day-to-day basis from a small office attached to the workshop. An industrial arrangement of that type, unlike the large, impersonal structure which prevails in much of industry today, was conducive to close contact and, therefore, a relatively high degree of identification between employers and employees. It was also conducive to a low degree of status-exclusiveness and hence formed, in part, the social foundation for the formation of the 'open' Rugby clubs of the North.

This structural base was probably reinforced by the mode of social ascent which prevailed in Britain prior to the modern era when the industrial was replaced by a mainly educational route. A man made money and then sought to add prestige to his new financial status by sending his sons to public school and by seeking access to the social circles of those with 'old' wealth, particularly the aristocracy and gentry. However, there was an intervening stage while he was still engaged in amassing a fortune and before he was ready to attempt to gain acceptance by the established élite. During this stage, he continued to retain his local identifications and his kinship and other connections with his class of origin, making no attempt to hide them. It may be that this helps to explain why some Rugby clubs in the North were open, whilst others were socially exclusive. The former, it is reasonable to suppose, were probably run by men whose families were in the intervening stage, the latter by men whose families had passed beyond it. It is certainly the case that, while they were still from the middle and upper middle classes, the leading members of the open clubs had, for the most part, received a local education. It is also the case that the membership of the exclusive clubs included a greater proportion of players and officials who had been to public school. Of course, few had attended the most prestigious schools such as Eton and Harrow. That is, they had not met with complete success in their mobility striving and remained, to that extent, socially marginal. That may help to explain why, in common with their counterparts in the South but unlike their socially less prestigious middle-class fellows in the North, they were status-exclusive as far as membership of their Rugby clubs was concerned.

7. The combination of socially exclusive and open Rugby clubs which came into existence in Lancashire and Yorkshire in the last quarter of the nineteenth century was a social configuration full of potential axes of tension. It was the social differences between them, in particular their different reference groups, i.e. in the one case the national ruling class and, in the other, the local community, which lay at its root. Its first effect was to produce a struggle for control over Rugby at county level.

Because they were the first to be founded, the exclusive clubs were the first to gain control. Their ascendancy was established as early as 1870 when the first match between Lancashire and Yorkshire, the first ever inter-county Rugby match, took place. Manchester RFC, in close collaboration with the Liverpool club, took charge of matters on the Lancashire side, pursuing policies fully in alignment with those of the RFU. However, these were regarded by the open clubs as irrelevant to the conditions under which Lancashire Rugby was played and so they set about gaining a share in control for themselves. They met with success in 1881, when, for the first time, a duly constituted and representative body for the government of Lancashire Rugby—'The Lancashire County Football Club'—was set up.[22]

In Yorkshire, county Rugby was placed on a more representative footing from the outset, control being assumed by a cabal drawn from the Leeds, Bradford, Hull and Huddersfield clubs. They constituted themselves as the 'Yorkshire County Football Club', meeting regularly from 1874 onwards and gradually widening the membership in response to pressure from newer and more open clubs. It was not until 1888 when the 'Yorkshire RFU' was founded that their hold over Yorkshire Rugby was broken. Nevertheless, they began from early on to introduce innovations which changed the face of Rugby in that county.[23]

Decisive in this respect was the introduction in 1876 of the 'Yorkshire Challenge Cup'. The idea for such a competition was proposed by A. E. Hudson of Leeds RFC, a mill owner, and seconded by H. W. T. Garnett, a borough magistrate, and F. Schutt, a wool merchant, both of the Bradford club. The cup was quickly a success, leading to the formation of many new clubs and becoming, within the space of ten years, the pivot around which Yorkshire Rugby revolved. In particular, since cup matches attracted large crowds, it played a crucial part in the emergence of Rugby as a spectator sport, hence providing the economic foundation for the transformation of the 'open' into 'gate-taking' clubs.

The success of the challenge cup can be traced to features specific to the Yorkshire social structure, in particular to the strong spirit of rivalry among its mill towns and mining villages. Such rivalry sprang primarily from the strong 'in-group' ties, the sense of 'community' within them. They were close-knit, often economically dependent on a single industry and, therefore, relatively homogeneous occupationally. Travel between them was costly and, hence, relationships tended to be formed within the town or village itself. It was, if we can be permitted to adapt Riesman's term, an 'inner-directed' existence.[24] Hostility and rivalry towards 'outsiders' followed as a natural corollary.

The Challenge Cup added a new dimension to this existence. The cup-ties attracted large, partisan crowds which identified strongly with their representatives on the field, seeing matches not just as exciting spectacles but as tests of virility between their community and another. The depth of identification of town with team meant that players were constrained to play, less for their own enjoyment and more for the glory which victory would bring to the community as a whole. With the attendant uncertainty about the final outcome, both of individual matches and the competition as a whole, Rugby cup-ties provided excitement and relief in the routinized, work-dominated lives of men (and women) in the towns and villages of Yorkshire. In addition, the matches themselves and, when the team was victorious, the ensuing communal celebrations, provided spectacle and colour in the drab environment of the urban-industrial North. As one can see, under the conditions then coming to prevail in Yorkshire, and to a lesser extent in Lancashire and some other Northern counties, Rugby began increasingly to express the values and social situation of the industrial classes, i.e. of the bourgeoisie and proletariat. It was this development which sowed the seeds for the controversy over amateurism and professionalism and, hence, for the split between Union and League. We shall examine the amateur-professional controversy in the next chapter.

7 Professionalization and the amateur response

1. In the last chapter, we showed how Rugby in Lancashire and Yorkshire began, as part of its democratization, to express the values of the industrial classes and how the 'open' clubs which drew their membership from the bourgeoisie and proletariat grew more powerful in a playing and organizational sense. In short, the game in those two counties underwent processes of 'bourgeoisification' and 'proletarianization'. This requires elaboration.

Bourgeois values were expressed in Northern Rugby in the formalization of competition through, for example, the introduction of cups and leagues. Above all, however, they were expressed in the growing 'monetization' of the game.[1] This involved charging for admission, the arrangement of matches which would attract large crowds, the payment of money to players and the use of material inducements to lure them from one club to another. Proletarian values were expressed in the use of Rugby as a source of material rewards, the perception of teams as representative of working-class communities, and in the stress which began to be laid on the game as a spectator sport. In short, in conjunction with its democratization, Rugby in Lancashire and Yorkshire began to emerge as what we would nowadays recognize as a 'professional' sport.

Such changes were not restricted solely to the level of values or confined in their effects to the North. Thus, by about 1880, a number of the socially heterogeneous, 'open' clubs had transformed themselves into 'gate-taking' clubs. The wealth they accumulated enabled them to emerge as the most powerful in Lancashire and Yorkshire. At the same time, the Yorkshire and Lancashire Unions, particularly the former, grew increasingly influential within the national RFU. Indeed, it seemed for a while in the 1880s and early 1890s that they might be able to establish dominance at a national level and, with it, the capacity to determine the overall character of the game. Growing Northern dominance, moreover, was not expressed simply in the organizational sphere but reflected also on the field of play where Northern clubs established superiority over their Southern counterparts and began, increasingly, to monopolize the membership of England sides.

These changes led the game in Yorkshire and Lancashire to diverge increasingly from the interests and values of the Rugby establishment. On the level of interests, it was their playing and organizational pre-eminence which were threatened and, on the level of values, the nature and objects of the game as they wished to see it played. They reacted with alarm concerning the possible spread of such developments to the South. Above all, they resented the fact that the momentum for change was being generated by what they regarded as alien and inferior groups. That is understandable given the fact that they had been principally responsible for the development of Rugby up until that time. This, they felt, gave them proprietorial rights. Their resentment was exacerbated by the fact that, increasingly, they were being beaten, quite literally 'at their own game', by members of these 'alien' and 'inferior' groups.

As one would expect, these developments in the North were resisted by the Rugby establishment. Battle was joined organizationally and ideologically. That is, members of the public school élite used their controlling position in the RFU and their influence over its regional affiliates in an attempt to stop the spread of professionalism in and from the North. At the same time, they developed a set of ideas by which they attempted to legitimize Rugby as a 'purely amateur' sport, and, as a corollary, to castigate professionalism as entirely 'beyond the pale'. To express it more technically, they began to fight for the establishment of 'amateurism' as the major organizational goal of the RFU. In other words, their emphasis became more focused, changing from a diffuse commitment to the promotion of and legislation for the game in general to a highly specific commitment to the promotion and legislation for it in a specific form.

It is this process of ideological development—the development of the 'amateur ethos'—which forms the principal subject of this chapter. The amateur ethos was not, of course, confined to Rugby. It was developed by the public school élite as a whole, not just its Rugby-playing sections, and sought to justify amateurism in sport in general. It emerged, moreover, 'dialectically', i.e. in opposition to the factual development of professional sport. Furthermore, even though it was couched in 'sport-specific' terms, at a deeper level it was based to a considerable extent on class hostility. This usually remained beneath the surface but occasionally, as we shall show, it was given clear expression. It follows from this discussion that our first task in this chapter must be to examine the factual developments which preceded the development of the amateur ethos and helped to produce it. In particular, we shall have to look at the growing dominance in a playing sense of clubs and players from Yorkshire and Lancashire, and at the incipient professionalization of Rugby in those two counties.

2. During the 1880s and early 1890s, the playing superiority of Northern clubs was expressed at every level. In a review of 'metropolitan' Rugby written in 1892, for example, an 'anonymous Londoner' admitted that: 'if we take the play of the Northern clubs as a standard, . . . we have to confess that

our average of play is an incredibly low one'. He then expressed the hope that London clubs would shake off their 'lethargy', adding chauvinistically that: 'What can be done in a Yorkshire village can surely be done here, . . . if nothing else will, at least the Tyke Yokel forging . . . ahead ought to touch our pride and galvanize our energies.'[2]

Northern dominance was expressed in the County Championship, too. That competition began in 1888–9, Yorkshire emerging triumphant in seven of the first eight seasons. Only in 1890–1, when Lancashire were the winners, did Yorkshire fail to win. It was not until 1897—after the clubs which formed the 'Northern Union' had seceded—that a Southern county, Kent, emerged victorious.[3]

The dominance of Northern Rugby also made its impact felt at international level. In 1871, the England XX for the first match with Scotland included six Northerners, all from the Manchester and Liverpool clubs. That is, they were Old Rugbeians or old boys of other Rugby-playing public schools. By contrast, the England XV which met the Maori touring side in 1888–9 contained ten Northerners, all from clubs which would have been unfamiliar to 1871 ears, viz, Broughton Rangers, Dewsbury, Heckmondwike, Bradford, Featherstone, Free Wanderers, Morley, Batley, Halifax and Hartlepool Rovers. In the following season, Yorkshire again provided five forwards and two backs for the England side against Scotland. We have been unable to obtain information on the educational and occupational status of these Northern members of early England sides. However, since none played for the socially exclusive Northern clubs, it is safe to assume that few, if any, had been educated at public schools and that some may even have been working-class.

The anonymous Londoner had no such doubts about the social composition of Yorkshire teams. They were, he contended, mainly composed of working men who had not learned the game at school, yet they were able easily to beat teams whose members had 'imbibed it with their Latin grammar'. He continued:

> One reads with amazement of villages in Yorkshire, whose names one cannot discover in Bradshaw, springing up like mushrooms as formidable fifteens, and tussling with the best for the Cup. They receive no recruits from without. How is it done? Why, by converting the indigenous talent into an enthusiastic machine, and by insisting on the fact that the machine is always in working order.[4]

Members of the public school élite in the late nineteenth century drew a sharp distinction between work and leisure. To train for sport and take it too seriously was, for them, tantamount to transforming it into work and, hence, to destroying its essence. According to the anonymous Londoner, their attitude amounted, in effect, to saying that: 'We can't be bothered with your training—we play for pleasure, and if we get beaten, we get beaten.' Few, he suggested, could accept that 'the day is at hand when if you play football at all, you must play it in earnest'.[5]

Playing for fun expressed the individualization and relative independence of the public school élite, the fact that they could use their leisure principally for themselves. They may have played as representatives of a school, university or profession but, for them, the representative character of the team was supposed not to take precedence over enjoyment. In the North, however, a different social configuration and different values were coming to prevail. There, the majority of players were not so individualized or independent. They played as members of a close-knit community with which they identified strongly. At the same time, the community identified strongly with the team, with the consequence that communal pressure was put on players to train and play seriously in order that victory might be ensured. In addition, the greater industrialization which had occurred in the North and the increasing dominance there of bourgeois groups unsullied by direct contact with the values of the public schools, meant that there was less opposition to charging for admission to matches and to providing players with material rewards in order to increase their commitment to the goal of securing victory on the community's behalf.

In such a situation, large crowds were attracted and the gate-money taken enabled top clubs to accumulate funds from which players could be paid. For example, a crowd of 22,000 watched Bradford play Halifax in the Yorkshire Cup in March 1893, and £410 was taken at the gate.[6] On 2 January 1895, a crowd of 10,000 was reported at the match between Bradford and Leeds and one of 4,000 at that between St Helens Recreation and St Helens.[7] On 23 January 1895, a crowd of 8–10,000 was reported at the Yorkshire Senior Competition match between Liversedge and Manningham.[8] By contrast, only 'upwards of a thousand' attended the match between Blackheath and London Scottish reported in *The Times* on 6 November 1886, while on 11 January 1895, no more than 1,500 are reported as having turned out to watch Kent play Midland Counties.[9] These data are admittedly sketchy. Moreover, it seems that the Blackheath–London Scottish gate was adversely affected by a rainstorm. Nevertheless, we are convinced that the differences between these Northern and Southern crowds are not an artefact of regional climatic differences or arbitrary selection on our part, but, on the contrary, symptomatic of the greater crowd-drawing power of Northern Rugby at that time.

It was developments of this kind—the 'monetization' of Northern Rugby, the increasing importance in the game there of spectators, and the growing pre-eminence of Northern clubs—which led the public school élite to counterattack. 'Professionalism', i.e. utilization of the game for material advancement, formed the main issue on which they made their stand. It is to the factual development of professional Rugby, therefore, that our attention must now be turned.

3. Money payments were introduced into Rugby in two principal forms: (i) 'broken-time' payments, or the reimbursement of working men for wages lost through playing during working hours; and (ii) professionalism *per se* with the payment of players in the hope of ensuring that they would always give their best and remain loyal to a club. Material inducements were also used in order to lure players from one club and one part of the country to another, and there is evidence that entrepreneurs tried to make a profit from the game. It is important, however, to stress that few players were able to use Rugby as their sole source of livelihood. Indeed, even after the break with the RFU, 'Rugby League' never developed the capacity to maintain a large body of full-time players such as are employed in soccer and cricket. Nor did the breakaway game come to serve on a large scale as a medium of commercial speculation. Moreover, despite what we have called the growing 'bourgeoisification', 'monetization' and 'professionalization' of Rugby in the North, the game there remained, even after the split, more or less firmly under amateur control. As we shall show, that is symptomatic of the general development of professional sport in this country.

It is difficult to gauge the extent of the two different forms of payment in the period immediately prior to the split. The reasons are inherent in the situation itself. Thus in 1886, faced with what it regarded as the mounting threat from the North, the RFU enacted legislation forbidding anyone to profit materially from the game. In order to remain members of their county unions and, hence, of the RFU, clubs in the North were forced to cover up the fact that payments were being made. A 'conspiracy of silence' was the result which means that most of our evidence about professionalism at that stage comes, perforce, from Southern sources. However, since Southern pronouncements on this issue were made in a conflict situation, they tended to exaggerate the extent of professionalization. Exaggerated claims helped members of the public school élite to rationalize the fact of increasing defeat. They cannot be held, however, to constitute an accurate picture of the extent of professionalization in the North.

The ideological character of the Southern sources is not our only cause of difficulty. After a while, the Yorkshire and Lancashire Unions were forced, largely by pressure from the 'open' or 'gate-taking' clubs, to try to get the RFU to legitimize 'broken-time' payments. It was this which led the split to occur. Its main significance for present purposes lies in the fact that, as part of their attempt to secure the legitimacy of such payments, the Northern Unions had to break the conspiracy of silence and admit that payments were being made. However, it is impossible to estimate how much of what they admitted as broken-time payment was, in fact, disguised professionalism. It is clear, nevertheless, that professionalism did exist on a widespread scale. In any case, broken-time payment and professionalism are both indicative of an attitude towards the role of money in sport different from that of the public school élite. They were symptomatic of the growing monetization of Rugby in a part of the country where industrialization was proceeding apace and where the power of bourgeois groups as yet 'uncontaminated' by direct contact with the public school élite was rapidly advancing.

A report by the Rev. Marshall of a Rugby tour of Australasia undertaken in 1888 shows how the RFU tried to combat professionalism and illustrates the sort of conflicts generated in Yorkshire in that connection. It was organized by Shaw and Shrewsbury, the professional cricketers,[10] but the RFU were unwilling to grant their patronage to a team 'organized for the benefit of individual promoters'. The tour's most memorable feature, according to Marshall, was the fact that J. P. Clowes of Halifax RFC, selected as a member of the touring party, was declared a 'professional' just beforehand and hence unable to go. The manner in which this transpired was as follows. Halifax were about to play Dewsbury in the Yorkshire Cup and three members of the latter side, a player called Lockwood and two Welshmen, Stuart and Stadden, were approached by a Mr Turner of Nottingham, the agent of Shaw and Shrewsbury, and offered £15 to purchase clothing for the trip. Lockwood and Stuart signed agreements with Turner but Stadden placed his in the hands of his club officials and Lockwood afterwards withdrew. Dewsbury—they had been victims of similar sharp practice at the hands of Halifax in 1882—then set a trap. They left Stuart out of their side and, on losing the match, appealed to the Yorkshire RFU for a replay on the grounds that Clowes was a professional. The Yorkshire Committee found for Dewsbury and informed the RFU who adopted the following resolution:

'The Rugby Football Union has decided, on the evidence before them, that J. P. Clowes is a professional within the meaning of their laws. On the same evidence they have formed a very strong opinion that others composing the Australian team had also infringed these laws, and they will require from them such explanation as they may think fit on their return to England.' On the return of the team each player was required to make an affidavit that he had received no pecuniary benefit from the tour, and there the matter ended.[11]

Twenty-one players and an umpire went on the 1888 tour. The umpire and two players had attended university and the captain, A. E. Stoddart, was a member of the London Stock Exchange and an architect.[12] That is, these four were at least upper-middle-class in social status. The remaining eighteen all played for Northern clubs, some in all probability being working-class and many probably also professionals. The RFU was unable to prove this but there is no doubt that its suspicions were, for the most part, well-founded. For example, the organizers, Shaw and Shrewsbury, were professional cricketers. For them and their agent, Turner, the tour was principally a money-making venture. As far as the Northern players were concerned, the honour of being chosen and the opportunity to travel and play in Australasia may have provided sufficient reward. However, it is unlikely that ordinary working men—or, for that matter, ordinary members of the middle class—would have been able and willing to forgo work and wages for eight months without being paid handsomely over and above the expenses and the £15 clothing allowance which, although they denied it, they undoubtedly received. Of course, the supposition that they were paid for taking part in the tour does not prove that they were also paid for playing for their clubs. We can only be relatively certain on that score about Stuart and Stadden, the Welshmen mentioned by Marshall. That is because it is reasonable to assume that material inducements had been used to lure them from their native Wales and that, in addition, they received regular payment for playing for the Dewsbury club.

Although, ideally, a fuller documentation would be desirable, this item showing how the Rugby establishment used its judicial power in the RFU and county unions must, for present purposes be enough. However, it did not simply respond judicially to professionalization but through the written word as well. From about 1880, numerous articles appeared in books and magazines defending amateur principles and attacking professionalism and the syndrome of related abuses held to be developing in the North. What was written is our main source of evidence about this social process. It is revealing, in particular, of the manner in which the sports ethos of the public school élite developed in response to the challenge to their erstwhile dominance created by the widening social base of the game.

4. Prior to the 1880s, the amateur ethos existed in a relatively inchoate form. It was, that is, an amorphous, loosely articulated set of values regarding the functions of sport and the standards believed necessary for their realization. However, with the threat posed by incipient professionalization in the North, the amateur ethos began to crystallize as a highly specific, elaborate and articulate ideology. As such, it came to attain the status of what Durkheim would have called a 'social fact'. It became, that is, a 'collective representation', an ideational product developed by members of one collectivity in opposition to the ideas and actions of the members of another. As such, it came to have an existence independently, not, as Durkheim would have had it, of individuals, but of specific individuals. This is not to say that every member of the public school élite adhered to every aspect of the amateur ethos or that their beliefs were of a uniform character or held with uniform intensity. A few, indeed, were totally opposed to sport.[13] Nevertheless, they were all, even the latter, as is evidenced by the strength of their reaction, subject to strong pressure to conform to its major tenets and this pressure increased with the mounting tension between North and South.

In its developed form, the amateur ethos can be reduced to three components. In order to be worthy of the name 'sport', an activity had, for members of the public school élite, to involve at least the following constellation of normative and behavioural attributes:

(1) pursuit of the activity as an 'end in itself', i.e. simply for the pleasure afforded, with a corresponding downgrading of achievement striving, training and specialization;

(2) self-restraint and, above all, the masking of enthusiasm in victory and disappointment in defeat;

(3) the norm of 'fair play', i.e. the normative equalization of game-chances between contending sides, coupled with a stress on voluntary compliance with the rules and a chivalrous attitude of 'friendly rivalry' towards opponents.

According to this ethos, sports had as their ideal aim the production of pleasure, i.e. an immediate emotional state rather than some ulterior end, whether of a material or other kind. The competitive element was held to be crucial but the achievement of victory was, for the public school élite, supposed not to be central. On the contrary, striving to win was supposed, at all times, to be kept subordinate to the production of pleasure. That is, it was supported only to the extent that it was consistent with the maximization of fun for those taking part and, as a result, hemmed in by rules and rituals of various kinds. To put it slightly differently, the 'mock-fight' character of sports was held by the public school élite to be essential for the achievement of their central aim, the generation of pleasure for the players. Too great a stress on victory could easily lead the delicate balance by which this aim was supposedly achieved to be upset and hence lead the 'mock fight' to be transformed into 'real' or 'serious' fighting.

One of the ways in which this balance was effected was by insisting that players and spectators should applaud the performance of the other side. Public school games players, according to Wilkinson, 'tempered the determination to win demanded by "house-spirit" with the amateur's enjoyment of sport for its own sake'.[14] Moreover, it was regarded as 'unsportsmanlike' and 'ungentlemanly' to show enthusiasm in victory and disappointment in defeat, i.e. sports were supposed to be engaged in without overt emotion and with an emphasis on outward form. This is brought out in a description of spectators at the Oxford–Cambridge match written in the 1930s. As one can see, the author realized that he was describing a tradition which, by that time, was on the wane:

> Every young breast is flaming with partisan fires, but youth is equally determined to give nothing away in bad manners. No cry but a formal antiphony of 'Oxford–Cambridge' goes up and everywhere there is repression of the passion which such a game between sides must create. This is the grand assembly of the Forsyte Commonwealth, the parade of the self-possessive class . . . one hears neither revilings, nor gloatings, equanimity is all . . . Twickenham is a sobering frame for the bright battle-scapes we put there. The man with a stiff upper lip is everywhere about it. So much is it a middle class institution that the ebullient

instincts are smothered at the gate. A spectator of Rugger in London has no kinship with the soccer fan; he retains his private life. Beyond the occasional shout, the discreet waving of a hat, he will not betray the agonies or ecstasies of strife. He will not sing, nor eat hot-dogs. His lips are guarded though his heart beat strong. Twickenham is the last fortress of the Forsytes and when the Welshmen come they seem to feel the chill of it.[15]

It followed as a corollary of the amateur ethos that the public school élite were opposed to cups and leagues. Such competitions were conducive, it was held, to an overemphasis on victory, to an 'overly serious' attitude to sport, to striving for extrinsic rewards such as medals, cups and shields, to an increase of violence, to a devaluation of the short-term goal of obtaining pleasure from particular matches and a corresponding elevation of the long-term goal of obtaining satisfaction from the kudos dished out to the ultimate winners. Montague Shearman summed up what was a widespread opinion at that time:

> Experience has conclusively shown that whatever be the class of the players, Rugby cup-ties give an opening for ill-feeling and the exhibition of unnecessary roughness ... As long ago as 1876, the Oxford Rugby Union decided to have a College Championship, and the competition was abandoned after two years' trial on account of the roughness of the game. The writer still has a vivid recollection of playing in the final ties in 1877, and can well recollect what a battered appearance was presented by his side when they met to celebrate ... There seems to be little doubt that in the excitement of a cup-tie, the old Adam in the breast of the footballer will have its way, and probably nothing but a team of Neo-platonists could play a Rugby Union cup-tie without roughness.[16]

Shearman was opposed to cup Rugby because, he felt, the introduction to the game of a highly valued extrinsic reward tended to transform it, independently of the social characteristics of the players, from a 'mock fight' into a 'real' one. Others, however, believed that cup competition had this 'de-civilizing' effect because it brought into Rugby players who were not 'gentlemen'. A. E. Hudson, for example, the man who proposed the introduction of the Yorkshire Challenge Cup, had come by 1881 to maintain that:

> ... the friendly rivalry which used to exist between clubs has now, in some cases, given place to unconcealed animosity, and certain players in the Cup Ties behave in such a brutal manner, that they have not only disgraced the clubs which still tolerate them, but have brought the game itself into disrepute.[17]

This sentiment was echoed by G. Rowland Hill. Cup competition, he contended had engendered foul play, betting and unhealthy excitement.[18] However, he admitted that none of these 'abuses' occurred in the cup-ties he witnessed in 1882, implying that they are not inevitable concomitants of cup competition. This provides testimony to the ideological component in his case for this qualification suggests that what really worried him was the introduction to the game of players unaccustomed to 'gentlemanly' norms. Apparently unaware of this inconsistency, he went on to argue that cup matches *as such* engendered an 'evil spirit', leading players to be more concerned with winning than abiding by the rules. They even played 'unfairly', he suggested, because it 'paid' to do so. Whether this was a reference to material inducements or simply to success in the game is not entirely clear. Here is the actual text of what he said:

> We believe that in some cases these matches have caused an evil spirit to arise, and that sometimes men are influenced more by the desire to win than to play the game in the true spirit. We are told that men intentionally play 'unfairly' because it pays to do so. If such is the case, it is certainly a most melancholy fact.[19]

Almond was less ambiguous in his pronouncements. In his view, cup competition was symptomatic of a deeper malaise, namely of an 'overly serious' attitude to sport and the elevation of the success-goal to supreme position in the hierarchy of sporting values. This attitude, he felt, was as prevalent in public schools as elsewhere. The introduction of extrinsic rewards into sport, he contended, whatever their form and whatever the context, was bound to lead to a downwards spiral, with professionalism and 'corruption' the inevitable end-results:

> Schoolmasters have been most unwise . . . in permitting . . . first and second eleven and fifteen 'blazers', jerseys, scarves, etc., and worse than all, barbaric gold and silver about football caps . . . Such things . . . detract from the simplicity and genuine character of sport, and introduce a fictitious sort of keenness, which is only too apt to lead to tricks of all descriptions. The cup-ties in Yorkshire . . . have done this. The executives of clubs will, in the first instance, do anything lawful to win. Next they will do what is doubtfully lawful. They will use inducements to procure recruits wherever they can get them, and these inducements are apt very soon to pass the limits of fair persuasion. The various steps on the downward course are too obvious to require any further description.[20]

The fact that Almond included public schools and universities among his targets, whereas these sporting 'abuses' were held by most members of the public school élite to be restricted to the North, points once more to the ideological component in the amateur ethos. Thus, even though the public school élite tended to couch their pronouncements in 'sport-specific' terms, claiming to be solely interested in preserving the 'essential character' of sport, class and regional hostility and resentment over the loss of their erstwhile dominance played an important part in what they said. This element of class and regional antagonism comes out most clearly in what they wrote about professionalism *per se*. In 1898, for example, E. K. Ensor described the northwards spread of football in the following terms. What he wrote illustrates the sort of contemptuous attitude towards Northern people widely held by members of the public school élite at that time:

> [Football] began in the South. Enthusiasts who faced jeers and taunts had their reward and the game made its way northwards. There it was passionately adopted by that people whose warped sporting instincts are so difficult to understand, even when they are quite familiar.
>
> For a time it was played as a game, money was not a disturbing element; but the warped sporting instincts asserted themselves—the main chance is not ignored for long north of the Trent—and the clubs began to import players from all sides, in order to gratify the prevailing desire to get the better of one's neighbour.[21]

He went on to use words such as 'contagion', 'defilement' and 'moral slough' in describing the spread of professionalism:

> So far the contagion has not spread to the South, where the influence of the public schools and universities is strong. Indeed the reason why Rugby remained an amateur game so much longer than 'soccer' is that it was always preferred by the better class of athletes . . . Association has touched pitch and been shockingly defiled. North and South are now alike, and soon the only football played, as used to be the case, for love of the game, will be seen amongst university men . . . The line of demarcation between the upper and lower classes which everybody professes to wish to see removed, is growing more distinct. The terms 'gentleman' and 'amateur' have now very different connotations. Gentlemen can now only play Association football with each other for they cannot risk plunging into the moral slough. Gentlemen must not run foot-races or ride bicycle races in open company. The unutterable corruption of amateur athletics during the last few years need not be dwelt upon; the betting and swindling, the feigned names, the selling of races, pace-making, that hateful travesty of sport, and many other abuses are notorious. Football is on the same road . . .[22]

Ensor's reference to the growing distinctness of the 'line of demarcation between the upper and lower classes' was apposite for the controversy over professionalism in Rugby occurred, as we shall show, at a time of mounting class tension. A similar view was held by Arthur Budd, the Old Cliftonian physician who became President of the RFU in 1888.[23] Professionalism, he contended, the issue 'which will most materially affect the destiny of . . . Rugby', had arisen because 'the working man has become so prominent an element in our game'. It is, he continued, an unwritten law of sport that professionalism leads to 'corruptibility, disrepute and sometimes absolute decay'. Cricket was an exception because amateurs devoted as much time to the game as professionals and were hence able to maintain 'equality of play' and 'monopoly of government'. He even suggested that to compensate working men for 'broken-time' would represent a form of discrimination against the middle class:

> If A.B. of the Stock Exchange were to ask for compensation for loss of time for a two-days' football tour, such compensation to be fixed on a scale commensurate with his earnings, the football community would denounce it as a scandal. A.B., the stockbroker, has therefore to stop . . . at his desk because he cannot afford to play, but C.D., the working man, is to be allowed his outing and compensation for leaving his work, which under any other circumstances he could not afford to abandon. If, to come to my second point, a man who gives his whole time to a game is bound to best the amateur, who devotes only his leisure to it, the inevitable law of the survival of the fittest must intervene, and it simply becomes a question as to how long the amateur can survive. It comes, then, to this, that . . . while you allow a man to play for money, you prevent another playing for love of the game without emolument. Is this sport? . . . the great game of football . . . was never invented by the schoolboy . . . to provide a livelihood for professionals and exclude amateurs, or to become a medium of speculation for gate-money financiers. These, if we legitimize professionalism, are the dangers . . . and the crisis is consummated in my last axiom, that no professional sport under its own government, and independently of amateur supervision, has ever yet permanently prospered . . . [The history of all sports over which professionals have gained sway] is a catalogue of corruptibility and decay . . . History repeats itself, and there is no reason to suppose that a Rugby football professional would be a more moral person than his fellow in any other branch, and spurn the temptations which fall across his path. On the contrary, the presumption is the other way . . . The profession of football . . . means a life of idleness while it lasts. But it is also a game at which a man cannot play for many years, and after his career is finished it leads to absolutely nothing, so that the superannuated professor, when his short day of activity is over, finds himself stranded without resources, and has to begin life again to get his bread.
>
> If, with the lesson before them, which facts such as these so cogently supply, . . . blind enthusiasts of working men's clubs insist on introducing professionalism, there can be but one result—disunion. The

amateur must refuse to submit himself to the process of slow extinction which has been going on in the sister game, and say at once that henceforth he will play and compete with his own class alone, and let professionals for the future look among themselves for opponents. And if this black day comes, which I hope never will, it will be the duty of the Rugby Union to see that the division of classes dates from the dawn of professionalism, and not to wait, before seeking to apply a remedy as the short-sighted Associationists have done, to see the whole of the North and part of the South denuded of amateurs and given up to subsidized players. To them, the charge of a game of great traditions has been committed, and, if they would be willing to consign the future of these to the baleful influence of professionalism, they would assuredly be betraying the trust imposed in them, and live regretfully to see the game of today, depraved, degraded, and decayed.[24]

Budd's impassioned plea summed up the central amateur objections to professionalism, giving notice of the fact that the Rugby establishment were willing to fight to retain a game-form which conformed to the tenets of the amateur ethos. They were unwilling to compromise even though their intransigence made disunion virtually inevitable. We shall examine the process by which disunion came about in the next two chapters. It is necessary, first, to look more closely at the element of class ideology in Budd's analysis. It emerges with special clarity from the non sequiturs in his argument.

The most striking example is contained in Budd's assertion that professionalism leads inevitably to the 'corruption' of sport, an assertion made despite his realization that this 'inevitable process' had not occurred in cricket. In order to fit this awkward fact into his argument, he suggested that amateurs had been able to retain a governmental monopoly in cricket and prevent its 'corruption', because they devoted as much time to it as the professionals. This enabled them to maintain equality of play and meant, Budd implied, that no challenge to their authority had been forthcoming. But that is tantamount to an admission that professionalism does not lead inevitably to a 'legitimacy crisis' for amateur rule. It only has that consequence, that is the implication, when professionals are able to devote more time to a sport than amateurs and are, hence, able to establish superiority on the field of play. It is to suggest, in other words, that the occurrence of such a crisis is a function, not of the balance between amateurism and professionalism *per se*, but of relativities of time and skill.

Implicit in Budd's analysis is the notion that, unlike their cricketing counterparts, amateur Rugby footballers would be unable to devote as much time to the game as professionals and, hence, would be unable to remain superior as players. However, he provided no rationale for such an assumption. He did not even see that such a rationale was demanded by the logic of his case. Instead, he simply asserted that working men who could not afford to play

Rugby should learn 'to do without it,' introducing the specious argument that to legitimize payment for 'broken-time' would constitute discrimination against stockbrokers and other wealthy men!

The virtually undisputed control that amateurs were then able to exercise over cricket depended basically on the existence of a class structure in which a few people inherited sufficient wealth to exempt them from the need to work. It was inherited wealth which enabled amateur cricketers to devote their summers to the game. Budd was, therefore, admitting by implication that Rugby amateurs did not come from such an exalted social position. In short, his argument is an example of a pattern common in class societies, i.e. of middle-class resentment of the underprivileged rather than of the highly privileged groups who stand at the summit of the social hierarchy.

Another non sequitur is contained in Budd's contention that, if professionalism were legitimized in Rugby, it would lead inevitably to the 'extinction of the amateur'. Again, however, it is difficult to follow his logic for such a policy would not have been able to prevent amateurs playing amongst themselves. Clearly, the main thing that disturbed him was not professionalism but his fear that professionals would become superior as players and steal from the upper and middle classes the kudos which attaches to being the source of the country's leading players. In this, he, and those who argued likewise, contradicted the amateur ethos by showing they played for glory as much as for fun. But it was not simply the fact that the prospectively superior players were professionals which disturbed the public school élite but the fact that they were working-class. In that way, the fear of professionalism in football was closely tied up with the fear, current at that time, of the growth of working-class power.

5. Simply to suggest that elements of class antagonism were bound up with the amateur ethos does not prove that its fundamental tenets lacked foundation, e.g. that professionalism would not 'destroy'—or at least fundamentally alter—the character of Rugby as a sport. However, the arguments of the public school élite went deeper than those discussed so far. Accordingly, it is necessary to look at what the amateur ethos had to say about sport *per se*, about the motivation of professionals and about spectatorship. As we shall show, even here, class ideology and class antagonism were never far beneath the surface.

According to Budd, 'sport' is 'a recreation pursued for love of itself and devoid of emolument'. This was echoed by Shearman who wrote in 1899 that: 'It is a rule allowed by most of us that a sport ceases to be a sport when it is played not for the enjoyment it affords, but for the pecuniary benefits it confers.'[25] The element of compulsion inherent in professional sport by virtue of its occupational character would, he suggested, decrease the enjoyment afforded to players by the activity itself. It would also destroy the non-pecuniary motivation for taking part and mean that sportsmen would only strive to the utmost when a financial reward was involved:

> Few of us get as much pleasure from what we must do as from what we can or not at our own will. When sport becomes a matter of pounds, shillings and pence, when players are paid and are but fulfilling their vocation in life the game must necessarily lose some of that delightful enthusiasm which characterized it before the advent of such consider-ations. In former times the game itself sufficed to stir up feelings of intense excitement; now unless there is some inducement forthcoming, unless some gain is offered, there can be no certainty that the paid player will do his best.[26]

Writing in 1892, C. Edwardes suggested that monetary rewards led to unscrupulousness and corruption.[27] Almond also subscribed to this view-point, adding that, whereas in soccer and cricket the referee or umpire can see and penalize unfair play, it is impossible in Rugby for the referee to see everything. Consequently, he said, for there to be a game at Rugby,

> . . . there must be a certain amount of *bona fides* . . . or it soon becomes no game at all. But from the professional player we cannot expect this *bona fides*. His object is to win, no matter how, for his livelihood depends upon his success.[28]

In other words, given the difficulties of imposing external control on Rugby with its close-packed scrummages, rucks, mauls and lineouts, the players must show 'good faith' and control themselves. Otherwise, it will be trans-formed from a 'mock fight' into a 'real' one. Professionals cannot be expected to show such good faith since their livelihood is at stake. Hence, for them, Rugby ceases to be a 'sport', a form of 'play', and becomes a form of fighting in earnest.

Ensor suggested that cups and leagues reinforce the tendency towards vio-lence produced by professionalization by adding to the pecuniary motivation of players that of spectators to see their representatives win. Under such circumstances, victory becomes the supreme value and spectators are willing to applaud the use of any means which helps in the achievement of that end:

> The effect of League matches and cup-ties is thoroughly evil. Men go in thousands, not to study and admire skill and excellence but to see their team gain two points or pass into the next round. The end, not the means, is everything. Rough play, so long as it escapes punishment by the referee, is one means to the end, and delights the crowd.[29]

According to Almond, the metamorphosis involved in the transformation of Rugby from 'sport' into 'spectacle' was conducive not only to violence and the destruction of its 'play-character' but degrading for players and spectators alike. This, he believed, was as true in the context of a school as in society at large:

> . . . no idle spectators should be allowed to stand looking on at school sides. The very sight of loungers takes the spirit out of players, and the loungers should be doing something else if they are too feeble for football. 'Spectating' is . . . the greatest of all football dangers.[30]

Shearman, too, spoke of the harm done to those who were 'induced to become spectators instead of players, preferring to watch the paid gladiators from Scotland . . .' to taking part themselves.[31] The analogy between professional and gladiatorial sport recurred in the writings of the public school élite. Even as late as 1929, Sir Cyril Norwood could write that:

> The wrong view, the un-English view, of sport, prevails widely, and is cutting deep into the national mind. It is the view that all sport is competitive, designed to be a spectacle of gladiatorial character, and to demonstrate the one team or individual who may be acclaimed as the best. It is the spirit which gloats breathlessly over international contests, and sees the signs of national decadence if England does not win every championship in every game.[32]

Thus, members of the public school élite identified their own ethos with that of the nation as a whole. Groups who adhered to different standards had betrayed their national heritage.

According to the amateur ethos, sports participation is physically and morally beneficial but spectatorship has no such desirable effects. However, the public school élite's dislike of spectator sports did not rest simply on this moral ground but was rooted, arguably more firmly, in the fact that spectatorship was increasing mainly among the working class and involved the congregation of large crowds who behaved in an openly excited manner. This ran counter, not only to their sports ethos with its stress on the controlled expression of emotion, but was perceived as a threat to public order. In 1884, for example when thousands of Blackburn supporters travelled to London to watch the FA Cup Final between Blackburn Rovers and Queen's Park, Glasgow—the first all-Northern final—they were contemptuously dismissed by an author writing in the *Pall Mall Gazette* as 'a northern horde of uncouth garb and strange oaths'.[33] And Edwardes described a recent match in which he said the referee was:

> . . . hooted and cursed every time he gave a decision, and one of the spectators went so far as to threaten to throw him into a pond. Immediately after the match he was snowballed, in addition to which mud was thrown at him, and he had to seek protection from the violence of the

spectators. He took refuge in the pavilion for some time, but when he went towards the public house where the teams dressed, he found that there was a large crowd waiting for him, and he was again roughly handled, his hat being knocked off, and he received a blow on the neck.[34]

An account of spectator behaviour at a match played in Shrewsbury on Easter Monday, 1899, provides further confirmation of the menace which such congregations were felt to represent:

> There were many thousands present at Shrewsbury on Easter Monday, and the concomitants of betting, drinking, and bad language were fearful to contemplate, while the shouting and horse-play on the highway were a terror to peaceful residents passing homewards.[35]

The aspect of such gatherings which frightened the upper and middle classes was brought out by Ensor when he wrote that: '. . . twenty thousand people torn by emotions of rage and pleasure, roaring condemnation and applause, make an alarming spectacle.'[36] As we suggested earlier, it does not seem too far-fetched to maintain that the alarm expressed by these authors was not simply a fear of the threat to public order posed by large assemblies but, more importantly, a fear of large *working-class* congregations. As we have said, the 1890s were a decade in which the power of the working class grew. As a result, class conflict became more intense and, correspondingly, members of the upper and middle-classes perceived the working class increasingly in hostile terms.

We shall explore the growth of working-class power and its effects on class consciousness and class conflict in Chapter 10. As we shall show, it had important consequences for the development of Rugby, helping to bring about the split between Union and League. However, before we deal with the part played by class and class conflict in this process, it is necessary to discuss the organizational dimensions of the emergent schism and the events by which it came about. It is to that task that we shall turn in the next chapter.

8   The split

1. The culmination of the developments discussed in the last two chapters was the bifurcation—the 'splitting up'—of Rugby into separate amateur and professional segments. This process was given institutional form in 1895 when twenty-two 'gate-taking' clubs, eleven from Yorkshire, nine from Lancashire and two from Cheshire, resigned their membership of the RFU and established the 'Northern Rugby Football Union'. The present chapter is concerned with the events through which 'the split' occurred. However, since other sports in late nineteenth century Britain, most notably cricket and soccer, also experienced crises over amateurism and professionalism but managed to survive intact with nationally unified rules and an organizational framework incorporating both amateurs and professionals, it will be necessary later to undertake a comparative analysis of the tensions generated in Rugby in that period and the similar tensions generated in cricket and soccer. Such an analysis is necessary to show why, in a period of general conflict over amateurism and professionalism in British sport, it was only Rugby which underwent a fully-fledged amateur–professional split. More precisely, it is only by means of a comparative analysis of that sort that we shall be able to penetrate the fundamental social processes which led to the bifurcation of Rugby. We shall undertake such a comparison in the next chapter. For the moment, we have set ourselves the more modest task of describing the events through which this process occurred.

2. The professionalization of Rugby in the North led, as we have seen, to a decrease in the power of the public school élite in the county unions there and to a corresponding increase in the power of those who controlled the 'gate-taking' clubs. At the same time, due largely to the success of the challenge cup in popularizing the game, the Yorkshire Union became the most powerful in the country. By 1890, for example, it had a membership of 150 clubs, some three-sevenths of the number then affiliated to the RFU. In the words of the Rev. Marshall:

> The future legislative problem is the relationship between the Yorkshire
> Union and the Rugby Union. The latter ... is threatened with the
> undesirable contingency that one district with its preponderate voting
> power may arrogate to itself the control of the destiny of the game.[1]

However, the problem was not simply that of a single county obtaining
electoral hegemony but that of the county where professionalization had
proceeded furthest achieving a preponderant influence in the formation of
national policy.

To say that those who controlled the gate-taking clubs had emerged as
the most powerful figures in Yorkshire Rugby by the 1890s, is not to imply
that they enjoyed monopoly control. Nor is it to suggest that a majority of
Yorkshire representatives on the RFU were in favour of full professionalism.
Indeed, in certain quarters—the Rev. Marshall is the prime example—
support for the amateur ethos continued undiluted. In general, however,
the social configuration within which the playing and administration of
Yorkshire Rugby took place was conducive to modification of its central
tenets. In particular, it led to the belief that the best means of inhibiting
professionalization and retaining amateur control would be to legitimate
'broken-time' payment. G. F. Berney offered the following comments on this
configuration:

> ... at this period the Yorkshire Committee included members ...
> tainted with professionalism and who subsequently went over to the
> Northern Union. Under the pressure of their constituents, ... even
> those of Marshall's colleagues ... who were amateur at heart, appear to
> have supported the various proposals ... from the clubs of the county,
> for amendment of the Rugby Union bye-laws and legalization of the
> principle of payment to players.[2]

Yorkshire supporters of the amateur ethos came into direct contact with
members of the clubs which paid their players and which had become
dependent on gate-money. They met them in the organization and playing of
matches, and shared with them the running of the County RFU. They were,
as a result, subject to direct pressure from that source. Since few had
attended public schools, and had, therefore, not received a thorough ground-
ing in amateur principles, it is hardly surprising that they were less than
steadfast in their commitment. Moreover, the fact that they were not integrated into the public school élite meant that, even though they were middle-
class, they did not, for the most part, share the class antagonism from which
the pristine amateur ethos derived much of its momentum. That is, they
tended to be tolerant towards working-class participation and not to perceive
working-class success as a threat to their self-image or interests, even when it
was contingent, or perceived to be contingent, upon the receipt of material
rewards. Indeed, many saw broken-time payment more positively, i.e. as a

device for increasing working-class participation. In any case, local patriotism caused them to resent what they regarded as the Southern dominance of the RFU. It led, in their opinion, to a failure to take Northern interests into account, causing them to identify with other Northerners even though they had to identify across the class and amateur-professional boundaries in order to do so.

Under such circumstances, the policy pursued by Yorkshire representatives on the RFU came to reflect a compromise between the interests of the gate-taking and other local clubs. It embraced three principal proposals: (i) that the RFU's annual meeting should be held alternately in London and at a Northern venue; (ii) that broken-time payments should be legitimized; and (iii) that county unions should be granted by the RFU the right to set up leagues. All three proposals were believed by the Rugby establishment to be conducive to 'creeping professionalism'. Hence, they fought them tooth and nail. It was numbers (ii) and (iii), however, which were decisive as determinants of the outcome of the amateur–professional struggle.

3. Matters came to a head at the RFU General Meeting held in London on 20 September 1893, when J. A. Miller and M. Newsom of the Yorkshire Union proposed and seconded respectively 'that players be allowed compensation for *bona fide* loss of time'.[3] The Rugby establishment learned of the Yorkshire intention some time prior to the AGM. They also learned that arrangements had been made to secure the attendance of a large Northern contingent. Thus forewarned, they formed an unofficial committee under the chairmanship of F. I. Currey, the Old Marlburian solicitor and President of the RFU from 1884–6.[4] It met at the Sports Club, St James's Square, a club formed exclusively by and for public school old boys. The objects of the committee were to ensure that amateurs realized the seriousness of the threat posed to their interests and values by recent developments in the North and to secure a large turnout and united front at the forthcoming meeting. One of its first acts was to draft a circular 'over the names of about 70 prominent football men' appealing for support for the amateur principle and to send it to sympathetic clubs.[5] At the same time, H. E. Steed of Lennox RFC was directed to contact clubs known to be opposed to broken-time payments and to obtain proxy votes from those unable to send representatives. When the fateful day arrived, and after the Yorkshire motion had been put, William Cail of Northumberland, a manufacturer, export merchant and currently President of the RFU,[6] and G. Rowland Hill, Hon. Secretary, proposed and seconded, respectively, the following counter-motion:

> That this meeting, believing that the above principle is contrary to the true interest of the Game and its spirit, declines to sanction the same.[7]

The counter-motion was carried by 282 votes to 136. However, 120 of the votes cast in its favour were proxy votes obtained by Steed. This means that voting among those actually present was considerably closer, i.e. 162 to 136. What would have happened had supporters of the Yorkshire motion also obtained proxy votes can only be guessed. It is clear, nevertheless, that they were caught out by these secret machinations of the Rugby establishment who had been spurred retroactively into achieving greater solidarity by the growing threat to their interests and values which they perceived in the industrial North.

Shortly after 20 September, a Special General Meeting of the RFU was held in order to alter the constitution. According to Berney, the object of the alterations 'was to crush any attempt to establish professional cells within the government machine'.[8] Bye-law number one, for example, was made to declare that:

> ... the name of the Society shall be the 'Rugby Football Union' and only clubs composed entirely of amateurs shall be eligible for membership and its headquarters shall be in London where all general meetings shall be held.[9]

In this way, the amateur principle, previously no more than an unwritten commitment of the Rugby establishment, became enshrined in the constitution of the RFU. However, such a constitutional innovation did not, by itself, mean that the trend towards professionalism had been halted. The protagonists of a professional game and the broken-time compromise may have suffered a reverse but they were, for the most part, unrepentant. They also continued in membership of the RFU and were, hence, still in a position to fight for alterations which would have made it more consistent with the realization of what they perceived as the interests of their clubs. To be sure, therefore, of maintaining a form of Rugby consistent with what they regarded as 'true' amateur principles, the establishment had to drive them out. It was with that object in mind that the RFU set about framing a more precise and comprehensive set of anti-professionalism regulations. Such rules, designed to expunge from the game all forms of monetary consideration beyond the reimbursement of travelling expenses and, at the same time, to prevent the recurrence of professionalization, were adopted on 19 September 1895.[10] So wide was the definition given to 'professionalism' by the new rules that a club or player could be held to be 'professional', and hence expelled or suspended, simply by awarding or receiving medals without the authority of the RFU, or simply for performing paid repair work to the facilities of his club. At the same time, professional soccer players were prevented from playing Rugby as amateurs, and any player, referee or touch-judge who knowingly played or officiated at the ground of an expelled or suspended club was himself liable to definition as a professional and hence to expulsion or suspension. Short of imposing an absolute taboo on the reimbursement of travelling expenses or prohibiting clubs from charging for admission, it is difficult to think of how more thorough-going anti-professionalism regulations could have been devised.

4. 'Re-amateurization' could have been secured in at least two ways: by a slow process of expelling clubs which had provably breached the new regulations; or by forcing the gate-taking clubs to resign *en bloc*. It was the latter course which prevailed and Yorkshire the county where the events took place which led the Northern gate-taking clubs to retire from the RFU and establish the rival 'Northern Union'. We shall now examine these events more closely.

The defeat in 1893 of the proposal to legitimize broken-time payments and the RFU's adoption in 1895 of more stringent anti-professionalism regulations was a major reverse for the Northern gate-taking clubs. The stranglehold which it had seemed they might be able to establish over the RFU had been effectively broken but it remained problematic whether the national union would be able to enforce the new regulations, particularly in Yorkshire where the administrative and playing power of the gate-taking clubs remained great. However, the power of the latter had been somewhat reduced, and that of local proponents of a purer type of amateurism correspondingly increased, by the victory of the amateur faction in the RFU. For the first time in at least a decade, amateurs in Yorkshire were in a position to resist the usurpation of control of the Yorkshire Union by the gate-taking clubs and to prevent them from running local Rugby in their own interests. However, it was not ostensibly on the issue of money payments that Yorkshire amateurs made their stand but that of competitive leagues. That is understandable for the gate-taking clubs would not have risked expulsion from the RFU by openly admitting that they paid their players. Nevertheless, professionalism and the growing dependency of the leading Yorkshire clubs on gate-money were the issues principally at stake. In any case, competitive leagues were just as antithetical to the pristine amateur ethos and, hence, just as potent a source of conflict.

Despite its opposition to leagues, where locally dominant clubs wished to introduce them, the RFU was powerless to prevent it. It could, however, attempt to ensure that such competitions were run in a manner consistent with what the establishment regarded as the interests of the game. It was with this end in view, and parallel with their attempt to eliminate material rewards, that in the 1890s the RFU introduced regulations designed to tighten their control over leagues, in particular to see that they were 'fairly' run.[11] It was this policy which formed the issue which led the Northern gate-taking clubs to resign from the RFU and form the 'Northern Union'.

By 1890, Yorkshire Rugby had come to be organized mainly on league principles. This form of organization was superimposed on the earlier 'knockout' system largely because it guaranteed more regular gates, a flow of money through the turnstiles and was, hence, more in accordance with the interests of gate-taking clubs. The twelve leading clubs in the county formed what they termed, the 'Senior Competition'; below them came the 'Second Competition', a third being added in February 1893.[12] Like clubs in the present-day Football League, the clubs in these 'competitions' contended each season for the position of 'champion club'. The 'competitions', however, were not 'divisions' in the sense in which these exist in the Football League for there was no promotion and relegation. This was largely because the clubs in the Senior Competition wished to maintain themselves as a self-perpetuating élite, a stance which, not unnaturally, was resented by the clubs in the Second and Third Competitions who were thus denied the chance of competing for the position of 'top' club in the county and hence of obtaining, not only the kudos which derived from that fact, but also the lucrative gate-receipts yielded by membership of the Senior Competition. This resentment of the junior clubs was fastened on to by the RFU as a stick with which to beat the gate-taking clubs. Chief among the regulations introduced for the control of leagues was one stipulating that such competitions would only be deemed legitimate if they involved promotion and relegation. Despite strong opposition from the gate-taking clubs, this was complied with by the Yorkshire Union who introduced a rule of their own providing that the two clubs finishing lowest in the Senior Competition should retire at the end of each season. The two top clubs in the Second Competition might then apply to take their place but the retiring clubs were provided with the right to apply for re-election.

The issue of promotion and relegation was thus made, not automatic as in the Football League, but dependent on the voting strengths of factions in the Yorkshire RFU. Such a compromise reflected the weakened power of the gate-taking clubs. They tried to increase their representation on the county committee but were rebuffed. Accordingly, towards the end of 1893, united in their resentment over what they regarded as unwarranted RFU interference in a purely local affair, and smarting over their failure to secure the legitimization of broken-time payments, they threatened *en bloc* to resign from membership of the Yorkshire Union. They were persuaded, on that occasion, to remain in membership but, in 1895, learning of the more stringent anti-professionalism regulations which the RFU planned to introduce and which, they realized, were designed primarily to make them toe the pristine amateur line or risk expulsion, they decided to act pre-emptively and form a union of their own.

The decision to establish the breakaway 'Northern Rugby Football Union' was taken at the George Hotel, Huddersfield, on 29 August 1895, i.e. three weeks before the publication by the RFU of its new anti-professionalism regulations. After the meeting, the following statement was issued to the press:

> The clubs here represented forming the late Senior Competition consider that the time is now opportune to form a Northern Rugby Football

Union and will do their utmost to push forward as rapidly as possible the establishment of such a Union.[13]

Eleven of the Senior Competition clubs sent in their resignations to the Yorkshire RFU immediately, Dewsbury being the only one not to do so. They were joined by nine Lancashire and two Cheshire clubs, making an initial NRFU membership of twenty-two. By the following season, the number had increased to fifty-nine.

Two items which appeared in Yorkshire newpapers on the day prior to the Huddersfield meeting illuminate the reasons why the antagonists in this dispute acted as they did. Thus, the author of a letter published in the *Leeds Daily News* suggested that the payment of players had become so widespread in the North that the proposed anti-professionalism regulations were unrealistic. It would, he said, be more honourable to permit clubs to reimburse players for 'broken time'. No danger of full professionalism would be entailed by such a course and it would also prevent the occurrence of discrimination against working-class players. Here is part of his text:

> I . . . draw attention to the class of men . . . now playing . . . in the North; and one will find it composed of working men at an average wage . . . of not more than 27/- a week . . . How do those gentlemen sitting on the English Rugby Union suppose these players can afford to lose time and wages for playing football? As a matter of fact they do not lose it, and the clubs in the North will certainly be acting in a more honourable way if they, instead of concealing these illegal payments, adopt the manly course of openly declaring themselves in favour of a Union which will allow them to make such payments, the like of which are made, and will be made in spite of all laws and rules yet framed by the present Union. One might reasonably limit the payment to 5s. a match for any one player, and I have no doubt all our clubs will be able to pay their way.
>
> Of what I know of the present class of players they would rather work during the week—when able—than be declared a professional. In fact they know perfectly well, also the leading men in the twelve clubs, that professionalism on such a scale as Association could not possibly come about.[14]

Thus, as the dispute approached a climax it became possible for the protagonists of the breakaway Union to speak openly of their reason for adopting such a course. That is, as the realization dawned that they would be unable to secure their interests within the framework of the RFU, they lost their fear of being prosecuted for breaches of the professionalism regulations. Accordingly, they ceased to fight their case solely on 'safe' issues, e.g. representation on the county committee, promotion and relegation, and brought out into the open the central issue which divided them from the pristine amateurs: namely, their wish to be able legitimately to pay players.

Yorkshire supporters of amateurism, too, identified this as the underlying reason for the dispute. For example 'Old Ebor', the football correspondent of the *Yorkshire Post*, had this to say on the eve of the Huddersfield meeting:

> . . . the only possible justification for a Northern Union is professionalism . . . The Yorkshire Union can . . . now stand before the country with clean hands. It declined to permit the recalcitrant clubs to rule and govern the fortunes of the County Union, and it is well for the reputation of the Union that it did so. It is pretty well known that uneasiness as to the operation of the new laws of professionalism has been at the bottom of the whole dispute, and I wonder what the Yorkshire Union would have looked like if a few of its clubs had managed to control the County's affairs during the next year or so. Exposure was inevitable. The clubs themselves admit . . . that the 'risk' was too great, and they must retire from the English Union in a body rather than be in danger of suspension by instalments. Their retirement saves the Yorkshire Union the indignity of having some of its chief members 'spotted' one by one for professionalism and expelled from amateur football. The clubs that have retired state that a great deal of professionalism will still remain in the Union's ranks. If so, it may be taken for granted that, having insisted upon their authority in one direction, the Committee of the Yorkshire Union will not be slow to use it in another.[15]

We saw earlier that the national power of the gate-taking clubs declined with their defeat at the 1893 AGM, with consequent repercussions for their local dominance. Nevertheless, Yorkshire amateurs could not have hoped to defeat them swiftly as long as they remained members of the RFU. Moreover, as long as the two factions remained locked within the existing organizational framework, each was bound to regard the presence of the other as 'contaminating'. Thus, when it came, the act of disunion by the gate-taking clubs performed a 'purifying' function. It enabled both parties to feel that they would be able to act henceforward in a more 'open' and 'honourable' manner. For their part, the protagonists of pure amateurism believed they had saved a portion of Rugby from the 'corrupting scourge' of professionalism. They also believed that the County Committee had been spared the indignity of carrying out a 'purge'. And for their part, the gate-taking clubs had managed to place themselves in a position where they would be able hence-forward to pay players openly and run their affairs in their interests as they saw them, independently of outside interference.

9 The class structure and the professionalization of British sport

1. The analysis in the last chapter focused almost entirely on *events* and did not penetrate the *deeper levels* of the social process by which the peculiar dual organization of Rugby was established. Above all, it failed to explain why, in a period of generally mounting tension over professionalism in British sport, only Rugby split. A comparison of professionalization in Rugby, cricket and soccer will provide an answer to this question and help to lay bare the deeper levels of this overall process. We shall pay special attention in this connection to changing class relations and the way in which they generated tensions in sport. Before we embark on this analysis, however, it is necessary to say how our approach to amateurism and professionalism differs from that currently dominant in the sociology of sport.

We remarked in Chapter 6 that the 1890s in Britain were a decade of mounting class tension. That is relevant for the development of Rugby because no sport can be insulated from the wider society in which it is played. Of course, the manner in which sports are implicated in the class structure is not the only way in which the wider society makes its impact felt. Nor does the interweaving of class and sport lead necessarily to the generation of overt conflict. Nevertheless, there is reason to believe that the changing pattern of class relations in nineteenth-century Britain and the tensions it gave rise to were crucial determinants of the amateur–professional struggle, in particular of the split of Rugby into 'Union' and 'League'.

This approach to 'professionalism' differs in several ways from that which is currently dominant. Stone's analysis can serve as an example. As we saw in the Introduction, he attributes the tensions generated by the professionalization of sports in the United States to the transition from 'work-centred' to 'leisure-centred' values. These tensions arose, he suggests, because Americans regarded as anomalous the transformation into 'work' of what had previously been regarded as 'play'. We are not competent to assess the validity of this explanation for the USA. However, it is inadequate regarding Britain in several respects. Thus, it does not locate these values in a wider social context and cannot account for the transition between them except by reference to general processes. That is, it fails to spell out the 'configurational dynamics' of the transformation. Moreover, it does not allow one to explain why, in

Britain, there were variations between sports in the degrees of tension aroused by professionalization and, consequently, different structural outcomes.

In our view, the differential intensity of these tensions cannot be explained by reference to properties inherent in the different sports.[1] An adequate explanation has to be sought in wider circumstances. Of critical importance, we believe, is the period in which professionalization began and the pattern of class relations prevailing at that stage in the development of society at large. It follows that we shall have to look closely at the location within the developing class structure of the groups involved in professionalization and at their relations with one another and wider social groupings. We shall also have to estimate the changing extent and intensity of class conflict and its effects on sport.

In short, we are suggesting that the problem of the differential intensity of the tensions generated by the professionalization of sports requires a developmental and configurational approach. To stress the need for such an approach is not to discount the possibility that value changes of the type discussed by Stone may have played a part. It is, however, to suggest that values are not disembodied ideals but structurally located, constructs generated by specific groups, expressive of their interests and which change in connection with the changing structure of society as a whole. Our task, accordingly, is to examine the professionalization of cricket and soccer in order to ascertain why, in the one case, virtually no tension was generated at all, and why, in the other, the tensions aroused did not reach a level where disassociation and the establishment of separate amateur and professional games became necessary.

2. Professional cricket, i.e. the chance for men to earn a living, either wholly or partly, from prowess at the game, emerged for the first time in the eighteenth century. The process of professionalization started when members of the aristocracy and gentry hired men, nominally as household servants or for work on their estates but, in fact, principally on account of their cricketing skills. Professional cricket in its initial form was thus based on aristocratic and gentry patronage and dependent on their wealth and dominance in society at large. It was from that social base that its most salient features derived, including the fact that it emerged peacefully and continued for some time to function without provoking major conflict.[2] The reasons why will emerge from an analysis of the social position of the eighteenth-century aristocracy and gentry, of their correlative values and of the part played by cricket in their social world.

We suggested earlier that the landed classes in the eighteenth century ruled over a society in which the balance of power between classes involved gross inequalities and in which, as a result, there was no effective challenge to their position as the dominant class. The secure character of their dominance was conducive to a high degree of status security on their part and this meant, in turn, that individual aristocrats and gentlemen were, as a rule, in no way seriously threatened by contact with social subordinates. Whatever the context, they knew who was master and so did everybody else. Such status security was extended to the leisure-sphere, including the game of cricket. The type of playing career which grew up under such conditions was based on unequivocal subordination of the professional to his patron and total dependency as far as life-chances were concerned of the former on the latter. No threat was posed by professionalism of that type to the interests and values of the ruling class. On the contrary, as can be seen from their central role in the initial development of the playing career, it was in their interests to promote it. The fact that a few lower-class men could earn a living by their cricketing prowess seemed to members of the aristocracy and gentry the simple extension of a social order full of 'natural' inequalities in which fate had decreed that they should be socially superior to and rule over others. Under such conditions, in marked contrast to those which came to prevail by the end of the nineteenth century, professional sport was neither morally nor socially suspect. All could be open and above board. There was no need to hide the fact that pecuniary advantage could be obtained from skill at games. A corollary was the fact that professional cricketers suffered no loss of status in the eyes of the ruling class. On the contrary, the latter competed for their services and, as long as they retained their skills and physical fitness, they were sure of steady, in some cases remunerative, employment.

Members of the aristocracy and gentry derived at least three forms of satisfaction from their patronage of cricket. They decked their teams out in their personal colours and led them onto the field like medieval war-lords leading armies into battle. This enabled them to derive satisfaction from participation in a type of 'war-game'. At the same time, they were able to act out personal and prestige rivalries with other members of their class and, in addition, gambling on the outcome of matches added spice to their enjoyment. As members of a leisure class, they had time to devote to the practice and improvement of their cricketing skills and this meant that, in many cases, they were able to participate meaningfully in sides composed mainly of professionals. For present purposes, however, the main significance of this pattern of professional sport lies in the fact that aristocrats and gentlemen could play alongside their socially inferior professional employees, change in the same dressing rooms, eat and drink with them in the convivial evenings which usually followed matches, and contemplate defeat and failure at their hands with complete equanimity. All that was at risk was their self-image as sportsmen. No threat at all—at least no serious or lasting threat—was posed to their self-image in general. That was independent of their self-image as sportsmen and, since it was based on the stability of their power and status in society at large, exceptionally secure.

However, like the pattern of class relations which formed the social base from which it grew, this pattern of professional cricket was not immutable.

As we saw earlier, industrialization, urbanization and the related process of *embourgeoisement* began, from the start of the nineteenth century, slowly to erode the foundations on which the dominance of the landed classes rested. As the social basis of their power crumbled, particularly as they became subject to a mounting bourgeois threat, so they began commensurately to experience status insecurity. And as that occurred, professional cricket emerged as a controversial issue and the old pattern of free and easy mixing on the cricket field gave way to a more class-exclusive pattern.

This is not the place for a lengthy discussion of that process. It must be enough simply to make one or two pertinent observations. The first thing to note is the fact that, by the end of the nineteenth century, professional cricket had become subject to the sort of hostile comment discussed in the last chapter in relation to Rugby and soccer. Writing in 1890, for example, an anonymous author suggested that the county game was now played in a manner which ran counter to the values cricket was supposed to instil: 'How can we expect our children to learn from playing cricket when the very matches they can watch during their school holidays—supposedly the zenith of cricketing achievement—carry the taint of jealousy, dishonesty and self-ishness?'[3] Twenty years later, C. E. Green, an amateur county player and later President of the MCC, declared that, in his opinion: 'County cricket has become too much of a . . . money-making concern. There is . . . very little sport in it now . . . and the feeling of *esprit de corps* which ought to exist in connection with real county cricket is fast disappearing.'[4]

These diatribes are representative of a wider body of criticism of trends believed to be occurring in cricket in the late nineteenth and early twentieth centuries. Nevertheless, the volume of antipathy aroused failed even remotely to approach the level generated over professionalism in Rugby. In fact, professionalism in cricket was rarely brought into question as such, merely the 'spirit' in which the county game was played. More significantly, in cricket, the tensions aroused by the struggle over amateurism and professionalism failed to reach a level sufficient, either in extent or intensity, to jeopardize the legitimacy of the controlling position of the MCC. Hence, there was no serious threat to the maintenance of a unified structure of rules and organization for the country as a whole.

The reasons why are not difficult to find. By the late nineteenth century, professional cricket had existed for more than a century. It had become, as a result, an accepted part of the English 'way of life', a 'national institution'. One of the consequences was that the sort of arguments raised against professionalism in soccer and Rugby either did not suggest themselves or did not apply, at least to the same extent. There was, for example, an established career structure for professional players and, given the fact that cricket had come to occupy a central place in the curriculum of public schools, ample opportunities existed for professionals whose active playing days were over to obtain employment as coaches. Moreover, as we saw in Chapter 7, amateur cricketers continued to play a prominent part in the county game.

Indeed, in the sphere of batting they were pre-eminent and this helped them to retain a monopoly of control. That was dependent on the continued existence in British society of a leisured élite and on the fact that full-time participation in county cricket as an amateur was regarded in élite circles as a meaningful and status-enhancing way for a 'gentleman' to spend the summers of his youth and early adult years.

Connected with this, however, and probably of greater significance in explaining why the tensions generated in cricket over the issue of professionalism failed to reach crisis proportions, is the number of aristocrats who remained actively involved in the MCC. In 1877, for example, out of a total membership of 2,291, 337, just under fifteen per cent, were members of the aristocracy. By 1886, the total membership had risen to 5,091 and the aristocratic component had fallen to 327, i.e. proportionally to just over six per cent. By 1915, the total membership had risen again, to 5,135. Meanwhile, the number of aristocratic members had increased to 452, i.e. to just under nine per cent.[5] We are unable to say what proportions were contributed to these figures by the gentry and the bourgeoisie. It is clear, nevertheless, that they reflect changes in the social composition of the British ruling class in the late nineteenth and early twentieth centuries and, above all, the continuing process of *embourgeoisement*. We shall return to this issue later. For present purposes, the main thing to note is that even though the aristocratic component in the membership of the MCC remained throughout this period relatively small—i.e. a fluctuating proportion ranging between six and fifteen per cent—their power and influence within cricket's ruling body were greater than their numbers and proportional membership would lead one to suspect. That is because the bourgeoisie in that period, the emergent ruling class, continued to use the aristocracy as a reference group, i.e. as a model on which to base their own social standards. To the extent that this continued, the power and influence of the aristocracy were sustained and this meant, in turn, that the traditional aristocratic attitude of tolerance towards professionalism could still be meaningfully invoked in the councils of the MCC.

It could not, however, continue to be invoked in unchanged form. *Embourgeoisement* had led to increased bourgeois involvement in the affairs of the MCC. As we have seen, they adopted the values of the aristocracy and gentry but *embourgeoisement* had led to an increase of status insecurity among the latter. This meant that a greater proportion of those with influence over cricket now viewed the working class as a threat. Consequently, it was no longer possible to incorporate professionals into the game on the comparatively open, i.e. non-status exclusive, terms which had earlier prevailed. That is, the British ruling class at the end of the nineteenth century no longer enjoyed the unequivocal social dominance of its eighteenth-century predecessor. Therefore, in any activity where its members participated jointly with lower status groups, special devices were needed in order to demarcate the increasingly rigid lines of social status. In county cricket, this took the form of subjecting professional players to varieties of ritual and symbolic subordination designed to exemplify and reinforce their social inferiority and, at the same time, to reduce the threat they posed to the dominant group. Principal among the forms of ritual and symbolic subordination introduced in this connection were the following: the use of separate changing facilities and separate entrances to the field of play for amateurs and professionals; the housing of professionals at away matches and on tours in separate, usually inferior accommodation; the printing of the professional's initials after his surname on the scorecard and those of the amateur before it; and the subordination of professional players to an amateur captain chosen more on account of his social status than his playing and tactical ability as a cricketer. In addition, professionals were expected, independently of relativities of age and skill, to call amateurs, 'Sir', and, particularly when young, to perform menial duties around the ground. In all these respects, first-class cricket came to reflect the threat of contamination which members of the upper classes felt was posed by close contact with lower-status men when the inferiority of the latter was not clearly expressed in ritual and symbolic terms.

These invidious rituals and distinctions seem to have been accepted by professional cricketers without resistance. That is probably because the career in cricket offered working-class men financial and status advantages coupled with the opportunity to perform work of an enjoyable kind which would not otherwise have been open to them. Of greater significance for present purposes, however, is the fact that the ritual and symbolic subordination of professional cricketers reflected the extent to which status insecurity had increased within the British ruling class by the end of the nineteenth century. Eighteenth-century aristocrats had little need for devices of that kind. Their social status was exceptionally secure and did not need continual bolstering artificially. However, even though, by the end of the nineteenth century, status insecurity had increased within the ruling class, its expression in cricket remained confined to the forms of ritual and symbolic subordination just discussed. It did not lead to significant opposition to professionalism as such or undermine the authority of the MCC. Hence that body was able to remain in control of a unified game which incorporated amateurs and professionals. That was also true of the Football Association. However, in the case of soccer, professionalization began considerably later, at a stage when *embourgeoisement* with its attendant consequences was more advanced. As we shall show, this meant that tensions of a more severe and potentially disruptive character were generated.

3. The professionalization of soccer began in the 1870s and the form taken by the professional game reflected from the outset the changes then occurring in society at large. That is, professional soccer emerged as a type of sports professionalism very different from that based on aristocratic and gentry patronage. It involved, for example, a more complex and impersonal

relationship between employers and employees. It also depended financially, less on the wealth and power of a particular class than on exploiting the commercial opportunities presented by the crowds who flocked to the game in urban centres. It thus involved a diffuse relationship between players and an anonymous mass of paying fans, mediated by those able to gain control of the gate-money from which the players' wages were principally paid. As far as we can tell, consistently with its urban context and the stage of *embourgeoisement* reached, such control was usurped in almost all cases by local businessmen.

There are several parallels between the incipient professionalization of soccer and that of Rugby. In soccer as in Rugby, professionalism first emerged in the North. Moreover, like their Rugby counterparts, Northern soccer teams quickly established playing dominance over their Southern rivals. There were, however, two principal differences in the regional location of the earliest development of professionalism in the two games. Thus, professional soccer started in the Midlands, not only in the North, most notably in the Birmingham region; and in the North, professional soccer began primarily in Lancashire while, as we have seen, it was in Yorkshire that the most significant early developments of professional Rugby occurred.

Of greater significance than these regional differences, however, is the fact that the tensions generated by the incipient professionalization of soccer, even though they were considerable, did not lead to the establishment of separate amateur and professional branches. That was the case, we believe, for two principal reasons: firstly, because of specific social differences between the soccer and Rugby establishments in the period when professionalism became a crisis issue; and secondly, because of the intensification of overt class conflict in British society which occurred in the interval between the eruption of the amateur–professional crises in the two games.

We have already looked at the unfolding of the amateur–professional crisis in Rugby. In order to bring out the social differences between the soccer and Rugby establishments and locate them within a context where they can be meaningfully compared, it is necessary to undertake a brief examination of the way in which soccer's amateur–professional crisis arose. We shall begin by referring to the playing of the game itself, focusing particularly on the early history of the FA Cup. Only later, will we turn to the organizational and value dimensions of the emergent conflict. It is in that context that we shall discuss the social differences between the soccer and Rugby establishments and the different social configurations within which they acted out their parts.

For eleven seasons following its inauguration, Southern teams composed principally of public school old boys enjoyed total supremacy in the FA Cup. The winners and their final opponents in that period were as follows:

1872 Wanderers v Royal Engineers
1873 Wanderers v Oxford University
1874 Oxford University v Royal
    Engineers
1875 Royal Engineers v Old Etonians
1876 Wanderers v Old Etonians

1877 Wanderers v Oxford University
1878 Wanderers v Royal Engineers
1879 Old Etonians v Clapham Rovers
1880 Clapham Rovers v Oxford University
1881 Old Carthusians v Old Etonians
1882 Old Etonians v Blackburn Rovers

The fact that a Northern team, Blackburn Rovers, reached the final in 1882 was symptomatic of an underlying trend: the entry into the competition of growing numbers of Northern and Midlands teams, many composed, solely or partly, of working men. This change in social composition first had a noticeable effect on the balance of playing power in 1878–9 when Darwen, a team from Lancashire, played two draws with Old Etonians in a preliminary round before being beaten. As we have seen, another Lancashire team, Blackburn Rovers, reached the final three seasons later. They were beaten 1–0 by Old Etonians. The Etonians were finalists again in 1883 but Blackburn was evidently a powerful centre of early soccer for, this time, the Etonians were defeated by Blackburn Olympic. The occupations of the winning side give a good idea of the way in which the social composition of the game was changing. They were: three weavers, a spinner, a cotton operative, an iron worker, a picture framer, a master plumber, a dentist's assistant, and two who, it is alleged, were disguised professionals.[6]

The paid players in the Blackburn Olympic side were two of a growing number employed in the North and Midlands from the 1870s onwards. It was principally soccer's crowd-drawing capacity which made this possible. While old boy teams were in the ascendant, comparatively few spectators had been attracted. The crowd at the FA Cup Final failed to exceed 5,000 during the first eight years. But, when teams representing Northern working-class communities became successful, the number of spectators expanded. 12,500 were attracted to the first all-Northern final, played in London at the Kennington Oval between Blackburn Rovers and Queen's Park, Glasgow, in 1884. 27,000 saw the cup-tie between Aston Villa and Preston North End in 1888. The Cup Final of 1893 drew a crowd of 45,000 and 80,000 was the average attendance at the final over the next ten years.[7]

Encouraged by spectator growth, Northern and Midland clubs began to charge for admission. When Aston Villa first adopted the practice in 1876, the takings amounted to 5s. 3d. Thirty years later the same club was able to take £14,329 at a single match.[8] Local businessmen took the lead in this monetization of Association football through the introduction of admission charges and the payment of money to players. It was they who gained control of the gate-receipts from which the wages of players were paid, though of course it is likely that, then as now, they augmented the financial resources available to a club and, hence, their own power in relation to it, by the more or less continuous injection of personal funds. Prominent among the businessmen thus involved in the early control of soccer were: Major Sudell, a Preston mill-owner who founded and ran Preston North End;[9] John

Houlding, a Liverpool businessman who played a central part in the constitution, first of Everton, and later of Liverpool, as professional clubs;[10] and J. H. Davis, a wealthy Manchester businessman who was principally responsible for the formation of Manchester United as a professional side.[11]

Paralleling what happened in Rugby, this development ran counter to the values and interests of the public school élite. Nothing illustrates the changing balance of playing power in soccer more clearly than the fact that, following the appearance of Old Etonians as losing finalists in 1883, no Southern amateur team again reached the FA Cup Final. That trophy remained in the North until 1901 when Tottenham Hotspur became the first Southern *professional* team to win it.[12] Faced with this situation, C. W. Alcock, the FA Secretary, wrote in *The Football Annual* as early as 1881 that: '. . . there is no use to disguise the speedy approach of a time when the subject of professional players will require the earnest attention of those on whom devolves the management of Association football.'[13] A year later, paralleling Budd's remarks discussed in Chapter 7, he commented ruefully on the growing seriousness and professionalization of the game:

> What was . . . the recreation of a few has now become the pursuit of thousands, an athletic exercise carried on under a strict system . . . by an enforced term of training almost magnified into a profession. Whether the introduction of so serious and business-like an element . . . is a healthy one or not, this is not the place to enquire, but there are many . . . who recall with no small satisfaction the days when football had not grown to be so important as to make umpires necessary, and the 'gate' the first subject for conversation.[14]

It was also in 1882 that the FA enacted legislation forbidding payment to players in excess of bona fide expenses and wages lost[15] but it was difficult to enforce and 'illegal' payments continued. A series of sub-committees were, therefore, set up to see if more stringent controls could be devised. A decisive moment came on 19 January 1884, when Preston drew with Upton Park in the fourth round of the Cup. Upton Park lodged a protest, alleging that Preston employed professionals. Such allegations had been made previously but had always been denied and were difficult to prove. Now, for the first time, Major Sudell of Preston openly admitted that his players were paid, claiming that it had become common in the North, essential for any club that wished to succeed. As a result of Sudell's honesty, Preston were disqualified from the Cup for that season and the FA enacted stricter legislation for the control of professionalism and the related practice of 'importing' players, i.e. of recruiting them from districts other than that which a team represented.

In order to assist in implementing the new legislation, the FA circulated a form requiring clubs to furnish information regarding all players on their books whose nationality was not English or who had come from another district. It also demanded information on the past and present occupations of such players, their occupational wages and reasons for their change of residence. This brought matters to a head. Realizing that, if they replied honestly, they would be expelled or debarred from paying players in the future, a number of Northern clubs, mainly from Lancashire, decided to form a separate 'British Football Association'.[16] Like the Northern Rugby Football Union, its principal object was to legitimize the payment of players.

Faced with the prospect of disunion and reduction of their national influence, the FA decided, after an internal struggle, to compromise and legalize professionalism under 'stringent conditions'. These were designed to halt the growing monetization and professionalization of the game and retain it under amateur control. This compromise was first proposed at an FA sub-committee meeting in November 1884 and finally passed at a Special General Meeting in July 1885. Thus, despite the fact that professionalism ran counter to the amateur ethos and the playing interests of the FA establishment, events built up to a legislative end-result directly opposite to that reached in Rugby some ten years later. That was principally because the balance of opinion within the ruling circles of the FA regarding the manner in which professionalism should be tackled was, in certain respects, the reverse of that which came to prevail in the ruling circles of the RFU. Thus, in soccer, it was principally the leading groups in the national association, members of the public school élite from the 'simon-pure' amateur South, who came to favour an accommodative stance, and groups from the North and Midlands, men of lower status from amateur clubs in districts where professionalism had taken firm hold, who argued against compromise. It must be enough if we cite just one or two examples of the opinions voiced on either side in the struggle over professionalism in soccer. Where we have been able to obtain the necessary information, we shall locate the proponents of rival views within the wider social structure by citing their occupational and educational characteristics. We shall deal with the opponents of professionalism first.

J. C. Clegg, a solicitor and representative of the Sheffield Association claimed that 'if professionalism is allowed it will only be placing greater power in the hands of betting men and encourage gambling'.[17] W. F. Beardshaw, also of Sheffield, maintained that 'the legalization of professionalism will tend to lower the game of football'.[18] This was echoed by C. Crump, of Birmingham, by occupation Divisional Chief Clerk at the Locomotive and Carriage Department of the Great Western Railway, who contended that 'the introduction of professionalism will be the ruin of the pastime'.[19] And W. H. Jope, also of Birmingham, argued that it was 'degrading for respectable men to play with professionals'.[20] Thus, opponents of professionalism in soccer raised arguments broadly similar to those of its opponents in Rugby.

Soccer's leading figures in the fight for a conciliatory policy included C. W. Alcock, the Old Harrovian, and Lord Kinnaird and Major Sir Francis Marindin, both Old Etonians. Also included were N. L. Jackson of Cambridge University, E. S. Morley, a doctor, and R. P. Gregson, a photographer.[21] The latter were both Lancastrians. The words of C. W. Alcock must suffice to show the sort of considerations advanced by those in favour of a conciliatory stance.[22] At the FA General Meeting in March 1895, he said:

> I cannot be called a supporter of professionalism, for when I played football it was only played by amateurs, but until professionalism is legalized the deadlock which now exists will continue. I consider that veiled professionalism is the evil to be repressed, and I am sure that it now exists in nearly every football district, 'pure' Birmingham not excepted.
>
> Professionals are a necessity to the growth of the game and I object to the idea that they are the utter outcasts some people represent them to be. Furthermore, I object to the idea that it is immoral to work for a living, and I cannot see why men should not, with that object, labour at football as at cricket.[23]

As we have seen, in soccer the tolerant attitude won the day. How can one explain the differences between Association and Rugby football in this regard, i.e. in the distribution of opinions regarding professionalism and the legislative end-results? As we suggested earlier, the social, especially the educational and related differences between the principal actors in the struggle over professionalism in the two games appear to be of particular significance in this respect. These are set out in Figure 9.1.

If the diagnosis implicit in Figure 9.1 is correct, the social differences between the principal actors in the struggle over professionalism in soccer and Rugby were as follows: (i) the ruling personnel in soccer had tended to attend higher-status public schools than their counterparts in Rugby;[24] and (ii) a proportion of the former had titles. Also significant is the fact that, in those areas where professionalism first gained a foothold, fewer professional soccer than professional Rugby clubs seem to have obtained direct representation in administration at the regional level. This meant that, in soccer, the struggle over professionalism occurred principally at the level of the national Association, whereas in Rugby, the struggle in the national RFU was preceded by a struggle in the Yorkshire and Lancashire Unions. This constellation of differences, it seems to us, can help to account for the different distribution of attitudes and opinions and, therefore, the different legislative outcomes regarding professionalism in the two games. Let us elaborate on this.

The fact that a proportion of the soccer establishment had attended high-status public schools and that some were titled meant that they were, to a considerable extent, recruited from higher reaches of the stratification hier-

	Social Characteristics	
Attitudes	Association Football	Rugby Football
In favour of 'legalized' professionalism	Leading groups in the Football Association. Majority had attended 'established', high-status public schools (A). Some with titles. Majority employed in upper middle-class, mainly professional occupations. Infrequent contact with 'professional' clubs and their members in a playing and social sense.	Leading groups in the Yorkshire and Lancashire Unions. Majority had attended low status, principally non-public schools. None with titles. Majority employed in middle- and lower-middle-class occupations, principally in business and industry. Frequent contact with 'professional' clubs and their members in a playing and social sense. Some served in local Unions as representatives of 'professional' (i.e. 'open' or 'gate-taking' clubs).
opposed to 'legalized' professionalism	Leading groups in local Associations, particularly in areas (Midlands and North) where professionalism had gained a foothold. Majority had attended low-status, principally non-public schools. None with titles. Majority employed in middle- and lower-middle-class occupations, principally in business and industry. Frequent contact with professional clubs and their members in a playing and social sense. Served in local Associations as representatives of amateur clubs.	Leading groups in the Rugby Football Union. Majority had attended newer and, therefore, middle- and lower-status public schools (B). None with titles. Majority employed in upper-middle-class, mainly professional occupations. Infrequent contact with professional clubs and their members in a playing and social sense.

A = schools such as Eton, Harrow, Charterhouse and Westminster.
B = schools such as Rugby, Marlborough and Cheltenham.

Figure 9.1

archy than their counterparts in Rugby. Of course, the numbers of Etonian, Harrovian and aristocratic soccer administrators cited above are only small but it is likely, nevertheless, that their general influence over the Association game, like that over cricket of the aristocratic component in the membership of the MCC, was, by virtue of their social status, greater than their numbers alone would lead one to suspect. That is, they are likely to have been trendsetters in the formation of opinions, followed by others who did not have strong grounds for taking an opposite view. More importantly, they are likely to have been relatively secure in identity and status, and therefore, less likely than their counterparts in the RFU to have perceived the working class as a threat. As a result, they were able to follow an 'open-door' policy and encourage working-class teams to enter the FA Cup. And, although they did not like professionalism, they had no wish to stamp it out or to drive its proponents out of the Association fold. On the contrary, they were confident in their ability to control it, feeling they would be able to guide the development of a combined amateur–professional game in a direction consistent with their own interests.

These social differences, more precisely the different location of the soccer and Rugby establishments within the upper and middle classes and their correspondingly different attitudes towards the working class, thus enable one to construct a plausible explanation of their different attitudes towards professionalization. However, the principal opponents of professionalism in soccer seem to have come from social backgrounds similar to those responsible for its initial development in Rugby. Thus, in this case, social differences *per se* cannot account for the attitudinal differences. One has to search for an explanation of a different kind. It is implicit in the analysis on which Figure 9.1 is based; namely, the assumption that the principal difference between these groups was the fact that the former all served on local Associations as representatives of amateur clubs from districts where professionalism had gained a firm foothold. They were, that is, representatives of clubs which had not grown dependent on gate-money. Such clubs are likely to have suffered directly at the hands of professional sides for they could not have hoped to compete effectively with teams composed of full-time players. They must have been frequently beaten by such sides and the resentment thus generated probably formed the principal source of the hostility of their officials toward professionalism. It can only have been exacerbated by the fact that, prior to 1885, professionalism had been declared illegal by the FA. Midlands and Northern soccer officials thus had good grounds for not following the high status FA leadership in their moderate attitude. Indeed, as often happens in the judgment of metropolitan by provincial élites, they probably found the recommendations of the latter hypocritical.

4. Reference to the constellation of social differences just discussed can provide no more than a partial explanation of the different attitudes and legislative responses of the soccer and Rugby authorities to incipient professionalization. As we suggested earlier, in order to obtain a more complete explanation, it is necessary to probe more deeply into circumstances in British society when these processes began. The first thing to note is the fact that, although the professionalization of both games began at a stage in the overall development of British society when, to define its parameters only

loosely, industrialization and *embourgeoisement* were relatively advanced, soccer became more rapidly established as a popular, more specifically as a spectator sport, than Rugby and hence began to undergo professionalization somewhat earlier.

In fact, there was something like a ten-year lag between the professionalization of the two games. A decade may only be a short time in the development of a society but, in that case, it was enough to bring about a marked change in the overall social climate and, hence, in the social conditions under which the crises in soccer and Rugby occurred. More specifically, the fact that the crisis over the legitimacy of professionalism in soccer came to a head in the middle 1880s, meant that it took place towards the end of the thirty-year period of relatively harmonious class relations referred to in Chapter 6. By contrast, the crisis over professionalism in Rugby erupted in the early 1890s, i.e. at a time when class conflict was mounting owing, on the one hand, to the maturation of the long-term changes taking place in the structure and social composition of the ruling class and, on the other, to the dawning realization by the working class of its latent power. It is to these long-term changes that our attention will now be turned. It is relevant to discuss them in detail since it was they that formed the deep structure which led Rugby to be the only sport in Britain to undergo a total amateur–professional split. We shall examine the changing structure and composition of the ruling class first.

The 1880s mark a crucial stage in the process of *embourgeoisement*, for it was in that decade that the aristocracy and gentry ceased to be the predominant element in the British ruling class. As Hobsbawm has expressed it:

> . . . the foundations of a British society dominated by the landed classes all collapsed together with and during the Great Depression. Landownership ceased, with some exceptions, to be the basis of great wealth and became merely a status symbol.[25]

This is not to imply that Britain was henceforth subject to dominance by a 'pure' bourgeoisie. That would be to oversimplify a complex social process. Rather, the British ruling class continued, as previously, to comprise 'bourgeoisified' aristocrats and gentlemen, and 'aristocratized', 'gentlemanly' bourgeois. Now, however, a stage of industrialization had been reached at which the balance swung more decisively in favour of the latter. In short, even at this stage, *embourgeoisement* remained incomplete. That is, industrialization had still not led to the eclipse of the landed classes. Thus, by increasing their financial dependency on industry and trade, sections of the aristocracy and gentry were able to retain their wealth and, hence, keep a foothold in the ruling class. By 1896, according to Perkin, '167 noblemen, a quarter of the peerage, were directors of companies'.[26] Simultaneously, however, the reverse process was occurring. Thus, just as a growing proportion of the aristocracy was undergoing 'bourgeoisification', so, at the same time, there began to emerge what historians call the 'industrial' or 'business aristocracy'. By the end of the nineteenth century, it was larger and more wealthy than the landowning class.

At the roots of its emergence lay the growth in the size and scale of financial, commercial and industrial enterprise which received its clearest expression in the spread of joint-stock companies. In 1844, excluding railways and other chartered or parliamentary companies, there had been 1,000 registered companies in Britain. By 1887, the number had risen to over 10,000.[27] The 'business aristocracy' comprised, on the one hand, those whose majority holdings enabled them to control the joint-stock companies and, on the other, the owners of family concerns which managed to increase the size and scale of their operations without a corresponding change in the legal form of ownership and control. They were, however, not an 'aristocracy' solely by virtue of their occupancy of commanding positions in the expanding pyramid of corporate wealth but also by virtue of their absorption in various ways into the ranks of the aristocracy proper, a process which took the form, on the one hand, of the creation of new peerages, and, on the other, of intermarriage with the existing aristocracy.

Perkin has identified as the central feature which distinguished the 'business aristocracy' from earlier generations of upwardly mobile entrepreneurs, the fact that they retained their business involvements at a career stage when, previously, these would have been renounced in an attempt to gain acceptance by the aristocracy and gentry.[28] Of course, the purchase of an estate remained an index of entrepreneurial success but improved means of transport and communication now enabled the hitherto more or less exclusive lifestyles of 'estate' and 'office' to be combined. At the same time, the business career began to be socially upgraded, coming to be regarded, even in the eyes of traditional sections of the aristocracy and gentry, as commensurate with 'gentlemanly' status. That was particularly true of the career in 'the city', i.e. in the worlds of banking and high finance, and not to anything like the same extent of the career in industry proper.

The reasons for such a change are not difficult to find. For one thing, finance and industry were now, quite unequivocally, the greatest seats of wealth and power. As such, they offered the greatest opportunities for building a fortune or replenishing an old one. But there were other factors connected with the changing nature of the business career itself. Thus the earliest entrepreneurs participated directly in production or exercised control from an office set just apart from the factory floor. However, as the size and scale of industrial operations grew, the office began to be separated physically and socially from production. Control began to be exercised, correspondingly, through the medium of a bureaucratic chain. In other words, entrepreneurial work came to be involved less directly with production and, as that occurred, the 'taint' of industry began to be removed. It began, in short, to be regarded as work which a 'gentleman' could perform. This was truest of the career in finance because, there, the connection with production was twice-removed. In this way the business career was socially upgraded within the reconstituted ruling class and the career in 'the city' came to be accorded highest status in ruling circles.

For present purposes, the main significance of this transformation lies in the fact that the reconstituted ruling class was one which, more than ever before, engaged in status-exclusive behaviour. As we have seen, *embourgeoisement* had already begun to push the landed classes in that direction. Now, however, the business aristocracy began to engage in similar behaviour. Prominent among the reasons was probably the status insecurity typical of *arrivistes* but this must have been coupled with fear of the increasingly powerful working class. It was as part of this transformation that the landed classes increasingly abandoned their ideals of paternalism and public service, and that the 'grand bourgeoisie' abandoned their values of hard work and asceticism, both in favour of more leisure- and consumption-oriented values.

However, the dominance of the reconstituted ruling class rested on foundations which were, in some respects, insecure. It was internally divided and lacked a consistent ideology. Hence, it experienced difficulty in legitimizing its position in the eyes of society as a whole. Moreover, appearances to the contrary, its members lacked self-confidence. By 1880, according to Perkin, though 'outwardly stable and triumphant and in complete moral and ideological control', they were 'inwardly divided and confused and crumbling in their conviction of moral superiority and their faith in their class ideal'.[29] As a result, they reacted with alarm and hostility to the growth of working-class power. For their part, members of the working class were stung into attacking a society which lacked clearcut legitimizing principles. It is to the growing power of the working class that our attention will now be turned.

5. The power of the industrial working class derived from two principal sources: (i) their concentration in cities and towns; and (ii) the chains of interdependence inherent in an industrial division of labour. The former was a factor largely because it was conducive to recognition of common interests and organization; the latter because it meant that, by organized withdrawal of labour, they could disrupt the intricate processes on which production in industrial societies depends.

At first, the power of the working class was only latent. It began to be transformed into 'real', i.e. organized and effective, power early in the nineteenth century when the 'craft' or 'artisan' unions and movements such as Chartism were formed. The next step came towards the end of the century with the establishment of trades unions by semi-skilled and unskilled workers, and the formation of the Labour Party. The crystallization of this second stage depended on wider developments, in particular on the increasing size and scale of productive establishments. Thus, correlatively with the emergence of the joint-stock company as the dominant form of industrial enterprise, leading firms began to employ hundreds, sometimes upwards of a thousand workers, often in a single factory. At the same time, the mechanization of production reached a stage where unskilled and semi-skilled machine operators, particularly the latter, became the most numerous and fastest-growing section of the labour force. It was they who formed the new unions. Given their work-situation, it is not difficult to see why. Their concentration into large establishments led quickly to the emergence of feelings of solidarity and consciousness of common interests. Probably more decisive, however, was the heavily mechanized and, therefore, repetitive and monotonous character of the work-tasks they performed. It was conducive to uniformity of experience and, hence, to low individualization and that, in turn, meant they had little resistance to taking part in collective action as a means of securing their interests.

The new unions were also formed as a response to the economic conditions of the 'Great Depression' and because, in the eyes of a growing number of working men, the reconstituted ruling class lacked the legitimacy of its predecessor. Other factors played a part as well but, for present purposes, it is sufficient just to note that, as a result of the formation of the new unions, the late 1880s and the 1890s were a period in which working-class militancy grew.[30] There began, accordingly, to occur a change from the relatively harmonistic perception that had characterized class relations between 1850 and 1880 to a more conflictual perception. A perceptual polarization of society took place into 'us' and 'them', the escalation of hostility on one side of the increasingly dichotomously perceived class system leading to a simultaneous escalation of hostility on the other. We shall now spell out in greater detail the way in which this transformation affected the development of sport, contributing, in particular, to the bifurcation of Rugby into 'Union' and 'League'.

6. Writing in 1884, a *Manchester Guardian* correspondent described Alcock's proposal to legalize soccer professionalism as 'the beginning of the end in an important social movement'. As he put it:

> The idea has been to bring together all classes in football and athletics on terms of perfect equality ... The first effect of the change will be to make the Rugby game the aristocratic one, and the Association game will probably almost die out in the South ... where it is already declining ... Again, a fresh excuse will be given for a tendency to exclusiveness which is even now sufficiently apparent. The Universities of Oxford and Cambridge have for some time past picked the clubs with which they deign to compete, and an example of this kind may be widely followed ... Perhaps this disruption was inevitable, and perhaps it may turn out to be slight and unimportant; but the indications of failure in a really great experiment should not pass unnoticed.[31]

Subsequent events proved this diagnosis substantially correct. That is, the late 1880s and the 1890s were a period of growing status-exclusiveness over the whole range of British sports. The 'important social movement', the 'great experiment' referred to by the *Guardian* correspondent, i.e. the attempt, as he put it, 'to bring together all classes in football and athletics on terms of perfect equality', had depended on the relative harmony in class relations which prevailed during the period 1850 to 1880. It had formed just one aspect of the general paternalism of the upper and middle classes in that period. However, the relative class harmony which made it possible rested, as we have seen, on a fragile base. The ongoing processes of industrialization and urbanization were producing fundamental changes in the deep structure of class relations. More specifically, *embourgeoisement* was bringing into being a reconstituted ruling class in which bourgeois elements and bourgeois values—admittedly in a changing form—were increasingly predominant. It remained, however, internally divided and lacked, above all, a coherent legitimizing ideology. Correlatively, the dawning realization by the working class of its latent power and the increase in the frequency and intensity of overt class conflict led the upper and middle classes to feel beleaguered. They came, correspondingly, to view the working class increasingly as a threat. As part of the same overall process, the belligerence of the working class towards those above them increased, with the result that the central precondition for the earlier trend towards class integration in sport—relative harmony in class relations—began to be whittled away.

For a while, members of the different classes or, what was increasingly in upper and middle class usage no more than a different expression for the same thing, amateurs and professionals, continued to play together but, in the social situation of the late 1880s and the 1890s, members of the higher classes grew less able to tolerate sporting defeat at the hands of what they perceived to be inferior and alien groups. Where such defeats did occur, they rationalized them by alleging that the victorious teams were composed, wholly or partly, of professionals. Whether such allegations were based on factual evidence or not, they helped members of the higher classes to cope emotionally and intellectually with the ignominy of defeat at the hands of social inferiors. That is, they helped to assuage the self-doubts to which, as members of a socially insecure ruling class, they were subject as a result of the inconsistency between their self-image as socially superior and their failure in sporting competition against what they perceived to be socially inferior groups. At the same time, such defeats symbolized what they feared most in society at large: political and economic defeat at the hands of the working class. It would be wrong, however, to view this aspect of the problem as merely symbolic. That is, class antagonism spilled over directly into the sports sphere leading, not infrequently, to an escalation of 'real' fighting; i.e. contests between teams representative of different classes ceased to be 'play fights' and became, increasingly, microcosmic enactments of the class war in society at large. There developed, accordingly, a pattern of segregated sports participation in which the different classes and, as a result, amateurs and professionals, were kept strictly apart.

In cricket, as we have seen, such segregation was expressed primarily through forms of ritual and etiquette designed to express the social inferiority of professionals. In soccer, the upper and middle classes began in the 1890s to abandon their old paternalism and withdraw into their own exclusive circles. Thus, deprived of their former dominance in the FA Cup, members of the public school élite used their influence over the FA to secure the institution of a separate competition for amateurs. Called the 'FA Amateur Challenge Cup' it was introduced in 1893. Old Carthusians, earlier winners of the FA Cup, reached the final three times in the first four seasons, winning twice. Soon, however, a further transformation was noticed within the amateur ranks. Clubs such as Tottenham Hotspur, Middlesbrough, Reading and Shrewsbury, all later destined to become members of the Football League, started to become 'nurseries' for professional sides, to make 'illegal' payments and, more importantly, to dominate the amateur cup. Unable to compete, indeed increasingly unwilling to do so, public school old boy teams moved into total isolation, forming their own competition, the 'Arthur Dunn Cup', in 1902. They were also influential in forming in 1907, the separate, 'Amateur Football Association', an organization which remained independent of the FA proper until 1914.[32] An important corollary of the tensions in the soccer world which gave rise to these developments was the fact that more and more public and grammar schools began to renounce Association football and switch to the 'simon-pure' amateurism of the increasingly class-exclusive Rugby game. As a result, soccer which had started out as a game of the most prestigious members of the public school élite, i.e. of Old Etonians and Old Harrovians, began to slip downwards in Britain's status hierarchy of sports and, accordingly, to be regarded by members of the upper and middle classes as inconsistent with the behavioural standards expected of a 'gentleman'. Rugby Union experienced a corresponding elevation. Nevertheless, despite their renunciation of playing contact with working-class teams and even their growing abandonment of soccer, the public school élite managed, for a considerable time, to retain a share in the overall control of the game and, above all, to maintain a nationally unified structure of rules and organization.

It was, as we have said, only in Rugby that it proved impossible to maintain even the semblance of class integration. Only there, that is, did the strains of British society in the late nineteenth century lead to the formation of completely separate organizations for amateurs and professionals, and, ultimately, to the emergence of different games. That, as the foregoing analysis shows, was because members of the Rugby establishment had, for the most part, attended newer and, therefore, relatively low-status public schools. They tended, as a result, to be marginal and relatively insecure in their membership of the public school élite and this made them anxious lest contact of too close or too direct a kind with members of the working class should contaminate their status. Hence, even prior to the 1890s, they were more socially exclusive regarding participation in their game than the establishments in cricket and soccer. They also adhered more rigidly to the amateur ethos and were less tolerant of the aspirations of the working class, whether in the field of sport or elsewhere.

However, even more significant as a determinant of the bifurcation of Rugby into 'Union' and 'League' was the fact that, owing to the ten-year gap between developments in soccer and Rugby, the Rugby establishment had to deal with the issue of professionalism in a period of mounting class conflict when the previously held goal of improving class relations through contact on the sports field had begun to fade from view. The bifurcation of Rugby was thus 'doubly-determined', caused by both the social marginality of the Rugby establishment with their rigid adherence to the amateur ethos and intolerance of the working class, and by the fact that the struggle over amateurism and professionalism in their game reached crisis proportions in a period of growing class tension, and, hence, of growing class segregation in British society. That, to put it in a nutshell, is why the conflict over amateurism and professionalism in Rugby proved irreconcilable and why the schism discussed in Chapter 8 took place.

We realize that this analysis may seem inconsistent with the fact that it was not only the Rugby establishment who were 'middle-class' but also the officials of the 'gate-taking' clubs and many Northern representatives on the RFU, i.e. the groups with whom the Rugby establishment were principally and most directly in conflict. Two sets of questions are raised by this apparent inconsistency. The first relates to the different attitudes towards professional Rugby held by people who ostensibly shared a common middle-class position. The second concerns the differential tolerance of middle-class groups towards the working class and what one might call their 'differential immunity' to the class tensions of British society in the late nineteenth century.

The answer to both sets of questions is implicit in our analysis so far, above all in our abandonment of the naïve concept of the middle class as an undifferentiated, internally homogeneous whole and in the fact that we have tried, accordingly, to take account of the regional, occupational, educational and other sources of difference within its ranks. Thus we have shown that the Rugby establishment were, for the most part, employed in professional occupations and that most had attended public schools. They were, that is, occupationally removed from industry and direct contact with members of the working class. Moreover, by virtue of their public school education, they had been integrated, albeit in a marginal capacity, into the national ruling élite.

By contrast, the officials and representatives of the Northern 'gate-taking' clubs were, as we have seen, mainly members of the business and industrial middle class. Few of them, as far as we have been able to ascertain, had attended public schools. That is, they were members of *local* élites, not yet integrated into the national ruling class. They were familiar with the sports ethos of the public school élite but had not been directly socialized into it. In fact, their values approximated more closely to those of a 'pure' bourgeoisie than was the case with the public school élite, i.e. they were more openly and unambiguously achievement-oriented and acquisitive and tended to place a money value on social relations and personal attributes of all kinds. As a result, they had few qualms about stimulating competition in Rugby through the introduction of cups and leagues or about charging for admission to matches and making money payments to players.

At the same time, the work and community situations in which they found themselves brought them into close and frequent contact with members of the working class. As a result, they experienced little need to distance themselves from the latter. Such a need would only have been felt had they sought integration into the public school élite but, as we suggested, the typical mode of social ascent in nineteenth-century Britain involved two stages. A man made money and then sought to increase his 'social honour' by sending his sons to public school and seeking access to the circles of those at the top of the national hierarchy. However, there was an intervening stage while he was still amassing a fortune and before he was ready to attempt to gain acceptance by the established élite. During this stage, he continued to retain his local identifications and connections with his class of origin. As we have shown, it is likely that the officials and representatives of the gate-taking clubs stood at this intervening stage of social ascent. They remained, that is, closely involved with the 'realities' of industrial life.

Hobsbawm has shown that the 1890s, correlatively with the general increase in the frequency and intensity of overt class conflict, were a decade of 'militant labour-baiting' and 'labour-smashing' by the British upper and middle classes. He suggests that attitudes and actions of that kind were commonest among 'businessmen [with] no experience of the realities of industrial life—stockbrokers, bankers and their like . . .'.[33] It is not unreasonable to suppose that members of the Rugby establishment were similar in this respect and that it was this which conditioned their attitude towards the working class and professionalism in sport. That is, the attitudes and policies which led to their intransigence towards the proposals put forward by the Northern gate-taking clubs were a sporting counterpart of the 'labour-baiting' of their colleagues in banking and finance.

Part III

The Development of Rugby Football as a Modern Sport

10 The professionalization of Rugby League

1. The men who ran the Northern Union[1] in the period immediately following the split were mainly members of the business and industrial middle classes. They were of broadly similar socio-economic status to the members of the RFU establishment but, as we have seen, there was a significant difference between these groups: the former had not, for the most part, attended public schools. This meant they were not integrated into the national ruling élite and hence retained their local ties and identifications. It also meant that, even though they claimed allegiance to the amateur ethos, they had not been socialized into its tenets directly and from an early age. As a result, their commitment to it was relatively weak.

Their commitment to amateurism was further weakened by their general values. In conformity with their overall social situation, these approximated more closely to the values of an 'ideal type' bourgeoisie than was the case with the public school élite. That is, they were more openly achievement-oriented and acquisitive, and showed a greater tendency to place money value on social relations and personal attributes of various kinds. As a result, they had few qualms about stimulating competitive Rugby through the introduction of cups and leagues. They also saw little wrong in monetizing the game, at least in the limited sense of charging for admission to matches and reimbursing players for wages lost. It was this combination of structural and value attributes which led them into conflict with the RFU. It would be wrong, nevertheless, to suggest that they were not genuinely committed to amateur principles. Their commitment may have been relatively weak in the sense that they did not appreciate the finer points preached by the public school élite but it was genuine enough. They were, however, pulled in opposite directions by national and local pressures and this led to considerable ambivalence on their part. This requires elaboration.

Prior to the 'split', the rulers of the future Northern Union were subject to pressure from the Rugby Union establishment to maintain an amateur game in the areas under their jurisdiction. Such pressure to conform with the currently dominant sporting ethos was brought to bear most strongly and directly on those who served as representatives on the RFU, for it was principally in that context that middle-class, non-public school Rugby men from

Yorkshire and Lancashire came into close contact with men who epitomized amateur values. They bowed to such pressure largely because amateurism was the ruling ethos in sport at that time, i.e. because no counter, 'professional' ethos had been articulated to serve as a basis from which to question the prevailing ideology. They also yielded on account of the prestige which the Rugby establishment enjoyed as members of the public school élite.

But local pressure simultaneously pushed the rulers of the Northern Union in the contrary direction, i.e. into deviance from amateurism in its pristine form. Principal among the sources of such pressure was the fact that, in the North, Rugby had begun to emerge as a major focus of community rivalry. This meant that club officials were subject to strong communal pressure to produce successful sides. The degree of competitiveness thus engendered was enhanced when they broke with the RFU because their commitment to the principle of compensation for 'broken-time' increased the dependency of clubs on money 'taken at the gate'.

Competitive pressure of that kind pervaded all levels of Rugby in the North and was soon transferred to administrators of the county game, many of whom, in any case, were representatives of gate-taking clubs. They claimed, in all honesty, that their sole aim in setting up the breakaway Union was to secure the legitimacy of recompensing players for 'broken time'. Such a policy, they maintained, far from destroying amateur Rugby, would strengthen it and nip incipient professionalism in the bud. They showed their sincerity by immediately enacting legislation requiring players to have full-time employment outside the game. But the local pressures to which they had been subject prior to the split were strengthened once they had broken from the national body. Whilst in membership of the RFU, they had enjoyed a degree of insulation because, in that situation, their weak commitment to the amateur ethos was reinforced by the strong commitment of the Union establishment. They could also claim that any proposal for change which smacked too strongly of professionalism ran counter to national policy. But once they had branched out on their own, they no longer had membership of the national union to act as a buffer and were thrown on the mercy of local pressures. As we shall show, their weak commitment to amateurism did not provide them with the will to offer strong resistance and they quickly succumbed. The result was that, by 1904, less than a decade after the break with Rugby Union, Rugby League had emerged as a fully professional sport.

It is this whittling away of the weak amateur commitment of the Northern Union authorities, which forms the first subject of the present chapter. As we shall show, in the competitive situation then emerging, the power of the players to demand payment in excess of broken-time compensation was enhanced and it was this which formed the main immediate stimulus for professionalization. It is important, however, to note that the form of professionalism which emerged was typically British in that it involved the subordination both of professional to amateur personnel and of professional to amateur conceptions of sport. That is, it did not emerge principally as a medium for financial speculation but was used by its promoters mainly as a means of social control.

It is this issue, that of the motives which led members of the Northern business and industrial middle classes to become involved in the promotion and running of Rugby clubs, which forms the second main subject of this chapter. As we shall show, their interest in the game as a vehicle of social control led them to promote it as a form of mass entertainment and it was in that connection that they introduced changes which led Rugby League to emerge as a distinctive game. Our analysis of this issue diverges from that of at least one authority on the subject, an anonymous author writing under the pseudonym, 'Tawd Vale',[2] who has suggested that Rugby League developed a different form because it was forged by the industrial workers of the North and came to incorporate their basic values. As such, he contends, it reflected the 'working class separateness' which emerged in the North of England in the late nineteenth century. Our analysis suggests, on the contrary, that Rugby League acquired a distinctive form because it was forged *for* Northern industrial workers by members of the middle classes with essentially middle-class interests in mind. That is, it reflected in its development the pattern of asymmetrical interdependence between the middle and working classes in the North of England, the fact that they were locked in a system of relationships which made them dependent upon one another but which involved, simultaneously, the concentration of power chances in the hands of the former, leading to a conflict of interests between them. This is a complex issue. In order to make our analysis clear, we shall present it in the form of a test of 'Tawd Vale's' hypothesis, concluding with a comparative examination of the development of Rugby in Wales. However, our first task is to examine the professionalization of Northern Union football and it is to that subject that our attention will now be turned.

2. We hinted earlier that the development of Rugby League after the split was, in one respect, typical of the general pattern of development of British professional sport. That is, it became a type of professionalism characterized by subordination, on the one hand, of professional personnel to amateur control and, on the other, of commercial and professional values to amateur conceptions of sport. The generality of this pattern can be illustrated by reference to soccer. It is arguably the most commercialized and professionalized of British sports yet, as late as 1935, Sir Frederick Wall, FA Secretary from 1895 to 1934, could write that 'the radical law in every sport, for its own good, is that the professional in status is subordinated to the amateur'.[3] Geoffrey Nicholson attributes such a structure to the 'puritanism' of the British. 'We are affronted', he suggests, 'by the idea of paying money for playing games and this accounts for the fact that our professional sportsmen are employed, not by "impresarios" but by "non-profit-making clubs which local business and professional men, and the occasional rich patron, run as a hobby.'[4]

It is an oversimplification to attribute the relative non-commercialism of British sport simply to our puritan heritage. As we have seen, the emergence of such a structure was centrally connected with the part played by public school amateurs in the establishment of Britain's sporting institutions and values. The fact that amateur personnel have retained a degree of influence in the determination of national affairs and that amateur conceptions continue to be influential, is testimony to the persistence of the public school heritage. So deep and lasting is its influence, that it permeates all levels and areas of sport. No class has been able to escape its effects, even when its own interests and values have clashed with those of the public school élite.

The development of Rugby League is no exception. Even though the men who led the breakaway Union were not public school amateurs themselves, they were middle-class and, despite the communal pressures that were forcing the game in the areas under their jurisdiction to change, they clung, albeit in a weakened form, to amateur conceptions of sport. As we have seen, they were initially determined to allow only payments for broken time. Indeed, the main reason for the break with the RFU was their belief that the trend towards payment could best be controlled if brought into the open. This emerges from an article published in a Yorkshire newspaper in 1896 in which the author suggested that the Northern revolt had been precipitated by the Rugby Union establishment's ignorance of the social conditions under which the game in the North was played. What, he asked, was the basis of the Northern Union? Was it a professional organization run for professional purposes? Was the amateur principle extinct within its limits? No, he maintained. He continued:

> The Northern Union is governed by amateurs who regard what others call professionalism as inevitable, and so, taking time by the forelock, they are prepared to do in football, just as has been done in cricket— legislate for the amateur and professional together, and preserve the purity of the game by retaining its control in amateur hands . . . and it is to the Northern Union, consequently, the public in the North are indebted that football does not follow in the wake of those other sports which have deteriorated under professional control.[5]

However, another correspondent suggested that the authorities were deluded in their belief that they could halt the gathering momentum of professionalism. As a purely local body, he suggested, the NU lacked the compelling authority of a national association and, hence, the insulation from local pressures they had formerly enjoyed. He singled out as critical in this respect pressure from players, in particular doubting whether Welshmen would be prepared to uproot themselves from their 'native soil' if all they got in return was compensation for 'broken time':

It is possible that some members of the Yorkshire clubs now seriously think that the professionalism on which they are about to enter is a . . . harmless thing, which they can limit with ease. But it must not be forgotten that their authority will be essentially a local thing. They will prevent, by means of a cast-iron transfer law, any 'poaching' among themselves. They will form, as it were, a 'preserved' circle. But the clubs will be free to roam in search of players far and near. These players put a value upon their services, and will naturally sell their skill to the highest bidder. Does anyone imagine that a man is coming, say from Wales, to Lancashire or Yorkshire for a miserable 6s. a day for time broken when playing football? It may be said that a club that's engaging men on terms enlarged beyond the standard of 'broken-time' remuneration will run the danger of suspension from the Committee of the new Union. The idea is excruciatingly funny. Fancy the Committee of the Northern Rugby League gravely conducting an enquiry into a charge of professionalism. It would be a monumental example of Satan rebuking Sin.[6]

This suggests that 'player pressure' for a level of remuneration beyond broken-time compensation was one of the principal sources of the trend towards outright professionalism in Rugby League. It was, apparently, strongest from players recruited from Wales and other distant parts of the country. It seems that, realizing their worth as crowd-pullers, players began to ask for more than the small payments officially permitted under Northern Union rules. This was resisted by officials of the smaller clubs on the grounds that it would drive their organizations out of existence. However, the power of players to secure their financial demands was enhanced by the fact that the majority of club officials, especially those from the larger, more prosperous clubs, were unwilling to limit payment in the manner officially decreed. It was, after all, they who had to deal with player pressure in a direct sense. Moreover, they had to do so in a competitive situation. That is, in order to maximize the chances of securing victory on the community's behalf, they had to compete with one another for the services of players. A successful team was vital for the maintenance of gates but, conversely, gate receipts were a necessary precondition for securing a successful team. In short, clubs were caught in a vicious circle: they needed good players in order to maintain gates but, at the same time, good gates in order to have the wherewithal to hire the best players. And in such a situation, good players, especially those recruited from far afield, were able to name a price for their services in excess of what they could have earned had they stayed at home.

It was, however, not simply the competitive situation in the game itself which enhanced the power and material life-chances of Northern Union players. The whole social configuration in the North tended to increase their power. As we have seen, the competitiveness in the game had arisen partly as a consequence of intense community rivalry and partly as a consequence of the growing involvement of sections of the working class. In such a situation, as representatives of local communities in a socially valued activity, players had adulation heaped upon them. And, as we have repeatedly stressed, Yorkshire and Lancashire were counties in which bourgeois attitudes to the monetization of social relations were coming to prevail. As a result, a growing number of club officials saw little wrong in offering financial inducements. But just as, in these and other ways, the social configuration in the North increased the power of the players to secure their material objectives, so, simultaneously, it reduced the power of the authorities to maintain an amateur game in which payment was limited to compensation for broken time.

In 1898, only three years after the break with the RFU, the Northern Union was forced to bow to these compelling pressures. A policy was adopted which made professionalism, or at least the abandonment of any attempt to restrict the payment of players, a fundamental part of the Northern Union game. This policy was expressed in the form of a four-point charter which decreed that professionalism in this sense should be openly adopted; that players should be properly registered; that they should have full-time employment in a 'legitimate' occupation outside football; and that severe penalties should be imposed for any breach of the professionalism regulations.[7] The third point merits intensive discussion. An analysis of its implementation will enable us to throw light on the way in which Rugby League was used by the Northern business and industrial middle classes as an instrument of social control.

3. The rule concerning full-time employment in a 'legitimate' occupation was not introduced in 1898 but dated from the inception of the Northern Union in 1895. It was designed to prevent players becoming financially dependent on the game and was introduced as a corollary of the initial determination of the authorities to allow broken-time payments but to halt the trend towards professionalism at that point. To that end, unemployed men were not to be allowed to take part in matches organized under NU auspices. However, that necessitated interference with and an attempt to control the working life of players and was inconsistent with the emergence in the wider society of greater freedom for the working class to determine whether and in what capacity they should work. As a result, it was not long before it began to cause irritation. As early as 1896, for example, an irate letter appeared in *The Yorkshire Post*:

> [T]ake the case of Franks, the Hull half-back . . . Franks, three weeks ago, played against Liversedge on the Monday at Liversedge, worked on the Tuesday, went to Cardiff by special permission of his employer on Tuesday night, stayed there on Wednesday, arriving back in Hull on Thursday morning at five o'clock, and went to work at six, worked all

day Thursday, Friday and up to noon Saturday and the Hull Football Club were summoned to explain why Franks had wilfully neglected his work.

Of course, they could not find a case against the player, but told him the next time he takes a day off he must report the matter to them, and apply for special permission . . . before he can play again. Isn't it carrying the game a little too far? . . .

Is it reasonable to suppose that, should a player want a day's holiday, he will apply for special permission to do so? Decidedly not. The sequel is—if found out—player suspended, club relieved of, well, anything from £50 to £1,000. The fact of the matter is this working clause, as at present interpreted, is neither workable, just, nor reasonable, and will only live until the next general meeting . . . Then clear the way for professionalism pure and unadulterated, with no employment clause to worry people's brains, no Emergency Committee to summon a club or player to travel about 200 miles at a moment's notice, to explain why so-and-so went 'rabbiting' on such a day, and why he didn't ask their permission. No, let us give a man the chance to make money while his football 'life' lasts. Let us remove these silly notions that because a man becomes a professional he is going headlong to the bad, and becomes a 'pub-moucher' . . . He is all the better for work during the week, but let it be optional . . . so long as he keeps himself in good condition and gives satisfaction to his employers, or if you like it better, his club.[8]

The idea that men should be allowed to earn money from Rugby and that, as long as they kept fit and strove to the utmost on the field of play, a club had no right to interfere with their non-football life, was in keeping with grass-roots opinion in the North at that time. The fact that the Northern Union retained its employment rule in 1898 when it abandoned the attempt to allow nothing more than 'broken-time' payments is an index of the determination of the middle-class men who ran it, not only to check the gathering trend towards professionalism, but also to keep it within the bounds of 'respectability'. In that, they reveal their interest in the game as a medium of social control. As the above letter shows, they were anxious to avoid the charge of encouraging 'idleness' and, worse than that, of promoting 'evils' such as gambling and 'excessive' drinking amongst the working class. To that end, players were required, not only to have regular employment but forbidden to take up 'disreputable' jobs such as 'bookie's runner' and 'public house waiter'. We have been unable to obtain data on the number and rate of 'prosecutions' for breaches of this rule but a few examples will illustrate the manner and consequences of its implementation. One player, Booth of Radcliffe, had his registration suspended when it was found he worked in a public house. Another, Fitzgerald, the Batley centre, was suspended for nearly two seasons for failing to find full-time employment.[9] Such was the strictness with which this regulation was interpreted, that a player could be suspended for failing to notify the NU that he had changed his job. That was the fate of H. Sinclair of Hull Kingston Rovers in 1899 when a fortnight elapsed before the club submitted notification of his change of employment. A similar fate befell R. Petrie of Seaton FC, whose case was investigated by the 'Cumberland Professional Committee' in 1903. He was employed as a blacksmith's striker by the London and North Western Railway Company at Workington and had previously played as a professional for Workington and Oldham. However, at the time of the alleged offence he was playing as an amateur for this small Cumberland club. If his story was correct, he was suspended for not notifying his club secretary that he had been sent home from work on the afternoon of 26 January. Alternatively, if the story believed by the Cumberland Professional Committee was correct, his 'offence' lay in not reporting the fact that he did not go to work until that afternoon.[10] But in neither case did his action have anything materially to do with his performance as a player. It followed solely from his failure to comply with the paternalistic employment regulations of the Northern Union and these are indicative of the determination of the authorities to do their utmost, in the face of the inexorable grassroots pressure for professionalism, to keep the game 'respectable' by ensuring that it did not form a means whereby a prestigious and socially visible section of the working class could languish in 'idleness' and 'corruption'.

The middle-class men who ran the Northern Union were thus engaged in an exercise in social control. Their personal interest in the game was probably high but, to recognize that, is not to gainsay the fact that, politically and socially, the growing popularity of Rugby was a godsend to them. Working men found the game meaningful and exciting, and the middle class were quick to realize that, by promoting it as a spectacle, they could compensate for an onerous, relatively impoverished life. In that way, the game could serve as a means of decreasing working-class dissatisfaction and of channelling their energies away from socially disruptive activities, e.g. of a political or criminal kind, into work and what, from a middle-class standpoint, was a socially harmless pursuit. But the grassroots pressure which had forced the NU authorities to employ working men as professional players gave rise to a dilemma: namely, the possibility that they would create a class of 'idlers', of men whose 'working' hours were short and who had at their disposal ample spare time and ample cash. Since such men were prestigious among the working class, they could easily have come to act as models with deleterious effects on work and social standards. Therefore, in order that Rugby League could properly perform its function as an agency of social control, its principal practitioners, the players, had themselves to be strictly controlled, i.e. made to have employment outside as well as inside the game. In that way, their prestige could be mobilized on behalf of the promotion of norms of 'hard work', 'sobriety', 'respectability' and 'stability'.

The employment rule survived until 1904. By that time, it had become clear that the anomalies which it gave rise to were a permanent consequence of the incompatibility between existing NU legislation and the syndrome of professionalism and 'player power' which was emerging at grassroots level. However, even after that date, most Rugby League professionals continued to follow another trade. Unlike the majority of professional soccer players, they do so to this day. That is because Rugby League never developed an economic base which would have enabled it to support a large body of full-time players solely dependent on Rugby for their livelihood. It follows that the fear of the NU authorities that abolition of the employment rule would create a class of 'idlers' was groundless. Indeed, it is possible that a dawning realization that, given the limited economic base of the game, such a regulation was redundant, may have formed one of the reasons why they swallowed their pride and, in 1904, gave way to the growing clamour and abolished it. But whether that was so or not, control of players' 'extra-Rugby' employment by explicit regulation gave way in that year to a more subtle form of control by 'economic forces'.

4. The abolition in 1898 of the official restriction on the amounts of money which could be paid to players and, in 1904, of the employment rule, marked the emergence of Rugby League in its modern organizational form. That is, only nine years after the split with Rugby Union, Rugby League had become organizationally what it is today, a professional sport, mainly dependent financially on money taken 'at the gate'. By 1906, it had also evolved the game-pattern which distinguishes it from Rugby Union. It is to this aspect of its development that our attention will now be turned. Our first task is to describe the step-by-step accretion of changes by which this process occurred.

The first two seasons of Rugby League were played under Rugby Union rules. However, changes soon became necessary in order to make it more consistent with the performance of its function as an agency of social control. In 1897, for example, it was decided that kicked goals would henceforward score only two points. In Rugby Union at that time, a 'dropped' goal counted for four points, a penalty for three, and the conversion of a try for two. The Rugby Union 'line-out' was also abolished to make way for a 'kick-in' or 'punt-out' from touch. And in addition, the scrum-half or 'half-back' as he was then called, who had previously been allowed to harry his opposite number, was required to retire behind the scrummage or risk a penalty. The 1897–8 season was played under these rules.[11] Then in 1899, it was decided that the Rugby Union 'play-the-ball' rule—which stated that when a man was tackled he had to put the ball down and play it with his feet—should give way for one which read that: 'if man and ball be fairly held the referee awards a scrum. If the ball is not held, the tackled man can pass or drop it at his feet, provided the ball is not dropped in a forward direction.' Such a rule was thought to be necessary because the previous one had led to contentious and 'scrappy' play.[12] During the 1899–1900 season, the 'punt-out' from touch came under fire on the grounds that it led to 'untidy charging and barging', while the Rugby Union 'knock-on' rule was criticized for being too harsh in penalizing a player for merely juggling with the ball before catching it. Both rules were amended in 1901. The punt into play was only retained when the ball had been kicked into touch. When it had been carried, a scrummage was awarded. It was also decided that a player should be allowed to make two or more attempts at a 'clean catch' and, in addition, that there was to be no 'knock-on' if a member of the opposing side caught the ball before it touched the ground. A further amendment was made in 1902 when the 'punt-out' was abolished and replaced by a ten-yard scrummage, thus indicating that the earlier compromise had not had the desired effect.

In 1904, clubs were ordered to take steps to prevent players packing down with more than three men in the front row, a change designed to stop barging and 'wheeling', i.e. changing the direction of the scrum. At the same time, the 'knock-on' rule was further amended to allow the opposing side to gain possession, even if the ball had first touched the ground. And in 1906, the number of players in a side was reduced to thirteen.[13] Agitation for this change had started prior to the break with Rugby Union and was renewed in 1903 when the cup final between Halifax and Salford was generally agreed to have been dull. This was attributed by the 'reformers' to the fact that fifteen players a side was too many with the result that 'mauling, scrambling and destructive' games were frequent.[14] It was the forwards who were held to have developed a 'destructive' game and when, in 1906, the thirteen-a-side rule was introduced, two of them were removed. With this change, the game-pattern of Rugby League had, in all major respects, acquired its modern form.

As we suggested earlier, an explanation of the emergence of Rugby League as a distinctive game was put forward in 1969 by an author writing under the pseudonym, 'Tawd Vale'. Basically, he argues, Rugby League evolved its specific form as a result of the growing 'political power', 'freedom' and 'separateness' of the late-nineteenth-century Northern working class. In the more industrialized regions of Yorkshire and Lancashire, he suggests, class conflict was at its most intense. And when the opportunity arose for working men to organize leisure activities independently of their social superiors, the tendency towards 'separateness' was given clear expression. Rugby appealed to them because its hard physical contact was consonant with the tough life they were accustomed to at work.

This hypothesis coincides, in some respects, with our own. We think, however, that it exaggerates the autonomy achieved by the Northern working class. Their power certainly increased in the 1890s and played a part, indirectly and unintentionally, in producing the split between Union and League but its direct effects were confined mainly to the industrial and political spheres. On the face of it, Northern working men may seem to have enjoyed greater autonomy in their leisure but we are not aware of any evidence which shows that they set out, in conjunction with what 'Tawd

Vale' calls their 'separateness', to develop a 'counter-culture'. Indeed, the currently available data suggest that, on the contrary, all the major changes which led Northern Union football to develop into Rugby League were initiated by middle-class legislators as part of an attempt to increase the game's entertainment value for working-class spectators. That is, such changes were introduced in connection with its function as a vehicle of social control. Members of the working class other than those registered as players were, for the most part, passive recipients of the changes made. Or rather, they participated in this process only indirectly and anonymously in their role as terrace fans. That this was so will emerge from a closer examination of 'Tawd Vale's' hypothesis.

We shall approach this task in two ways. First, we shall look at evidence concerning the motives of the Northern Union legislators in introducing the changes which led Rugby League to develop as a separate game: this will enable us to show that it was not the 'separateness' of the Northern working class but the political needs of their middle-class 'superiors' which led to this development. And second, we shall undertake a comparative analysis of the development of Rugby in Wales. This will enable us to probe 'Tawd Vale's' hypothesis more critically and deeply because the industrial base of the principality is similar to that of the North of England and certainly no less conducive to class conflict. Moreover, the Welsh working class, because, for example, of the English cultural orientation of its upper and middle classes, did develop 'separateness' to a considerable degree. Under such conditions, there developed a greater degree of working-class participation in and, more crucially, control over Rugby than in the North. Therefore, if 'Tawd Vale' was right, Rugby in the principality should have undergone 'separate development', too. However, it did not and that, coupled with the fact that the Welsh have resisted attempts to transplant Rugby League, shows that, in the exaggerated form in which he presents it, 'Tawd Vale's' hypothesis is false. We shall return to this issue in a moment. Our first task is to examine the evidence concerning the intentions of Northern Union legislators in introducing changes which led Rugby League to evolve its separate form.

5. The motives of the middle-class men involved in the formation and running of the Northern Union and its constituent clubs were undoubtedly comprised, in part, of a mixture of local patriotism and simple love of the game. In part, however, their motives derived from the fact that they were engaged in an exercise in social control. They may have lived in a part of the country where barriers to class interaction were relatively low but it remained the case that their interests were threatened by the growing power and militancy of the working class. As a result, they came to believe that their interests could be protected by the promotion of forms of mass entertainment which would divert the attention of the 'lower orders' from an exploitative socio-economic structure and which could serve, simultaneously, as a

means of inculcating and reinforcing standards of 'hard work', 'sobriety', 'cooperativeness' and 'thrift'.

Rugby was exciting as a spectacle and required diligence, application and team-work for success. Therefore, it fitted the bill in both respects. It had showed its spectator appeal prior to the split with Rugby Union. However, the establishment of a Northern Union committed, at first, to broken-time compensation and, from 1898 onwards, to the payment of wages restricted only by the game's economics, meant that the dependency of clubs on paying spectators grew. This meant that the interests of spectators—or, rather, what the Northern Union authorities perceived their interests to be—increased in importance as a determinant of the game.

We saw earlier how the form of Rugby inherited from the RFU was a closed, discontinuous and relatively static game. Evidence that the Northern Union authorities believed that the game in that form would not enable them to increase spectator support comes, in the first instance, from critics of the changes introduced. Thus Almond complained as early as 1893 that the dependency of the Northern clubs on gates was leading them to ruin the game by making it too fast.[15] He made a similar complaint in 1896, this time directed towards the proposal for one of the rule-changes with which we are presently concerned:

> [You cannot] find a stronger proof of the prevalent tendency to care more about what pleases spectators than what interests players than the proposal of some Northern clubs to reduce the number of the latter. Such a proposal strikes at . . . the main purpose for which games are played . . . Let all who have this purpose at heart . . . make Rugby football as interesting as possible to all players . . ., and let them treat the preferences of spectators as a very unimportant matter.[16]

But for Rugby League to survive as a professional sport, it had to attract spectators. Without them, it would have been unable to pay the wages of players or perform its function as an instrument of social control. Of course, the simple *presence* of spectators does not require the introduction of changes in a game. Middle-class Rugby Union spectators in the late nineteenth century evidently found the game entertaining enough in its existing form. As we have seen, they could derive considerable enjoyment from 'timing the prolonged equipoise of a well-balanced scrummage'. But Rugby Union was not *dependent* on spectators. Playing before an audience may have heightened the game's appeal to some players but it was organized with *them* and *not* spectators in mind. The opposite was true with Rugby League. Moreover, the spectator-orientation of the latter was reinforced by the fact that, once organized on a professional basis, it had to compete with soccer for spectator support. As a result, the authorities were forced to introduce changes in order to try to increase the game's spectator appeal. However, this argument requires elaboration, especially since it may seem inconsistent with the fact that Northern Rugby had been able to attract large gates prior to the split.

The experience of Rugby in Lancashire and Yorkshire in the period before the split shows that it is possible for a static, closed and discontinuous game to attract spectators if its teams represent social units with which the spectators identify and if it forms a means for expressing values central to the social units concerned. But such a game will tend to lose support in competition with another which is more open, continuous and exciting if teams in the latter represent equally meaningful social units and if it symbolizes the same values. That was the case with soccer in the late nineteenth and early twentieth centuries. Taylor has suggested that early professional soccer 'was associated with a set of autonomously working class values, values born of struggles and isolation, victories and defeats'. The most important of these values, he contends, 'were those of *masculinity, active participation* and *victory*'.[17] We shall question later whether it is correct to characterize these values as *autonomously* working-class but there is no doubt concerning their applicability to the Northern working class in the period with which we are concerned. Soccer had come by that time to emphasize movement, speed, continuity and passing, and the result was an open and 'dynamic' game which was a serious threat to Rugby's spectator support. That is why the Northern Union authorities saw it as desirable to make their own game more open and exciting, for only in that way could they hope to compete effectively with soccer.

The urgency of their task was increased by the fact that Northern Union clubs had, to some extent, to rebuild their support after the split with Rugby Union. That was necessary for two main reasons: firstly because they lost some of the middle-class support they had previously enjoyed; and secondly, and perhaps less obviously, because their working-class support, e.g. that of 'deferential' workers who remained loyal to the pristine amateur ethos, declined as well. The critical nature of the situation faced by the Northern Union will emerge from a discussion of its early financial difficulties, of its official diagnosis of the situation and of the sort of measures believed by its authorities necessary to effect a cure.

In their first year, the Northern Union and its member clubs were conspicuously unsuccessful in a financial sense. Indeed, the limited data available at present suggest that, without remedial action, it would have been impossible for them to maintain even a limited professional structure. As a correspondent in the *Yorkshire Daily Post* pointed out:

> There is no use blinking facts . . . the game has dwindled in popularity in the very quarters where . . . it should be most expected to succeed. There are exceptions . . . but of the forty-two clubs . . . the successful exceptions can be numbered on the fingers of one hand . . . the clubs forming the Yorkshire section of the Northern Union are those which have hitherto drawn the greatest 'gates'. Under the new system it was expected

these gates would not only be maintained but increased, and one is justified in thinking that the novelty of a new régime would command success in the first year whatever happened afterwards. But they have neither been maintained nor increased in the great majority of cases and it is only by the exercise of rigid economy—and I am afraid by making men play for less money than they got before—that some of the clubs have been kept on their legs at all . . .[18]

Several clubs were brought to the verge of bankruptcy in the first year. Bradford was one of the main sufferers and, in 1896, a circular was issued by the management drawing attention to its plight. The club's liabilities were set forth at £10,300, made up as follows: £4,500, £2,000 of which was due in February 1897, was owed on the purchase of the ground; an overdraft of £4,000 had been taken with the club's bankers; and the remaining £1,800 was owed for the construction of roads and extensions agreed to when the ground was purchased.[19] The circular did not blame the Northern Union for the club's misfortunes but it was pointed out in local newspapers at the time that, when Bradford had been a member of the RFU, it had made a yearly profit of between £1,000 and £2,000. One such report concluded:

> . . . there does not seem to be the remotest prospect of the club meeting its liabilities out of quasi-professional football, indeed . . . the season just about to close has proved more disappointing than the most determined anti-Unionist could have predicted. Even Manningham, who hold now front position . . . and have doubtless taken away a considerable share of Bradford's support, have not received that financial benefit which their success would lead one to expect . . .[20]

Faced with such a situation, some of the men who ran Northern Union clubs showed that they were more interested in profit and/or social control than the game itself by hiring out their grounds to Association clubs. Others tried to capitalize on their major asset by running soccer as well as Northern Union sides. However, according to a Yorkshire journalist, such practices merely served to exacerbate their difficulties and to increase the threat from the rival game:

> [They] show they have no confidence in their new Union by establishing the rival game on their own ground; in other words they seek to repair their Rugby weakness by killing it by the Association code. When clubs in the Northern Union find Bradford, Halifax and other teams not taking 2,000 and 3,000 spectators to see their away engagements, they wonder where the public have gone to. They read of Association games played on the club's own ground with gates of 2,000 and 3,000. Need they wonder where the missing public are? They are at home enjoying a rival code.[21]

This recognition of the rivalry between Rugby League and soccer is further brought out in a report of the Northern Union's first AGM. It shows that the NU authorities believed the roughness of Rugby League to be one of its most problematic aspects. A sub-committee had been appointed to change the laws in order to make the game less violent, more attractive for spectators and to increase its chances of competing successfully with soccer:

> In order to improve the game the sub-committee recommended an alteration in the half-back play and no one, he thought, dare say that the change made had not been a success. They had removed one cause which had been responsible for a great amount of rough play, and which had also been a means of getting some of their spectators into disgrace. It was the intention of the Union to lose no opportunity of further improving the game.[22]

The change in half-back play referred to was that which required the 'scrum-half' to retire behind the scrummage or be penalized. Its significance for present purposes lies in the fact that it was introduced ostensibly in order to reduce the opportunities for roughness among players and spectators. As one can see, the authorities believed that the violence of Rugby League was dysfunctional for the maintenance of spectator support. This issue, i.e. the relationship between the roughness of Northern Union football and its spectator appeal, is one which merits special consideration. Some figures on the deaths and serious injuries incurred in Yorkshire Rugby prior to the 'split' can serve to introduce the discussion. They are given in Table 10.1. These figures do not tell how many Rugby players there were in Yorkshire in that period or how regularly they played. Nevertheless, assuming them to be reliable, a total of seventy-one deaths in one county in a three-year period, to say nothing of 366 broken legs, arms, collar bones and other injuries, is suggestive of death and injury rates which, in the context of a game, can only be described as alarming. We do not have comparable data for the period following the break with the RFU but evidence that Rugby League remained physically dangerous comes from the fact that, in 1910, the Essex and Suffolk Insurance Company refused to continue insuring players.[23] And the Northern Union minutes of April,

Table 10.1[24]

	Deaths	Broken legs etc.	Arms	Collar bones	Other injuries
1890–1	23	30	9	11	27
1891–2	22	52	12	18	56
1892–3	26	39	12	25	75
TOTALS	71	121	33	54	158

November and December 1900, reveal that sums of £25, 25 guineas and 15 guineas were voted to the relatives of three men who received fatal injuries whilst playing.

That it was not only the game but spectators who were violent is brought out by an extract from the minutes of the Northern Union 'Cup Committee' for 24 March 1902:

> Mr. Marshall (the referee) reported the Rochdale Hornets spectators for misconduct at the close of their match with Huddersfield on Saturday last. The Committee found the charge justified, and suspended the Hornets ground up to and including April 5th and the Hornets team from taking part in football in the Rochdale district to that date.
>
> Mr. Ashton reported the Dewsbury spectators for mobbing and kicking him after their match against Salford on Saturday last. The Dewsbury ground was suspended up to and including April 26th.

It is reasonable to suppose that what happened in these two cases is that the referee was attacked because his decisions were perceived as biased in favour of the opposition and hence as instrumental in preventing the Hornets and Dewsbury from achieving victory. In short, they are indicative of the high emotional investment of spectators in the victory of their teams. However, that, and the parallels with 'hooliganism' in present-day soccer, is less significant for present purposes than the fact that the Northern Union authorities sought from early on to reduce the violence of their game and to prevent outbreaks of unruly fan behaviour. In both respects, their actions are symptomatic of the problems they faced in seeking to use the game as a vehicle of social control.

The violence inherent in Rugby League at that stage presented the authorities with an acute dilemma. They must have realized that it constituted one of the main sources of the game's spectator appeal. That is, Rugby League was seen by Northern working men as a means of expressing the tough and aggressive norms of masculinity they adhered to. Indeed, 'cauliflower ears' and other signs of injury received in the game remain to this day a major source of pride to players and a symbol of their prestige in the local community. But there are several reasons why the authorities were forced to try to reduce the level of violence in the game. Thus, players were valuable assets in whom, particularly when transfer-fees had been paid, considerable sums of money had been invested. A game in which the injury rate was high would have reduced the clubs' chances of securing a return on their investments. Moreover, it must have been difficult in such a game to maintain settled teams capable of regularly producing peak performances. That is because, under such conditions, the chances would have been high of losing one or more team personnel either for the remainder of a match or for matches in the weeks to come. But, just as importantly, the authorities could not condone a game which was overly rough for fear that it might encourage the use of physical violence outside the game. That is, they had to seek to 'civilize' the game and its supporters because working-class violence was a threat to their interests. But they had to carry out this 'civilizing' task without 'emasculating' Rugby to such an extent that it could no longer serve as a vehicle for celebrating the 'manliness' norms of players and spectators.

Analysis of the data available at present thus suggests that 'Tawd Vale' was wrong and that it was not 'working class separateness' which led Rugby League to evolve as a distinctive game but the actions of the middle-class authorities in their effort to use the game as a vehicle of social control. They were forced, in that connection, to 'civilize' it and make it faster, more open and more attractive so that it could compete more effectively with soccer. The example of Welsh Rugby, we believe, similarly negates 'Tawd Vale's' hypothesis for, as we suggested earlier, the game there developed under social conditions parallel in many ways to those which he claimed existed in the North of England. In fact, among the Welsh working class forms of 'separateness' developed which were, if anything, more extreme than those he attributes to the North of England. The Welsh working class also gained a greater measure of control over Rugby. Thus, if 'Tawd Vale' was right, the game in Wales should have developed in a direction similar to Rugby League. It did not, because the crucial condition for such a development was absent, namely a middle class able and willing to use the game for purposes of social control. Rugby Union retained the allegiance of Welshmen, eventually emerging as their national sport. A brief analysis of the development of the game there will show how this peculiar structure came into existence and enable us, simultaneously, to refute 'Tawd Vale's' hypothesis, we think conclusively.

6. At the beginning of the 1870s, no Rugby clubs had been established in Wales. By the end of that decade, however, each main town and many villages in the industrialized South had teams. As in England, the game derived its original impetus principally from public schools and universities, but 'old boy' influence was never as great. That was probably because the Welsh aristocracy were mainly of English descent and because the native middle class tended to migrate to England. It was as a result of such a social structure that the lower middle and working classes came to predominate in Welsh Rugby, not simply in the sense of providing the majority of players and spectators but of administrators, too. This dominance was reinforced by the fact that middle-class Welshmen who did not migrate to England were apparently apathetic towards the administration of the game, seemingly not grasping its potential as a vehicle of social control. In 1929, Rowe Harding lamented that:

> ... the efficiency of the Welsh Union has compared unfavourably with that in other Unions, because the leading citizens in our towns, though

they attend Rugby matches and become members of Welsh clubs, do not consider it worth their while to assist in the management of a mere sporting club, nor in the administration of Rugby . . . This criticism . . . is not inspired by any class prejudice. Rugby in Wales is a democratic institution, and it is right that the miners and manual workers who form the bulk of the players . . . should be represented by members of their own class; but an organization with an income of over £10,000 a year, and which is responsible for the prestige of a national sport, should attract men of social standing and business ability, and unfortunately the number of such men on the Union is too small. Of course, every member of the Union does his best; but some members are not fitted either by education or experience to guide the destiny of Welsh Rugby and they should be supplanted by men of better social standing and with a better grasp of affairs . . .[25]

The orientation of locally dominant groups to an alien ruling class and culture, coupled with the tendency for the middle class to migrate, probably reinforced the fervour with which the people who remained became attached to indigenous cultural forms. Hence their fervent support for Rugby, especially when Welsh sides meet English ones. But for present purposes, the main significance of the social configuration alluded to by Harding is that it was evidently conducive to the emergence of playing, spectating and even administrative dominance by working men. In Wales, as in England, a central axis of Rugby tension was that between the upper and middle and the working classes, but, given the predominance achieved by the latter in Wales, the pattern of discrimination operated in the reverse direction. At least, that is what Harding hinted when he complained that, if it continued to rely on its traditional bases, Welsh Rugby could not hope to keep abreast of 'scientific' developments in the game. If they wanted to become an international 'Rugby force', he suggested, the Welsh would have to look to the products of native public schools and to Welshmen trained at Oxford and Cambridge. It seems, however, that the working men who ran the game were unwilling to do this:

I have attempted to explain the cause of the apparent decline in Welsh club Rugby . . . I say 'apparent' . . . because I think . . . that English Rugby has advanced while Welsh Rugby has stood still. That explanation does not, however, altogether explain the consistent failure of Welsh national teams, because there have been available players with Welsh qualifications who have had the benefit of assimilating the new theories . . . in England . . . They have been consistently ignored by the Welsh selectors who have preferred players from the native clubs who stick obstinately to the old theories because they know of no other.[26]

Of course, such discrimination was probably as much the result of what we nowadays call 'Welsh nationalism' as of class hostility. That is, as men who had attended English universities and schools, the more 'scientific' players were branded as 'traitors'. However, more germane for present purposes is the fact that, if this analysis is correct, Welsh Rugby was controlled from early on mainly by working men who did not adhere to the amateur ethos. As a result, the game there developed a character different from that of the game in those parts of England where the public school élite remained in control. It became, that is, a popular sport, a game for spectators as well as players and large crowds meant that big money entered club houses. However, since the game was not controlled by men whose social-ization and social situation led them to adhere firmly to the amateur ethos, sums of money in excess of 'legitimate' expenses soon found their way into the pockets of top-class players. As Morgan and Nicholson put it, 'clubs were soon making enough money to pay players' . . . expenses, if not more'. The figures of Cardiff RFC, they say, are representative. It obtained £364 2s. 3d. at the gate in 1884–5, £720 3s. 9d. in 1885–6, £1,223 16s. 10d. in 1890–1, £1,985 in 1891–2, and £2,472 in 1901–2. And that is to say nothing of the sums obtained from members' subscriptions, 'ground tickets' and, when they were introduced in 1891, 'workmen's tickets'.[27]

Early Welsh players were local heroes. They epitomized locally dominant values, representing them in competition with 'outsiders', especially the English 'foe'. Therefore, in the eyes of local inhabitants, they deserved to be rewarded. However, since there was no restraining amateur ethos to inhibit money payment, not even in the weak form in which such restraints were at first operative among the men who ran the Northern Union, the rewards given soon surpassed the simple prestige of being local and national celebrities and took a monetary form.

Such monetization appears to have been established as a permanent fea-ture of Welsh Rugby. Reports continue to allege that clubs there persistently disregard the Rugby Union rules which prohibit the payment of money in excess of 'legitimate' expenses. In no case, however, have these reports been *publicly* substantiated. For example, in 1953, the Welsh Rugby Union called upon a BBC commentator, G. V. Wynne-Jones, to prove his allegation that players were receiving payment and, on his failure to do so, banned him from broadcasting from any ground under its jurisdiction.[28] However, what Wynne-Jones was penalized for was breaking a 'conspiracy of silence' regard-ing a well-known fact for there is no doubt that money payments are made in Wales. They form an integral part of Rugby Union there as the following examples show. Thus, in a 'ghosted' article written for a Sunday newspaper after he had signed for the Rugby League club, Bradford Northern, Terry Price, a former Welsh international, wrote: 'Oh yes, there's an expenses racket in the lilywhite, simon-pure Rugby Union . . . There's ticket-spivvery too.'[29] Writing in the same newspaper, Billy Boston offered insights into the manner in which money payments are made. He tells how he joined the Neath club in order to gain a first-team place and how they had 'generous ideas about expenses'. 'A similar system', he concluded, 'operates in Welsh representative Rugby, too':

> A former Welsh Union star, now in the League in Lancashire, told me of the time he went to collect his expenses for playing in a final Welsh international trial. The man handling the money just swept a pile of notes towards him. 'Will this do?' he asked, without enquiring about details. My mate nodded dumbly and shot off to count his loot. He'd been paid £10.[30]

These reports appeared in a 'sensationalist' newspaper and may have been motivated by a desire for revenge. However, the general picture they presented was corroborated by the Welsh club which, in the late 1960s, gave £1 a week 'rent' to every player on its books. Another told us that London Welsh are known to have paid 'travelling expenses' from Wales to players who live in London, and a Welshman who went on to play Rugby League in Yorkshire, replied as follows when we asked him: 'What money did you get from playing Rugby Union?'

> £1, 30/-, £2. I got £1 for the first two games . . . No, I played a mid-week game and I got £1 for that, and after that I got 30/- and £2, all unofficial. But before I came up North, I was only a youngster of 18, the last game I played was against X club and I can't say I had a particularly good game because we lost about 20–0, but I played reasonably well and X club officials approached me and offered me £5 a game to go to them.

The Welsh Rugby Union knows that such 'illegal' payments are made. Indeed, if Boston's allegations are correct, some of its officials actively connive at this breach of regulations. The other national unions, too, know that players in Wales are paid. Yet, even though 'shamateurism' runs strongly counter to the official rules and ethos of the game, they maintain cordial relations with the Welsh RFU. They also allow their club and national sides to play regularly against Welsh teams comprised, wholly or partly, of 'shamateur' players. However, in order for this to be possible, all parties have to subscribe to the fiction that Welsh Rugby is, and remains, an amateur game. They also have to suppress any attempt which is made publicly to substantiate the fact that Welsh players are paid. That is the case because, if the degree to which 'shamateurism' has taken root in the principality were brought into the open, they would face a potentially disruptive conflict similar to that of the 1890s. In short, the fiction that Welsh Rugby remains true to pristine amateur standards is an essential precondition for the maintenance of the framework of international cooperation which has been carefully built up and painstakingly nurtured in the century which has elapsed since the foundation of the RFU.

Our purpose in drawing attention to the fact that money payment has come to form an integral part of Welsh Rugby has not been to highlight the hypocrisy of the Welsh and other national governing bodies. We undertook this examination in order to test 'Tawd Vale's' hypothesis that it was Northern working class 'separateness' which led Rugby League to develop as a distinctive game. Had his hypothesis been correct, a similar process should have taken place in Wales. The fact that it did not and that, despite the degree of 'shamateurization' which occurred there, the Welsh remained firmly committed to Rugby Union, shows, we think conclusively, that 'Tawd Vale's' hypothesis is false.

It might be objected that the cultural differences between the Welsh and Northern English working classes render our comparison invalid. Thus it is conceivable that it was some peculiarity of working-class culture in Wales which made them cling to Rugby Union. But, whilst there are certainly differences between the Welsh and Northern English working classes, they are to some extent counteracted by the industrial similarities of the two areas, e.g. by the concentration of coal-mining and heavy industry in both. However, even if that were not the case and the differences were sufficiently great to make our comparison totally invalid, 'Tawd Vale's' hypothesis would still be wrong for it rests on the spurious assumption that Rugby League developed as an autonomously working-class affair. As we have shown, that was not the case. The players and spectators of Northern Union football may have been predominantly working-class but the men who ran it were mainly members of the business and industrial middle classes. They were primarily interested in the game as a means of social control and it was that which forced them to introduce changes in the rules.

Their task was made especially urgent by competition with the more established Association game. This suggests a further reason why the Welsh retained their allegiance to Rugby Union, namely the fact that soccer never penetrated deeply into Wales. To this day, there are only four Welsh Football League clubs, Cardiff, Wrexham, Swansea and Newport. Thus, even though the existence of working-class predominance in Welsh Rugby led the amateur ethos to be contravened, there was no effective competition from a rival game for spectator support. Hence, besides the fact that their class position did not lead to an interest in Rugby Union as a vehicle of social control, there was no pressure on those who ran the game to change the rules or switch their allegiance to Rugby League.

It remains to explain why, after fighting to prevent the professionalization of Rugby in Lancashire and Yorkshire, the RFU has remained seemingly content to live with 'shamateur' Rugby in Wales. The answer, we think, is principally twofold. It lies partly in the fact that, as long as the conspiracy of silence can be maintained and it is not publicly proven that Welsh players are paid, the RFU have no wish to rock the boat and risk another bout of internecine warfare similar to that which produced the split in 1895. But the answer lies partly in the fact that Welsh Rugby does not come under the RFU's direct jurisdiction. Were it to do so, e.g. if a *British* RFU amalgamating the English, Irish, Scottish and Welsh Unions were formed, then the currently dominant groups in the English Union would probably feel it their duty to fight Welsh 'shamateurism' tooth and nail. However, there seems little chance at present that such a development could occur. Welsh, Scottish, Irish and, dare one say it, English 'nationalism' militate against it. Moreover, there is little stimulus for such a process of unification in a game which, up until the 1960s, had hardly spread internationally beyond Australia, France, New Zealand and South Africa.

Postscript

We could have written more about Rugby League but, for present purposes, it must be enough simply to add a postscript which explores two main points: firstly, the fact that Rugby League has failed to spread – in Britain – beyond the Northern context in which it originated;[31] and secondly, the fact that its spectator appeal has tended recently to decline.

Attempts to transplant Rugby League to other parts of the country have been made on several occasions, e.g. to London, the Midlands and South Wales in the inter-war years and to West Wales in 1949. However, each proved a failure in the sense that no permanent administrative apparatus, no permanent teams, no body of players and no spectator following were established. The reasons why are basically twofold: firstly because Rugby League could not hope to gain support in working-class areas where soccer was already entrenched; and secondly because its 'cloth cap' image and professionalism meant that it could not compete effectively with Rugby Union for middle-class allegiance. So it was destined, virtually from the outset, to be a regionally limited, minority sport.

However, this applies *in toto* only to the professional game, for amateur Rugby League has proved to be a slightly more successful Northern export. A 'Southern Amateur Rugby League' consisting of twelve teams was founded in 1965 and, in the early 1970s, an attempt was made to set up a similar organization in Corby, Northants. The spur for this spread of amateur Rugby League was provided by the live television coverage of the professional game which began in the early 1960s and exposed Rugby League to a national audience. This might appear to be indicative of the current vitality of the game. However, most commentators take the opposite view, seeing television as the principal cause of Rugby League's decline as a spectator sport.[32]

Although television has undoubtedly affected match attendances, this is probably an oversimplification. That this is the case is suggested by the fact that a comparable decline has occurred in virtually all British sports, even those such as soccer where, up until about 1990, live television used to be forbidden. In short, live TV coverage is probably only one factor in a larger constellation, most of them connected with deeper changes in the Northern working class.

The following changes in the British working class generally can be singled out as likely to be of especial importance in this connection: the break-up of traditional working-class cultures due to the pressures and opportunities of life in an 'affluent society'; as part of this, the availability of alternative leisure pursuits and the effects of car-ownership on leisure patterns; the effects of 'slum clearance' on traditional working-class communities; and many more, some perhaps peculiar to the North. In addition, in order to provide a complete explanation, account would have to be taken of the organizational inefficiency of the Rugby League and the continued adherence of its administrative personnel to variants of the amateur conception of sport. That is because it is this, or so it is reasonable to suppose, which has made them slow to respond to the current crisis and which has led them, when they have finally acted, to introduce measures which are often inappropriate and irrelevant to the crisis actually faced.

But, whether or not these few points constitute the germs of an adequate explanation, of one thing there can be no doubt: namely, that Rugby League is declining as a spectator sport, at least in the sense of direct match-attendance by spectators. This can be seen from the attendance figures at home matches reported by Featherstone Rovers for the years 1953 and 1973 (see Table 10.2). Similar figures could be reported for other clubs. Thus, Featherstone Rovers attracted a total of 87,500 spectators to their home matches in 1953 and 66,770 in 1973, a drop of 20,300 over the twenty-year period. It would have been even greater had the 1973 figures not been boosted by attendances at the matches against Salford, Rochdale and the Australian touring side. The first two were Cup matches and the third against a visiting national side. Matches of that kind have evidently retained their drawing power. It is at 'bread and butter' league games that the drop has principally occurred.

These figures compare unfavourably with those for professional soccer. Teams in the Fourth Division may not attract many more spectators but even the lowliest First or Second Division side has match-by-match and annual attendance figures considerably in excess of those for Featherstone Rovers. Indeed, top sides regularly attract crowds for a *single match* which approach or are in excess of the number of spectators attracted *annually* by their counterparts in Rugby League. In an inflationary era when even soccer clubs are experiencing financial difficulties, attendance figures such as these are indicative of a professional sport whose finances are, to put it mildly, in a parlous state. Of course, Rugby League is not financially dependent solely on money taken at the gate: additional sums are obtained from television rights, from corporate sponsors such as the John Player Tobacco Co. who, in 1975, injected £22,800 into the game,[33] from wealthy individual patrons and from the fund-raising activities of supporters' clubs. However, the money obtained in this manner, even together with that taken at the gate, is barely sufficient to keep Rugby League afloat. It is certainly not enough to enable the game's authorities to take the sort of action which would be necessary to combat its long-term decline as a spectator sport. We may

Table 10.2 Match attendance figures at Featherstone Rovers, 1953 and 1973*

1953		1973		1953		1973	
No.	Opponents	No.	Opponents	No.	Opponents	No.	Opponents
3,300	Hull	1,000	Hunslet	6,100	Hull Kingston Rovers	4,000	Castleford
2,800	Halifax	1,370	Halifax	7,800	Leeds	2,450	Whitehaven
4,000	Barrow	9,300	Salford	3,500	Harrow	1,400	Hull
4,200	Doncaster	1,290	Bramley	3,500	Hull	3,100	Wigan
2,500	Oldham	8,200	Rochdale	4,500	Keighley	3,700	Warrington
5,000	Leeds	1,670	Hull Kingston Rovers	3,700	Hull Kingston Rovers	1,900	Keighley
10,000	Huddersfield	2,400	Huddersfield	2,400	Hunslet	5,000	Australia
3,500	Wakefield	2,000	Hull	4,400	Rochdale Hornets	4,600	Wakefield
3,200	Whitehaven	4,690	Wakefield	3,500	Castleford	1,300	Oldham
3,900	Bradford	5,500	Leeds	4,700	York	1,800	Whitehaven

* These figures were obtained for us by R. Harrison who graduated in Sociology from the University of Leicester in 1974. They are for the latter half of the 1952–3 and 1972–3 seasons, and the first half of the 1953–4 and 1973–4 seasons.

even be witnessing at the moment the early stages in a process of 're-amateurization'. In short, the wider social process may be unintentionally producing an end-result which the Rugby Union authorities at the end of the nineteenth century strove for but were unable to obtain. Paradoxically, however, there is occurring, parallel with this 're-amateurization' of Rugby League, a 're-professionalization' of Rugby Union. Again, the authorities appear powerless to prevent it. It is to this seemingly inexorable, unintended social process that we shall turn our attention in the next chapter.

11 Rugby Union as a modern sport: bureaucracy, gate-taking clubs and the swansong of amateurism

1. In marked contrast to Rugby League, Rugby Union has expanded since the beginning of the present century. However, its development has been far from crisis-free. Expansion has produced a number of unintended and unforeseen consequences, leading in particular to developments which run counter to amateur principles. More specifically, in the course of its expansion, Rugby Union has:

(i)   begun to be bureaucratically controlled. Since it remains in its early stages, this process is best described as 'incipient' bureaucratization. Its main interest for present purposes lies in the fact that it has necessitated an increase in the employment of paid personnel on the Twickenham staff;

(ii) developed a rank-hierarchy of clubs. Initially, this depended on social as well as sporting criteria but it soon opened up and Rugby ability *per se* increased in importance as a determinant of status. Later, however, when the hierarchy became national in scope, it hardened once more in the sense that the relative positions of clubs became virtually frozen;

(iii) seen the rise once more of gate-taking clubs, i.e. of clubs which are compelled to contravene the amateur ethos by paying attention to the interests of groups other than players. Indeed, as we shall show, not only the gate-taking clubs but also in subtle ways the RFU itself has grown financially dependent on spectator support.

These structural developments were interrelated and accompanied by parallel changes in the rules, ethos and organization of the game. Again, there are three main indications that such a transformation has occurred:

(i)   as a result of the growing dependency of the RFU and the gate-taking clubs on spectator support, the rules have gradually been altered to meet spectator interests. For a while, this was unrecognized ideologically and the old player-centred ethos continued to be stressed. However, such a 'cultural lag' could not continue indefinitely and, latterly, the changed dependency pattern and rules have been accompanied by corresponding ideological changes. This transformation is still in its early stages and is best described as a change from a 'player-centred' towards a more 'spectator-oriented' form of amateurism;

(ii) at the playing level, Rugby Union is now approached in a more serious and dedicated manner. Extensive preparation in the form of fitness training, coaching and pre-match tactical sessions is now more fully accepted. In this sense the game has become more 'professional', especially at the highest levels;

(iii) organizationally, the game has witnessed growing pressure for the introduction of a centrally organized competition based on knock-out ('cup') or continuous ('league') principles. After strong initial resistance, the RFU bowed to such pressure and introduced, in 1971, a knock-out competition and, in 1976, a system of 'merit-tables', i.e. of 'leagues', although, of course, wishing to maintain the distinctness between Rugby Union and Rugby League, the RFU is understandably reluctant to use that term.

These developments have gradually led Rugby Union to assume a form which contradicts the pristine amateur ethos. Despite the resistance of 'traditionalists', it is being forced, seemingly inexorably, into a modern sporting mould. Thus, the competitive element within it is being directed into formal channels. At an attitudinal level, achievement-orientation is increasing, manifested in victory-striving as the ultimate short-term goal and in a longer term striving to raise standards. This is coupled with intense seriousness of purpose and an emphasis on training, coaching and pre-match planning. Moreover, as in modern sport more generally, each Rugby encounter is coming to form just one moment in a longer chain. There has also occurred an 'intellectualization of the game, i.e. people think about and plan it more. And coupled with this, there is the tendency for spectator interests to challenge, if not take precedence over, those of players.

Until the 1960s, the conflicts which contributed to, and which in their turn, were produced by, these developments, were in a minor key. That is, no organized groups emerged and they were not related to tensions in society at large. However, the 1960s saw an end to this pattern and the problems generated by expansion began to reach crisis proportions. For the first time since the 1890s, organized groups crystallized around proposals for reform and maintenance of the *status quo*. In other words, open struggle broke out concerning the structure of Rugby Union, taking on an undisguisedly ideological form. The stage was thus set, or so it was widely believed, for repetition of the events of the 1890s.

It is the crisis generated by the expansion of Rugby Union which forms the subject of this last chapter of our book. What we shall attempt to show in this connection is the step-by-step accretion of changes which have led the game at top level to become, to all intents and purposes, a professional sport. Indeed, apart from ideological amateurism, the only remaining differences between it and, say, professional soccer, are that top-level players are not paid, at least not openly, that they have full-time occupations outside Rugby, and that they claim, in the majority of cases quite sincerely, allegiance to amateur principles. As a result, the crisis is not overtly about money-payment but issues such as the desirability of spectators, modern methods of training and coaching, and the role in the game of formal competition. At a deeper level, however, money and professionalism are what is at stake. In our view, that is necessarily the case for, in capitalist societies, there is an inexorable tendency for sports to become bound up with money values.

As we have said, our main task in the present chapter is to explore the expansion of Rugby Union and the correlative developments which led the present crisis to occur. We shall begin with an examination of the expansion *per se*, paying special attention to the class characteristics of clubs. We shall try in that connection to establish whether, like its nineteenth-century counterpart, the twentieth-century expansion of Rugby Union involved a process of democratization at least in the minimal sense of diffusion down the social scale.

2. In 1893 the number of clubs in membership of the RFU was 481. In 1898, three years after the formation of the Northern Union, the number had dropped to 383 and, by 1903, to 244.[1] Subsequently, however, the game has gone from strength to strength.[2] The pattern of its spread is shown in Table 11.1 which reports the number of clubs founded decade by decade up to 1969, revealing some of the regional variations in that process. The table shows the effects on Rugby Union's expansion of the 'split' and the two world wars. Thus, the twenty years, 1890–1909, and the two decades, 1910–19 and 1940–49, were periods of slow growth. The 1920s and 1960s, followed closely by the 1870s, 1930s and 1950s, witnessed the fastest growth. The growth in the 1870s was probably a function of the formation of the RFU, i.e. of the fact that the new national organization was effective in promoting the game. That of the 1920s and 1930s probably marks the beginnings of the 'switch' of grammar schools from soccer to Rugby and the resultant formation of Rugby clubs by grammar school old boys. It is reasonable to suppose that this trend is also reflected in the figures for the 1950s and 60s. In short, the twentieth-century expansion of Rugby Union appears to have formed part of the long-term trend towards class-exclusiveness in British sport which started in the 1890s when all but a handful of public schools turned from soccer to Rugby Union.

Michael Green argues that television has led to the emergence of a less class-exclusive game. In the 1960s, he says, Rugby Union 'began to be discussed in workshops as well as boardrooms . . . and few clubs bother about where a player went to school'.[3] Our data do not support this variant of the popular *embourgeoisement* thesis. This can be seen from Table 11.2 which uses the Registrar General's occupational scale to give the social class of players selected for

Table 11.1 Foundation of clubs in membership of the RFU in 1970 by decade and County Championship Division

| | County Championship Divisions | | | | | |
Decade	Northern	Midlands	South-Eastern	Southern	South-Western	Totals
Before 1870	16	2	21	5	7	51
1870–79	42	22	34	3	31	132
1880–89	28	13	15	1	15	72
1890–99	14	7	19	5	19	64
1900–09	10	9	11	2	17	49
1910–19	2	12	14	2	3	33
1920–29	56	49	78	20	28	231
1930–39	29	18	51	13	18	129
1940–49	15	27	24	13	19	98
1950–59	30	32	42	23	26	153
1960–69	43	25	69	23	16	176
TOTALS	285	216	378	110	199	1,188

This table was worked up from the figures cited in Titley and McWhirter, op. cit. pp. 187–207. It is incomplete in the sense that they were unable to discover the foundation dates of all clubs and that they deliberately excluded all but a few school clubs.

Table 11.2 Class composition of England Rugby sides (1902–71)*

Social class	1902–11	1912–21	1922–31	1932–41	1942–51	1952–61	1962–71	Totals
I	50 (34%)	18 (33%)	33 (30%)	21 (29%)	21 (30%)	3 (4%)	21 (20%)	167 (26%)
II	46 (31%)	15 (27%)	50 (45%)	30 (41%)	34 (49%)	57 (75%)	58 (56%)	290 (46%)
III (non-manual)	2 (1%)	0	1 (1%)	2 (3%)	1 (1%)	8 (11%)	9 (9%)	23 (4%)
III (manual)	8 (5%)	1 (2%)	6 (5%)	4 (5%)	3 (4%)	3 (4%)	5 (5%)	30 (5%)
IV	1 (1%)	0	2 (2%)	0	0	0	0	3 (0.5%)
V	0	0	0	0	0	0	0	0
Not known	40 (27%)	21 (38%)	19 (17%)	16 (22%)	11 (16%)	5 (7%)	10 (10%)	122 (19%)
TOTALS	147	55	111	73	70	76	103	635

* These figures were obtained from information in the biographical section of Titley and McWhirter, *op. cit.*

England between 1902 and 1971. These figures show that no fewer than 70 per cent of the men who played Rugby Union for England between 1902 and 1971 were members of Classes I and II, that is, men engaged in professional and what the Registrar General terms 'intermediate' occupations. During that entire seventy-year period, however, not a single man whose occupation falls into the Registrar General's Class V was selected. Thus Rugby Union has remained throughout the present century a primarily middle-class sport. Only a handful of players or, more accurately, of those selected for their country, have come from the lower middle and working classes.

A postal survey which we carried out in 1972 confirms this picture,[4] suggesting that the figures in Table 11.2 reflect the exclusive character of the game in general and not just class bias in the selection of national teams. The results are set forth in Table 11.3.

A similar picture of an exclusively middle-class sport emerges from Table 11.4 which reports the types of secondary school attended by players selected for England between 1902 and 1971. It shows how, over that period, the public schools contributed no less than forty-three per cent to the membership of England sides. Indeed, between 1922 and 1931, the proportion was as high as fifty-seven per cent.

These figures have to be seen against a measure of the proportion of the male population at large who go to public schools. It is difficult to reach a precise definition of a 'public school' but the Public Schools Commission calculated in 1968 that 'independent' schools contribute five per cent to the total number of pupils attending British schools and that 'public schools', more narrowly defined, contribute 1.4 per cent.[5] This is a gross estimate since the Commission's figures are for Britain as a whole and not broken down by age or sex. Moreover, they refer only to a single year and signify nothing about changes which may have occurred in the ratio of the public to the total school population. Nevertheless, it seems that, for most of the present century, schools attended by somewhere between 1/20th and 1/60th of the total school population have contributed about half to the membership of national Rugby sides.

Over the same period, the proportion contributed by grammar schools

Table 11.3 Social class of Rugby players and officials, 1972

Social class	No.	%
I	113	34.5
II	191	58.4
III (non-manual)	4	1.2
III (manual)	18	5.5
IV	0	0.0
V	1	0.3
TOTAL	327	99.9

Table 11.4 Types of schools attended by England Rugby players (1902–71)*

Type of school	1902–11	1912–21	1922–31	1932–41	1942–51	1952–61	1962–71	Totals
Public	62 (42%)	28 (51%)	63 (57%)	35 (49%)	27 (39%)	30 (40%)	27 (26%)	272 (43%)
Grammar	14 (10%)	1 (2%)	1 (1%)	8 (11%)	9 (13%)	19 (25%)	36 (35%)	88 (14%)
Board, Secondary modern, etc.	2 (1%)	3 (5%)	0 (0%)	2 (3%)	4 (6%)	2 (3%)	5 (5%)	18 (3%)
Other	28 (19%)	11 (20%)	16 (14%)	9 (13%)	18 (26%)	12 (16%)	22 (21%)	116 (18%)
Not known	41 (28%)	12 (21%)	31 (28%)	18 (25%)	12 (17%)	12 (16%)	13 (13%)	139 (22%)
TOTALS	147	55	111	72	70	75	103	633

* This table is based on information contained in the biographical section of Titley and McWhirter, op. cit.

was fourteen per cent and by secondary moderns and equivalent, three per cent. Thus, since public and grammar schools are educational preserves mainly of the middle class, measured by types of school attended by players selected for England, Rugby Union appears to have remained an almost exclusively middle-class sport. Close inspection of the time-series in Table 11.4, however, suggests that, in the course of its expansion, the game did undergo some democratization. Thus, the proportion contributed to England teams by grammar schools increased decennially from 1922 onwards. By 1962–71, their contribution exceeded that of public schools (thirty-five as opposed to twenty-six per cent). Our 1972 survey provides further confirmation of this trend for fifty-two per cent of our sample had attended grammar and only thirty per cent public schools.

Although there is considerable overlap, public schools in general are attended by boys from higher, grammar schools by boys from lower sections of the middle class. These figures, therefore, suggest that, in the course of its expansion, Rugby Union spread down the middle-class hierarchy, i.e. from the 'upper middle' to the 'middle middle' and 'lower middle' classes. It seems, however, that its diffusion came to a virtual standstill at the boundary between the middle and working classes. Therefore, Green and those who argue likewise appear to be wrong. Despite its downwards diffusion, Rugby Union remains almost exclusively middle-class. It follows that any changes which occurred in connection with its expansion cannot be attributed to its spread to the working class. That is true, for example, of the process of bureaucratization which has begun to take place at the level of central administration. It is to that issue that our attention will now be turned.

3. Rugby Union's amateur ethos is a variant of the middle-class ethic of voluntary association. That is, it involves a stress on unpaid labour for the performance of administrative tasks and the maintenance and improvement of playing facilities. This is held at, and at the same time held to refer to, all levels, from the meanest club right up to the RFU and international teams. Yet, despite this supposedly universal commitment, expansion has made it necessary to contravene the ethos of voluntary association at the level of central administration and, virtually from the outset, to rationalize, bureaucratize and, in certain respects, professionalize the game.

1904 was a key year in the early stages of this process. By then, the administrative load of the RFU had grown to an extent sufficient to require the appointment of a salaried secretary and assistant secretary.[6] At the same time, the scope of its financial transactions had grown to a level sufficient to warrant granting the treasurer the services of a clerk at an annual salary of £15. By 1974, the RFU had come to employ twenty-seven paid personnel on its Twickenham staff. Their posts and, where we have been able to discover them, the years in which they were created, are as follows: 1904: Secretary, Assistant Secretary (renamed Administrative Secretary, 1970); 1909: Head

Groundsman (renamed Clerk of the Works, 1963); 1946: General Administration Clerk (later renamed Match Operations Officer); 1969: Technical Administrator; 1972: Schools and Assistant Coaching Administrator; 1974: Administrative Officer, Administrative Officer (Tickets), Finance Officer. There are, in addition, four female secretaries (one part-time), five female clerks (two part-time), and eleven tradesmen and groundsmen. Two more people are employed on a seasonal basis to help with match applications and a variable number of occasional helpers are paid for specific services when a big match is held.[7] We do not wish to exaggerate the degree of bureaucratization and professionalization implied by these figures. The bulk of the RFU's work is still performed on a voluntary basis and an aura of amateurism—in the sense of a commitment to fun and a desire to resist formal rationality—pervades its operations, thus indicating an organization which remains at an early stage in these processes. Nevertheless, it is true that bureaucratization and professionalization have started, leading to contraventions of the amateur ethos. This can be seen from an examination of the employment of paid ground and administrative staff.

Paid groundstaff are employed by Rugby clubs all over the country, not just at Twickenham. By itself, that practice does not lead necessarily to contravention of the amateur ethos. Where an ordinary club pays for its ground to be maintained and continues to perform only administrative work on a voluntary basis, it expresses the divorce between intellectual and manual labour and the higher status in our society of the former, but it does not, by that fact, contravene amateur principles. However, a distinction must be drawn between an amateur sport in which the wages of groundstaff are paid from players' subscriptions, bar-receipts, fund-raising dances, etc., i.e. from the income and *non-playing* efforts of club members, and one in which, as is the case with Twickenham groundstaff, wages are paid to a greater or lesser extent from gate-money, i.e. from the deliberate organization of the game, or a specific portion of it, as a spectacle. In the latter case, the game has moved, however slightly, towards professionalism because player performance has become subject to an economic exchange. Spectators pay money in the expectation of obtaining satisfaction. For their part, the players, even though they may not be paid a money wage, receive benefits from this financial transaction, e.g. superior ground facilities and the ego-enhancement which comes from being considered good enough to play representative Rugby in front of large crowds. This may be obvious in the case of superior playing facilities but it is no less true of matches played in front of large crowds, for the stadia which permit large-scale spectator attendance are costly to build and run and paid for primarily out of match receipts.

Similar considerations apply to the employment of paid administrative staff. Again, no necessary contravention of the amateur ethos is implied by that practice but, where the salaries of administrative personnel are derived in part from gate-money, a sport can no longer be considered purely amateur. Since the administrators' salaries are at least partly dependent on spectator money, it has moved towards professionalism. That has happened in the case of Rugby Union where administrative salaries are met principally out of revenue from matches at Twickenham and only to a lesser extent out of membership subscriptions. Against this, however, it must be noted that the RFU employ paid personnel, not simply in order to perform the routine tasks involved in running a national organization but also, and from their viewpoint more importantly, to promote amateurism at the playing level. In short, administrative expertise is employed on behalf of the amateur ethos. Paradoxically, however, this serves only to undermine amateurism even further since, to the extent that the paid administrators bring rationality and efficiency to the performance of their task, the game's expansion is facilitated and the trend towards bureaucracy and professionalism, of which their own existence is an expression, is reinforced.

Bureaucratization and professionalization are thus artefacts of Rugby Union's expansion. The same basic process has led, in addition, to the stratification of clubs and, understandably in a market society, to the emergence once more of gate-taking clubs. It is to these aspects of the process, i.e. to the stratification of clubs and the growing monetary orientation of some of them, that our attention will now be turned.

4. Without the occurrence of the degree of bureaucratization and professionalization just discussed, the expansion of Rugby Union would have involved a proliferation of clubs and an increase in the number of players but it would have been a simply numerical process. That is, it would not have involved the emergence of a unified national framework through which teams from different areas play regularly together and which permits the selection of representative sides. That is because inter-area matches cannot be organized on a continuous basis without a degree of central coordination. Moreover, central control is a precondition for the selection of representative sides. However, it remains to be explained why the demand for inter-area and representative matches should have arisen in the first place. The answer to this question will provide a clue to the stratification of Rugby clubs and the emergent dependency of some of them on gate-receipts.

The demand for inter-area and representative sport is, we think, inherent in modern society. No comparable demand arose in pre-industrial Britain because the lack of effective national unification and poor means of transport and communication meant there were no common rules and no means by which participants from different regions could be regularly brought together. At the same time, the 'localism' inherent in society at that stage meant that play-groups perceived as potential rivals only groups with which they were contiguous in a geographical sense. However, modern Britain is different on all these counts. It is relatively unified nationally, has superior means of transport and communication, sports with common rules, and a degree of 'cosmopolitanism' which means that local groups perceive as potential rivals, and are anxious to compare themselves with, others which are not geographically adjacent.

More narrowly, modern sport is organized in a manner which reinforces the demand for inter-area and representative matches. Of central importance in this respect is the fact that each sporting encounter is a contest with three possible outcomes: a team may win, lose or draw. In addition, the contestants tend to be involved in some longer-term struggle for superiority, whether formally to win a league or cup, or informally for the prestige of being regarded as a 'first-class' club. It was in the context of this longer-term struggle that the stratification of clubs arose.

If such struggles were carried out under conditions analogous to those which economists describe as 'perfect competition', there would be neither permanent winners nor permanent losers: each team would win, lose and draw with equal frequency. But in the 'real' world, sport corresponds more closely to what economists call 'imperfect competition' or 'oligopoly', i.e. some teams tend regularly to win and others regularly to lose. It is the degree of permanence in this respect which has to be explained. Put simply and crudely, we think it is a function of inequalities in the distribution of rewards in the wider society, i.e. of the class system more generally. Teams with the greatest resources are likely to emerge victorious. It may be tautologous to say so but the relevant resources are those necessary for regularly securing victory, i.e. for maximizing team-performance and/or ensuring the recruitment of superior players.

In the case of Rugby Union after the 'split', public school old boys were able to recapture their erstwhile dominance simply because the withdrawal of the Northern Union restored the virtual monopoly of playing skills which public school attendance had previously conferred. In short, public school dominance was a function of the unequal distribution of the game at that stage, of the fact that Rugby Union was a minority sport, played only at public schools. Some schools produced more good Rugby players than others mainly because they devoted more time and resources to the game, i.e. because they regarded it as of greater educational importance. It was the old boys of such schools who formed the nuclei of the first great Rugby Union clubs. For a while, public school attendance was as important a criterion of membership as Rugby ability but, as the game spread to grammar schools, the competitive pressure grew. At the same time, the balance between 'old school tie' and playing ability as criteria for membership of first-class clubs began to change in favour of the latter. As that occurred, the best players, independently of social origins and education, began to join the most successful clubs and, hence, the emergent system of stratification among them was given a degree of permanence.

Under such conditions, dominant clubs no longer found it satisfying to play their weaker local counterparts and *vice vèrsa*. The latter were no match for the former. Encounters between them lacked meaning. They were predictable and served neither to generate excitement nor as adequate vehicles for testing identities. Consequently, the demand arose for matches against teams which had risen to the top of *other* local hierarchies. Top teams from different regions got to know of each others' reputations informally in the first instance, either through gossip channels within or related to the game, or through the national media. For many years, such 'first-class' fixtures were organized informally without causing dissatisfaction, but in the 1960s the demand arose for formal, centrally organized competitions such as cups and leagues. We shall return to that issue later.

Matches between regionally separated teams provide clubs and players with the chance to establish wider reputations, at the same time generating spectator interest which, in a market society, permits charging for admission and, hence, the emergence of gate-taking clubs. One might have thought, given the conflict caused by the formation of gate-taking clubs in the late-nineteenth-century North, that the Rugby Union authorities would have striven to prevent such clubs from re-emerging. But, however contrary to the amateur ethos the practice of charging for admission may appear, the RFU has never, not even in the period of retrenchment following 'the split', officially resisted such a practice. Ideologically, of course, they have re-peatedly stressed the player-oriented character of their game. However, in practice, their official energies in defence of amateur principles have been expended, almost entirely, in preventing individual players from benefiting materially from the game. Thus in 1932–3, a prohibition was enacted against any player, referee, club or RFU official writing articles or broadcasting on the current game for payment.[8] And in 1933–4 when several breaches of the RFU's 'professionalism laws' were brought to light, a 'well-known' player was expelled.[9]

Similar official resistance has not been offered to material gain by clubs. The reason why is probably twofold: the fact that leading groups in the RFU have come, overwhelmingly, from the major clubs, many of which levied admission charges even before the split with Rugby League; and the RFU's commitment to the goal of raising standards. However, in the resultant climate of ideological support for the player-centred, amateur ethos and official inaction regarding the spread of a potentially serious threat to that ethos, the formation and development of gate-taking clubs was able to pro-ceed unhindered. By 1973, their number had risen to forty. Their names, together with some other pertinent facts about them, are set forth in Table 11.5. They are split into regional divisions in order to show their spread around the country. Thus, all but two of the present gate-taking clubs—Fylde (1920) and Penzance and Newlyn (1945)—were founded in the nine-teenth century. And, out of the seventeen which responded to our request for the date at which admission charges were introduced, nine began such a practice before 1900. It follows that most of the gate-taking clubs were founded by public school old boys or soon attracted such players to their ranks. At first, membership was determined by social as well as sporting criteria but, as we saw, the latter always tended to predominate. Since the

Table 11.5[10] Gate-taking clubs in membership of the RFU (1977)

Name	Founded in	Became a gate-taking club in	Ground capacity	Highest ever gate	Total number of spectators (1975–6)	Total gate-receipts (1975–6)
North						
Birkenhead Park	1871					
Bradford	1866	Turn of century	16,000*	16,000	—	£150–£200
Broughton Park	1882*		12–15,000			
Fylde	1920*		2,500			
Gosforth	1877					
Halifax	1872**	1873	11,000*	3,000	10,000	
Headingley	1879*		10,000			
Liverpool	1857	1860	5,400	2,500	5,000	£1,000
Manchester	1860		3,300	3,000		
New Brighton	1875	1875	6,000	4–5,000		
Northern	1876**	1947	2,000	1,500		
Sale	1861	Probably early 1930s	5,000	4,500		
Waterloo	1882					
Midlands						
Bedford	1886	1886	4–5,000	6–8,000	19,867	£7,045
Coventry	1874**	1874	17,000	20,000		ca.£6,000
Leicester	1880	1890	25,000	31,000	26,000	£13,500
Moseley	1873	1883	7,500	9–10,000		£10,753
Northampton	1880*					
Nottingham	1877					
Nuneaton	1879*		2,500	1,800		£664
Rugby	1875*					

London and Home Counties						
Blackheath	1858*					
Harlequins	1866*		2,000	2,000	20,000	£2,212
London Irish	1898	1946				
London Scottish	1878**					
London Welsh	1885*					
Richmond	1861		5,000			
Rosslyn Park	1879		3,000	2,500	10,000	£4,173
Saracens	1876			3,500	10,000	£3,500
Wasps	1867*	After World War II	5,000			
West						
Bath	1865	About 1894	17,000			
Bristol	1888		22,000*			
Cheltenham	1889	1901	10,000	6–7,000		
Exeter	1872	1872	26,000	20,860	20,000	£1,435
Falmouth						
Gloucester	1873	About 1913	17,000		31,000	
Penryn	1872		15,000			£1,599
Penzance and Newlyn	1945	1945	12,000	9,000		ca. £2,000
Plymouth Albion	1876		7,000			ca. £1,000
Redruth	1875		26,000*			ca. £1,000

* Information from *The Guardian*, 12 Feb. 1975
** The following foundation dates were given in *The Guardian*: Halifax, 1866; Northern, 1875; London Scottish, 1876.

public schools were virtually the only institutions in the late nineteenth century and early twentieth centuries at which a boy could learn Rugby Union, most first-class players had attended such schools. That is, there was at that stage a high correlation between public school attendance, ability at Rugby and membership of top-level clubs.

The social homogeneity of Rugby Union's personnel in the early twentieth century and the fact that most players had been socialized into amateur conceptions of sport, meant the game was characterized by a high degree of consensus on amateur values. This was reinforced in two main ways by the split with Rugby League: by the fact that dissident players who wished to 'cash in' on their Rugby prowess could join clubs which played the professional code; and by the fact that the withdrawal of what were in the late nineteenth century the principal Northern gate-taking clubs restored the social homogeneity by which the game had been characterized prior to its spread down the social scale in Lancashire and Yorkshire.

In the 1920s, when its spread to the grammar schools began, Rugby Union started to become socially heterogeneous again. However, since the sports ethos taught at such schools was that of traditional amateurism and since the English middle class tends to embrace the values of its social superiors, this spread down the middle-class hierarchy did nothing fundamentally to alter the value-consensus by which Rugby Union had hitherto been marked. Yet it still began to change, and, particularly at the highest level, to diverge from pristine amateurism. This process became visible in the game-pattern through rule-changes introduced from 1956 onwards.

5. The transformation which began to become manifest in Rugby Union in the late 1950s is best described as a change from a 'player-centred' towards a more 'spectator-centred' form of amateurism. Ideologically, the authorities have continued to proclaim allegiance to the traditional, player-oriented ethos. In their actions, however, they—i.e. successive memberships of Rugby Union's law-making body, the 'International Board'—started to introduce changes which cumulatively increased the game's spectator appeal. For example, new offside laws were introduced to curb reliance on 'spoiling' defensive tactics; players are no longer required to play the ball with their feet after a tackle; penalty kicks no longer have to travel ten yards, thus making it possible to start passing moves from them; the 'knock-on' law, which in its old form was most likely to be infringed during the execution of intricate, crowd-pleasing moves such as the 'scissors', was eased thus reducing the number of set-scrums for handling infringements; the value of the try was raised from three to four points in an effort to encourage this *spectacular* element of the game; threequarters were required to stand ten yards behind the line-out; and kicking directly into touch was restricted to players within their own 25-yard areas.

The latter change—in 'law 27'—produced the most dramatic effects and is worth discussing at length. It was first introduced in 1968–9 on an experimental basis and reduced at a stroke the number of line-outs, simultaneously increasing the emphasis on running and passing. Because it originated in Australia and was introduced due ostensibly to Australian pressure, it was known at first as 'the Australian dispensation'. The Australians are said to have introduced such a change because the topography of their country 'favours' an 'open', running and passing game. The real reason, however, was the need to win back spectators who had been switching to Rugby League. Since that could not be openly acknowledged by the RFU as the reason for a proposed change, it had to be cloaked behind a plausible, geographical explanation.

In an attempt to gain material with which to silence opponents and, at the same time, reassurance that such a change was welcomed by the majority of players, the International Board sent a short questionnaire to constituent bodies and clubs in 1969. They received 627 replies, 585 expressing approval and a desire to see the change continued and only thirty expressing disapproval.[11] The uncertainty which prompted the International Board to dispatch this questionnaire was matched by the embarrassment of the Union authorities as they tried to explain the inconsistency between such spectator-oriented legislation and the player-centred ethos to which they claimed allegiance. Their typical rationalization was to maintain that changes had been introduced for the benefit of players and that any increase in spectator-attractiveness was an incidental by-product. However, perhaps because their life-chances are more centrally connected with the game's spectator appeal, Rugby journalists have tended to be less equivocal. Commenting in 1968 on the proposal to experiment with 'law 27', Clem Thomas wrote: 'the game must now inevitably be speeded up and become more adventurously alive: . . . the new law should help close the gap between soccer and Rugby as a spectator sport.'[12] And when, four years later, again following what was initially an Australian suggestion, the 'knock-on' law was amended and 'fumbling' ceased to be a punishable offence, David Frost suggested: 'This proposal is clearly designed to bring continuity to the game and so to afford greater entertainment for spectators.'[13] Commenting in 1975 on the effects of these changes, Michael Green wrote that: 'Crowds for the big occasions increased dramatically. Every international became a sell-out. Gates for the Middlesex sevens rose from 20,000 to 50,000.'[14]

A rough time-series (Table 11.6) showing the annual attendance figures for seven gate-taking clubs suggests, however, that spectator attendance of club matches overall has declined since the immediate post-war period. Assuming them to be reliable, these figures suggest that one of the principal reasons why the gate-taking clubs pressed for spectator-oriented changes was the fact that, in a period of mounting inflation, the gates on which they had grown financially dependent were declining. However, these figures cannot tell us why the RFU flew in the face of its commitment to a player-centred ethos and bowed to such pressure. The puzzle gets more intriguing when one realizes that, at the

Table 11.6[15] Annual match attendances of seven gate-taking clubs

Club	Season			
	1949–50	*1959–60*	*1969–70*	*1975–76*
Halifax	12,000	12,000	10,000	10,000
Liverpool	9,000	4,500	2,500	5,000
Bedford	47,449	16,628	8,934	19,867
Leicester	21,000	20,000	24,000	26,000
Saracens	1,500	5,000	7,000	10,000
Cheltenham	50,000	20,000	10,000	8,000
Exeter	29,000	25,000	22,000	20,000
TOTAL	169,949	103,128	84,484	88,867

same time, Rugby Union began to be accompanied by crowd behaviour of the kind which advocates of Rugby's traditional 'virtues' claim are peculiar to soccer. According to Michael Green, at Twickenham 'long-haired youths in jeans now throw toilet rolls and jeer, and, in 1965, a fire was started in a bar by students who 'put out the flames by urinating on them'. Moreover, local residents 'complain of hooliganism by crowds outside the ground'.[16]

So far such incidents have been relatively few. Nevertheless, 'Rugby hooliganism' has taken place and with a frequency sufficient to cause alarm in RFU circles. Given that and the embarrassment caused by the discrepancy with the player-centred ethos, one can see that the motives which led the International Board to introduce and persist with crowd-pleasing changes must have been compelling.

6. One or two clues to the constraints which led to the introduction of spectator-oriented changes are implicit in the discussion so far. For example, it is clear from the so-called 'Australian dispensation' and the fact that the new 'knock-on' law introduced in 1972 was proposed by Australia, that the spread of the game to countries where Rugby authorities do not cling so tenaciously to pristine amateur values, played a part. Closely bound up with this was the competitive tension generated by international diffusion. This led to a chauvinistic concern to ensure the success of the national XV and, when that was not easily forthcoming, the Rugby establishment became more willing to countenance change. Or more precisely, they became willing to countenance change as long as they could convince themselves that it did not threaten the game's amateur foundations.

Constraints generated domestically played a part in the introduction of these changes, too—prominent among them pressure from the gate-taking clubs which resulted from their growing dependency on spectator support. In its earliest stages, this pressure was diffuse but it became organized in 1969 when the 'Association of Gate-Taking Clubs' was formed. Starting with thirty-two clubs, this informal association had, by 1973, a membership of forty. It is without fixed rules, member clubs pay no subscriptions and its principal object is to act as a pressure group to secure the interests of the larger clubs. However, not only the gate-taking clubs but the RFU itself has grown financially dependent on spectator appeal. This has resulted in pressure 'from within'. In short, the 'sacred' amateur ethos has begun to be 'profaned' even at Twickenham, i.e. at a level where one would have expected it to remain inviolate. This requires elaboration.

In speaking of the RFU's dependency on spectators, we are not referring to the fact that some of its offices are held by members of gate-taking clubs. Although it exists, it is not that kind of 'covert dependency' that we have in mind. Nor are we anticipating the achievement by the Association of Gate-Taking Clubs of one of its principal aims: direct representation on the RFU. On the contrary, we are suggesting that the RFU *itself* has become dependent on spectators for fulfilling the functions it is expected to perform. This was established as soon as it began to levy admission charges for the international and other representative matches staged under its auspices. More correctly, it was established as soon as the RFU began to extract a surplus by that means and use it as a supplement to the affiliation fees of clubs for financing day-to-day administration and longer-term projects. However, the RFU is not financially dependent on spectator support simply in this direct sense. In 1927–8, the BBC began to broadcast from Twickenham and was charged a fee for the right to do so.[17] In 1937–8, televised Rugby and payment for TV rights began.[18] These two developments expanded the audience of the game but, at the same time, created for the RFU an indirect dependency on viewers and listeners, mediated by the TV and broadcasting authorities.

The extent of the RFU's financial dependency on direct and indirect spectator support can be gauged from what the Mallaby Committee tells us about the RFU's finances for 1974. Its total income for that year was about £148,000. Only about £3,000 of this, however, came from affiliation fees. The rest was made up as follows: gate receipts, etc., from internationals at Twickenham, about £95,000; TV and broadcasting fees, about £27,000; gate receipts, etc., from the Middlesex Seven-a-Side Competition, about £14,000; interest on loans and bank deposits about £9,000.[19] Thus by 1974, assuming that to have been a typical year, the RFU had grown dependent for more than ninety per cent of its average annual income on Rugby Union's spectator and audience appeal.

The RFU's dependency on spectators means that junior clubs are indirectly locked into and benefit materially from such a relationship, too. That is partly because affiliation fees would have to be raised if the revenue from internationals, radio, TV and, latterly advertising and commercial sponsorship, were not forthcoming. But it is also because the RFU operates a policy of giving low-interest loans to clubs to enable them to pay for ground improvements. In 1966–7, for example, £56,000 was lent to clubs and, at the end of April 1967, the outstanding balance of loans made to 167 clubs totalled £250,648 out of original advances totalling £424,283.[20]

The dependency of Rugby Union on spectator money involves, in part, a circulation of funds from one segment of the game's fraternity to another. For example, the crowds at international matches are composed mainly of schoolboy, junior and former players. Hence, a two-way transfer of funds takes place: from these three categories of spectators to the RFU. The latter then recycles funds back to the lower levels through its policy of low-interest loans. This cycle may, at first, have been more or less completely closed, i.e. it may have involved a circulation of funds solely or mainly within the Rugby community. However, that ceased to be the case with the advent of broadcast and televised Rugby, for these developments implied a growing financial dependency on the mass media and, through them, on a wider, in part non-Rugby-playing, audience.

It was the existence of this wider audience which led to the injection of money from advertisers and commercial sponsors into Rugby Union. At the end of 1973, the RFU signed a contract with Arena Sports for the placement of advertisements at Twickenham. We have been unable to discover how much the RFU earns in this manner but we do know that Arena Sports look after the advertisements at Cardiff Arms Park and that these were worth £22,000 to the Welsh Rugby Union over five years.[21] Commercial sponsorship was established somewhat earlier, being first accepted by the RFU when Watney-Mann, the brewing firm, sponsored the Universities Athletic Union Championship to the sum of £6,500. But that was chicken-feed compared to the £100,000 injected by the tobacco manufacturers, John Player and Sons, into the National Knock-Out Competition in 1975.[22] Although it was stated on each occasion that the RFU would retain strict control over the use of these monies and would in no way allow either advertising or commercial sponsorship to harm Rugby Union's amateur status, each further increment in the game's dependency and that of its controlling organization on outside finance posed another threat to the RFU's autonomy and to the amateur ethos in its pristine form. It is to the transformation of that ethos in the 1960s and the struggles which accompanied it that we shall now turn.

7. The player-centred ethos which Rugby Union developed in the late nineteenth century was not seriously challenged in the first half of the twentieth. However, from the 1950s, the realization slowly dawned that contemporary developments were a threat to amateurism in its pristine form. Thus, in 1954, Howard Marshall felt the need to reaffirm the player-centred ethos in the face of what he perceived as the inexorable transformation of the game at the highest levels into a money-oriented, spectator sport. He wrote:

> ... modern Rugby ... is a serious affair ... expresse[d] ... in gigantic stands; its success is measured in gate-receipts; the spectator is an

integral part ... I say that Rugby ... continues ... in spite of the spectator not because of him. He may ruin the game in the end, but there are still club matches where the spirit of true Rugby ... persists.[23]

In the 1950s, there was still little need to reaffirm traditional values. In the 1960s and 70s, however, as the consequences of Rugby Union's gradual transformation into a spectator sport became manifest, and particularly as spectator-oriented changes were introduced into the rules, such comments became part of Rugby journalism's standard fare. For example, Wilfred Wooller expressed the fear that contemporary pressures might lead the RFU to concern itself exclusively with 'star' players and gate-taking clubs. 'Rugby squares like me', he wrote, 'believe the game is for the player and the spectator is but an incidental attachment. The art of coarse Rugby is its true strength.'[24] H. B. Toft reintroduced the puritanical argument that spectatorship is morally wrong for fit young men, suggesting that a spectator-orientation might lead 'soccer-style' crowds to be attracted to Rugby Union.[25] And, alarmed by the mounting pressure for more formal competition, Rupert Cherry, writing in the *Daily Telegraph* in 1969, felt compelled, not only to reaffirm traditional values but to essay an explanation for the 'regressive' changes currently occurring:

> ... the most important point in making any change ... is that it should help the player ... The Rugby Union never cease to stress that ... yet so many men when they ... become club officials forget this and endeavour to turn their club into big business. This makes them look at an innovation like competitive Rugby from the angle of 'what will the club get out of it?' which to my mind is wrong. 'How will it benefit the player?' is all that matters.

Our survey data suggest that this explanation is inadequate and that the principal deviants from the player-centred ethos are not club officials but members of gate-taking clubs, players as well as officials, and independently of the level at which they play, players born after World War II. They also give an idea of the extent to which ideological deviancy has occurred in Rugby Union and show which groups—they are still numerically in the majority—continue to pay at least lip-service to traditional ideals. Respondents were asked how much notice they thought should be taken of spectator-interests in determining (a) the rules ('laws') and (b) the general management of Rugby Union. Their replies are summarized in Table 11.7.

It is not surprising that the 'laws' of the game are regarded as more sacrosanct than its management and administration. Thus, three times as many members of the RFU committee—eighteen per cent as opposed to six per cent—were willing to pay 'a lot' of attention to spectator interests in the latter than in the former regard. Our data also suggest that the views of the RFU Committee are in this respect representative of the opinions

Table 11.7 Opinions regarding the importance of spectator interests in determining the Laws and General Management of Rugby Union

Amount of attention to be paid to spectator interests	RFU Committee		Secretaries, Senior clubs		Players, etc.,* Senior clubs		Secretaries, Junior clubs		Players, etc.,* Junior clubs		TOTAL SAMPLE	
	Laws	Mgt	Laws	Mgt	Laws	Mgt	Laws	Mgt	Laws	Mgt	Laws	Mgt
A lot	2 (6%)	6 (18%)	6 (21%)	6 (21%)	15 (16%)	13 (14%)	3 (6%)	4 (8%)	22 (18%)	14 (12%)	48 (15%)	43 (13%)
Very little	21 (62%)	20 (59%)	16 (57%)	11 (39%)	50 (53%)	47 (49%)	26 (52%)	15 (31%)	61 (51%)	40 (33%)	174 (53%)	133 (41%)
None at all	11 (32%)	8 (24%)	6 (21%)	8 (28%)	30 (32%)	18 (19%)	16 (32%)	14 (28%)	35 (29%)	36 (30%)	98 (29%)	84 (26%)
Did not answer	0	0	0	3 (10%)	0	17 (18%)	5 (10%)	17 (34%)	2 (2%)	30 (25%)	7 (2%)	67 (20%)
TOTALS	34	34	28	28	95	95	50	50	120	120	327	327

* Includes club officials other than secretaries

of participants in the game generally, i.e. that there is a numerical majority in favour of the traditional ethos. We shall not speculate on whether this is indicative of the democratic character of the RFU or whether it reflects either the tendency for the lower sections of the British middle classes to model themselves on and act deferentially towards their social superiors or the skill of the game's establishment as manipulators and moulders of opinion. It is sufficient just to note that the highest proportions of adherents to the minority view, i.e. who believed that spectator interests should be important as determinants even of the 'sacred' laws of Rugby Union, came from three categories of respondents: secretaries of Senior clubs (twenty-one per cent), players and officials (other than secretaries) of Senior clubs (sixteen per cent), and players and officials (other than secretaries) of Junior clubs (eighteen per cent). In short, it was the Senior, i.e. gate-taking club officials, and, independently of the type of club to which they belonged, the players in our sample, i.e. members principally of the generation born after World War II, who were most likely to deviate from Rugby Union's traditional ethos. Neither of these facts is very surprising: the first reflects the growing dependency of gate-taking clubs on spectator support; the second the general tendency of younger people to question the values of their elders.

A distinct fear exists in Rugby circles that the changes currently occurring could herald a process of deterioration similar to that which they believe has taken place in soccer. This serves to reinforce their commitment to the traditional ethos and stiffens their resolve to resist the current trend. But this trend is powerful, affecting all levels and areas of the game. Nowhere is it revealed more clearly than in the transformation of attitudes to training and coaching. Accordingly it is to that issue that our attention will next be turned.

8. Perhaps the best index of the traditional Rugby Union attitude to training and coaching is the fact that, until the 1950s, the achievement of victory was held to be subsidiary to other aims such as character formation and gentlemanly behaviour. However, during that decade, as the growing competitiveness caused by the spread of the game grew more transparent, it became necessary to reaffirm this aspect of the traditional ethos, too. For example, commenting in 1956 on the 1930 British Lions tour of Australasia, F. D. Prentice, RFU Secretary from 1947 to 1962, felt obliged to include the following exhortation: '. . . let us remember that a British touring side does not . . . [have] the sole object of winning . . . or setting up . . . scoring records. . . . Rugby should . . . be played for the love of the game.'[26]

Since victory was supposed to be subsidiary, training and coaching were necessarily relegated to a subordinate position, too. Howard Marshall expressed this neatly when he wrote that: 'The game is not intended for highly trained athletes but for reasonably fit men who like their exercise on a Saturday afternoon.'[27] Commenting on Cambridge University's visit to

America in 1934, K. C. Fyfe recalled that a major reason for the tour was: '. . . to . . . impress on . . . people . . . that the game was . . . meant to be enjoyed by businessmen . . . and . . . not in need of the specialization or intensive training which . . . Americans bring to their . . . sports.'[28] His report of the team's consternation on reading American press reports of what they regarded as a 'hard work-out' suggests that the traditional attitude to training was not simply verbal but translated into deed:

> We had a hard puntabout—or so we thought—for an hour and a half, and we went off the field feeling very fit; imagine then our consternation when we read our evening papers and discovered that we had 'indulged in a gentle loosening-up exercise'.[29]

These views were expressed, not simply as descriptions of the past, but in order to defend traditional amateurism against the encroachment of forms of specialization and intensive training similar to those which the Cambridge players deplored in American sports. However, such practices have now become the norm in Rugby Union. That they are approved by the majority connected with the game can be seen from Table 11.8 which reports the attitudes of our sample to the currently dominant approach to training and coaching. This table speaks for itself. The overwhelming majority of our sample, and in this they are probably representative of the people at present connected with the game, have abandoned this aspect of the traditional ethos and approve unreservedly of the serious-minded approach which now pre-dominates. However, a feeling of unease has developed regarding the prob-lems this has generated at the top levels of the game. A few quotations from statements made by first-class players will illustrate the sorts of pressures to which they claim to be currently subject. In 1972, for example, the Welsh international, Barry John, was asked to explain his 'premature retirement' at the age of twenty-seven and said: 'In a nutshell, I had reached a point . . . where I was public property with no home or family life'[30] Bob Hiller, the former England and Harlequins captain, when asked why he had chosen to stop playing international Rugby replied: 'Basically we play Rugby for fun. It was never meant to carry the pressures it now does.'[31] A similar picture of pressure and diminishing autonomy and privacy, emerges from Green's description of the schedule which led David Duckham to drop out of the 1974 'Lions' South Africa tour. What with committee meetings and club, county and international matches and training sessions, he was, apparently, spending at least five nights and two afternoons a week on Rugby:

> 'It's not just playing frequently that causes the stress,' he said, 'it's the feeling of never getting away from the game. You're under a micro-scope the whole time. Even if you go for a drink someone starts to talk Rugby when all you want to do is rest. You find you're thinking about nothing but Rugby. And these days success is so much more

Table 11.8 Attitudes to training and coaching

	RFU Committee		Secretaries, Senior clubs		Players, Senior clubs		Secretaries, Junior clubs		Players, Junior clubs		Totals	
	Training	Coaching	Training	Coaching	Training	Coaching	Training	Coaching	Training	Coaching	Training	Coaching
Approve of current approach	17	15	23	17	82	74	39	37	105	95	266 (81%)	238 (73%)
Approve, with reservations	15	15	4	6	10	16	8	9	7	16	44 (13%)	62 (19%)
Disapprove of current approach	2	4	1	5	3	5	3	4	8	9	17 (5%)	27 (8%)
TOTALS	34	34	28	28	95	95	50	50	120	120	327	327

important. You feel the Press watching every move. It's like living in a goldfish bowl.'[32]

David Irvine reports a Rugby Union international who was 'amused'

> ... by a BBC interview with a Stoke City forward who claimed that he was 'exhausted' after playing almost 60 league and Cup games. 'I reckon to play that many every season, train two nights a week, occasionally on Sunday, and do a full week's work besides.'[33]

Such are the amounts of time and energy committed in first-class Rugby that, according to the Welsh international, J. J. Williams:

> We're virtually full-time players. The only difference between us and the soccer professionals is that we don't have to hang about the club every day.[34]

And he continued:

> They'll have to pay us in the end, you know. Scrap all this nonsense and let us earn a bit from something we can do well.[35]

Such is the degree of commitment to amateurism which remains in Rugby Union—or such the fear of recrimination by the RFU—that it is rare for players to countenance the possibility of payment so openly. Nevertheless, it is clear that, at top-class level, the game has begun to undergo a process of professionalization similar to that in the late-nineteenth-century North. Thus, top clubs and players are oriented towards crowds and take the game seriously. Considerable time is devoted to preparation for, travelling to, and playing matches. In fact, as we said earlier, though remaining amateur in name and continuing to rationalize its existence in terms of amateur values, top-class Rugby Union has become virtually indistinguishable from a professional sport. The only major difference is that players are not bound to clubs by financial contract. They can, however, benefit materially from the game. According to Nicholson:

> The pressure ... comes from outside the sport—from newspapers, publishers, television, commerce, P.R. and advertising. In these days, any kind of fame is a convertible asset. You notice it in small ways: the Adidas bags going into the changing room, the level at which players are entertained, the constant appearance of photographers when they go about their everyday jobs or take their wives to a restaurant, the constant mixing with the George Bests, Graham Hills and Henry Coopers at receptions and club openings, this centenary, that charity function. In a decade their life-style has altered out of all recognition.[36]

That the official introduction of financial compensation for clubs or players may be imminent was suggested in a discussion between Carwyn James
and Roy McKelvie reported in the *Guardian* in 1973. After expressing commitment to the amateur ethos, James noted, firstly, that employers 'are sub-
sidizing the players, and the game as well, by not docking salaries and wages',
and secondly, that tours abroad 'can make up to half a million profit',
McKelvie then suggested that 'a simple solution would be for the unions to
reimburse the employers for the money they paid out to players involved in
representative Rugby'.[37]

If such a solution were adopted, the money paid would not be called a
'wage' or 'broken-time' payment. Nevertheless, players would still be financially subsidized for their Rugby from spectator money. The only real difference between that and the existing situation would be that, instead of money
changing hands through a dyadic transaction, i.e. from employers to players
ostensibly as payment for occupational duties, it would pass through a chain
of four, i.e. from spectators to the Unions, thence to the employers, and
from them to the players as part of their occupational salaries and wages. In
return, the employers would receive free of charge the benefits for which they
now covertly subsidize the game, e.g. the kudos of employing top-class
sportsmen, the psychological satisfactions from close association with first-
class athletes, and the exploitation of players' reputations for commercial
gain, e.g. by employing them as salesmen.

9. Even though the process of professionalization which top-class Rugby
Union is currently undergoing represents the greatest contradiction of the
amateur ethos, it is either not seen or not admitted by many of the game's
personnel as the greatest and most immediate threat. Or to put it more precisely, it is not over professionalization in a direct sense that the majority of
antagonists have, to paraphrase Karl Marx, 'become conscious of the conflict
and are fighting it out'. On the contrary, the issue of formal competition, more
specifically of cups and leagues, is seen to represent the greatest threat. By the
same token, it is cups and leagues which the opponents of traditional amateurism are striving to incorporate into the game. But what they are unintentionally
contributing to is the emergence of Rugby Union as a spectator-oriented professional sport just like any other in the modern world. A brief review of the
major events in this process will help to document our case.

Matters came into the open in January 1969 when thirteen Northern gate-
taking clubs and twelve leading Surrey clubs held meetings. The former
decided unanimously to ask the RFU for permission to organize a league. A
majority of the latter were in favour of introducing some form of cup. On 17
January, the RFU Secretary issued a statement rejecting league organization as
'against the interests of an amateur game'. This formed the catalyst which led
to the formation of the Association of Gate-Taking Clubs, thus transforming what had hitherto been largely unorganized into an overtly organized

struggle. Faced for the first time by organized pressure, the RFU set up a special sub-committee to discuss how an open competition could be started. Since league organization had been rejected, and since the gate-taking clubs did not wish to precipitate another split or lay themselves open to the charge of having done so, a knock-out competition was the only feasible possibility. Hence it was in that form and after two years' wrangling that the RFU agreed to launch a national competition. It was to be known as 'the National Knock-Out Competition', to commence in 1971–2 and, consistently with the amateur ethos, no trophy was to be awarded. Our survey data show how respondents viewed the new competition shortly after its introduction. As one can see from Table 11.9, the overwhelming majority (seventy-eight per cent) looked on it with approval. A feature of the figures in this table is the fact that the highest rates of disapproval were found, not, as one might have expected, among members of Senior and gate-taking clubs but among members of the RFU Committee and secretaries of Junior clubs, i.e. by and large among the older age groups. The highest rates of approval were found among players, i.e. the younger age groups, independently of type of club. In short, it tends to be the older members of the Rugby fraternity who support the amateur ethos in its pristine form and younger ones who tend to deviate.

The events leading to the establishment of the National KO Competition were just the opening skirmishes in a struggle which has continued, without decisive resolution, to the present day. Nevertheless, it is clear that in the long term, the supporters of traditional amateurism are waging a losing battle. Their first capitulation came in 1969 when they agreed to the setting up of the special subcommittee; their second in 1971 when they submitted to the introduction of the KO Competition. Subsequent capitulations have involved: agreeing to the award of a cup and allowing the competition to be called 'the National Knock-Out Competition'; more crucially, submitting in 1975 to sponsorship by the John Player Tobacco Company and allowing the competition to be called 'the John Player Cup'; and, most recently of all, agreeing in 1976 to the introduction of 'merit tables', i.e. in effect giving official blessing to league organization. Our survey data are again of relevance to an understanding of this issue. They are summarized in Table 11.10.

These findings coincide with those of the Mallaby Committee who reported that '. . . there is more support for a Club Knock-out competition at national level than there is for any national league system of clubs.'[38] But, assuming our data to reflect attitudes in the game as a whole, this hides the fact that more than one-third (thirty-five per cent) of the present Rugby Union fraternity would approve the establishment of leagues. Only among officials and members of the RFU Committee do less than one-fifth (twelve per cent) approve of competitions of this type. And in the case of Senior players, there is a clear majority, fifty-seven per cent, in favour.

The ostensibly democratic fact that a majority of the Rugby fraternity (sixty-one per cent in the case of our sample) regards league organization as incompatible with amateurism has not deterred the proponents of leagues

Table 11.9 Attitudes to the National Knock-Out Competition

	RFU Committee	Secretaries, Senior clubs	Players, Senior clubs	Secretaries, Junior clubs	Players, Junior clubs	Totals
Approve	22 (65%)	22 (79%)	77 (81%)	33 (66%)	100 (83%)	254 (78%)
Ambivalent	4 (12%)	1 (4%)	7 (7%)	5 (10%)	8 (7%)	25 (8%)
Disapprove	8 (24%)	5 (18%)	9 (9%)	12 (24%)	12 (10%)	46 (14%)
No reply	0	0	2	0	0	2
TOTALS	34	28	95	50	120	327

Table 11.10 Attitudes to the establishment of Leagues in Rugby Union

	RFU Committee	Secretaries, Senior clubs	Players, Senior clubs	Secretaries, Junior clubs	Players, Junior clubs	Totals
Approve	4 (12%)	13 (46%)	54 (57%)	11 (22%)	32 (27%)	114 (35%)
Ambivalent	1 (3%)	2 (7%)	2 (2%)	3 (6%)	5 (4%)	13 (4%)
Disapprove	29 (85%)	13 (46%)	39 (41%)	36 (72%)	83 (69%)	200 (61%)
TOTALS	34	28	95	50	120	327

from pressing their claims. Rebuffed by the RFU, their first act was to establish unofficial 'merit tables' up and down the country and at least one newspaper, the *Daily Mail*, began to award a pennant annually to the winners of such a 'league'. Further support came from developments outside England. Thus, 1975 saw the establishment of leagues in Scotland and a commitment to introduce such a system in Wales. It was also in that year that the match secretary of Coventry RFC proposed the setting up of an 'Anglo-Welsh Merit Table' consisting of nineteen leading clubs within a 120-mile radius of Bristol.

Thus, in a Rugby world increasingly characterized by cups, leagues and more or less open 'shamateurism', the RFU found itself isolated as a proponent of pure amateur principles. The Mallaby Committee was set up in 1972 in the hope that its recommendations might help to defuse or diffuse the crisis generated by the demands of the gate-taking clubs. It reported in 1974, suggesting that such clubs 'could be afforded official recognition and given appropriate representation', adding that 'the title "Major Clubs" would more accurately represent what they are'.[39] However, the RFU rejected this almost entirely, proposing, instead of direct representation, the formation of a 'Major Clubs Sub-committee', thereby bringing into the open once more a conflict which had for two years been fought principally behind closed doors as different interest groups strove to influence the Mallaby recommendations.

As part of their attempt to gain direct representation, the gate-taking clubs circularized the rest with a letter, signed by representatives of the Rosslyn Park and Liverpool clubs, setting forth their case. An immediate response was produced among the representatives of junior clubs. One of the leaders was Les Boundy, a former player and international referee who, in an interview published in *The Sunday Times*, urged junior clubs to vote against direct representation at the forthcoming AGM, asking those unable to send a representative to submit proxy votes. His comments in support of this position are revealing:

> 'The gate-taking clubs' he said, 'say that they are the game's shop window, but it is the junior clubs which furnish them with players. Players in the latter have to pay subscriptions and match-fees, buy their own kit and contribute to a "beer-kitty" for the visiting team, whereas senior players pay nothing and do not have to worry about administration. Anyway, senior clubs are already represented at the RFU through their constituent bodies. Their ultimate sanction would be to break from the RFU': 'So what?' asks Boundy. 'In five years they would be replaced by other clubs equally as strong. There was exactly the same position in 1893 . . . But did it harm Rugby Union in the end? Not on your life! The game that is growing at the moment is Union, not League. The same would happen again.'[40]

Boundy's stress on the interdependence of Senior and Junior clubs was correct. It will remain as long as the former continue to recruit players from the latter. However, although he apparently failed to recognize it, the implication of his suggestion that the major clubs would resurrect themselves following another split, points to the recurrent dilemma, inherent in modern sport and which Rugby Union is unable to avoid, namely the tendency for clubs and performers to become stratified and for those at the top to attract paying spectators.

In the event, the Junior clubs won the day. The Rosslyn Park–Liverpool motion at the 1975 AGM was defeated by 583 votes to 137. That is hardly surprising given the constitutional dominance of the Junior clubs. At the same meeting, the establishment of a 'Major Clubs Subcommittee'—on which the RFU and the major clubs each have eight representatives—was overwhelmingly approved.[41] But, even though this went against the wishes of the gate-taking clubs, it did result in change for it required the RFU to break with the traditional fiction that all clubs are equal and designate some as 'major'. In 1976, they followed by setting up four regional 'merit tables' for the leading English clubs, thus moving even closer to meeting the demands of the gate-taking clubs.

It remains to be seen whether this latest compromise will satisfy either 'major' or 'minor' clubs, or whether we are on the threshold of another split. It is clear, however, that history is repeating itself in certain respects. Thus the RFU is again at loggerheads with gate-taking clubs, although this time they do not come exclusively from the North and the issues of 'broken-time' payment and professionalism have not yet been explicitly raised. A further difference is that the membership of the present gate-taking clubs is predominantly middle-class. However, that does not necessarily mean the two situations are *structurally* different. Thus, a smaller proportion of the middle-class personnel who run the gate-taking clubs have attended public schools than is the case with members of the RFU Committee. In other words, the public school/non-public school division within the upper and middle classes which was important in the late-nineteenth-century crisis is, to some extent, paralleled in the crisis which the game is witnessing today. Moreover, the present crisis is also taking place in a situation of intense and overt class conflict in society at large. The combination of these structural and historical facts *could* have consequences similar to those of the 1890s.

In our view, however, that is unlikely for several reasons. Thus, the regional dimension of the nineteenth-century crisis is lacking. And, as we have stressed, the lower middle and middle middle class in Britain, or at least those sections represented in the Rugby fraternity, tend to be deferential towards social superiors. In other words, although the current crisis involves conflict between different sections of the middle class, the subordinate sections identify socially with their superiors. And that means that the sports dimensions of the crisis are not reinforced by non-sports criteria. In short, even though the public school/non-public school division *could* represent a source of escalation of the current crisis, such an escalation is less likely than was the case in the nineteenth century.

However, whether we are on the threshold of another split or not, it is significant that the power of the public school élite in Rugby Union leads others to accept their definition of the situation and to blind them to the facts, especially to the fact that, at the top level, the game is already virtually professional or at least no longer amateur in any meaningful sense. Thus, as we have shown, the RFU and the top clubs have grown dependent on spectator support. Moreover, first-class players do not have to pay to play but have their travelling and accommodation expenses and often their kit provided. And they are, in many cases, allowed time off to play Rugby by their employers. Since they suffer no loss of wages on that account, this means they are subsidized to play. In short, independently of whether first-class players are rewarded by the payment of sums in excess of legitimate expenses, their Rugby is financed either out of money paid by spectators, advertisers and sponsors to their clubs, or by employers. In that sense, they are 'professionals'. Increasingly, also, they are 'time-professionals' in the sense in which Christopher Brasher defined that term,[42] i.e. they devote increasing amounts of time and energy to the pursuit of Rugby. This means that it has come, for them, to form a major life-interest, pushing other interests such as marriage, family, education and occupation into the background.

This development, along with the others traced in this and earlier chapters, shows the strength of the pressures in modern society which lead to the professionalization of sports. Thus, even an organization such as the RFU which set itself steadfastly for more than eighty years to the goal of defending the 'amateur ideal' is unable, under modern conditions, to maintain a game-form consistent with that ideal. What, then, are the social conditions that make the maintenance of amateur sport an impossible ideal, particularly at the highest levels? That is an issue we have touched on several times in our text. We shall attempt to tie the threads together in the conclusion. We shall also return in that context to the other theoretical issues raised in the Introduction.

Conclusion

Sociological reflections on the crisis in modern sport

1. Our principal task in this conclusion is to bring together the threads of our analysis and to tease out its implications for the theoretical issues outlined in the Introduction. There are three such issues: (i) the light our study sheds on the reasons why Britain was not only the first industrial but also the first 'sporting nation'; (ii) the implications of our analysis for Elias' theory of the 'civilizing process', more specifically for his hypothesis that there has occurred in West European societies, a long-term change in standards of violence-control; and (iii) the light thrown by our study on the structural sources of the worldwide trend towards greater seriousness of participation in, and greater cultural centrality of, sport. Most of our attention will be devoted to the second and third issues. We shall begin, however, by briefly considering the first.

2. Our study sheds light in several ways on the structural features in Britain's social development which led it to form what Huizinga called 'the cradle and focus of modern sporting life'. We rejected the overly simple view which sees the fact that Britain was the 'first sporting nation' as an automatic reflex of industrialization and stressed, instead, the emergence of a social configuration which enabled the ruling classes to retain a degree of independence from the monarchical state. This, we suggested, enabled them to resist total absorption into court society and to retain a life-style containing strong rural elements and with a heavy emphasis on outdoor pursuits. They were less constrained than their continental counter-parts, e.g. in France, to participate in highly formalized, stylized and ritualized courtly activities, retaining the independence to use their leisure-time as they wished. Consequently, it was outside the context of the court, namely on their country estates, in rural villages and in the public schools, that the more elastic, less rigid, stylized and ritualized antecedents of modern sport grew up. It is also reasonable to hypothesize that the same social configuration, with its judicious mixture of central control and independence, was one of the central structural sources of the fact that Britain became the first industrial nation.

As we showed, it was the public schools that were the crucial 'model-making centres' as far as the initial modernization of football was concerned. Again, it was the peculiar balance between freedom and control established in these institutions that formed the necessary condition for the occurrence of this process. Such a balance, we suggested, could not have been established in social institutions that were either more authoritarian or more anarchic. It formed, it is reasonable to suppose, one of the central preconditions for the initial development in Britain of sport-forms that were destined subsequently to spread all over the world.

It is worth pointing out, particularly in sociology at its present juncture, that, in order to explain the genesis of this balance at the 'micro-structural' level, we found it necessary to trace its dependency on 'macro-structural' developments, that is, on developments at the level of British social structure as a whole. Of critical importance in this connection, we suggested, was the process of *embourgeoisement* which we redefined to mean the growing power of the industrial middle classes at the societal level with its attendant consequences for institutions and values. However, since that process took place within the framework of an established system of dominance by the aristocracy and gentry, it remained in crucial respects incomplete. That is, Britain's industrialization was accompanied by growing bourgeois power but the industrial middle classes were forced to accommodate to the aristocracy and gentry and to adopt some of their values. At the same time, the reverse process also occurred, i.e. the landed classes were forced to 'bourgeoisify', to adopt a number of values which are characteristically bourgeois.

This process of mutual accommodation between the earlier and the later ruling-class was, we suggested, the principal structural source of the persistence of amateur structures and values in British sport, even in those which are professional. It has served to insulate them against commercial pressures, weakening the impact of the latter and making British sport in general far less commercialized than its counterparts in the United States. This difference in the degree of commercialization of American and British sport is largely a reflection of the fact that American society represents a 'purer' type of capitalism. That, in its turn, reflects the fact that industrial capitalism in Britain developed within the frame-work of an established system of dominance by the aristocracy and gentry whereas, in the United States, no serious or lasting barriers to the establishment of bourgeois dominance existed.

The development in British sport of an amateur-dominated structure can be regarded as symptomatic of the structure and development of British society as a whole in the nineteenth and twentieth centuries. Its counterpart in industry is a managerial and employing class in which 'gentlemanly' values continue to loom large. However, just as these values have come, in recent decades, to form one of the principal sources of Britain's inability to compete effectively with other industrial nations, so, too, the amateur-dominated structure of British sport has created difficulties for competition with sportsmen from elsewhere. For years, Britain was the world's supreme industrial and sporting power. The advantages conferred by being the country where industry and modern sport originated enabled Britain to dominate the international scene. Subsequently, the *dis*advantages of coming first began to accrue. The British found themselves hampered by obsolete equipment, organization and values, and unable to compete so easily against countries which entered the industrial and sporting scenes later. Yet the memory of past glories has persisted, helping in both spheres to generate expectations which it is impossible for a small country with obsolete structures and values to realize in a world where industry and sport have spread.

Such a discrepancy between expectations and performance constitutes one element in what one might call Britain's current 'sporting crisis'. The other elements are the alleged growth in violence, and the conflict over amateurism and professionalism. It is to these issues that our attention will now be turned. We shall pay special attention in this connection to their implications for Elias' theory of the civilizing process and to the light they shed on the world-wide trend towards greater seriousness and achievement-orientation in sport.

3. It is widely believed that we are currently witnessing an increase in violence in and around sport. On the face of it, such an increase would seem to represent a clear refutation of Elias' theory. Indeed, the fact that it does so has been explicitly suggested by the German sociologist, Kurt Weis. In a recent essay, he wrote:

> . . . Elias has indicated that in the process of civilization the degree of active aggression and violence decreased and that the joys of violence were transferred from participation to observation. Considering the latest development in sports-related violence, this optimistic view may have to be modified. Not only is there . . . general agreement on an overall escalation of spectator violence, but, at least in Europe, it is again the British who enjoy a leading position among soccer hooligans, although the margin of their leadership is constantly narrowing.[1]

This is based on an overly simple interpretation of Elias' theory. As we hope to show, far from being in any sense a refutation of it, the current increase in 'sports-related' violence—and we shall not commit ourselves yet as to whether it has really occurred—can only be explained by reference to that theory. This may seem paradoxical so, in order to set the matter straight, we shall now consider the implications of our study for Elias' theory.

In the sense that its formal rules legitimize a relatively high degree of violent physical contact, Rugby football is undoubtedly one of the roughest contemporary sports. Nevertheless, our study of its development seems to confirm a limited aspect of Elias' theory: namely that which relates to the social control of violence. Thus the period we have covered witnessed the emergence of Rugby out of the earlier, relatively undifferentiated and violent folk matrix as a modern sport, 'civilized' in four senses which were lacking in the ancestral forms. More specifically, modern Rugby is civilized by: (i) a complex set of formal rules which demand strict control over physical violence and which prohibit it in certain forms, e.g. 'hacking'; (ii) clearly defined intra-game sanctions, i.e. 'penalties', which can be brought to bear on offenders and, as the ultimate sanction for serious and persistent rule-violation, the possibility of exclusion from the game; (iii) the institutionalization of a specific role which stands, as it were, 'outside' and 'above' the game and whose task it is to control it, i.e. that of 'referee'; and (iv) a nationally centralized rule-making and rule-enforcing body, the RFU.[2]

This civilizing process did not take the form of a continuously progressive development of the kind modern sociologists tend to attribute to their nineteenth-century predecessors. On the contrary, it occurred in two main spurts, subsequently reaching relatively stable plateaux: the first took place at Rugby School, principally during and immediately after the headship of Thomas Arnold; the second occurred in the wider society when the public controversy over 'hacking', itself an index of the civilizing process that was occurring in British society at large, contributed to the constraints which led Rugby clubs to unite and form the RFU. What happened in each of these cases was that the *standards* of violence-control applied in the game advanced in the sense of demanding from players the exercise of a stricter and more comprehensive measure of self-control.

The long-term development of Rugby thus tends, in our view, to confirm a limited aspect of Elias' theory. However, since it seems to be a difficult theory to grasp, it will probably help the reader if we spell out in greater detail what we take Elias to have argued and what we think our findings show. The first thing to note is that Elias' theory and our own findings both relate primarily to *standards* of violence-control, i.e. to the social norms applied in that respect. It is these which have developed in the long-term in a civilizing direction, demanding that Rugby players exercise stricter control in respect of physical violence, at the same time, attempting to ensure that they do so via the imposition of specific sanctions by specialized controlling personnel.

That such a development of civilizing standards has taken place seems to us to be undeniable. What is more problematic is whether *rates* of violence in the game, as measured, e.g. by numbers of injuries and deaths per thousand man-hours played, have undergone a correlative decline. That is a complex and difficult issue. Neither the historical nor the contemporary data are sufficiently detailed and precise to enable one to substantiate what has happened in this regard. For reasons that we shall spell out later, it is, we think, probably the case that we are currently witnessing a factual increase of violence in the game. However, if it is occurring, such an increase, we should like to suggest, is an increase *within* the higher level of civilization at which the game currently stands. That is, it does not represent a regression sufficient in extent to make the modern game comparable with the violent antecedents out of which it grew. That is the case because all groups, even the transgressors of 'civilized' standards, claim to deplore the alleged current trend, and that means that less civilized standards have not yet become the norm. They are not, as was formerly the case, socially tolerated and legitimate, that is, built into the rule-structure of the game. Moreover, since it results from the application of the very standards whose development Elias has documented, it can also be said that the current outcry over violence in Rugby provides further confirmation of his theory. This requires elaboration since it may seem either inconsistent or paradoxical that we can believe the theory of the civilizing process to be confirmed, whilst at the same time admitting that a factual increase of violence may be currently occurring.

The first thing to note is that the present outcry over violence in Rugby provides further confirmation of his theory. Since it occurs in a minority, middle-class sport, Rugby violence has not been accorded as much prominence by the mass media as 'soccer hooliganism' but it has been given some. We noted a few examples of reports of hooligan behaviour by Rugby spectators in Chapter 11. An extract from an article which appeared in *The Sunday Times* in February 1978 must suffice in this context as an example of the current outcry over violence on the field of play. The author, an Irish barrister, wrote:

> Recently punching and kicking have become increasingly prevalent in rugby and soccer . . . Rugby was once a gentlemen's game, providing ample opportunity for violent contact within the rules. But gentlemen didn't take advantage of the rules to kick and punch. This is not so any longer.
>
> It is quite clear . . . that Common Law assaults are prevalent in the modern game. In a TV interview some time ago a famous Lions forward let it be known that the motto on tour was 'get your retaliation in first'.[3]

We could give more examples but they are unnecessary in this context. It is sufficient just to note that mass media and official responses to Rugby violence—and to its more publicized counterpart in soccer on and off the field—have all the trappings of a 'moral panic'. That is, for reasons we shall explore in a moment, the nature and extent of the violence appear to be exaggerated. Moreover, the allegedly violent present is compared with an idyllic past when men are held to have played robustly but stuck to the rules. To say this is not to deny that violent infractions of the rules occur in modern Rugby or that they may be on the increase. Nor is it to deny that the more general perception of our own as a violent age corresponds, in some respects, with observable facts. The modern world is undoubtedly violent in at least two ways: firstly in the sense that modern weapons are capable of inflicting death and destruction on a hitherto unprecedented scale, thus providing a factual core on which the current belief may, in part, be founded; and secondly, in the sense that present-day international relations are, in a real sense, anarchic, characterized by growing interdependence without effective central control. Standards for the conduct of international relations are beginning to emerge but, in the absence of a world state, there is no means of ensuring that they are universally adhered to or uniformly applied. As a result, naked power, unrestrained by civilizing standards, tends to operate to a greater extent in the international arena than is the case in the domestic affairs of industrial nation-states. The potential for violence inherent in such a situation is realized in fact in a number of cases, thus providing another real buttress for the current belief.

But to recognize these real sources of violence in the modern world is not to deny the valid core of Elias' theory. Growing international violence is what one would predict from the theory in a world in which international interdependence is growing, unaccompanied by effective state-centralization at an international level, i.e. by the emergence of a world state. At the same time, the evidence currently available about the social control of violence at an *intra*-state level, including that advanced in our own study, provides strong support for Elias' contention that a long-term civilizing process has occurred *within* the more advanced nation-states of Western Europe. But *inter*-state tensions and conflicts act as a brake on the occurrence of this process 'domestically', i.e. *within* particular nation-states, contributing, for example, to the continued training of specialized personnel in the use of arms. Yet the majority of citizens rarely encounter violence directly. Like birth, death, sex and other 'natural functions', it is 'pushed behind the scenes'. However, the majority do regularly witness violence *vicariously* in the mass media, especially TV, either in the form of news reports or 'mimetically' in the form of plays and films.[4] The media definition of violence as 'news' and the fact that reports of incidents, selected from wherever in the world the worst violence is currently occurring, are brought nightly into the homes of ordinary citizens, is a further buttress of the popular belief that we live in an excessively violent age. More important for present purposes, however, is the fact that the apparently insatiable popular demand for violence on stage and screen is attributable, at least in part, to the civilizing process as outlined by Elias.

This is a complex issue but it is possible to discuss it briefly. Thus modern nation-states are characterized domestically by growing interdependence and competitiveness. At the same time, their citizens are hemmed in and controlled by strict, 'civilizing' standards which prohibit resort to physical violence and which are backed up by the imposition of severe sanctions on those whose transgressions are discovered by or brought to the attention of the agencies of the state. The size and consequent impersonality of modern nation-states compounds the problem. Their members find themselves recurrently in competitive situations, frequently with adversaries whom, if they are aware of them at all, they recognize only dimly. These adversaries may be, for example, tax inspectors or employees of multi-national corporations, that is, strangers by whom a person feels slighted, exploited or in some other way maltreated and against whom they develop feelings of anger.

Unable to release these feelings because it is socially taboo, what they can do is develop aggressive fantasies and these can, to some extent, be satisfied vicariously by acting out or witnessing violence in the mimetic sphere, e.g. in sport or the theatre. Thus, if we are right, it is not only modern standards of violence-control which provide support for Elias' theory. The modern demand for mimetic violence supports it, too. The same is true of the perception of our own as an excessively violent era and, as part of it, of the perception of violence as increasing in modern sport. This is another complex issue. Again it is possible to discuss it briefly.

The first thing to note is that the evidence introduced in the empirical part of our book supports the view that a civilizing process has occurred within the restricted sphere of sport. And, until it can be shown that there are sound reasons either for believing that such a process was specific merely to sport or, more narrowly, to Rugby, or that it occurred independently of and perhaps contrary to the direction of development in society at large, it is reasonable to suppose that it provides more general confirmation of Elias' theory; i.e. it suggests that a civilizing process has occurred with respect to the control of violence, i.e. that standards have emerged which demand in this regard the exercise of greater self-control. But, and this is the nub of our criticism of sociologists such as Weis, this means that our perception of violence is filtered through these very standards, thus increasing the range of behaviours which are regarded as violent and contributing to a perceptual magnification of the rate of violence both in sport and society at large. In short, the emergence of more civilized standards of violence-control means that acts that formerly would have been dismissed as mere 'horse-play' or excusable 'high spirits' are nowadays regarded as abhorrent.

To say this is not to deny that an increase in sports-related violence has recently occurred. As we suggested earlier, there are reasons for believing that to be the case and we have now reached a point where it is appropriate to spell them out. Put succinctly, the current factual increase in sports-related violence is primarily attributable, in our opinion, to the growing cultural centrality of sport, to the fact that sport in modern societies has become a phenomenon which, *pace* Huizinga, can be described without exaggeration as quasi-religious. This has led people to pursue their sports seriously and to place an increasing emphasis on success. In its turn, this has led to a growth in the competitiveness of sports, contributing to an increase in the rate and intensity of sporting interaction, in that way leading to a growth of violence, both intentional and accidental. However, both the civilizing process and the growing cultural centrality and seriousness of modern sport can be attributed, in part, to the same deep-structural trend: to what Elias calls 'functional democratization'.[5] If we are right, it is functional democratization which accounts for the trend in modern sport which was identified but not, in our view, adequately explained by Huizinga, Rigauer and Stone. Let us attempt to demonstrate how that is so.

4. In order to accomplish such a demonstration it is necessary for us first to recall the 'amateur ethos', the dominant sports ideology in modern Britain. As we showed, the central component of this ethos is the ideal of playing sports 'for fun'. Other aspects such as the stress on 'fair play', voluntary adherence to rules and non-pecuniary involvement, are essentially subordinate, designed to secure the achievement of that end, i.e. to make sporting contests into 'play-fights' in which pleasurable excitement can be generated. However, if we are right, the industrializing, urbanizing, increasingly complex and impersonal society which has emerged in Britain since the eighteenth century, means that it is no longer easy for groups, whether dominant or subordinate, to participate in sport for fun. Such a society is characterized by what Durkheim called high 'moral' or 'dynamic density', i.e. by a high concentration of population and a high rate of social interaction.[6] Durkheim believed that the competitive pressures generated in such a society would be reduced and perhaps eliminated by division of labour. It would, he suggested, have that effect in two main ways: by creating 'bonds of interdependence' and by siphoning competitively generated tensions into specialized occupational spheres. However, Durkheim's analysis contains a fundamental flaw. It derives from his failure to recognize that functional interdependence does not lead necessarily to harmonious and cooperative integration but is conducive, even in its 'normal' forms, to conflict and antagonism. In short, his concept of the society based on 'organic solidarity' is utopian. A more realistic concept of interdependence is that proposed by Elias.

According to Elias, the social transformation which is usually referred to by terms relating to specific aspects such as 'industrialization', 'economic growth', the 'demographic transition', and 'political modernization', is, in fact, a transformation of the total social structure.[7] And, he contends, one of the sociologically most significant aspects of this total social transformation consists in the emergence of longer and more differentiated 'chains of interdependence'. That is, it involves the emergence of greater functional specialization and the integration of functionally differentiated groups into wider networks. As we have described it so far, Elias' analysis may not seem very different from Durkheim's. Its difference, more strictly speaking its greater 'object-adequacy' as a conceptual representation, becomes apparent when the analysis is taken one step further.

According to Elias, there occurs concomitantly with this overall social transformation, i.e. with the emergence of what one might call 'urban-industrial nation-states', a change in the direction of decreasing power-differentials within and among groups, more specifically a change in the balance of power between rulers and ruled, the social classes, men and women, the generations, parents and children. Such a process, he maintains, occurs because the incumbents of specialized roles are dependent on others and can, therefore, exert reciprocal control. The power-chances of specialized groups are further enhanced if they manage to organize since, then, they are able to disrupt the wider system of interdependences by collective action.

It is in ways such as these, according to Elias, that increasing division of labour and the emergence of longer chains of interdependence lead to greater reciprocal dependency and, hence, to patterns of 'multipolar control' within and among groups.

The relevance of this deceptively simple theory for the present analysis is manifold. Thus, in urban-industrial societies, multipolar controls operate in all spheres of life, including sport. This means, for example, that top-level sportsmen are not and cannot be independent. That is, they no longer play solely for themselves but as representatives of wider communities such as cities, counties and nations. As such, they are expected to produce a 'sports-performance', i.e. to produce the sorts of satisfactions that the controllers and 'consumers' of the sport demand, e.g. the spectacle of an exciting contest or the validation through victory of the 'self-image' of the community with which the controllers and/or consumers identify. The 'material density' of modern sport works in the same direction. That is, the sheer number of people involved means that high achievement-motivation, long-term planning, strict self-control and renunciation of short-term gratification are necessary in order to get to the top. Moreover, given the impersonal character of the modern nation-state, sport has come to form an important channel for obtaining recognition, i.e. of having individual and group identities validated, not simply in a local context but nationally and even internationally, a process in which the mass media play an important part.

In each of these respects, the social configuration, the pattern of inter-group dependences, characteristic of an urban-industrial nation-state generates constraints which militate against the practical realization of the amateur ethos with its stress on enjoyment as the central aim of sport. Or more specifically, it generates constraints which militate against the realization of immediate, short-term enjoyment, against each sporting contest as an 'end in itself', and leads to its replacement, even for spectators, by longer-term goals such as victory in a league or cup, i.e. by satisfactions more centrally concerned with identity. Moreover, such constraints are not confined to top-level sports but reverberate down to the lowest levels of sporting achievement. That is partly because top-level sportsmen form a media-promoted reference group who set standards which others try to follow. However, it is also partly a consequence of the pressures generated by competition for the material and prestige rewards which can be obtained by getting to the top. More centrally, however, it is a consequence of the pervasive insecurities and anxieties generated in a society characterized by multipolar controls and in which traditional props of identity and status such as class, occupation, sex and age, all connected with the division of labour, have been eroded by functional democratization, i.e. by the equalizing process which, according to Elias, is inherent in the division of labour itself.

5. So far, we have provided an explanation for the tendency towards increasingly serious involvement in sport. We have not, however, accounted for the related development in the course of which its cultural centrality and significance have grown. Accordingly, it is to that process that we shall now turn our attention. It seems to us that a constellation of at least six interacting determinants have contributed to this process. They are: (i) the fact that sport is not linked necessarily to the division of labour; (ii) the changing balance between work and leisure; (iii) the growing secularization of beliefs and social institutions generally; (iv) the function of sport as a source of mimetically generated excitement; (v) the fact that it has become a key enclave for the expression of masculine identity; and (vi) its function as a means of social integration. Let us elaborate briefly on the components of this 'causal nexus'.

The fact that the growing cultural significance of sport in modern society can be attributed partly to its lack of necessary linkage with the division of labour is easy to explain. It is simply that its importance as a source of identity and status has grown as that of division-of-labour-linked sources has declined. Its importance has been further increased by the changing balance, ideological as well as factual, between work and leisure. Thus, as the leisure-time available to people has increased and as leisure has come more and more to form a central value, so the cultural significance of sport has grown simply by virtue of the fact that it is a leisure activity, i.e. an activity which is freely chosen, or, more precisely, one in which the balance between freedom and compulsion is weighted more heavily towards the former than is the case with work. Secularization has also contributed to this process. Indeed, the fact that sport seems ideally suited as a medium of collective identification has probably enabled it to some extent to fill the gap left in this regard by the decline of religion.

More positively, sport serves as an important source of emotional arousal for people in routinized and 'civilized' societies characterized by multipolar controls where it is necessary to exercise continuously a high degree of emotional restraint in ordinary, everyday life. Of course, this emotional arousal is itself subject to civilizing controls, as our earlier discussion shows. That is, sport functions as a sphere for the generation of excitement in a form which is socially limited and controlled. Change is liable to occur when the excitement generated is perceived as either too high or too low according to current standards. Thus, on the one hand, the rules of a sport can become so controlling that it is unable to perform its function with regard to emotional arousal and new, less affect-dampening rules have to be introduced. On the other hand, the excitement generated can exceed the bounds of what is considered socially tolerable with the result that the authorities intervene. That is what seems to be currently happening with football hooliganism in Britain. That is a subject to which we shall return.

The fact that sport has come to form a key enclave for the establishment, expression and testing of masculine identity seems to us to be related to the same constellation of social changes. Our norms of 'manliness' still show signs of their origins in the pre-industrial division of labour when men were warriors and protectors of their families. But, in modern society, military functions are the preserve of specialized armies, and protection of the family is undertaken by state agencies such as the police. Of course, to the extent that international conflict makes mass conscription necessary, men are still required to play a fighting role. But it remains true that our norms of masculinity have not changed commensurately with these wider social changes. The result is that a sphere of social life is needed where traditional ideals of masculinity can be developed and expressed. The need for such a sphere has also grown to the extent that functional democratization has increased the power of women relative to men and, correlatively, the threat posed by the former to the latter. Contact sports, with their stress on strength, toughness and physical courage, are an ideal medium in this regard though, of course, the reverse is also true; namely that contact sports have helped to perpetuate traditional standards of masculinity.

The function of sport as a medium of social integration is a subject which demands treatment at greater length. The first thing to note is that it is enabled to perform this function by means of its inherently oppositional character. This means that it lends itself to group identification, more precisely, to 'in-group' and 'out-group' formation on a variety of levels. The oppositional element is crucial in this regard since opposition serves to reinforce in-group identification. Indeed, it is reasonable to suppose that sports such as football contribute to the social integration of urban-industrial societies in a manner not dissimilar to the segmentary lineage systems of some simpler societies.[8] This can be illustrated by means of a hypothetical example. Thus, the people of Liverpool are divided when Liverpool FC play Everton but united when either of these Liverpool teams plays Manchester City or Manchester United. In similar fashion, the people of Lancashire unite in support of any Lancashire team which plays one from Yorkshire, and the people of the North unite in support of any Northern team which plays one from the South. And finally, the country as a whole unites in support of the national team when it plays one from abroad. In short, the oppositional character of sport means that it can serve as a means for the expression of regional and other group identifications.

To the extent that regional identifications remain important in a society, it is characterized by what Durkheim called 'mechanical solidarity', that is, united by 'bonds of similitude'.[9] Such bonds are functionally less significant in industrial societies than the 'bonds of interdependence' established through the division of labour, but they continue to exist. The degree of compulsion towards identifications of a mechanical solidarity kind is also lower in industrial societies than in their pre-industrial counterparts. Never-theless it varies, principally with social class, being highest for groups at the bottom of the social hierarchy. The choices available to such groups are severely restricted. They have comparatively few chances for mobility, particularly of an occupational kind. They tend to fail educationally, to be employed only casually or in unskilled jobs and to be among the first to suffer when the rate of unemployment rises. Their occupational and general life-experiences are relatively homogeneous. As a result, their social horizons tend to be narrow. They mistrust strangers and find difficulty in adjusting to the demands of life in a differentiated urban-industrial society. Their strongest ties are with others who belong to the same regional and class subculture. That is, they are linked by 'bonds of similitude', to others who are like themselves. Strong enmity—not, as is commonly supposed, simply towards people at higher levels in the class structure but also towards different groups whose social situation is similar to their own—follows as a natural corollary. It is from such groups, i.e. from the poorest, educationally and occupationally most disadvantaged sections of the working class, that the football fans officially labelled as 'hooligans' are principally recruited. However, if we are right, it is neither their poverty *per se* nor their resentment of the higher classes that leads them to behave in a manner that attracts this label but the complex of experiences that leads them to be bonded in mechanical solidarity form. We shall conclude by offering a few remarks on football hooliganism and what we take to be its relationship to mechanical solidarity.

Our earlier suggestion that sports such as football contribute to social integration in a manner similar to segmentary lineage systems serves to highlight the predominantly ritual character of football hooliganism, i.e: that the bulk of 'hooligan' behaviour involves ritual posturing and that open fighting represents only a comparatively small proportion of the behaviour that attracts official and media condemnation. The songs and chants of the 'hooligans', with their near-military unison in delivery and expressions of unswerving loyalty to their team and of implacable hostility to the opposition and its supporters, are an example of such ritualized aggression. The behaviour of the 'hooligans' contrasts markedly with the more restrained and individualized expressions of support and excitement of the rest of the crowd. Yet, though it may have been consistent with this ritual aspect of 'hooligan' behaviour, our earlier discussion was oversimplified in at least one respect, namely in its characterization of the pattern of unity and opposition between rival fan groups from the same local area. Such a characterization was inconsistent with one of the principal aspects of mechanical solidarity, i.e. with the tendency for mechanically bonded groups to be hostile to others who are like themselves. Thus it is well-known that so-called 'local derbies' have traditionally been occasions for spectator disorderliness and violence. The aspect of contemporary football hooliganism which appears to be new, therefore, is not spectator violence as such but the fact that fan groups are no longer restricted to their immediate locality, but motivated, and enabled by their capacity to pay, to travel to distant parts of the country in support of their teams. And this means that the violence, ritual and actual, which has always tended to accompany confrontations between groups of young males from sections of the working class characterized by mechanical solidarity has spread correspondingly. In short, what was once a phenomenon restricted to particular localities has now become nation-wide.

Ritual and actual violence, we should like to suggest, is an almost inevitable concomitant of the meeting of groups characterized by mechanical solidarity. The confrontations between rival fan groups before, during and after football matches appear to be a special form of the gang warfare common amongst youth in all parts of the world whose social experiences lead to this form of unification. Such confrontations serve as means for enabling them to express their standards of masculinity, e.g. of establishing reputations as 'tough', 'real men' who can fight, who do not run away and who remain loyal to the group in a crisis. These standards are developed and expressed in all-male settings and are indicative of both the extreme male-dominance and the rigid sexual segregation found in close-knit groups characterized by mechanical solidarity. Such groups have been subjected to civilizing pressures externally, e.g. from the higher classes and the state, but their lack of internal differentiation means that they have not been subject endogenously to the pressures of multipolar controls to the same extent as other groups. Moreover, their low life-chances in the educational and occupational spheres mean that they are not constrained to defer gratification in the hope of achieving future rewards. They live for the moment, especially for the excitement of their weekly confrontations. Their socialization teaches them to return blow for blow and does not inculcate in them strong inhibitions with respect to physical violence. Not surprisingly, their behaviour causes repugnance in groups whose social standards stress greater restraint though, of course, it would be wrong to view hooligan behaviour as unregulated. It is not. It is rather that their code demands overt physical aggression whereas the standards which are dominant in society at large demand the exercise of stricter self-control in this regard.

The behaviour of the so-called football hooligans, however, appears to be only marginally related to football. They are seemingly unable to gain adequate satisfaction from watching a relatively 'civilized' mock-fight on the football field and appear to need a more direct type of excitement from taking part in 'real' fighting. Football is tailor-made for their activities because group opposition and norms of manliness are intrinsic to it. However, such activities can, and do, take place in other contexts, too. Hooligan behaviour also has its own dynamics which appear to be only marginally related to events on the field of play. Victory for their team undoubtedly provides the hooligans with an opportunity for boastful posturing and defeat with an excuse for recrimination against the rival fan group. But their behaviour appears to be more centrally bound up with traditional working-class rivalries of a mechanical solidarity kind, such as those between North and South, London and the provinces, adjacent towns and sections of towns. It is also linked with occurrences at previous encounters and involves the consumption of alcohol, the latter serving to release inhibitions and as another source of masculine identity. Indeed, these informal, secondary play-fights—of course, they are primary from the standpoint of the participants—seem to be, in many ways, an urban counterpart of the old folk-contests with their expression of community rivalry and opportunity to pay off old scores. Such a parallel is not surprising if we were right to argue earlier that contemporary football hooliganism is largely rooted in the continued existence of social structures which generate close approximations to pure forms of mechanical solidarity.

But this analysis assumes that the behaviour labelled as 'football hooliganism' is all of a piece. There is reason to believe, however, that there are at least two types, one of which is more closely connected to events on the field of play. We are referring to crowd invasions of the pitch. These, it is reasonable to assume, are an attempt to affect the outcome of a match, an extension of chanting, booing or whistling to put a player off his kick, i.e. an attempt to assert control. As such, they are indicative of an overly strong pattern of team-identification, of a degree of involvement among certain fans with the fortunes of their club that is so strong that they cannot bear to see it lose in a status-enhancing competition such as the FA Cup or in the struggle to maintain First Division status. So bound up is their self-esteem with the success of their club that they reject the traditional division of sporting roles in which a select group of specialist players battles symbolically on their behalf and, in the only way open to them, join the fray themselves. Indeed, a further transformation of traditional values seems to be involved in the sense that pitch-invasion appears to be a process that occurs under the stress of a severe identity threat, leading to the redefinition as secular and profane of something previously regarded as sacred, namely the pitch. It is, we think significant that the football pitch is often referred to as the 'sacred' turf, a usage which presumably denotes the fact that it is the location of an activity which is socially highly valued.

However, whilst the first type of hooligan behaviour may interrupt a match accidentally when fighting spills over on to the pitch or be defined as a threat to public order and deter some potential spectators from attending, it is not inherently antithetical to sport. Indeed, in an informal, unorganized way, it is a kind of sport, a modern counterpart of the kind of activity from which sports such as football have sprung. By contrast, pitch-invasion is totally antithetical to sport for it involves the attempt on the part of some spectators to suspend the element of sporting competition. This destruction of the play-element does not occur, as Stone would have it, because the presence of spectators induces the players to engage in display. It is, rather, the spectators in a direct sense who act as destroyers. And they act in this way because the players are unable to provide the level of satisfaction they demand.

This insatiable spectator demand for success is indicative of a kind of anomie. It is fanned by the mass media with their attempts to inject false excitement into the reporting of sports events. But, in our view, that is not the central cause of such behaviour. We suggested earlier that pitch-invasion involves the redefinition as profane of something traditionally regarded as sacred. But it is not only the pitch that is regarded in this manner. For some groups in our society, football itself has become a phenomenon of quasi-religious proportions, and it is in that that the roots of pitch-invasion seem to lie. Evidence of the transformation of football into a quasi-religious phenomenon is provided by the fact that it has become traditional for some deceased supporters of Liverpool FC to have their ashes strewn on the Anfield pitch. Whilst this may be peculiar to the Liverpool club, at least in such an extreme form, it is, we think, symptomatic of the more general elevation of football to the status of a central value. As such, it is part and parcel both of the trend towards the increasing cultural centrality of sport and of that towards greater seriousness which we attributed earlier to functional democratization. However, and this is the point we wish to stress at present, given the 'zero-sum' character of football, i.e. the fact that, as in any other sport, there are necessarily always losers, such high expectations are bound to lead to cases of intense frustration and probably also of disorderly behaviour which is destructive of the play-character of the game.

6. It only remains for us now to tie the threads of our analysis together. We have argued that the trend towards the greater seriousness and cultural centrality of sports has led to an intensification of competition and hence to a real increase in violence and related behaviour on and off the field of play. We have also suggested that some of the behaviour labelled as football hooliganism can be accounted for in this manner but that there is also another type which appears to be related to the mechanical solidarity and correlative norms of masculinity of the poorest working-class groups. The former type, it seems to us, is inherently antithetical to sport but the latter is not. Indeed, it, too, appears to be a form of play-fighting, though it is more spontaneous, less highly organized, and controlled by standards which demand a greater readiness to engage in physical violence.

The growing cultural centrality of sport has led the mass media to focus on it and to the mobilization of 'civilized' values in relation to violent incidents both on and off the field of play. This leads, in turn, to perceptual distortion and magnification of the nature and extent of the violence that actually occurs. But there is class bias in this process, and that leads, simultaneously, to distortion in the opposite direction, namely to the perception of sports-related violence as a mainly working-class phenomenon. As we have seen, however, there is Rugby 'hooliganism', too, and Rugby Union is a mainly middle-class sport. We are not referring simply to violence on the Rugby field or to the disorderliness of Rugby spectators but also to the beer-swilling antics of what has been aptly called the 'après-Rugby' scene. We do not wish to imply that the behaviour of Rugby players after the match is identical to that of football hooligans in all respects but it, too, takes place in an all-male setting, involves heavy alcohol consumption and leads frequently to the destruction of property. The principal difference seems to lie in the fact that the element of group confrontation is restricted to the controlled and socially acceptable setting of the Rugby match and that, no matter how violent the exchanges on the field of play may have been, they are forgotten in the friendly antics that take place afterwards in the bar. Moreover, the anti-normative behaviour of 'Rugby hooligans' takes place in private, mainly in the bars of club-houses, hotels and universities. By contrast, that of 'soccer hooligans' takes place in public. It is, as a result, more visible to the authorities, the media and the general public. And finally, whilst the behaviour of working-class hooligans is branded as 'delinquent' and defined as a serious 'social problem', that of their middle-class counterparts tends to be excused as 'youthful high spirits'.

Despite these differences, soccer and Rugby hooliganism seem to spring from broadly similar roots, namely from the fact that the socialization of males in our society leads, independently of social class, to the enjoyment of physical group confrontation. That is, play-fighting, whether in the organized, relatively controlled and 'civilized' context of a Rugby match or the less organized, less controlled setting of a 'hooligan' confrontation, provides the opportunity for generating pleasurable excitement and establishing and testing masculine identities. This suggests a possible solution to the problem of football hooliganism. It will only be possible to *eradicate* such behaviour by removing the social structures which generate it but, in the short term, it may be possible to *institutionalize* it by persuading the so-called hooligans, at school and elsewhere, to play Rugby. In that way, they would be given the opportunity for generating the pleasurable excitement of a playfight and for establishing masculine identities in a controlled and socially acceptable setting. If it were implemented, such a proposal might help, not only to diminish the problem of football hooliganism but also to raise the standard of the game by spreading it to groups whose norms and values seem ideally suited to the creation of Rugby players. But, apart from the fact that the 'hooligans' are likely to reject any attempt to influence them from sources they regard as 'official', there is an obvious obstacle in this respect, namely the class prejudice which has characterized Rugby Union up to now. This is ingrained so deeply that we are sure that our proposal will be greeted with horror by the Rugby Union establishment and probably also by the majority of players, too.

This brings us to our final point. We have argued that our data support Elias' theory of the civilizing process but that an increase in real violence is occurring in modern sport. Although it, too, tends to be exaggerated, such an increase is probably occurring in the wider society as well. This suggests that the analysis can be taken one step further. Thus, it may be the case that the civilizing process is 'curvilinear', more specifically that one of its central determinants, functional democratization, produces consequences which are, on balance, 'civilizing' in its early stages but that it produces effects which are 'decivilizing', i.e. conducive to disruptive conflict, once a certain level has been reached. It may be that such a level has been reached in Britain today. It remains to be seen whether we are on the threshold of a downswing of some duration in the civilizing process or whether it will be possible to find modes of integrating subordinate groups whose power chances are increased by the modern structure of social interdependences at a new and higher level of 'civilization'. If the authorities and players of Rugby Union prove willing to incorporate 'football hooligans' into their game, that would be one indica- tion that such a process could successfully occur. However, we are by no means optimistic in this regard. That is because the class prejudice of Rugby Union seems to us to be merely symptomatic of the deeply-rooted class prejudice of British society as a whole. Such prejudice is the major obstacle to reform in Britain, whether in the wider society or the more limited sphere of sport. Until it is eradicated or at least significantly softened in its effects, it will be impossible to satisfy the aspirations of the British people for industrial and sporting success.

Afterword

The continuing commercialization and professionalization of Rugby Union

The publication in 1979 of *Barbarians, Gentlemen and Players* constituted, we venture to suggest, an event of some academic significance. It was the first monograph-length sociological study of sport undertaken using an 'Eliasian', that is, 'figurational' or 'process-sociological' perspective.[1] Indeed, it was one of the first book-length studies in the sociology of sport to be published *per se*. As such it marked—and, we like to think, made a small contribution to—the growing maturity of what then still remained a fledgling field of sociological endeavour: the sociology of sport. It is a field that has subsequently grown apace and has since become one of the most vibrant areas of the subject overall.

The publication of *Barbarians, Gentlemen and Players* was met by largely favourable reviews, non-academic as well as academic. Among the most complimentary non-academic reviews was that by Geoffrey Nicholson in the Northern edition of *The Observer* (22 April, 1979). Perhaps unsurprisingly, given his journalistic background, Nicholson was not entirely positive. He described some of our sociological language in the book as 'gobbledygook',[2] and took exception to the first word of our title. This, he insisted, would signify Barbarians FC to most people concerned with rugby. Since the Barbarians were originally a 'gentlemen's' club, and are still associated with a particular style of play, we admit that our title is ambiguous and perhaps confusing. It was, of course, our intention to play on the ambiguity. More particularly, by juxtaposing 'barbarians' with 'gentlemen' and 'players', we were, on the one hand alluding to the famous club and, on the other, seeking to signal what we regard as the three main stages in the development of the game. This process is the principal subject of our book and we remain convinced of the appositeness of our title.

Nicholson was also critical of the fact that, despite there having been two of us to do the proof-reading, we allowed the infelicitous phrase, 'get your intimidation in first', to be substituted for the famous (infamous?) and far subtler battle cry of the victorious 1971 British Lions, 'get your retaliation in first', a battle cry attributed to Carwyn James. This, however, was small beer compared with Nicholson's praise. He went on to suggest that it is 'rare to find a book on rugby written with such detachment, . . . so scrupulously

researched' and that 'nobody who has ever heard himself described . . . as a "thinker on the game" – especially a thinker on its future – can very well afford not to read it'. However, he recognized that, since few rugby players had bothered to read the report of the Mallaby Commission of 1974, it was unlikely that they would be forming queues outside their local book shops to purchase *Barbarians, Gentlemen and Players*! This was unfortunate, Nicholson suggested, especially because our diagnosis of the undercover and incipient professionalization of the Rugby Union game was prescient and timely. As he expressed it: 'Everybody knows, although no one is prepared to give specific examples, that already there are men being paid—meagrely, perhaps, but paid—for playing rugby. If this is not to be a return to 1895, then rugby must make up its mind where to draw the line. And *Barbarians, Gentlemen and Players* could help them to do so'.

Other reviewers were not so generous. A reviewer in *Rugby World* (15 June, 1979) argued, contrary to Nicholson, that we had exaggerated the extent of shamateurism in Wales. This, he suggested, was because we had been overly reliant on ghosted articles in Sunday newspapers by bitter converts to Rugby League. The consequence was that '. . . lo and behold, the cross-references which made the book so authoritative disappear in favour of anonymous tip-offs'. We understood why this reviewer felt it necessary to deny what every player and ex-player in Britain probably knew at the time. However, we had to protect our sources. One of our principal informants, a team-mate of Ken Sheard in the Leicester University First XV, was Terry Price, the Welsh international Rugby Union, British Lion and Rugby League full-back, now sadly deceased. We protected him, together with Llanelli Rugby Club, by utilising his ghost-written 1969 article in *The People* (24 September, 1969) instead of his much more revealing and potentially more damaging private recollections when still a Rugby Union player. The *Rugby World* reviewer also drew attention to an embarrassing typographical error which we have corrected in the present edition. We realize, of course, that it was incorrect to suggest that, 'At the beginning of the 1890s, no rugby clubs had been established in Wales . . .' (Dunning and Sheard, 1979 p. 223) and that this should have read 'the 1870s'. (See Sheard, 1972 p. 326.) Nevertheless, even in the context of a sneering review – there are references in it to 'half-truths and garbage' and 'Meanwhile, back on Earth'—the author grudgingly acknowledged that 'you may still find that the book is important enough not to be missed'.

This re-publication of *Barbarians, Gentlemen and Players* provides us with an opportunity to correct another of the serious mistakes made in our original text. It was first brought to our attention by Andy White in 1997[3] and later remedied in print by Tony Collins in his *Rugby's Great Split* (1998). On page 220 of the first edition of *Barbarians* (p. 187 in this), we cited some figures from the *Wakefield Express* (8 April 1893) which we interpreted as indicating that, in the years 1890–1893, there occurred a total of 71 deaths and 366 serious injuries among Rugby players in Yorkshire. Collins correctly points out that these figures were included in a 'Football Notes' column and were not restricted either to Yorkshire or the Rugby code. According to Collins, furthermore, the *Wakefield Express* had obtained these figures from a series of articles which had appeared in the *Pall Mall Gazette* over the three preceding years. They had been used as part of a campaign to discredit football generally by highlighting the dangers of the game. They were widely commented on at the time as being unreliable. However, research by Sheard reveals that they were not too wide of the mark. More particularly, a survey of *The Lancet* for the years 1891–93, reveals that 54 deaths and 320 serious injuries were reported in that journal as having occurred in Association and Rugby football, whilst in the years 1894–99, 42 deaths and 148 serious injuries were reported as having occurred in the two main football codes (Sheard, 1998, p. 77). Together with the additional and more reliable evidence furnished by Collins (1998 pp. 129–30), this is supportive of the more general point that we were trying to make, namely that, by the emergent standards that were coming increasingly to predominate in late nineteenth century Britain, football, especially the Rugby form, was viewed as a hazardous activity and subjected to critical scrutiny as a result. Such as they are, moreover, the *Lancet* figures are also consistent with the occurrence of a decline in football injury and death rates in the 1890s. More particularly, during that decade, the annual average rates of football injuries and deaths reported in that journal fell from 106.6 and 18 in 1891–3 to 24.6 and 7 in 1894–9.

In *Barbarians* we were also critical of the hypothesis proposed by 'Tawd Vale', an anonymous author writing in 1969, that the specific form of Rugby League emerged as an expression of the growing 'political power', 'freedom' and 'separateness' of the late-nineteenth century Northern working class. (Dunning and Sheard, 1979 p. 205ff.) This hypothesis, we suggested, exaggerated the part played in this process by working class groups and minimized that of the industrial middle classes. We stand by that critique but are less sure of what we wrote in that connection about South Wales. Despite similarities in social structure with the North, Rugby League failed to take root in South Wales, we contended, because a crucial condition was absent, namely 'a middle class able and willing to use the game for purposes of social control'. (Dunning and Sheard, 1979, p. 222). However, as a number of Welsh historians have since convincingly pointed out, this is precisely what Wales *did* have (Smith and Williams, 1980; Williams, G. A. 1982, 1985; Andrews, 1996). For example, whilst we argued, following an analysis proposed by Rowe Harding in 1929, that 'middle class Welshmen who did not migrate to England were apparently apathetic towards the administration of the game, seemingly not grasping its potential as a vehicle of social control' (Dunning and Sheard, 1979, p. 223), Andrews (1996) succeeds in showing that the Welsh urban middle class did, in fact, come to dominate Welsh Rugby between 1870 and 1890 and that what 'saved' Wales for Rugby Union was the success of the Welsh industrial middle class in harnessing 'the divergent interests, aspirations and backgrounds of the flourishing but potentially disruptive Welsh industrial workforce' to a unifying Welsh national identity (Andrews, 1996 p. 53). Identification with the nation's Rugby side played a major role in this process.

Were we to be writing *Barbarians, Gentlemen and Players* today, nationalism is a subject to which we would have paid more attention. This suggests in its turn that we should have paid greater attention in writing the book to the developing globalization of Rugby football and the part played by the international media, especially satellite television, in that process. This is something we shall attempt to remedy in this postscript.

Whatever the errors and omissions in our original text—the historian of the Rugby League, Robert Gates, suggested that many of these derived from our being first in the field[4]—we have been proved right in one major prediction, *viz* our forecast regarding the virtual inevitability of the full and open professionalization of Rugby Union, a process that we attributed to the 'inexorable tendency' for sports in capitalist societies 'to become bound up with money values' (Dunning and Sheard, 1979 p. 234). It is to the continuing developments in this direction after 1979 that we shall now turn our attention. Four of these were of particular importance: the increasing commercialization of the game led by that bastion of pristine amateurism, the RFU itself and epitomised by the activities of its Twickenham staff; the continuing formalization of national and international competition; the introduction and success of the Rugby World Cup; and the attempt to 'cherry pick' élite competitions for support by groups with international media interests.

The ongoing commercialization of Twickenham

During the 1980s, in conjunction with increasing commercialization and the growing formal institutionalization of national and international competitive structures, money began to 'flood' into the Rugby Union game. By comparison with 'conventional' (i.e. non-sports) business, top-level soccer and professional sport in the USA, these sums were small. For a still nominally amateur sport, they were staggering.

Initially, the majority of this money was concentrated at the national level, with the RFU attempting to capitalize on the growing sponsorship market in what RFU representatives claimed were the interests of Twickenham and hence the game as a whole. These were the years in Britain of the 'Thatcher revolution' when business groups were said to be being liberated from the 'shackles' of an 'over-extended' 'nanny' state. It was a process that can only be fully understood by reference to a context of increasing globalization and the emergence of digital technology.[5] The intensity of economic competition increased and growing numbers of entrepreneurs, corporate managers and television personnel began to see the prestige and high profile of sport as potentially advantageous for advertising products and services and hence as a source of profit.

In nominally amateur Rugby Union, however, the intrusion of business into the supposedly autonomous world of sport was widely seen at first as anathema. For example, when, in 1982, Adidas rewarded international players with cash and other gifts for wearing their boots, this was perceived as a 'scandal' (Wyatt, 1995 p. 21). However, the power of top-level players was growing, the pressures towards the 'marketization' of sport were increasing, and more and more RFU personnel realized that they would have to reach an accommodation. Accordingly, rather than expressing outright condemnation, reinforcing existing shamateur practices and risking a repeat of 1895, they sought to bring such activities under RFU control. By 1985, in fact, Twickenham had appointed a marketing manager. They had also initiated a deliberate and aggressive marketing policy. The question, by this time, was no longer whether the commercialization of Rugby Union was desirable but more about who should benefit. The RFU was clear that it should be them and only indirectly the top players. As they themselves saw it, Twickenham personnel were concerned with benefiting the game at all levels.

Early in its existence, the RFU Marketing Department was given responsibility for generating revenue from sources other than gate-receipts. The first income of this type involved sponsorship of the RFU through what were called 'Elite Sponsorship Packages'. These were initially limited to eight companies which included Save and Prosper, ICL Information Systems, the Gateway Building Society, the Ford Motor Company, Nike, Courage and Imperial Tobacco, all prestigious national or transnational companies. Match sponsors were also procured, enabling the RFU in 1988 to generate over a million pounds from these sources alone. The leasing of 'Executive Boxes' added a further £400,000 of income. Further revenue was obtained from sponsorship of the various RFU competitions. In 1987, Courage Breweries sponsored the Clubs Championship (new national Leagues) to the tune of £1.6 million; the electronics company, Toshiba, sponsored the County Divisional Championship for £400,000; and John Player continued their support for the Clubs Knockout competition with annual sponsorship of £125,000. By 1993, the estimated financial return from an annual Home International series was estimated to be around £1.8 million. Significantly, less than half this sum (£750,000) was generated from ticket sales. The rest came mainly from television fees (£550,000), perimeter advertising (£200,000) and merchandising and programme sales (£90,000) (*Guardian*, 6 February, 1993). To an extent, these marketing activities reflected the pattern of Rugby Union spectatorship at that time. Even for the élite clubs, attendances at Saturday fixtures rarely reached five figures and, for some clubs in Division One, barely averaged 3,000. International fixtures and the finals of Cup Competitions were by far the most popular, with sell-out crowds virtually guaranteed. Thus, relative to the élite clubs, the RFU was in the enviable position of being able to generate substantial sums of money with comparative ease. It was this financial base which facilitated the redevelopment by the RFU of the North, East and West stands that transformed Twickenham into a thoroughly modern 75,000 all-seater stadium. This re-development was completed in 1994 at an estimated overall cost in excess of £60 million.[6] It established Rugby Union as the only major sport in Britain to own its national stadium.[7] Symbolically, however, it marked the emergence of Rugby Union, at least at the national level, as a fully fledged spectator sport and thus represented a further nail in the coffin of pristine amateurism.

In this situation, the RFU found itself increasingly locked into a spiral of escalating constraints which led its representatives, on the one hand to search more and more for new revenue sources and, on the other, to develop closer relations with television interests. These two aspects of the spiral were closely interrelated. Pressure grew as well to utilize Twickenham for big matches more often. This strained relations with the élite clubs. Although these clubs were at one level beneficiaries, especially the leaders among them, from more competitions with a 'competitive edge', the requirement to release key players more frequently for internationals exposed such players to greater risk of injury. In that way, the revenue-spinning League and cup chances were potentially (and, in some cases, factually) threatened, constraining the clubs to recruit larger squads which, in turn, heightened the need to generate further income.

In this emergent context, too, the RFU found it necessary to expand its employment of paid administrative staff at Twickenham. More particularly, by 1993 the paid staff there had increased from the 27 employed in 1974 to over 100 (*Report to the Bishop Commission*, RFU, London, 1994). Developments at Twickenham and in the Union game more widely were thus both products of, and gave further impetus to, the accelerating and interrelated processes of professionalization and bureaucratization which, as we put it in 1979, were major 'artefacts of Rugby Union's expansion' (Dunning and Sheard, 1979 p. 242). A process of 'de-amateurisation' was involved as well.

The formalization of national and international competition

During the last two decades of the twentieth century, the formalization of national and international Rugby Union competition, the beginnings of which we had analyzed in *Barbarians, Gentlemen and Players*, continued at an accelerating rate. A significant UK event in this regard was the announcement in 1987 by Courage Ltd of its £1.6 million, three-year sponsorship of the game and the replacement of the two-year-old John Smith's 'Merit Tables' with the national 'Courage Leagues'. Until 1987, English rugby had lacked a nationally organized League competition, something which overseas visitors and UK sports-people more familiar with the organizational principles of Association Football and Rugby League, found baffling.

We sought to shed light in *Barbarians* on the long-term historical processes which had led the RFU's amateur administrators to view such structures as anathema. But there were anomalies and contradictions in the amateur structures they were fighting to preserve. Central among them was the fact that the informal organization of competition flew in the face of the merito-cratic principles which lie at the roots of modern sport, allowing the senior clubs to operate a fixture cartel which enabled them to preserve their own élite status while excluding ambitious junior clubs. The cartel system also helped to perpetuate a diet of so-called 'friendly' fixtures, many of which lacked a serious competitive edge, allowing the big clubs to maintain their status to some extent regardless of playing success. The standard of the national side reflected what Gage (1997 p. 29) called this 'complacency'.

The system of informal merit tables went some way towards resolving this contradiction. However, since clubs were not obliged to play all the others in their table and some played more matches, the merit tables were not an accurate reflection of relative playing strengths. Nor did they permit the unambiguous establishment in any season of who the overall 'champions', 'runners-up' etc. were. Moreover, since they lacked provision for automatic promotion and relegation, merit tables failed to provide a ladder for success-ful clubs to climb and for failing clubs to fall. In such a situation, pressures arose for ensuring that all clubs in a given table should play each other and that they should also play the same number of matches.

The emergence of such a structure virtually ensured that, despite the continued opposition of powerful groups in the RFU, officially recognized, more full-blown Leagues would eventually be introduced (Gage, 1997, p. 30). In the event, the introduction of the 'Courage Leagues' in 1987 not only extended the League structure to 1,128 clubs in 106 Leagues throughout the country but, by giving formal expression to what one might call the 'Rugby-specific (i.e. game-related) rank hierarchy' among clubs, increased the frequency of intense and meaningful contests, hence facilitating the gener-ation of greater revenue both from sponsorship and at the gate. In a survey conducted part way through the inaugural season of the Courage Leagues, the *Rugby World and Post* (September 1987) quoted David Cooke, the former Harlequins Captain and England flanker as having said: 'If it (the League) is properly organized and advertised it will hasten the arrival of professional rugby'.

The World Cup

1987 was also the year of the first Rugby Union 'World Cup' Competition. In 1983, an earlier attempt to inaugurate such a competition by a group who called themselves 'Sports Sponsorship International Limited' was rejected by the IRB on account of what they saw as its inherent organizational and financial difficulties. IRB members also argued that a competitive structure of that kind would 'inevitably' lead to professionalism. However, pressure from players, spectators and representatives of the Southern Hemisphere Unions eventually led to the IRB agreeing to hold an inaugural tournament in Australia and New Zealand. Details of the first three occasions on which this quadrennial event was held are presented in Table 1 (below):

Table 1 The Development of the Rugby World Cup Competition, 1987–1995

	1987	1991	1995
Host Unions	2	5	1
Venues	11	19	9
Spectators	501,000	1,135,000	2,800,000
TV viewers	300 million	1.75 billion	2.5 billion
TV countries	17	103	125
Surplus	£1.5 million	£5 million	£20 million
Participating Unions (including qualifiers)	16	40	52
Number of matches (including qualifiers)	32	87	106
Media contingent (excluding TV personnel)	445	1,000	1,200

Source: Rugby World June, 1995: 50
Notes: Host Unions: 1987 New Zealand/Australia; 1991 UK and Ireland; 1995 South Africa.

The rapid development of the Rugby Union World Cup as a revenue-generating and media event between its inception in 1987 and the threshold of open professionalism in 1995 emerges with crystal clarity from these figures. Correlatively, the game spread as an international sport. For example, in 1986, the IRB had eight members but, ten years and three World Cups later, no fewer than 76 countries were affiliated (Malin, 1997 p. 9). As the Cup gained in popularity with attending spectators, TV viewers and National Unions, its commercial appeal increased. One measure of this was the attraction of major sponsors, including Coca Cola, Toyota, Visa and Heineken. It soon became established as the fourth largest world sports festival, being eclipsed only by its soccer and cricket counterparts and the Olympic Games. As this process continued, growing financial surpluses began to be generated in the Rugby Union game (*Rugby World*, June 1995 pp. 48–50).

The cherry-picking of élite competitions

In *Barbarians, Gentlemen and Players*, we sought to analyze what we called the 'incipient professionalization' of Rugby Union. After 1979, this process continued apace, becoming more and more compelling in the sense that the hands of those advocating variants of more open professionalism were strengthened, while those attempting to stay the professional tide and preserve an amateur game were correlatively weakened. The intensification of global Rugby Union competition that was both reflected by and reciprocally enhanced through the inauguration of the World Cup proved decisive in this process. Crucial, too, was the increasing involvement of media interest groups and entrepreneurs with media and commercial connections who sought to 'cherry-pick' élite Rugby Union competitions, in that way signalling that a commercial infrastructure was emerging in the game sufficient to merit the attention of people searching for opportunities for secure revenue-generation and profit. The first serious attempt was made in this regard in 1983 by Australian 'promoter-journalist', David Lord. His intention, allegedly with the backing of board members of the South African Rugby Union (SARFU), had been to gather together a 'professional troupe' of up to 200 Rugby Union internationals to play competitive matches in a number of countries on a touring basis. The scheme was modelled on the marketing of televized cricket internationals by Kerry Packer, the Australian media tycoon, in the 1970s. Lord claimed that, by April 1983, 136 players from seven countries had signed 'preliminary optional contracts' and that, subject to the confirmation of TV rights and commercial backing, the tournament would be launched at London's Wembley Stadium or the Sydney Cricket Ground, Australia, the following year.

In the event, this scheme was destined to fail. This resulted partly from the disclosure that Lord was an undischarged bankrupt, partly from South Africa's fears that involvement in such a competition would weaken their chances of being allowed back into the fold of officially sanctioned Rugby competition—this was a period when apartheid still appeared to be deeply entrenched—and partly from the refusal of Adidas and the drinks company, Pernod, to underwrite the venture. The Secretary of the (English) RFU was nevertheless prompted in this situation to write to 120 top English players spelling out what the consequences would be if they surrendered their amateur status and requiring their signatures to a document confirming their commitment to amateur rugby (*Rugby World*, October 1983 12–14).

The second attempt to introduce such a scheme proved to be of more lasting significance. It came some twelve years later, shortly after the 1995 World Cup in South Africa. Prior to this event, the Southern Hemisphere Unions had been concerned over what they perceived as the threat to their interests posed by a new transnational Rugby League competition—the 'Super League'—recently introduced and financed by the satellite TV division of Rupert Murdoch's News International Company. Officials of the Southern Hemisphere Unions believed that, unless drastic counter-measures were taken, this competition would attract Rugby Union players and spectators to the rival code. It was thus in order to forestall the mass defection of Rugby Union players and spectators to Rugby League and to prevent the feared marginalization of Rugby Union as a televized spectator sport that the Unions of South Africa, New Zealand and Australia set up a tri-nations tournament between them, along with a competition between twelve regionally-based teams – the 'Super Twelve' tournament – and sold the television broadcasting rights to News Corporation for a reported £360 million over a ten-year period.

This deal was announced on the eve of the 1995 World Cup Finals, a tournament which was probably the most significant event in the transition from incipient, undercover professionalism to professionalism that was above board and full. The third Rugby Union World Cup was not only the commercially most successful to that date but also the most successful in terms of numbers of participating countries, numbers of spectators and TV viewers, and simply as a televisual 'show'. Perhaps more importantly, however, it involved the gathering together in a single location of the cream of the world's best players, many of Rugby Union's top administrators, and the representatives of a number of major commercial interest groups. In such a situation, top players came directly into contact with commercial interest groups, among them representatives of the World Rugby Corporation (WRC). The organizers of the latter included Ross Turnbull, the former Australia team manager, ex-international forward and New South Wales IB representative. Turnbull was acting as agent for Kerry Packer. Also included were representatives of such TV interests as the ESPN pay-per-view television network and the South African Broadcasting Corporation. The aim of the WRC was to recruit players for a two-tier tournament involving eight 'national teams' (Australia, South Africa, New Zealand, Western Samoa, England, Scotland, France and Wales) and up to twenty-two 'provincial teams'. Turnbull was reported as offering players signing-on fees of £175,000 and salaries for the tournament at a similar level. His strategy involved approaching players who were believed to be nearing the end of their international careers. They, in their turn, were supposed to recruit their teammates, a goal which was successfully achieved in the case of South Africa when virtually all members of their World Cup-winning side signed up.

In this situation, growing numbers of players began to signal a willingness to play for money for new, explicitly finance-orientated organizations and, as this happened, the main threat to amateur structures and values began to come, especially for the Southern hemisphere Unions, not so much from Rugby League as from within Rugby Union itself. The threat was increased as more and more players began to 'buy-in' to 'Thatcherite' individualistic and money-orientated values. SARFU, the first Union to respond, did so by making it clear that they would not purchase any of the WRC's franchises and that they would refuse in future to pick any players who signed for the WRC for international matches. Although these threats were partially successful, SARFU's most convincing move came when they agreed to offer their players salaries reported to be in the region of £140,000, guaranteed for three years, which came close to matching those of the WRC. Revenue to finance these payments was 'guaranteed' through the News Corporation deal agreed earlier. By contrast, the backers of the proposed WRC scheme had yet to confirm the sources of long-term revenue on which the scheme was to be based. In the event, the offer of substantial professional contracts to South African, Australian and New Zealand players induced them to remain affiliated to their respective Unions, and the WRC's challenge to News International collapsed, leaving the latter holding the television broadcasting rights to both the Union and League codes in the Southern Hemisphere. Such an outcome to the competitive struggle for the services of Rugby personnel, that is, essentially the players, represented a significant moment in the transition to full and open professional Rugby. As we have seen, it was a development that was underpinned by growing television and commercial interest in the game, a process that cannot be fully understood without taking account of the emergent 'Thatcherite hegemony'. In this process, the 1995 World Cup Final proved to be crucial. By the end of that summer, the IRB had sanctioned the full-scale professionalization of Rugby Union football. On the surface, they seemed to have abandoned their commitment to amateur values but, in reality, what they did in effect was to accommodate to and formalize the then-existing *status quo*.

The interdependency of English rugby and global professionalization

In English Rugby, the growing competitiveness which had led to, and which was further encouraged by, the setting up of a National Knock-Out Cup in 1971 and the introduction of national Leagues in 1976 and 1987, was reflected in a greater 'seriousness' of involvement of Rugby Union players and club officials in their sport. This increasing competitiveness was stimulated and expressed by a process of internationalization that was both symbolized and formalized by the inauguration of the World Cup in 1987. Such a development towards increasing seriousness and greater 'attitudinal professionalism' was more or less accepted by both players and administrators in the major English clubs as being necessary to a modern sport. However, it was not just a question of changing attitudes and values for, during the 1980s and early 1990s, there also took place the gradual establishment and increasing acceptance of a developing professional structure in Rugby Union on a world-wide scale. It is difficult to imagine that 'Thatcherism' and its American variant 'Reaganomics', both expressions of economic individualism and arguably themselves linked both causally and consequentially to wider processes of globalization, did not play an important part in this regard.

English Rugby Union clubs were intimately involved in these developments, of which there were at least six main strands. First there was the gradual institutionalization of direct, if disguised, payments to players. These took the form of payments in cash for playing and training at all levels, including 'colts'[8] and women's Rugby, and as inducements to move clubs. These payments were, of course, illegitimate under IRB regulations and illegal from the standpoint of the state to the extent that they were not declared for income tax purposes. Second, indirect payments to players grew in extent and importance. These consisted of 'no cost to play' benefits at one end of the spectrum (that is, the payment of expenses incurred for medical treatment, insurance, kit, travelling and accommodation) through to the provision at the other end of employment, housing and cars. Top international players also increasingly had trust funds set up for them and became heavily involved in product endorsement and promotional activities for commercial companies and public bodies. Such payments and activities were supposed to be limited and controlled by IRB regulations, but some national Unions were more liberal in their interpretation and application of the regulations and others were more punitive. The differences between Northern and Southern hemisphere nations in this regard tended to be particularly pronounced, with the Southern hemisphere nations inclining towards the more liberal pole. Third, there was the development of an informal 'transfer market'. This often consisted of little more than informal approaches by players or club officials to the members of other teams. However, it could also involve more formal arrangements such as the establishment of official or semi-official 'recruitment officer' structures and functions. A variety of 'inducements' were offered to players to move clubs or even countries, ranging from cash, clothing, jobs (some sinecures, some merely a front to support rugby playing), through to mortgage support and match appearance money. The informal transfer market which started to develop at élite club level was a sophisticated one, with the international migration of players becoming increasingly common. New Zealand players, for example, were to be found in club sides throughout the world; many Australians spent the 'close season' in Italy; British and Irish players were similarly scattered around France, while Western Samoans turned up in the New Zealand national side. Tongans, Australians and New Zealanders were conspicuous by their presence in the Japanese side (see Maguire, 1999). Fourth, the lengthening and broadening of interdependency chains which the commercialization and corresponding globalization of Rugby Union involved, led to increased structural complexity. In its turn, this was conducive to an expansion and corresponding professionalization of managerial and administrative functions and the professionalization of bureaucratic structures, first at governing body level and then increasingly at the level of clubs. Coaching and team management also became increasingly professionalized with substantial salaries becoming common at élite club level. In 1995, for example, Ian McGeechan, the ex-Scotland and British Lions coach, joined the English club, Northampton, for a reputed £40,000 per annum. Fifth, there was an increasing formalization of player/club, player/governing body, club/governing body, relationships. This involved such developments as the emergence of player representative groups (both formal and informal), the creation of such bodies as the English Senior Clubs Association to represent the interests of the élite groups in their negotiations with the RFU, and the formalizing of both the financial and representative roles of such bodies. Sixth, as we have seen, at both local and national level, team sponsorship deals and marketing arrangements grew increasingly significant (White, 1994; Sheard, 1996; Malcolm, Sheard and White, 2000). The RFU was faced during the 1980s and early 1990s with the task of controlling, or attempting to control, all of these developments and is generally recognized as having been less than successful (Jones, 1993; 2000; Gage, 1997). Sociologically, of course, that is hardly surprising. It is extremely unlikely that the administrators of an erstwhile amateur game, schooled in the ethos and values of voluntary association and community service, would have been able to adjust quickly to the increasingly rapid occurrence of interrelated processes of commercialization, professionalization, lengthening and broadening of interdependency chains, bureaucratizaton and globalization.

It is clear that, by the start of the 1990s, rugby players at the top British clubs, although not necessarily professional in terms of the regulations of the RFU and the IRB, were professional in any sociologically meaningful sense of that term. They were certainly not amateur. Hence our insistence here on using the term '*openly* professional' to describe developments after 1995.[9] Indeed, in his nine-point typology, Dunning cites Rugby Union prior to 1995 as being on the cusp of the covert, non-legitimate and the overt-legitimate types of sports professionalism (Dunning, 1999; Malcolm, Sheard and White, 2000).

The 'professionalism crisis' in British Rugby Union came rapidly to a head in the early 1990s. The England tour to South Africa in 1994 had led to accusations by English players and officials that South Africans were being paid to play at both the provincial and international levels. It was also clear that, following the end of the 1995 Rugby World Cup, there were going to be major alterations in the regulations relating to amateurism and professionalism. In August 1995, a report by the Amateurism Working Party, 'the Pugh Report', was presented to the IRB meeting in Paris. This report, which outlined the pros and cons articulated by all parties to the amateurism–professionalism debate, came to the conclusion that: 'The concept of amateurism as a central philosophy of the game is redundant. Many may regret its passing, but its resurrection is not possible.' The report continued, providing further evidence of the fact that the author recognized that all associated with the Union game were caught up in a compelling social process:

> Whether or not we promote it, the game will be openly professional within a very short space of time. If we do not participate in and direct and control that change, the IRFB and the Unions as we now know them may no longer be running the game.

The IRB subsequently declared that the amateur principles upon which the game had been founded should no longer constitute the basis for its organization and that it should become what they called an 'open game'. This decision to allow an 'open game' was subsequently ratified by the International Board at a meeting in Tokyo on 28 September 1995. Pugh's words about control over the game proved prophetic for, by the beginning of May 1996, the RFU found itself in dispute, not only with the other 'Home Unions' (those of Ireland, Scotland and Wales) over how best to share the increased television money being offered to the game, but also with the recently emerged and named association of English Professional Rugby

Union Clubs (EPRUC) over who was to control the game and how best to finance professionalism (Sheard, 1996).

Before we go on to examine some of the more significant changes which followed the open professionalization of Rugby Union in England, we wish to take note of the fact that one of the more immediate and dramatic consequences was the rapid and, given what had happened during and since the 1890s, extremely surprising, thaw in relations with the 'old enemy': Rugby League. This was epitomized in the so-called 'Clash of the Codes' contests which took place in May 1996. The League champions of the respective codes, Wigan (Rugby League) and Bath (Rugby Union) competed against each other in two matches, one under League rules at Maine Road, Manchester —home of Manchester City soccer club—and the other under Union laws at Twickenham. It came as little surprise, at least to rugby lovers, that both Wigan and Bath convincingly won the matches in their own codes. Much more significant than the results, however, was the fact that the matches had taken place at all (Malcolm, Sheard and White, 2000).[10]

A further feature of this thawing of relations was the fact that it spelled an end to the practice of prohibiting Rugby League players—whether current or past—from playing Rugby Union. The move to summer Rugby League which accompanied the introduction of 'Super League'[11] in Europe meant that the opportunity now existed for players of both codes to move freely from one to the other and take part in year-round rugby. Although, initially, a number of 'League players' took advantage of this opportunity (most notably the Wigan players Jason Robinson and Robbie Paul at Bath, and Gary Connolly at Harlequins), this practice has since become relatively less common. This is partly a consequence of the rather limited success of 'League players' in Union—interestingly, since 1996 no professional 'Union player' has moved in the opposite direction—but also to the concern expressed in the media and by the administrators of both codes over the heavy physical demands on players that all-year-round playing would inevitably entail. More common was the reversion of former 'Union players' who had previously chosen to become Rugby League professionals—Jonathan Davies, Scott Quinnell, Alan Tait, John Bentley were among them—to their erstwhile code (Malcolm, Sheard and White, 2000), while several high profile Rugby League players opted for the Rugby Union game, attracted no doubt by the lucrative signing-on fees and wages on offer.

Club structure

Following the rapid post-1995 spurt of professionalization, in order to cope with the new financial and other demands of professional rugby many clubs were constrained to alter their ownership patterns and organizational structures. English, Scottish and Welsh rugby clubs increasingly moved from being 'members clubs' towards having professionally staffed, commercially orientated corporate structures. This process did not only involve changes in organizational structures and forms but also the professionalizing of functions that had previously been carried out by volunteer amateur committee members. At the national level, the continuing professionalization of administrative functions both engendered new and exacerbated existing tensions between the professional administrators and the amateur, member-elected committees which had previously been the principal rulers of the game (Malcolm, Sheard and White, 2000). The in many ways dysfunctional character of this hybrid structure is illustrated by the fact that, in 1998–99, the RFU was anticipating a loss of around £2.3 million, having already lost £10.3 million in the previous two years. The RFU sought to excuse this state of affairs by revealing that, since the onset of open professionalism, its costs had risen by over 300%. Francis Bacon, however, Twickenham's new Chief Executive Officer who was appointed in 1999, felt moved to condemn the absence of even the most basic and standard business practices in his new place of work. Not surprisingly, one of his first acts on taking office was to sack 191 headquarters personnel (Smith, 2000, p. 173). Smith suggests that the scale of the Twickenham losses and the complete absence of effective corporate management 'confirmed the survival of amateurism of the very worst kind at the highest level of the English game'. Indeed, many commentators believe that Twickenham's still unwieldy structure is inappropriate for a professional sport and continues to inhibit the development of the game (Jones, 2000). Of course, similar things are said about the governance of English soccer, English cricket and, although perhaps less frequently than used to be the case, English industry and business more generally.[12]

The Senior Clubs were less tardy in adapting to the requirements and pressures of open professionalism. Indeed, even prior to the declaration of 1995, clubs like Northampton and Leicester effectively anticipated the sorts of changes that would be required in an era of open commercialization and professionalization and began significantly to alter their management structures (Nier and Sheard, 1999). Moreover, only two months after the IRB's 1995 announcement, Sir John Hall, the entrepreneur, property developer and already owner of the soccer club, Newcastle United FC, offered Rob Andrew of Wasps and England £750,000 over five years to move Newcastle Gosforth from the bottom of Courage Division Two to the Division One Championship title. This, Andrew had achieved by May 1998. He was aided by Hall's willingness to invest, the club's incorporation as a limited company, and—or so we are led to believe—the adoption of modern business practices. Hall, however, recognized that a capacity crowd of 6,000 would fund neither the sort of record-breaking transfer fees he had set in motion nor the inflated wage bills he deemed necessary for rapid success. For this, television money would be crucial (Smith, 2000) and we shall return to its key role shortly. Before we do, it will be instructive to provide details of two of the more significant structural developments which accompanied professionalization and which were epitomized by Sir John Hall, namely the growing prominence in clubs' economic affairs of a benefactor/owner and their (the clubs') incorporation as limited companies. These details are provided in Table 2:

Table 2 Aspects of the Ownership Structure of Elite Professional Rugby Union Clubs (1997)

Club	Ltd Co.	Major investor (business interests)	Investment	Notes
Bath	Yes	Andrew Brownsword (greetings card business)	£2.5m	Changed name from Bath Football Club to Bath Rugby plc.
Bristol	Yes	Arthur Holmes. (Shares held by membership)	Loan of approx. £1m	Linked to merger with Cardiff RFC whose major investor was Peter Thomas
Gloucester	Yes	Tom Walkinshaw. (25% shares held by membership, 73% by Walkinshaw)	£2.5m	
NEC Harlequins	Trust	Peter and John Beckwith (Riverside Leisure Plc)	£3m	Changed name to NEC Harlequins after sponsorship by NEC, a trans-national Japanese electronics co.
Leicester	Yes	Planned share issue to membership	n/a	
London Irish	No	Remains a 'membership club'	n/a	
Newcastle Falcons (Promoted from League 2)	Yes	Sir John Hall (Entrepreneur/ Property Developer)	£5m	Part of local Sporting Club group owned by Hall which includes Newcastle United FC, ice-hockey and basketball clubs. The rugby club changed its name from Newcastle Gosforth to Newcastle Falcons after Hall's investment
Richmond (Promoted from League 2)	Yes	Ashley Levett (Metals trader)	£2.5m	
Sale	Yes	Shares owned by membership		

| Saracens | Yes | Nigel Wray (Executive Chairman of Burford Holdings, a property company; also has a financial interest in Nottingham Forest FC) | | Now located at Vicarage Road, the ground of Watford Town FC |
| Wasps | Yes | Chris Wright (Crysalis Records/Trocadero plc) | £3m | Wright also has a financial interest in Queens Park Rangers FC on whose ground Wasps were to play their home games. (In 2002, the latter moved to Adams park and the two clubs became part of the Loftus Road Group (plc) quoted on the Alternative Investment Market.) |

Source: Adapted from Malcolm, Sheard and White, 2000.

A similar pattern of combining investment and limited liability status was evident among clubs which were in the Allied Dunbar Premiership (ADP) League Division Two in 1997/98. Bedford, London Scottish, Nottingham, Wakefield, Orrell, Coventry, Blackheath and Moseley all became limited companies and, with varying degrees of success, attracted outside investment. With the financial assistance of millionaire Cecil Duckworth, Worcester RFC were promoted from the old Courage League Division Four (North) at the end of the 1996/7 season. He is reported to have supported them to the tune of £2 million when they competed in the newly-founded Jewson National League Division One in 1997/98.[13] In a word, there is strong evidence to support the view that, in the face of increasing competitiveness and growing opportunities in rugby football overall, clubs in the lower divisions were increasingly modelling themselves on their elite counterparts.

There appears to have been a high degree of structural homogeneity in the responses of the élite clubs as they adapted to the constraints and opportunities of a professional game by transforming themselves into limited liability companies. What are believed to be sound commercial reasons reinforced this pattern. Firstly, limited company status, either by guarantee or by shares, indemnifies the membership and managing committee from claims against them should the club make a loss. Secondly, the search for outside investors is facilitated by the expedient of having a limited company backed by assets against which investments can be made. Thirdly, the existence of share capital facilitates the transfer of ownership to a greater degree than in a membership club where the role of the investor is limited to one of benefactor rather than owner. Fourthly, the majority of the investors had obtained their wealth from the ownership of family companies or personally created business organizations. They were, that is, predominantly from entrepreneurial backgrounds and thus comfortable in the area of new and emerging business ventures, albeit with a preference for limited liability companies to reduce personal risk. Finally, the success of clubs in ADP League Division One, such as Wasps, Bath and Harlequins, and of promoted clubs Richmond and Newcastle,[14] with the trinity of structural attributes—limited liability, major investor and major sponsor—facilitated the acquisition and retention of better players, in that way reinforcing the logic of such an approach. In contrast, the fate of relegated clubs, West Hartlepool—which remained a members club—and Orrell—who were unable to attract major investment or sponsorship despite having limited liability status—provided salutary lessons of the probable consequences of a failure to adjust (Malcolm, Sheard and White, 2000).

There was, nevertheless, some diversity in the responses of élite rugby clubs to the exigencies of professionalization. As can be seen from Table 2, a number of clubs – among them Gloucester, NEC Harlequins, Newcastle, Saracens and Wasps – appear to have become additions to the portfolios of wider sports and/or leisure groups. A similar pattern was evident in Division Two where boxing promoter Frank Warren's 'Sports Network Group' took a 50% share ownership in Bedford,[15] and an eight-man consortium including Chairman of Aston Villa FC, Doug Ellis, took an 80% share ownership in Moseley. This suggests that élite level Rugby Union was beginning at this time to be perceived as full of commercial opportunities and that it was coming, as a result, to be more deeply integrated into the growing sports industry/entertainment/leisure network. Richmond's then owner, Ashley Levett, commented on the attraction of this situation by pointing out that: 'The initial entry price into rugby is very small compared with other sports' (Malcolm, Sheard and White, 2000).[16] Of course, a corollary of this was that the chances for profits were correspondingly lower, too.

In a second group of clubs, limited liability and share issues were also the preferred option but the ownership of the shares, and hence the ownership of the clubs, was retained by the members. For example, Bristol's approximately 2,000 members were each given four hundred £1 'Founder Shares'.[17] Leicester introduced a similar share ownership scheme for their 10,000 members, and at (Manchester) Sale, shares are owned by the members. Whilst London Irish managed to survive as a membership club for the first three years of 'open' rugby, financial difficulties led, in June 1999, to a three-way merger between themselves, Richmond and London Scottish. In November 1997, a 'cross-code' merger between Leeds Rugby Union Club (itself the product of an earlier merger between Headingly and Roundhay) and Leeds Rugby League Club was agreed after the former accepted a takeover bid from Paul Caddick, a businessman with a controlling interest in the Rugby League club.

Two general points can be made with regard to these developments. The first relates to the emergence of clubs as tradeable entities, with either partial or total ownership being achieved through the transfer of shares. Some clubs have recognized the possibility of loss of control over the organization which is inherent in this situation and have retained a 'golden share' to allow some degree of veto over the use of the club by investors. The second relates to the existence of evidence that English Rugby Union in its commercial development is increasingly being penetrated by transnational ownership, sponsorship, television, financial and marketing groups. Of particular importance in what Bale and Maguire (1994) call this expanding 'financescape', a key element in the globalization of sports,[18] is the potential it contains for transnational commercial organizations to add English Rugby Union clubs to their corporate portfolios through the simple expedient of acquiring shares. The transition to limited company status by the majority of English clubs, as one aspect of a continuing commercialization process, facilitates this development (Malcolm, Sheard and White, 2000). Although we cannot quantify it at the moment, a corollary of this process is English/British involvement in transnational corporations and hence, among other things, in the purchase of shares in rugby clubs overseas.

Rugby Union and television

The RFU began to grow more financially dependent on the mass media, and in part on a non-rugby playing audience, with the advent of broadcast and televised rugby in 1927 and 1937 respectively.[19] However, such a process became particularly marked during the 1970s as TV audiences grew and income from advertisers and commercial sponsors rose.[20] With the advent of open professionalism, the RFU signed a deal with BSkyB in 1996 in which the English Union were to be paid £87.5 million over five years for the exclusive rights to televise internationals, including Five (later Six) Nations matches played at Twickenham. BSkyB also obtained the rights to show selected matches from the Allied Dunbar Premiership, attracting a total of 5.5 million viewers in the 1997–8 season. BSkyB seems to have seen Rugby Union as a sport which would help attract new customers to their satellite channels, not only selling dishes but also advertising. Consequently, it has been prepared to invest large sums of money for the right to cover matches (Malcolm, Sheard and White, 2000).

Above all else, it was the prospect of widespread television coverage that attracted many new sponsors to the game, in that way contributing in part to the change in club structures. The electronics giant, NEC, became one of the first transnationals to inject money into the professional game when it agreed a three-year contract with Harlequins at the start of the 1996 season (see Table 2). However, these sponsors did not necessarily get the anticipated return on their investments. The audiences which BSkyB attracted were viewed by many as disappointing. The numbers watching televised club rugby on Saturdays rarely exceeded six figures, while Channel 5's highlights programme struggled to approach the two million that sometimes tuned in to BBC2's 'Rugby Special' (Malcolm, Sheard and White, 2000). Corporate sponsors began to question whether club rugby could produce a level of exposure comparable to other sports (Smith, 2000). For example, in 1998 NEC were prepared to make public their dissatisfaction with Harlequins. In 1996, senior figures in the electronics giant had believed that Harlequins offered them such things as a long-standing association with wealth, high status and the City of London. They were, at the time, London's most successful club and the team of Will Carling, both England's captain and her most famous player. For NEC, with its reputation for hi-tech quality products, this was the perfect marriage (Smith, 2000 p. 160). By 1998, Carling had gone and 'NEC Harlequins' were struggling in the League; 'divorce seemed imminent' (Smith, 2000). Fortunately for Harlequins, their results improved and the NEC sponsorship was still in place in September 2002. What this shows is how dependent many of the major clubs have become on their sponsors and how exposed they are to major financial difficulties should the sponsors withdraw from contract negotiations or greatly reduce their cash donations to the clubs.

It follows from what we have discussed so far that the fortunes of the RFU, its clubs, especially but not solely the top ones, and the players and officials (match as well as organizational), have all become, in an age of open professionalism, inextricably intertwined with those of the media and the firms and industries that are the principal providers of sponsorship and advertising revenues. It is above all clear that top teams, especially those with multinational sponsors, now need to appear on television regularly in order to retain their credibility as marketable assets. Similarly the players—especially once the initially unrealistic salaries and signing on fees started to become more attuned to the clubs' ability to pay—have begun to expand their PR and promotional activities, a development aided by the traditionally prosperous image of English rugby and one which allowed Polley to anticipate a 'professional élite of Rugby Union players emerging, with economic and cultural advantages over footballers and Rugby League players to allow them more quickly to exploit their situations' (Polley, 1998 p. 125; Smith, 2000 p. 187). He was, of course, alluding to the traditionally middle and upper middle class character of the Rugby Union game. In Bourdieu's (1984) terms he was referring to the correlative 'cultural capital' of its players relative to those of the two other major British forms of football, soccer and Rugby League, many more of whom have families of origin which are working class.

The defenders of traditional amateurism have long expressed concern about the anticipated effects of such a degree of media involvement on the structure and ethos of the game. These concerns still run deep as a recent survey of top clubs has indicated (Malcolm, Sheard and White, 2000). The effects of media involvement all stem from the need to woo spectators and can be divided into effects on the structure of the game itself; effects on the scheduling of matches; effects on the ethos and 'spirit' of the game; and effects on its spectator base (Malcolm, Sheard and White, 2000 p. 82).

It is difficult to separate out changes to a game which are designed to maintain an enjoyable tension-balance between polarities such as defence and attack for the players themselves,[21] those which are orientated in this regard towards spectators,[22] and those which are more or less equally orientated towards both groups. In *Barbarians*, we established as fact that claims that legislators have been making the game 'too fast' have been heard since at least 1893 (Dunning and Sheard, 1979 p. 217). It is undeniable nevertheless that many of the law changes which have been introduced into the game since open professionalism have contributed to increasing its speed, kept the ball in play for longer and with fewer stoppages, and have increased the appeal and entertainment value of Rugby Union for many 'live' spectators and television viewers. Such structural changes have been quickly accepted by players and have probably enhanced the pleasures of playing as well as watching the game. They do, though, require greater fitness. Nor have such 'drastic' changes resulted in the abolition of the line-out or the reduction of the numbers of players in a team, changes which some commentators suggested would be required by full professionalism and which would bring Rugby Union into closer and closer correspondence with the pattern of play associated with Rugby League (Malcolm, Sheard and White, 2000, p. 83).

Changes have been introduced to the scheduling of the game which are certainly attributable in large part to the influence and requirements of the media. For example, kick-off times have been altered to fit in with television schedules but this has not so far had the radical consequences it has had for other sports. Nor has it received the same weight of criticism.[23] International matches have sometimes been played end-to-end so that—to take just one example—on Saturday 6 March 1999, the France v Wales match (k.o. 2.00 pm) and Ireland v England (k.o. 4.00 pm) could both be viewed by television audiences. English club games have kicked off slightly earlier or later to accommodate television schedules while some clubs have opted to play on Sundays. This latter change, however, has not always been imposed by television companies, but is usually a pragmatic decision of the clubs themselves to maximize attendances. Sometimes it is dictated by their ground-sharing arrangements with soccer clubs (Malcolm, Sheard and White, 2000) and sometimes, e.g. in cases where a city or town has top-level soccer and rugby clubs, by the police in order to minimize the chances of traffic congestion and crowd disorder. In France, the game at élite level has long been organized with a view to attracting the maximum number of spectators. Matches are sometimes scheduled for 8.00 pm to enable players of junior sides and clubs to attend, or for 3.00 pm on Sundays, so that shop workers are also available (Nier and Sheard, 1999). The French, of course, are more easily able to be pragmatic in this regard because they lack the legacy of 'pristine amateurism' which goes back in England to the nineteenth century.

The English professional clubs were quick to recognize that their interdependence with television companies, sponsors and advertisers meant that, not only would they have to strive to retain their existing levels of support but that, in competition with the attractions of other sources of entertainment, they would have to adapt to what some perceived to be a consumer demand for a 'total entertainment package'. Despite the Mintel Crowd survey of 1989 appearing to indicate that the introduction of American-style 'razzmatazz' was not a major factor in attracting British crowds to sporting events,[24] several rugby clubs experimented with a variety of spectator 'attractions' including cheerleaders, fireworks, pre-match and half-time entertainments, remote-control kicking-tee deliverers, and musical accompaniment to successful goal-kicks and tries. The intention behind these changes in what has routinely come to be understood as the 'marketing' of Rugby Union has, of course, been to attract new spectators and to retain existing ones. That there has been some success in this regard is suggested by rising spectator attendances. For example, 1997–98 Premiership One figures rose by 22.4% on those of the previous season (Smith, 1999; Malcolm, Sheard and White, 2000). Attendances in 2001–02, it has been claimed, were up by 40% over 2000–2001 (*Guardian*, 30 August, 2002). The following examples point in the same direction. In September, 2002, Ken Nottage, the Gloucester RFC Chief

Executive, reported that their season ticket sales had increased over a three-year period from 1,700 to 4,750 and that their annual turnover had increased from £1.8 million to £5 million (*Guardian*, 24 September, 2002). Gloucester's League match against Northampton on 2 November 2002, was an 11,000 sell-out, while Leicester's match against Wasps on the same day attracted a capacity crowd of 16,700 (*The Observer*, 3 November, 2002). It is still not clear to what extent increased attendances have involved changes in the social characteristics of rugby crowds although letters sent to the magazines, *Rugby World* and *Rugby News* in 1998 did voice complaints about the behaviour of a presumed new group of Saracens fans, the 'Fez Boys'. The condemnation of these fans—or, more particularly, of their new style of supporting—focused on their drunkenness, foul language and threatening behaviour. Such letters provide a limited indication that the spectator base of the sport is both changing and increasingly contested. That appears to be particularly the case where clubs have moved to new locations with a view to attracting spectators and where they have attracted some who appear not to be well acquainted with the traditional ways of supporting Rugby Union (Malcolm, Sheard and White, 2000).

Players as assets

The grounds, buildings and shares of Rugby Union clubs are visible representations of their assets and make them potentially vulnerable to takeover bids, an eventuality the likelihood of which has increased with professionalization and the greater money-making potential of clubs. However, the players themselves, without whom, obviously, the clubs would cease to function, have also assumed greater importance as assets as the processes of professionalization and commercialization have continued. Rugby football is a physical contact sport which places great demands upon players' bodies; indeed, according to Sports Council data, rugby has a higher rate of participant injury than any other sport in Britain.[25] With professionalization, as players become 'commodities' and part of the human 'capital' of commercially organized and orientated clubs,[26] the conflict between the pressures to utilize that capital to the full, whilst also protecting a valuable asset, means that the demands upon players have to be carefully managed. There are several ways in which clubs seek both to protect their assets and/or to lessen their reliance upon a few skilled personnel. Firstly, to minimize the risk of injury, they can limit the number of matches in which players are required to take part. Secondly, they can carry large squads of players of similar or complementary abilities so that player rotation can take place and to ensure that adequate replacements are always available. These, of course, are a 'cost' and have to be paid for. Thirdly, the clubs can take steps to improve and/or protect the physical condition of players so as to lessen, as far as possible, the risk of injury. Such steps include, for instance, the use of protective padding and muscle/ligament support not only for matches but also for training and practice sessions. Also included under this category is the employment of trained physiotherapists and medical personnel. Fourthly, clubs can seek an improvement in refereeing standards, encourage the introduction of more 'protective' refereeing (Malcolm, Sheard and White, 2000), and try to ensure that players abide by the rules (laws), especially those concerned with the control and limitation of physical violence in the game. Let us examine how far such policies have been pursued.

(a) Limits on the number of matches played

Players in any professional sport, but perhaps especially a hard physical contact sport such as Rugby Union, are subject to a variety of often contradictory pressures and constraints. Some of these are self-imposed (for example, the desire to play even when injured because players' identities and sense of self-esteem are so closely bound up with their sporting performance)[27] but others stem from their employers' desire to make money or return a profit. In contrast to soccer where the clubs themselves are the primary generators of income,[28] in Rugby Union the income generated from ticket sales and the sale of television rights for international games is highly significant. Added to this, most of the home Unions are carrying substantial loans for new stadium construction. In 2002, for example, the RFU still had a £21m debt to repay for the redevelopment of Twickenham (*Touchline*, August 2002), p. 2.[29] Consequently, pressure has arisen to increase the number of international matches played and thus unintentionally increasing the demands on players. Here, the interests of the national governing bodies are in conflict with those of the major clubs. There is an understandable reluctance on the part of the clubs to release expensive 'assets', if not so much for home international matches as for training sessions, overseas tours,[30] or matches against touring sides. Not only do they lose the services of international players but the players involved run an added risk of injury. Further to this, the economic future of the leading clubs depends on their maintaining their membership of the élite divisions and/or winning prestigious championships and cups. Positive and negative feedback loops are evident whereby playing success enables a club to retain key personnel and recruit new stars which increases the likelihood of further playing success, and *vice versa*, failure on the field of play tends to be similarly self-perpetuating. Given this, even though RFU contributions constitute a major source of revenue for elite clubs, as much as 90% of their income, it is not surprising that there is a degree of ambivalence in their support for the national side (Malcolm, Sheard and White, 2000).[31]

The advent of 'open' rugby has brought about an increase in such contradictory pressures and desires. Most clubs have seen an increase in the number of matches they play and there is a widespread feeling among coaches that players are playing too much rugby. Coaches are more likely than owners to experience close up the damage done to players through over-playing, and they are beginning to demand fewer games. Whether they are listened to or not will depend upon the power relations at particular clubs. Similarly, the players are subject to a range of constraints some self-imposed, some imposed by others.[32] Lawrence Dallaglio, the England back-row-forward expressed the resultant tensions very clearly. In December 1996, he was reported to have described as 'madness' the fact that he had played ninety-one matches in a season, and expressed his intention to reduce this to thirty-five (Malcolm, Sheard and White, 2000).[33]

(b) Squad sizes

Given the demands imposed upon players in the 'open' professional game, it would appear to be in the interests of both clubs and players for large squads of players, all capable of playing at first fifteen level, to be established. In the pre-open days, some clubs were so successful in recruiting players, with the best players tending to concentrate at clubs like Leicester and Harlequins, that the RFU was constrained to contemplate placing limits on the number of players who could be registered with any club. As early as the first year of open professionalism, it became clear that the richest clubs were again entering the market to strengthen their squads and to deny their rivals the services of top players. This has not been a linear process, though, as competition, rising costs and lower than projected profitability have constrained clubs to reassess their priorities and to re-examine the number of players they can afford to place under contract. Some clubs, indeed, have even gone bankrupt. In February, 1998, the Premiership Second Division club, Moseley, went into administration, laying off a dozen players as their debts passed the £1 million mark.[34] In March 1999, Richmond called in the administrator when Ashley Levett made the decision to cut personal losses approaching £8 million and announced 34 redundancies.[35] As noted earlier, Richmond went on to merge with London Scottish[36] and London Irish. Richmond's fate stung the Premiership sides into agreeing to limit their wages bills to between £1 million and £1.5 million (Smith, 2000), although, under pressure from Northampton and Leicester, a salary cap of £1.8 million was eventually agreed. Rugby is, of course, in advance of soccer in the introduction of such legislation.

(c) Physical conditioning

Part of the reason for assembling large squads is that élite rugby clubs—or perhaps more accurately the coaches of élite rugby clubs: and this is a feature shared by top-level sport more generally—are increasingly aware of the physical demands placed on players and that the effects of these demands need to be minimized if players are to reach and remain at an optimal level of preparation for match-play. Most top clubs have begun to take steps to help ensure that players are in good physical shape so they can resist the rigours of the sport. These steps have included: the 'scientization' of training and fitness conditioning; the development of more adequate medical monitoring and control; the provision of more professionally trained and readily available physiotherapy support; and the implementation of better dietary and nutritional regimes. However, the effectiveness and general availability of such provision is only now starting to be adequately assessed and, if the example of Association Football, a richer sport which has been fully professional for far longer, is anything to go by, the quality of such provision, and its role in the protection of players, cannot be taken for granted (Malcolm and Sheard, 2002; Roderick, Waddington and Parker, 2000; Waddington, Roderick and Naik, 2000).[37]

One obvious way in which players can minimize the risk of injuries is through the use of protective equipment. Rugby Union *aficionados*, whether players, administrators or spectators—and the same is true, though to a lesser extent, in Rugby League—have traditionally resisted the introduction into their game of American football-style body armour, taking pride in what they perceived to be the more 'manly' character of their chosen sport. Indeed, until recently, much of this body protection had been banned by the RFU. Protecting the head by the use of scrum caps, and the teeth and jaw by gum-shields, have long been accepted (although most players used to prefer to protect their ears through the judicious use of adhesive tape, and scrum-caps were seldom seen), but shoulder padding and the use of upper body 'harnesses' were not only against the regulations of the RFU but regarded by many in the game as 'effeminate'. A small amount of padding was officially permitted, mainly to protect an injury, but before 1996 this protection was limited to light padding which had to be sewn into the lining of a shirt. In 1997, the laws were altered to say that protection could be taped to the body, but the use of shoulder pads was explicitly banned.

In 1996 the RFU sanctioned the use of approved head protection and, in 1998, the use of equipment to protect the upper body.[38] Since then, more and more players at all levels of rugby have taken advantage of the new regulations in an attempt to protect their bodies from the rigours of the game. It should not go unremarked, however, that the use of such protection is potentially as much *offensive* as it is defensive. Players wearing body 'armour' are not only protected from the 'hits' of others—the increasing use of this term in preference to the more traditional 'tackle' is revealing in itself —but are able to 'hit' their opponents harder with less risk of damaging their own bodies in the process.[39] It has been suggested that an apparent increase in injury rates since open professionalism may be attributable to the use of protective clothing (Garraway *et al.*, 2000), but others have suggested that such an increase, if indeed it has occurred, is more likely to have been caused by heavier, stronger, fitter, faster players engaging in more prolonged physical contact (Malcolm, Sheard and White, 2000; Malcolm and Sheard, 2002).

d) Officiating and refereeing of matches

The administrators of Rugby Union have, over the last few years but especially since the advent of open professionalism and with increasing globalization, come under increasing constraint to alter the laws of the game in order to create a more regularly free-flowing and spectacular 'product' or 'commodity' and one which is safer for players under professional conditions. It was argued in 1997 that, although touch judges had long been empowered to draw the attention of the referee to dangerous play, under professionalism their power could be anticipated to increase. Referees themselves might be expected to become more punitive (Sheard, 1997; Malcolm, Sheard and White, 2000). To this end, the sin bin was introduced for the 1997/98 season and referees now have recourse to this as an alternative to the more severe punishment of sending players off for the duration of the match. In addition to implementing these rule changes, match officials have been charged with dealing with their potential contradictions. More particularly, they have to protect players and the 'spirit of the game', apply the laws consistently, recognize the interests of spectators and clubs and help in the production of an exciting 'spectacle', whilst bearing in mind all the time their own career interests.[40] It is also noticeable that, nowadays, referees and touch judges at all levels of the game talk more or less constantly to players, issuing instructions designed to obtain quick release of the ball, prevent infringements by means of anticipation, and discouraging players from incurring penalties (Malcolm, Sheard and White, 2000). Whilst officiating is probably always going to be a thankless task in all varieties and at all levels of sport, it seems to us that Rugby Union referees and touch-judges have so far made an important contribution to the professionalization and spectacularization of this until recently amateur, not openly professional sport. It remains to be seen how well they will continue to cope if and when the earnings of players begin to approach those of their soccer counterparts. Let us close this postscript by returning to the academic reception of our book and figurational contributions to the sociology of sport more generally.

The academic reception of *Barbarians, Gentlemen and Players* and the figurational sociology of sport

Among the most noticeable academic developments to have taken place since 1979 when *Barbarians, Gentlemen and Players* first appeared has been the emergence of the systematic study of sport as a major field in sociology, anthropology, psychology, history, geography, economics, politics and law. It is a development which evidently corresponds to the rising social importance and correlatively increasing cultural centrality of sport itself.

Prominent among the contributors to this academic development since 1979 have been the cultural studies/hegemony theorists, central among them—and we cite them in no particular order—John Hargreaves, Jenny

Hargreaves, Rick Gruneau, Alan Ingham, John Sugden, Alan Tomlinson, Ian McDonald and Peter Donnelly. We like to think that we, the figurational sociologists, have made some useful contributions, too.

Figurational studies in the sociology of sport started in 1959 and have now been carried out over more than four decades. In that time, the figurational tradition of sport studies has come to be reasonably well established in two countries, the United Kingdom and the Netherlands, and roots are beginning to be laid down in six more, France, Germany, Canada, Brazil, Japan and Korea.[41]

In the UK, there have now been five generations of figurational sociologists of sport: (i) Norbert Elias; (ii) Eric Dunning; (iii) Patrick Murphy, Kenneth Sheard and Ivan Waddington; (iv) Grant Jarvie and Joseph Maguire; (v) Sharon Colwell, Graham Curry, Dominic Malcolm, Louise Mansfield, Martin Roderick and Stuart Smith.[42] Indeed, it might be argued that Daniel Bloyce, Ken Green, Andrew Smith, Jason Tuck and Andy White constitute a sixth generation. *Barbarians, Gentlemen and Players*, as one can see, was a product of collaboration between the second and third generations, and it appeared some seven years before the publication of the key figurational sport text, Elias and Dunning's *Quest for Excitement: Sport and Leisure in the Civilizing Process* which appeared in 1986.

1986 was a year which also saw the appearance of John Hargreaves's influential *Sport, Power and Culture* (Oxford, Polity). On its sleeve we are told that: 'This book provides the first systematic analysis of the links between sport and power in Britain'. We thought at the time, and still do, that *Barbarians, Gentlemen and Players* was more deserving of such an accolade, having beaten John Hargreaves to that goal by a full seven years. Of course, had the 'blurb' read 'the first neo-Marxist' or 'first hegemony theory analysis', it would have been closer to the mark. That is because our analysis in *Barbarians, Gentlemen and Players* is based on a figurational approach and thus, we contend, manages to avoid the economic reductionism which mars Hargreaves's book even though he is explicitly – and rightly – critical in it of other forms of Marxist approach on precisely these grounds.[43]

Interestingly, Jenny Hargreaves and Ian McDonald (2000 p. 56) continue to assert that economically determined class power is universally and eternally more 'fundamental' than other power sources. In a word, they stick to a law-like form of explanation in a field where, if Elias was right as we believe him largely to have been (Elias, 1974), forms of explanation more attuned to the complexity and fluidity of social relations are needed if we are to advance the body of sociological knowledge bequeathed to us by our nineteenth and early twentieth century 'founders'. Elias called these forms of explanation 'structure and process explanations' and that is what we were seeking to construct in *Barbarians, Gentlemen and Players*.

Judging by the book's reception, we think it fair to say that we were not entirely unsuccessful. Although they were writing of figurational contributions to the sociology of sport more generally, in 1987 John Horne and

David Jary summed up as follows what they called our 'main achievements'. They said we had provided:

i)   an account of the rule-governed character of modern sport in which 'mock fights' on the whole replace true violence.[44]

ii) an analysis and historical account of sport and society in which changes in the division of labour and class relations are shown to be central to the development and institutionalization of modern sports and games.

iii) a neo-Durkheimian account of the important 'symbolic' role of sport in providing significant 'representations' of nation and community in modern society, and the source also of 'personal identities' . . . (Horne and Jary, 1987 p. 97).

Horne and Jary went on generously to refer to 'the historical detail and considerable subtlety' of the figurational sociology of sport. Understandably though, perhaps especially given the fact that what Hargreaves and McDonald (2000) call 'paradigm wars' remain characteristic of our subject, they followed this by a lengthy and trenchant critique of the figurational contributions. In this, they reached the conclusion that the work of cultural studies/hegemony theorists represents a 'complementary but broader' approach (Horne and Jary, 1987, p. 103). We do not entirely disagree. For example, whilst it is true that Elias's (1939; 2000) study of the early stages of Western European, especially French, state-formation constitutes one of the foundation-stones of our work, it is equally true that, as Horne and Jary point out (p. 109, note 5) and with the exception of Maguire's pioneering work on sport and globalization (Maguire, 1999), figurational sociologists have not devoted much attention to the development, specifically, of capitalist nation-states and not much either to the development of sport in such contexts. It is important to point out that, as Chris Rojek suggested in 1985, despite their differences, figurational sociologists and hegemony theorists share a lot in common. Both sets of scholars advocate forms of historical approach; both stress the importance of power in social relations and follow Marx's suggestion—we are paraphrasing—that 'people make their own history but under circumstances they have inherited from the past and which they did not choose'; and both were early relative to the advocates of other forms of Marxism and other 'schools' of sociology to spot and seriously study the rising significance of sport.[45] In our view, the dialogue between us has been largely fruitful and constructive and we hope it will continue.[46] Let us turn now to Horne and Jary's critique. Given limited space we shall, perforce, be selective in this connection.

According to Horne and Jary, figurational sociologists claim that their paradigm is 'methodologically distinctive' or 'unique'. We make no such claims, although we did have to fight hard on behalf of 'historical', 'developmental', or 'process sociology' in the 1950s and 60s when static forms of functionalism and empiricism reigned supreme. What we do claim is that, with his radical concept of process, his stress on the need for 'structure-and-process' explanations, his non-economistic, relational concept of power, his insistence on the need for a constant two-way traffic between research and theory, and his eschewal of a *homo clausus* (closed person) in favour of a *homines aperti* (pluralities of open people) approach to the study of humans, Norbert Elias did make a sociological breakthrough relative to the classical and functionalist inheritance which was available in the mid-twentieth century.

Horne and Jary also challenge what they call 'any thesis of the distinctiveness of the concept of "figuration" ', going on favourably to cite Zygmunt Bauman's dismissive suggestion that 'there exists a clear affinity between the idea of figuration and such rather household notions as "pattern" or "situation" ' (p. 98). Apart from the fact that 'situation' is a term largely devoid of structural connotations, which is presumably why it figured in Popper's (1957) advocacy of 'methodological individualism', what this misses is the centrality of a non-harmonistic understanding of interdependence in Elias's concept of figurations, that is, the fact that he conceptualized them as power fields characterized by variable and labile balances between conflict and co-operation, centripetal and centrifugal pressures. In this, of course, he anticipated by some thirty or forty years a variant of the concept of social fields later successfully pioneered in France by Pierre Bourdieu (1984).

Probably central among Horne and Jary's criticisms of figurational sociology is what they refer to as 'a tendency to latent evolutionism' in our work (p. 100). They expand on this—in typically balanced fashion—as follows:

> On the positive side, . . . the concept of the 'civilizing process' is responsible for the focus on 'combat sports' and the codification and the domestication of these in their modern forms. It provides a systematic—if only one—rationale for focus on class, class emulation and class conflict. Against this, however, and variously at odds with some elements of figurational sociology's own methodological self-definitions, functionalist, evolutionary and related assumptions associated with the concept of the 'civilizing process' have been rightly questioned, for example: 'the apparent irreversibility of the process' (Lasch, 1985), its 'irrefutability' (Smith, 1984), its explicit or implicit reference to 'societal needs' and 'functional requirements'. Of course, there need be no outright objections to functional analysis or the use of 'untestable' general frameworks in sociology—indeed the productiveness of the concept of the 'civilizing process' in these respects is apparent. But there are aspects of the concept of the 'civilizing process' and its implicit functionalism and evolutionism which are one-sided in the questions raised . . .
>
> Noting this, some observers have wanted to locate figurational sociology clearly in the ranks of the 'social order' and 'social control' sociologies, as presenting leisure as performing 'compensatory' functions (Stedman Jones, 1977). Others also note the figurationists' relative

neglect of countertendencies to the civilizing process (e.g. public displays of sexuality, the 'barbarism' of modern warfare ... and some modern sports) and their tendency to overlook more 'negative' aspects of modern social control (e.g. attacks on privacy, pervasive surveillance ...). It is an 'oversocialized' and 'one-dimensional' conception of the person and society that emerges in Elias and Dunning's work ... In general, there is a neglect of the overall 'hegemonic' and contested functions of sport within a capitalist society (e.g. the role of sport in fostering competitiveness and possessive individualism). Instead, a focus on 'affect-control' and the new domestication of sport holds the centre stage ... (Horne and Jary, 1987 p. 100).

We accept some of the criticisms put forward here but most of them are, in our view, wide of the mark. We accept, for example, that figurational sociologists have so far not examined the relationships between self-control and surveillance in the patterns of social control in societies the members of which, especially of their dominant groups, consider themselves to be 'civilized'. We also accept that figurational sociologists have so far neglected 'the role of sport in fostering competitiveness and possessive individualism'. However, we firmly reject the charges of 'functionalism' and 'latent evolutionism'. This raises complex issues and we cannot hope to deal with them here in the depth and detail they deserve. We shall briefly rebut the charge of 'functionalism' first.

Norbert Elias argued for the retention of the concept of function in sociology because, as he put it:

> ... it is symptomatic of the transition from prescientific to scientific ways of gaining knowledge that the tools of thought people use should slowly cease to be concepts of *action* and become concepts of *function*. A growing recognition of the relative autonomy of a field of investigation as a special kind of functional nexus is a *prerequisite* of the two operations characteristic of scientific procedure. These are the construction of relatively autonomous theories about the relationships between observable details, and the testing of these theories against systematic observations (Elias, 1978 p. 56).

So, for Elias, a concept of function is necessary in sociology because the latter is an emergent science of relationships, more particularly of figurations or interdependency networks as a 'special kind of functional nexus'. No ideas of 'societal needs' or 'functional requirements' are implicit and certainly not explicit here. In fact, Elias developed his concept of function partly in direct opposition to the now largely discredited 'structural functionalism' of writers like Talcott Parsons (1951) and R. K. Merton (1957). What he wrote on this is worth quoting at some length. According to Elias:

The concept of 'function', as it has been used in some sociological and anthropological literature, especially by 'structural-functionalist' theorists, is not only based on an inadequate analysis of the subject matter to which it relates, but also contains an inappropriate value judgment . . . The inappropriateness of the evaluation is due to the fact that they tend —unintentionally—to use the term for those tasks performed by one part of the society which are 'good' for the 'whole', because they contribute to the preservation and integrity of the existing social system. Human activities which either fail or appear to fail to do that are therefore branded as 'dysfunctional'. It is plain that at this point social beliefs have become mixed up in scientific theory . . .

(In figurational sociology, by contrast), the term 'function' is not used as an expression for a task performed within a harmonious 'whole' . . . (L)ike the concept of power, the concept of function must be understood as a concept of a *relationship*. We can only speak of social functions when referring to interdependencies which constrain people to a greater or lesser extent . . . The difficulty in using the concept of function as a quality of a single social unit is simply that it leaves out the reciprocity, the bi-polarity or multi-polarity of all functions. It is impossible to understand the function A performs for B without taking into account the function B performs for A . . .

. . . (W)hen one person (or group of persons) lacks something which another person or group has the power to withhold, the latter has a function for the former. Thus men have a function for women and women for men, parents for children and children for parents. Enemies have a function for each other, because once they have become interdependent they have the power to withhold from each other such elementary requirements as that of preserving their physical and social integrity, and ultimately of survival.

To understand the concept of 'function' in this way demonstrates its connection with power in human relationships (Elias, 1978 pp. 77–78).

It is not our intention to imply through this lengthy quotation that every aspect of Elias's argument is necessarily correct. It is rather to try to show that the attempt by writers such as Horne and Jary to read elements of structural-functionalism into his work involves a distortion of what he actually wrote.

The same, we believe, holds true regarding the charge that elements of 'evolutionism' are inherent in figurational work. It is a charge that is more generally levelled against us (Giddens, 1984; Williams, 1991; Giulianotti, 1999; Armstrong, 1998; Hobbs and Robins, 1991). However, neither Horne and Jary nor any of these other authors specify what is, in their view, wrong with 'evolutionism'. They are also evidently unfamiliar with the work of Stephen Toulmin (1972) and Stephen K. Sanderson (1990) on this score, especially with Toulmin's distinction between 'evolutionist' and 'evolutionary' formulations. Sanderson explains this distinction as follows:

> . . . (T)he philosopher Stephen Toulmin has suggested that social scientists have created enormous confusion for themselves by persistently failing to distinguish between *evolutionist* and *evolutionary* formulations. Toulmin argues that this conflation was especially characteristic of the nineteenth century, but that these separate notions have not been completely disentangled even in contemporary social science. For Toulmin, evolutionist formulations are those that account for long-term social changes 'in some mysterious way, as the "conclusions" of a Cosmic Argument, which unfolds "logical implications" operative throughout the whole History of Society . . .' Evolutionary formulations on the other hand, are those that, like Darwin's account of biological evolution, attempt to explain changes as responses to the particular requirements imbedded in specific historical situations (Sanderson, 1990 p. 3).

If it was not the case that we agree with Elias (1983) on the need to talk of 'social development' rather than 'social evolution' because social developments are reversible whereas social evolution is not, we would accept the argument that our own position might be 'evolutionary' in this sense. We would not, however, speak of 'requirements' being 'imbedded in specific historical situations'. In any case, people who level the 'evolutionist' charge against us, cannot have read *Barbarians, Gentlemen and Players* very carefully because, in the Introduction, introducing the reader to our usage of the concept of stages, we wrote:

> These stages in the development of Rugby were not stages in an 'evolutionary' process in the sense that each was 'immanent in' or grew 'automatically' out of the one preceding it. On the contrary, the transition from one to another was largely determined by the structure and dynamics of the overall social context within which, at any given time, the game was played. Nevertheless, they do represent a 'developmental' order in at least two senses: the first is that the later bear discernible traces of earlier stages, i.e. they contain elements which show that they developed out of the antecedent forms; the second is that the order was necessary, not in the 'strong' sense of being inevitable but in the 'weaker' sense that fully-fledged modern forms of football could not have been born as such into the world but had to develop, as part of a long-term process, out of earlier and structurally more simple forms (Dunning and Sheard, 1979 pp. 3–4).

Apart from the fact that, nowadays, we might strive to inject greater elements of contingency and individual agency into our formulation, this is an argument with which we stick.

Another interesting, insightful and, like that of Horne and Jary, generally constructive critique of our work was provided by social historian, Douglas A. Reid, in his own words 'an historian trained partly in the empirical, partly in the Marxian school . . .' (Reid, 1988 p. 235). It is a critique confined to our examination in Chapter One of *Barbarians, Gentlemen and Players* of folk football and its decline, and it suggests to us the possibility that history may be in some ways a more mature discipline than sociology. We say this because Reid seems to us to be less concerned than some sociologists tend to be with positional, paradigmatic and ideological point-scoring than he is with the complex and difficult task of establishing empirically and theoretically the 'facts of the case'. As sociologists, we have learned a lot from his critique and will endeavour to integrate much of what he writes into our future work.[47] Let us deal with our points of agreement with him.

Although he is exaggerating, we agree with Douglas Reid that our evidence in Chapter One, particularly regarding aristocratic and gentry involvement in folk football, can be described as 'sparse'. We also agree that we 'fail to provide. . . evidence for the eighteenth century' (p. 225), and that we ought to have paid more attention in our explanation to 'the climate of evangelical moral reformism, and to the demand for "rational recreation" ' (p. 231). Indeed, our case would have been strengthened had we conceptualized these latter two as 'civilizing offensives', that is as deliberate (but not necessarily successful) attempts by people who considered themselves to be 'civilized' to 'improve' the manners and morals of people whom they considered to be 'less civilized' or 'barbaric'. The relationship between 'civilizing offensives' and 'civilizing processes', the former being intentional, the latter 'blind', unplanned and, so far in human history, largely uncontrollable, is an interesting, important and, up to now, neglected area of figurational research.

Although our terminology would be different, we also accept that 'one has to take into account the evolution of a political will to suppress popular sport, not simply the means of state coercion'. Reid is also right to draw attention to 'curtailed space', 'limited time' and 'religious sensibilities' (p. 229) as influences on the decline of folk football. In fact, however, most of this was part of our own argument. We wrote:

> This decline was a complex process. One of its aspects probably lay in the effects of industrialization on the time available to 'ordinary' people for participating in this kind of pastimes. According to Malcolmson, the tightening of labour discipline had a similar effect. So, too, he argues, did the declining availability of open space (Dunning and Sheard, 1979 p. 40).

In a word, Douglas Reid uses part of our own case to attack us! He also suggests that we pay too much attention to the period 1780–1850, apparently not realizing that this periodization comes from the work of eminent social historian, Harold Perkin, of whose work we were largely supportive but critical on this point. Thus, we wrote: 'This ("civilizing") change was not confined within the seventy-year period identified by Perkin but formed part of a long-term process which started before 1780 and continued afterwards' (Dunning and Sheard, 1979 p. 40). We should, of course, have written 'after 1850' instead of 'afterwards', a correction we have incorporated into the present text.

Perhaps the most complex issue raised by Douglas Reid's critique relates to the roles of the royal court, the aristocracy and the gentry in the decline of folk football and the development of modern sport more generally. This aspect of Reid's critique runs as follows:

> Dunning and Sheard erroneously minimize changes in aristocratic norms which took place before the late eighteenth century. Certainly, they refer to Dennis Brailsford's 'description of the "civilizing" function of the "courtly movement" ' of the sixteenth century (p. 38), but they do not make clear that football was precisely at issue in this movement. To Sir Thomas Elyot, in his influential book *The Governour* (1531), football was 'nothing but beastly fury and extreme violence'. Instead, Dunning and Sheard dismiss the 'courtly movement' on the grounds that the limited nature of English monarchy in the seventeenth and eighteenth centuries meant that the court failed to act in the manner of French absolutism as a 'civilizing agent' (p.38). It is worth noting that this dismissal of the effects of the sixteenth century 'courtly movement' is *not* based on research into English history, but on Elias's theoretical interpretation of French history. That is to say, it is a deduction from Elias's theory about the French monarchy, masquerading as an explanation of events in England (Reid, 1988 p. 232).

This passage suggests that Douglas Reid has failed fully to grasp the nuances of a complex sociological argument. It is based on two main strands: Elias's comparative study of the developmental trajectories of England, France and Germany (only the first two need concern us here); and the partly evidence-based, partly speculative conclusions that we drew from the ostensible fact that equivalents of the relatively 'advanced' or 'sportized' folk-football-like Cornish game, 'hurling to goales', described by Carew as early as 1602, do not appear to have spread widely through the country at that time. To this, we should have added that, whilst 'sportized' forms of cricket, boxing, horseracing and foxhunting began to emerge early in the eighteenth century, the bulk of the currently available evidence suggests that it was not until the nineteenth century that 'sportized' forms of football began to emerge. We shall deal with these issues one by one.

Pace Douglas Reid, Elias's work on the English 'civilizing process' is not based 'on Elias's theoretical interpretation of French history' but on three pieces of theory-guided research: the *'excursus'* on England, France and Germany referred to above and which appears in *The Civilizing Process*, Volume Two, more specifically on pages 261–268 of the revized single volume edition published in 2000; Elias's (1951) study of the genesis of the naval profession;[48] and his research, some of it undertaken with Eric Dunning, into the early development of modern sport. This research programme led Elias to the conclusion that there emerged in pre-industrial England a social configuration comprising a class of comparatively free peasants, a class of untitled landowners, that is the gentry the topmost ranks of which were rich, a class of titled aristocrats, and a monarchy which was unable to achieve the degree of power and central control (the 'absolutism') of its French counterpart. Prior to industrialization, the landed classes, i.e. the aristocracy and gentry, also remained dominant relative, not only to the peasantry and urban working classes, but also to the commercial and professional bourgeoisie.

This social configuration was one involving lower social distance all round than was the case in France prior to the revolution of 1789. Above all, assuming that our diagnosis is pointing in the right direction it facilitated greater social fluidity, mobility and class interaction than there was in France and formed an important precondition for the fact that England in the seventeenth and eighteenth centuries came to be the principal social locus of the so-called 'scientific', 'industrial' and 'sporting' revolutions. It also meant that members of 'Society' met each other in two principal venues besides the royal court: in parliament during the 'season' and on their country house estates. In this way, the civilizing impact of the court was lessened and England developed earlier than France as a relatively democratic, relatively egalitarian society. It was this, we hypothesized, which facilitated a degree of aristocratic and gentry involvement in the games of the common people. However, Douglas Reid interprets the term 'involvement' in a narrow sense to mean 'direct involvement' or 'playing', whereas we were using it sociologically in a wider sense to mean, not only playing, but providing facilities, encouragement and support, watching, starting, administering and encouragement of any kind. Interpreted in this way, the rate of aristocratic and gentry involvement is shown by Reid's own data to have been higher than he wishes us to believe.

There is much more we could say on this and related issues but, for present purposes, this must suffice as a reply to Douglas Reid. Let us bring this Postscript to a close by briefly discussing one more issue. In our Preface to *Barbarians, Gentlemen and Players*, we wrote that 'sociologists attempt to study people and the societies they form, scientifically, i.e. in a detached, dispassionate or objective frame of mind' (p. vii). This is not adequate as a description of the 'figurational' or 'Eliasian' position and from it we can see part of the reason why Horne, Jary (p. 102) and others (e.g. Hargreaves, 1994) repeatedly accuse us of espousing a crude doctrine of 'value-free' or 'value-neutral' research.

In fact, we follow Norbert Elias (1987) in believing that the only 'value-free' human is a dead one or perhaps a catatonic schizophrenic. Elias's view was considerably more complex than our formulation implied. He argued that our values and involvements are important for the research process because they can provide us with degrees of interest and engagement in, and insider knowledge of, the topics we are researching. However, he also advocated what he called 'a detour *via* detachment' and 'secondary reinvolvement'. The first is used during the research process itself because detachment maximizes our chances of understanding the research object *per se*, whilst in the process of 'secondary reinvolvement', we return to our values in the hope that improved knowledge will increase our chances of securing desirable outcomes that are more in conformity with them. Of course, we might have to change our values as well. Treating them as eternal verities is, we feel, one of the major problems of our field. Steering a path between fixity and fluidity, absolutism and relativism is certainly not easy but it is, we think, something that is necessary when one tries to put sociological findings into practice.

Acknowledgements

We are extremely indebted to Dr. Andy White for permission to use in this Postscript unpublished material gathered by him, but never used, for his PhD thesis; title: *A Sociological History of Gloucester Rugby Football Club: Implications for the Object-Adequacy of Figurational Sociology and neo-Marxian "Hegemony" Theory Explanations of Sports Processes*, University of Leicester, 2000.

Bibliography

D. Andrews, 'Sport and the Masculine Hegemony of the Modern Nation: Welsh Rugby, Culture and Society, 1890–1914' in John Nauright and Timothy J. L. Chandler (eds) *Making Men: Rugby and Masculine Identity* (London, Frank Cass, 1996), pp. 50–69.

G. Armstrong, *Football Hooligans: Knowing the Score* (London, Berg, 1998).

J. Bale and J. Maguire (eds), *The Global Sports Arena: Athletic Talent Migration in an Interdependent World* (London, Cass, 1994).

Z. Bauman, 'The Phenomenon of Norbert Elias', *Sociology*, 13, 1 (1979), 117–125.

P. Bourdieu, *Distinction: a Social Critique of the Judgement of Taste* (London, Routledge and Kegan Paul, 1986).

C. Brookes, *English Cricket: the Game and its Players Through the Ages* (London, Weidenfeld and Nicolson, 1978).

T. Collins, *Rugby's Great Split: Class, Culture and the Origins of Rugby League Football* (London, Frank Cass, 1998).

S. Colwell, 'The Letter and the Spirit: Football Laws and Refereeing in the 21st Century', in J. Garland, D. Malcolm and M. Rowe (eds) *The Future of Football: Challenges for the 21st Century* (London, Frank Cass, 2000), pp. 201–214.

E. Dunning, *Sport Matters: Sociological Studies of Sport, Violence and Civilization* (London, Routledge, 1999).

E. Dunning, D. Malcolm and I. J. Waddington (eds), *Sports Histories* (London, Routledge, 2004).

N. Elias, 'Studies in the Genesis of the Naval Profession', *British Journal of Sociology*, 1, 4 (1950), 291–309.

N. Elias and E. Dunning, 'Dynamics of Sport Groups with Special Reference to Football' in *Quest for Excitement: Sport and Leisure in the Civilizing Process* (Oxford, Basil Blackwell, 1986).

N. Elias, *The Civilizing Process* (revised edition) (Oxford, Basil Blackwell, 2000).

J. Gage, *Rugby's Blazered Buffoons* (Leicestershire, Kairos Press, 1997).

J. Garland, D. Malcolm M. Rowe, (eds), *The Future of Football: Challenges for the 21st Century* (London, Cass, 2000).

W. M. Garraway, A. J. Lee, E. B. A. W. Russell and D. A. D. Macleod, 'Impact of Professionalism on Injuries in Rugby Union', *British Journal of Sports Medicine*, 34 (2000), 348–351.

A. Giddens, *The Constitution of Society* (Cambridge, Polity, 1984).

R. Giulianotti, *Football: a Sociology of the Global Game* (Cambridge, Polity, 1999).

C. Gratton, 'The Peculiar Economics of English Professional Football' in J. Garland, D. Malcolm and M. Rowe (eds), *The Future of Football: Challenges for the 21st Century* (London, Cass, 2000), pp. 11–28.

J. Hargreaves, *Sport, Power and Culture* (Cambridge, Polity 1986).

J. Hargreaves and I. McDonald, 'Cultural Studies and the Sociology of Sport', in J. Coakley and E. Dunning (eds), *Handbook of Sports Studies*, London, Sage, 1986), pp. 48–60.

R. Hobbs and D. Robins, 'The Boy Done Good: Football Violence, Changes and Continuities', *Sociological Review*, 33, 3 (1991), 531–48.

J. Horne and D. Jary, 'The Figurational Sociology of Sport of Elias and Dunning: an Exposition and Critique', *Sport, Leisure and Social Relations* (London, Routledge and Kegan Paul, 1987), pp. 86–112.

S. Jones, *Endless Winter: The Inside Story of the Rugby Revolution* (Edinburgh and London, Mainstream, 1993).

S. Jones, *Midnight Rugby: Triumph and Shambles in the Professional Era* (London, Headline, 2000).

C. Lasch, 'Historical Sociology and the Myth of Maturity: Norbert Elias's "Very Simple Formula"', *Theory and Society*, 14 (1985), 705–20.

J. Maguire, *Global Sport* (Cambridge, Polity, 2000).

D. Malcolm, K. Sheard, and A. White, 'The Changing Structure and Culture of English Rugby Union Football', *Culture, Sport, Society*, 3, 3 (2000), 63–87.

D. Malcolm and K. Sheard, 'Pain in the Assets: The Effects of Commercialization and Professionalization on the Management of Injury in English Rugby Union', *Sociology of Sport Journal*, 19, 2 (2000), 149–169.

I. Malin, *Mud, Blood and Money: English Rugby Goes Professional* (Edinburgh, Mainstream, 1997).

R. K. Merton, *Social Theory and Social Structure* (Glencoe, Ill., Free Press, 1957).

Mintel Survey, 'Spectator Sports', *Leisure Intelligence*, 3 (1989).

O. Nier, and K. Sheard, 'Managing Change: the "Economic", "Social" and "Symbolic" Dimensions of Professionalization in Five Elite European Rugby Clubs', *European Journal for Sports Management*, 6, 2 (1999) 5–33.

T. Parsons, *The Social System* (Glencoe, Ill., Free Press 1951).

H. Perkin, *The Origins of Modern English Society 1780–1880* (London, Hutchinson, 1969).

M. Polley, *Moving the Goalposts: A History of Sport and Society Since 1945* (London, Routledge, 1998).

K. Popper, *The Poverty of Historicism* (London, Routledge and Kegan Paul, 1957).

D.A. Reid, 'Folk-Football, the Aristocracy and Cultural Change: a Critique of Dunning and Sheard', *The International Journal of the History of Sport*, 5, 2 (1988), 224–238.

Report of the Mallaby Committee (RFU, Twickenham, 1974).

Report of the Bishop Commission (RFU, Twickenham, 1994).

B. Rigauer, *Sport and Work* (New York, Columbia University Press, 1981).

H. Risse, *Soziologie des Sports* (Berlin, Reher, 1921).

M. Roderick, I. Waddington and G. Parker 'Playing Hurt: Managing Injuries in English Professional Football, *International Review for the Sociology of Sport*, 35, 2 (2000), 165–180.

C. Rojek, *Capitalism and Leisure Theory* (London, Tavistock, 1985).

S. K. Sanderson, *Social Evolutionism: a Critical History* (Oxford, Blackwell, 1990).

J. J. Sewart, 'The Commodification of Sport', *International Review for the Sociology of Sport*, 22, 3 (1987), 171–190.

K. Sheard, *Rugby Football: A Study in Developmental Sociology* (Unpublished MPhil thesis, University of Leicester, 1972).

K. Sheard, 'The Professionalization Process and English Rugby Union Football', *8th Canadian Congress on Leisure Research* (Ottawa, University of Ottawa Press, 1996), 250–254.

K. Sheard, "Rugby Union" in *The Encyclopaedia of World Sport: From Ancient Times to the Present*, in D. Levinson and K. Christensen (eds), (Santa Barbara, California, ABC-CLIO, 1996), p. 832–844.

K. Sheard, ' "Breakers Ahead!" Professionalization and Rugby Union Football: Lessons from Rugby League', *International Journal of the History Sport*, 14, 1 (1987), 134.

K. Sheard, *Boxing in the Civilizing Process* (Unpublished PhD thesis, Anglia Polytechnic, 1992).

K. Sheard, 'Aspects of Boxing in the Western "Civilizing Process" ', *International Review for the Sociology of Sport*, 32, 1(1997), 31–57.

A. Smith, 'An Oval Ball and a Broken City: Coventry, its People and its Rugby Team', 1995–98, *International Journal of the History of Sport*, 16, 3 (1999), 147–157.

A. Smith, 'Civil War in England: The Clubs, the RFU and the Impact of Professionalism on Rugby Union, 1995–99' in *Amateurs and Professionals in Post-War British Sport*, A. Smith and D. Porter (eds), (London, Frank Cass, 2000), pp. 146–188.

D. Smith, 'Established or Outsider', *Sociological Review*, 32 (1984), 367–89.

D. Smith, and G. Williams, *Fields of Praise: Official History of the Welsh Rugby Union 1881–1981* (WRFU, Cardiff, 1980).

Sports Council, 'Injuries in Sport and Exercise' (London, 1991).

G. Stedman Jones, 'Class Expressions versus Social Control: A Critique of Recent Trends in the Sociology of Leisure', *History Workshop Journal*, 4 (1977), 162–70.

S. Toulmin, *Human Understanding*, Vol 1 (Princeton, Princeton University Press, 1972).

I. Waddington, M. Roderick and G. Parker, *Managing Injuries in Professional Football: The Roles of the Club Doctor and Physiotherapist* (University of Leicester, 1999).

I. Waddington, M. Roderick and R. Naik, 'Methods of Appointment and Qualification of Club Doctors and Physiotherapists in English Professional

Football: Some Problems and Issues', *British Journal of Sport Medicine*, 34 (2000), 48–53.

A. White, 'The Professionalization of Rugby Union Football in England: Crossing the Rubicon' (unpublished MSc. thesis, University of Leicester, 1994).

G. A. Williams, *The Welsh in their History* (London, 1982).

G. A. Williams, *When Was Wales? A History of the Welsh* (London, 1985).

J. Williams, 'Having an Away Day: English Football Spectators and the Hooligan Debate', in J. Williams and S. Wagg (eds), *British Football and Social Change*, (Leicester, Leicester University Press, 1991), p. 160–184.

Notes and References

Series Editor's Foreword

1 Kumar, K. (2003). *The Making of English National Identity*, p. 7. Cambridge: Cambridge University Press.
2 See, especially, Adrian Harvey, *English Football's First Hundred Years: The Untold Story* (forthcoming in the Routledge series Sport in the Global Society in 2005).
3 I recall with special pleasure my first meeting with Eric Dunning at a Leicester University conference on the English Public School in 1974. We enjoyed a late, bibulous evening, during which we mutually lamented the curious myopia of too many academics regarding the value of social anthropological and sociological concepts to historical research, and pledged to do something about it.
4 By chance, as Dunning and Sheard were bringing *Barbarians* to a finish, I was mid-way through writing *Athleticism in the Victorian and Edwardian Public School*, first published by Cambridge University Press in 1981 and in it utilized social anthropological concepts in a discussion of ritual and the games ethic.
5 See *Athleticism in the Victorian and Edwardian Public School*, the Cass edition, 2002, chapter 7, for a consideration of the significance of the public school house system. For a description of public school period anarchic behaviour, see my chapter entitled 'Bullies, Beatings, Battles and Bruises: "great days and jolly days" at one mid-Victorian public school', in M. Huggins and J. A. Mangan, *Disreputable Pleasures: Less Virtuous Victorians at Play*, published in the Routledge series Sport in the Global Society in 2004.
6 Dunning, E. and Sheard, K. (2004). *Barbarians, Gentlemen and Players*. London: Routledge.
7 Ibid., p. 7.
8 Frank Cass responded enthusiastically to the suggestion that *Barbarians* appeared in the series Sport in the Global Society. His part in the republication should not be overlooked.

Preface to the Second Edition

Dunning, E., Maguire, J. A. and Pearton, R. (eds) (1993). *The Sports Process*. Champaign: Human Kinetics.
Gruneau, R. (1983). *Sport, Class and Social Development* (1st Edition). Champaign: Human Kinetics.
Gruneau, R. (1999). *Sport, Class and Social Development* (2nd Edition). Champaign: Human Kinetics.
Maguire, J. and Young, K. (2002). Back to the Future: Thinking sociologically about

sport. In J. Maguire and K. Young (eds), *Theory, Sport and Society* (pp. 1–22). Oxford: Elsevier Press.

Introduction

1 These games are discussed in Morris Marples, *A History of Football*, London, 1954.
2 Norbert Elias, *Über den Prozeß der Zivilisation*, 2 vols, Berne, 1939; 2nd ed., Berne and Munich, 1969. English translation of vol. 1 entitled, *The Civilizing Process: the History of Manners*, New York and Oxford, 1978.
3 David Riesman and Reuel Denney, 'Football in America: A Study in Culture Diffusion', in Riesman's, *Individualism Reconsidered*, Glencoe, Ill., 1954, pp. 242–57; repr. in Eric Dunning, *The Sociology of Sport: A Selection of Readings*, London, 1971, pp. 152–67.
4 According to American mythology, baseball was invented by General Abner Doubleday at Cooperstown, New York, in 1839. It is interesting to note that Rugby, too, is widely supposed to be the invention of a single individual, William Webb Ellis. We subject the Webb Ellis myth to critical scrutiny in Chapter 2. For a searching examination of the Doubleday myth, see Paul Gardner, *Nice Guys Finish Last: Sport and American Life*, London, 1974, pp. 64ff.
5 Johan Huizinga, *Homo Ludens: a Study of the Play Element in Culture*, trans. R. F. C. Hull (after Huizinga's own translation), London, 1949; an extract appears in Dunning, *op. cit.*, pp. 11–16, under the title, 'The Play Element in Contemporary Sport'.
6 Norbert Elias, 'The Genesis of Sport as a Sociological Problem', in Dunning, *op. cit.*, pp. 90, 91.
7 See Norbert Elias, *Was ist Soziologie?*, Munich, 1970. English translation: *What is Sociology?*, London and New York, 1978.
8 Huizinga, *op. cit.*
9 Gregory P. Stone, 'American Sports: Play and Display', in Dunning, *op. cit.*, pp. 47–65; see also his 'Wrestling: The Great American Passion Play', *ibid.*, pp. 301–35.
10 Bero Rigauer, *Sport und Arbeit*, Frankfurt, 1969.
11 Huizinga, in Dunning, *op. cit.*, pp. 223–4.
12 Stone, in Dunning, *op. cit.*, pp. 53–4.
13 Rigauer, *op. cit.*, p. 7.
14 It is not, of course, a question of interdependence simply between players and spectators but among *all* the personnel involved, e.g. players, spectators, managers, coaches, trainers, club officials, representatives of sports associations, pressmen, the police, etc.
15 This is less true of Stone than of Huizinga and Rigauer. Even he, however, does not structurally locate the conflicts and tensions which, as he remarks, accompanied the professionalization of sports in the United States. Instead, he attributes them to Protestant 'dualism', that is to a generalized ideology. But he does not attempt to relate this ideology to a structural base.
16 This is not entirely true. Amateur Rugby League has spread southwards in recent years where it is played, among other contexts, in some universities. However, it has not spread far enough or become sufficiently firmly established seriously to contradict the validity of this statement.
17 Emile Durkheim, *The Rules of Sociological Method*, London, 1964, p. 79.
18 Emile Durkheim, *The Elementary Forms of the Religious Life*, London, 1976, p. 95.
19 For a discussion of this issue, see Norbert Elias, 'The Sciences: Towards a Theory', in R. M. Whitley (ed.), *Social Processes in Science*, London, 1974, pp. 21–42.

Chapter 1

1 See, e.g., Geoffrey Green, *The History of the Football Association*, London, 1953, p. 6; also Peter McIntosh, *Sport in Society*, London, 1963, p. 29.

2 See, e.g. William Andrews, *Old Church Lore*, London, 1891, p. 11; quoted in M. Marples, *A History of Football*, London, 1954, p. 2. See also U. A. Titley and R. McWhirter, *Centenary History of the Rugby Football Union*, London, 1970, pp. 19 and 20.

3 See, e.g., Marples, *op. cit.*, pp. 6 and 7; and Percy M. Young, *A History of British Football*, London, 1968, p. 3.

4 See W. B. Johnson, 'Football: A Survival of Magic', *Contemporary Review*, CXXXV, 1919, pp. 225–31; discussed in Marples, *op. cit.*, pp. 11ff.

5 These references are discussed extensively in Marples, *op. cit.*, and Young, *op. cit.*; see also F. P. Magoun, *A History of British Football from the Beginnings to 1871*, Cologne, 1938.

6 Quoted in Magoun, *op. cit.*, p. 33. The fact that such prohibitions were not unique to Britain but enacted in continental countries, too, is established by Marples (*op. cit.*, p. 25). It is less well-known, at least on the eastern side of the Atlantic, that they were also enacted in colonial America. For example, the following order was promulgated in Boston in 1657: 'For as much as sundry complaints are made that several persons have received hurt by boyes and young men playing at foot-ball in the streets; these are therefore to Injoyne that none be found at that game in any of the Streets, Lanes and Inclosures of this Town, under the penalty of twenty shillings for every such offense' (quoted in Gardner, *Nice Guys Finish Last*, p. 96).

7 *Certayne Collection of Anchiante Times, concerninge the Anchiante and Famous Cittie of Chester*, published by D. Lysons in his *Magna Britannia*, London, 1810, p. 585.

8 C. H. Cooper, *Annals of Cambridge*, Cambridge, 1843, p. 71.

9 Johan Huizinga, *Herbst des Mittelalters*, Munich, 1924 (published in English as *The Waning of the Middle Ages*).

10 C. W. Farrer, *The Marblers of Purbeck*, papers read before the Purbeck Society (1859–60), pp. 192–7.

11 See, e.g. Christina Hole, *English Sports and Pastimes*, London, 1949.

12 Sir Richard Carew, *The Survey of Cornwall*, London, 1602, pp. 75–6.

13 Sir George Owen, *The Description of Pembrokeshire*, 1603, H. Owen (ed.), Cymmrodorion Soc. Res. Ser. no. 1, 1892, pp. 270–82.

14 *Oswestry Observer*, 2 March 1887, quoted in G. L. Gomme, *The Village Community*, London, 1890, and Hole, *op. cit.*, pp. 51–2.

15 See Reinhard Bendix, *Max Weber: an Intellectual Portrait*, London, 1960, p. 298.

16 Richard Mulcaster, *Positions wherein those Primitive Circumstances be examined which are necessarie for the Training up of Children*, 1561, R. H. Quick (ed.), London, 1881, pp. 105–6. Mulcaster was Headmaster of the Merchant Taylors' School from 1561 to 1586, and High Master of St Paul's School from 1596 to 1608.

17 *The Letters of Monsieur Cesar de Saussure to his Family*, London, June 1928; Mm. von Muyden, London, 1902, Letter xii, pp. 294–5. Quoted in Young, *op. cit.*, p. 54.

18 Young, *op. cit.*, p. 24.

19 *ibid.*, p. 37.

20 Montague Shearman, *Athletics and Football*, London, 1887, p. 263.

21 Dennis Brailsford, *Sport and Society: Elizabeth to Anne*, London, 1969, p. 83.

22 See Elias, *op. cit.*, for an illuminating discussion of this issue. See also his *Die Höfische Gesellschaft*, Neuwied and Berlin, 1969.

23 Peter Laslett, *The World We Have Lost*, London, 1965, p. 41.

24 Joseph Strutt, *The Sports and Pastimes of the People of England*, London, 1801, p. 168.

25 Robert W. Malcolmson, *Popular Recreations in English Society, 1700–1850*, Cambridge, 1973, pp. 99 and 109.
26 Harold Perkin, *The Origins of Modern English Society, 1780–1880*, London, 1969, p. 280.
27 Edward Moor, *Suffolk Words and Phrases*, London, 1823, p. 66.
28 Marples, *op. cit.*, p. 106.
29 Thomas Carlyle, *Chartism*, 1839, quoted in Perkin, *op cit.*, p. 182.
30 Quoted in Perkin, *op. cit.*, p. 183.
31 Anon., *Reminiscences of Eton*, Chichester, 1831, p. 47.
32 Quoted in Magoun, *op. cit.*, pp. 123–4; and Marples, *op. cit.*, p. 100.
33 Marples, *op. cit.*, p. 101.
34 *ibid.*, pp. 102–4.
35 *ibid.*, p. 100.
36 James Walvin, *The People's Game*, London, 1975, p. 180.
37 *ibid.*, pp. 20–1.
38 Philip Stubbes, *The Anatomie of Abuses*, 1583; F. J. Furnivall (ed.), New Shakespeare Soc., ser. VI, no. 6, 1879, I,p. 137.

Chapter 2

1 David Newsome, *Godliness and Good Learning*, London, 1961, p. 86.
2 G. W. Fisher, *Annals of Shrewsbury School*, London, 1899, p. 313.
3 J. B. Oldham, *A History of Shrewsbury School*, London, 1852, p. 231.
4 Foundation Deed of Winchester College, 20 October 1382, in A. F. Leach (ed.), *Educational Charters and Documents*, London, 1911, p. 325.
5 V. Ogilvie, *The English Public School*, pp. 24–5.
6 They tended, in any case, to come from relatively low social backgrounds. Thus, John Foster, appointed to the Eton headship in 1765, was the son of a tradesman. His successor, Jonathan Davies, appointed in 1788, was the son of a barber. See, e.g., Christopher Hollis, *Eton*, London, 1960, p. 159.
7 E. C. Mack, *Public Schools and British Opinion, (1780–1860)*, London, 1938, p. 80.
8 *ibid.*, p. 81.
9 *ibid.*, p. 80.
10 *loc. cit.*
11 *loc. cit.*
12 H. C. Adams, *Wykehamica: A History of Winchester College and Commoners*, London, 1878 pp. 143–51.
13 Quoted in W.H.D. Rouse, *A History of Rugby School*, London, 1898, pp. 182–5.
14 G. T. Keppel, Earl of Albemarle, *Fifty Years of My Life*, New York, 1876, p. 26.
15 Quoted by Bernard Darwin in *The English Public School*, London, 1929, p. 47.
16 Quoted in Hollis, *op. cit.*, p. 196.
17 Matthew Bloxam, *Meteor*, no. 157, 1880 (*Meteor* is the name of the school magazine at Rugby). See also *The Origins of Rugby Football* (pamphlet), The Old Rugbeian Society, Rugby, 1897.
18 Captain F. Markham, *Recollections of a Town Boy at Westminster*, London, 1903, pp. 92–5.
19 E. P. Eardley-Wilmot and E. C. Streatfield, *Charterhouse Old and New*, London, 1895, pp. 74–6.
20 G. S. Davies, *Charterhouse in London*, London, 1922, p. 295.
21 Quoted in A. H. Tod, *Charterhouse*, London, 1900, p. 154.
22 Anon., 'Rugby Football in the Sixties', *Cornhill Magazine*, Nov. 1922, pp. 571–81.
23 Adams, *op. cit.*, pp. 366–7.
24 Oldham, *op. cit.*, p. 231.
25 Wasy Sterry, *Annals of Eton College*, London, 1898, p. 325.

26 A. Gibson and W. Pickford, *Association Football and the Men Who Made It*, London, 1906, vol. 2, p. 25.

27 Oldham, *op. cit.*, pp. 231–8.

28 Davies, *op. cit.*, p. 294.

29 Bloxam's version of the Webb Ellis myth appeared in *Meteor*, no. 157, 1880, i.e. in the edition of the Rugby school magazine referred to in Note 17.

30 i.e. *The Origins of Rugby Football*, referred to in Note 17.

31 See, e.g., T. W. Bamford, *The Rise of the Public Schools*, London, 1967, p. 77.

Chapter 3

1 We are using the concept of *embourgeoisement* in a wider sense than is currently fashionable. Thus, according to present usage, it refers to the assimilation of the working into the middle class. As we are using it, however, it refers to the gradual emergence of the bourgeoisie as the ruling class, to their growing control of major institutions, and to the consequent spread of their values through society. That is, in our usage, it is not simply the working class which experiences *embourgeoisement* but society as a whole. It is, therefore, as meaningful to talk of the *embourgeoisement* of the aristocracy and gentry as of the working class.

2 See, e.g., W. O. Aydelotte, 'The Business Interests of the Gentry in the Parliament of 1841–47', included as an appendix to G. Kitson Clark, *The Making of Victorian England*, London, 1962.

3 See, e.g., Asa Briggs, 'Thomas Hughes and the Public Schools', in his *Victorian People*, Harmondsworth, 1965, pp. 148ff.

4 This section of our analysis is based largely on the discussion in Mack, *op. cit.*

5 Ogilvie, *op. cit.*, p. 129.

6 Perkin, *op. cit.*, p. 298.

7 Ogilvie, *op. cit.*, p. 144.

8 Mack, *op. cit.*, p. 239.

9 *loc. cit.*

10 Newsome, *op. cit.*, p. 38.

11 The boys came near to open revolt in 1833 when Arnold, after a complaint from a local landowner, expelled six boys for fishing in the Avon. However, the prefects closest to Arnold persuaded the others not to rebel. See T. W. Bamford, *Thomas Arnold*, London, 1960, pp. 72–3. As we shall show, this near-revolt was connected with the anti-aristocratic character of Arnold's reforms.

12 Quoted in A. P. Stanley, *The Life and Correspondence of Thomas Arnold*, London, 1858, vol. II, p. 324.

13 Bamford, *op. cit.*, ch. 6.

14 Arthur Reynolds (ed.), *Dean Stanley's Life of Dr. Arnold*, London, 1903, p. 66.

15 These percentages were worked out from the figures in T. W. Bamford, 'Public Schools and Social Class, 1801–50', *British Journal of Sociology*, XII, no. 3, Sept. 1961, p. 225.

16 Alicia Percival, *Very Superior Men*, London, 1973, p. 121.

17 Anna Merivale, *Family Memorials*, London, 1884, p. 330.

18 Quoted in J. R. de S. Honey, *The Victorian Public School, 1828–1902: The School as a Community*, unpublished D.Phil. thesis, Oxford, 1969, pp. 20–1.

19 Lytton Strachey, *Eminent Victorians*, London, 1934, p. 207.

20 'Athletics', *Encyclopedia Britannica*, 1967, p. 681.

21 N. Wymer, *Dr. Arnold of Rugby*, London, 1953, p. 119.

22 *loc. cit.*

23 Thomas Arnold, *Introductory Lectures on Modern History*, London, 1874, pp. 16–17.

24 Theodore Walrond, *Dictionary of National Biography*, vol. II, London, 1885, p. 115.

25 C. R. Evers, *Rugby*, London, 1939, p. 52.

26 Wymer, *op. cit.*, p. 45.

27 Thomas Hughes, *Tom Brown's Schooldays*, Harmondsworth, 1971, p. 103.

28 Rouse, *op. cit.*, pp. 238–40.

Chapter 4

1 See C. C. P. Brookes, *Cricket as a Vocation: A Study of the Development and Contemporary Structure of the Occupation and Career Patterns of the Cricketer*, unpublished Ph.D. dissertation, University of Leicester, 1974.

2 Reported in 'Martello Tower', *At School and at Sea*, London, 1899, p. 25; quoted in Honey, *op. cit.*, p. 230.

3 Support for this hypothesis can be found in E. M. Goulbourn (ed.), *The Book of Rugby School*, Rugby, 1856, p. 59.

4 Arnold's essay was first published, in pamphlet form, in 1851. It was reprinted in Goulbourn, *op. cit.*, pp. 147–69.

5 Bloxam, *loc. cit.*

6 Hughes, *op. cit.*, pp. 83–4.

7 *ibid.*, p. 89.

8 *ibid.*, p. 90.

9 *ibid.*, pp. 90–1; our italics.

10 Marples, *op. cit.*, p. 116.

11 An Old Rugbeian, *Recollections of Rugby*, London, 1848, pp. 131–2.

12 H. C. Bradby, *Rugby School*, London, 1900, p. 197.

13 *ibid.*, p. 192; see also Rouse, *op. cit.*, p. 321.

14 Rouse, *op. cit.*, p. 322.

15 *loc. cit.*

16 Hughes, *op. cit.*, p. 87.

17 Rouse, *op. cit.*, p. 246.

18 W. D. Arnold in Goulbourn, *op. cit.*, p. 151. Goulbourn was the successor to A. C. Tait as Rugby headmaster. Tait, in turn, had succeeded Thomas Arnold.

19 *ibid.*, p. 338.

20 See, e.g., Marples, *op. cit.*, p. 137; and Titley and McWhirter, *op. cit.*, p. 27. A copy of the 1845 rules can be found in the library at Rugby School. To our knowledge, Frances J. Woodward is the only author so far to have written on this subject to be aware of their existence. See her *The Doctor's Disciples*, London, 1954, p. 183.

21 Woodward, *loc. cit.*

22 *The New Rugbeian*, vol. III, 1860; quoted in Evers, *op. cit.*, pp. 177–9.

23 This date was given to us in 1961 by Sir Robert Birley, then Head Master of Eton.

24 Oldham, *op. cit.*, p. 231.

25 This date was given to us in 1961 by J. D. Carleton, then Head Master of Westminster.

26 This date was given to us in 1961 by R. H. Crawford, then Master in charge of football at Charterhouse.

27 J. R. Witty, 'Early Codes', in A. H. Fabian and Geoffrey Green (eds.), *Association Football*, 4 vols., London, 1960, vol. I, pp. 140–2.

Chapter 5

1 The games cult involved four main changes in the public schools: (i) a tendency to promote and appoint staff in terms of sporting rather than academic criteria; (ii) the selection of prefects on the basis of ability at sport; (iii) the elevation of sport to a prominent, in some cases, pre-eminent, position in the curriculum; and (iv) participation by members of staff in the organization and playing of

their pupils' games. For a useful analysis of the games cult, see Marples, *op. cit.*, ch. X.

2 *ibid.*, p. 138. Such schools were formed as an aspect of the continuing expansion of the middle class.
3 Honey, *op. cit.*, pp. 246a ff.
4 Marples, *op. cit.*, p. 138.
5 Quoted in Honey, *op. cit.*, p. 230.
6 *loc. cit.*
7 Quoted in Ogilvie, *op. cit.*, p. 169.
8 Quoted by Peter McIntosh in his 'The British Attitude to Sport', in Alex Natan (ed.), *Sport and Society*, London, 1958, p. 18.
9 Quoted in Ogilvie, *loc. cit.*
10 Oldham, *op. cit.*, p. 232.
11 Green, *op. cit.*, p. 15.
12 *ibid.*, pp. 15 and 16.
13 *ibid.*, pp. 16 and 17.
14 *ibid.*, pp. 18 and 38.
15 *ibid.*, p. 16.
16 *ibid.*, p. 18.
17 *ibid.*, p. 38.
18 Our data on Sheffield FC were obtained from Young, *op. cit.*, pp. 76–8.
19 *ibid.*, p. 77.
20 *ibid.*, p. 84. According to the Harrow School Register, J. F. Alcock became a merchant and shipowner. C. W. Alcock became a solicitor.
21 *loc. cit.*
22 *ibid.*, p. 90.
23 Our discussion of these meetings is based on that in Green, *op. cit.*, pp. 19–33.
24 *ibid.*, p. 27.
25 *ibid.*, p. 28.
26 *ibid.*, p. 32.
27 *ibid.*, p. 26.
28 *ibid.*, pp. 28–9.
29 *loc. cit.*
30 *loc. cit.*
31 *loc. cit.*
32 *ibid.*, p. 44.
33 Titley and McWhirter, *op. cit.*, p. 75.
34 Marples, *op. cit.*, p. 147.
35 *loc. cit.*
36 Titley and McWhirter, *op. cit.*, p. 66.
37 Marples, *loc. cit.*
38 An Old Rugbeian, 'Rugby Football in the '60's', *op. cit.*, pp. 579–80.
39 *The Times*, 27 Nov. 1869.
40 *The Times*, 30 Nov. 1869.
41 Titley and McWhirter, *op. cit.*, p. 69.
42 Quoted in Marples, *op. cit.*, p. 144.
43 Quoted in Rouse, *op. cit.*, p. 292.
44 Quoted in Marples, *op. cit.*, pp. 144–5.
45 An Old Rugbeian, *op. cit.*, p. 577.
46 *loc. cit.*
47 *The Times*, 23 Nov. 1870.
48 *The Times*, 26 Nov. 1870.
49 *The Times*, 28 Nov. 1870.
50 *The Times*, 30 Nov. 1870.

51 *loc. cit.*
52 *The Times*, 2 Dec. 1870.
53 *Punch*, vol. LIX, Dec. 1870, p. 252.
54 *Punch*, vol. LX, Jan. 1871, p. 19.
55 Marples, *op. cit.*, p. 153.
56 *ibid.*, p. 154.
57 O. L. Owen, *The History of the Rugby Football Union*, London, 1955, p. 60.
58 They can be found in Owen, *op. cit.*, pp. 66–72.
59 Titley and McWhirter, *op. cit.*, pp. 79–80.
60 Percy Royds, *The History of the Laws of Rugby Football*, Twickenham, 1949, p. 1. The allowable dimensions of the Rugby pitch were not subject to written specification until 1879.
61 Rouse, *op. cit.*, pp. 325–6. It was in that year that the school adopted Rugby Union rules.
62 C. J. B. Marriot, *The Rugby Game and How to Play It*, London, 1922, p. 15.
63 R. W. Irvine, 'International Football: Scotland', in Rev. F. Marshall, (ed.), *Football: The Rugby Union Game*, London, 1892, p. 202.
64 Montague Shearman, *Football*, London, 1889, pp. 33–4.
65 In this period, according to Arthur Budd, 'to put one's head down in a scrummage was regarded as an act of high treason' (quoted in Marples, *op. cit.*, p. 155).
66 *loc. cit.*
67 Thorstein Veblen, *Imperial Germany and the Industrial Revolution*, New York, 1915.

Chapter 6

1   J. R. Jones, *An Encyclopaedia of Rugby Football*, London, 1960, p. 90.
2   Marshall, *op. cit.*, p. 390.
3   These data were obtained from T. T. Heywood, *New Annals of Rochdale*, Rochdale, 1931, p. 201, and Duncan and Mills, *Rochdale and District Commercial Directory*, Rochdale, 1891.
4   Our data on these clubs were obtained from L. R. Tosswill's revised edition of Marshall's, *Football: the Rugby Union Game*, London, 1925.
5   *ibid.*, p. 418.
6   White's *Directory of Halifax*, 1899.
7   Marshall, *op. cit.*, p. 421.
8   Kelly's *Directory of Hull*, 1899.
9   Marshall, *loc. cit.*
10 *loc. cit.*
11 Kelly's *Directory of Hull*, 1899.
12 G. Nicholson, *The Professionals*, London, 1964, p. 65.
13 R. Brook, *The Story of Huddersfield*, London, 1968, p. 264.
14 See S. G. Checkland, *The Rise of Industrial Society in England, 1815–1885*, London, 1964, pp. 248–9.
15 See Geoffrey Best, *Mid-Victorian Britain, 1851–75*, London, 1971, p. 209.
16 Walvin, *op. cit.*, p. 53.
17 Checkland, *op. cit.*, p. 363.
18 Walvin, *op. cit.*, pp. 56–7; see also Marples, *op. cit.*, p. 167, and Young, *op. cit.*, pp. 111–2.
19 Walvin, *op. cit.*, p. 61.
20 Charles P. Korr, 'Working Class Football in London: the Founding of the West Ham United Football Club', *Occasional Papers of the Centre for International Studies*, University of Missouri, St Louis, no. 761.
21 Marples, *op. cit.*, p. 179.
22 Marshall, *op. cit.*, pp. 375ff.

23 *ibid.*, pp. 421ff.
24 David Riesman, *The Lonely Crowd*, New York, 1953.

Chapter 7

1 We use this term in order to convey a growing reliance on money and money values. We could have used the more obvious term 'commercialization' but avoided it since there is little evidence of use of the game, in a direct sense, for private profit.
2 'Metropolitan Football', by 'A Londoner', Marshall, *op. cit.*, pp. 323 and 330.
3 Titley and McWhirter, *op. cit.*, p. 186.
4 Marshall, *op. cit.*, p. 329.
5 *ibid.*, p. 330.
6 *Wakefield Express*, Sat. 11 March 1893.
7 *Liverpool Daily Post*, Wed. 2 Jan. 1895.
8 *Liverpool Daily Post*, 23 Jan. 1895.
9 *Liverpool Daily Post*, 11 Jan. 1895.
10 They played for Nottinghamshire.
11 Marshall, *op. cit.*, pp. 499–503.
12 Titley and McWhirter, *op. cit.*, Biog. section, part II.
13 See, e.g., Alec Waugh, *The Loom of Youth*, London, 1917.
14 Rupert Wilkinson, *The Prefects*, London, 1964, p. 33.
15 Ivor Brown, 'The Best Game to Watch', in H. Marshall (ed.), *Rugger Stories*, London, 1932, pp. 158–60.
16 M. Shearman, *Athletics and Football*, London, 1887, pp. 330–1.
17 *The Football Annual*, 1881, p. 108.
18 *The Football Annual*, 1882, p. 78.
19 *loc. cit.*
20 H. H. Almond, 'Football as a Moral Agent', *Nineteenth Century*, Dec. 1893, pp. 909–10.
21 E. K. Ensor, 'The Football Madness', *Contemporary Review*, Nov. 1898, pp. 751–60.
22 *loc. cit.*
23 Titley and McWhirter, *op. cit.*, Biog. section, part I.
24 Marshall, *op. cit.*, pp. 131–8.
25 Shearman, *op. cit.*, p. 175.
26 *loc. cit.*
27 C. Edwardes, 'The New Football Mania', *Nineteenth Century*, vol. 32, 1892, pp. 622–31.
28 H. H. Almond, 'Football as a Moral Agent', *op. cit.*, p. 909.
29 Ensor, *op. cit.*, p. 758.
30 H. H. Almond, 'Rugby Football in the Scottish Schools', in Marshall, *op. cit.*, p. 62.
31 Shearman, *op. cit.*, pp. 274–5. He was alluding to the fact that the first professional soccer players are reputed to have been Scots.
32 C. Norwood, *The English Tradition of Education*, London, 1929, p. 106.
33 Quoted in Marples, *op. cit.*, p. 173.
34 Edwardes, *loc. cit.*
35 Quoted in Marples, *op. cit.*, p. 173.
36 Ensor, *loc. cit.*

Chapter 8

1 Marshall, *op. cit.*, pp. 416–7.
2 G. F. Berney, 'Progress of the Rugby Football Union from Season 1892–3 to the

Present Time', in L. R. Tosswill's updated edition of Marshall, *op. cit.*, London, 1925, p. 57.

3 O. L. Owen, *op. cit.*, p. 97.
4 Titley and McWhirter, *op. cit.*, Biog. section, part I.
5 Berney, *op. cit.*, p. 59.
6 Titley and McWhirter, *op. cit.*, p. 113.
7 O. L. Owen, *loc. cit.*
8 Berney, *op. cit.*, p. 62.
9 O. L. Owen, *op. cit.*, p. 98.
10 *The Times*, 20 Sept. 1895.
11 See, e.g., Berney, *op. cit.*, p. 62.
12 *Wakefield Express*, 25 Nov. 1893.
13 *Yorkshire Post*, 30 Aug. 1895.
14 *Leeds Daily News*, 28 Aug. 1895.
15 *Yorkshire Post*, 28th August, 1895.

Chapter 9

1 Thus, although cricket is a non-contact sport, opportunities for social contamination as great as those inherent in contact sports such as soccer and Rugby arise, for example, in the changing room. Moreover, even though Rugby and soccer have a more fluid division of labour than cricket, the example of public school football in the early nineteenth century shows that invidious distinctions can easily be used as a means of role-allocation in such games.
2 Early in the eighteenth century, before the dominance of the aristocracy and gentry was complete, there was some bourgeois criticism of their cricketing activities, especially their gambling. This is discussed in Brookes, *op. cit.*
3 Anon., 'Chaos in Cricket', *Belgravia*, Aug. 1890.
4 C. E. Green, in W. A. Bettesworth (ed.), *Chats on the Cricket Field*, London, 1910, p. 183.
5 These figures were obtained from Brookes, *op. cit.*, p. 364.
6 Marples, *op. cit.*, p. 171.
7 *ibid.*, p. 172.
8 *ibid.*, p. 177.
9 G. W. Keeton, *The Football Revolution*, Newton Abbot, 1972, p. 16.
10 Walvin, *op. cit.*, p. 83.
11 *ibid.*, p. 84.
12 Green, *op. cit.*, p. 592.
13 *ibid.*, p. 96.
14 *ibid.*, p. 97.
15 *loc. cit.*
16 *ibid.*, pp. 102–3.
17 *ibid.*, p. 101.
18 *ibid.*, p. 104.
19 *ibid.*, p. 103.
20 *ibid.*, p. 105.
21 *ibid.*, p. 194.
22 According to Green, Jackson and Marindin were only 'lukewarm' in their attitude towards professionalism (*op. cit.*, p. 101). Indeed, Jackson later became an outright opponent, proposing in 1896 the division of the FA into separate amateur and professional sections (*ibid.*, p. 157).
23 *ibid.*, p. 105.
24 It is important to bear in mind that, in the late nineteenth century, soccer and not Rugby was the game of the highest-status schools. The status relativities of the

two games only began to change as the social process at present under analysis gathered momentum.

25 E. J. Hobsbawm, *Industry and Empire*, London, 1968, p. 170.
26 Perkin, *op. cit.*, p. 435.
27 *ibid.*, p. 430.
28 *ibid.*, pp. 431–2.
29 *ibid.*, p. 453.
30 See, e.g., David Thomson, *England in the Nineteenth Century*, Harmondsworth, 1950, p. 187.
31 *Manchester Guardian*, 30 Nov. 1884.
32 These developments are discussed in Green, *op. cit.*, see esp. pp. 426ff.
33 E. J. Hobsbawm, *Labouring Men*, London, 1864, pp. 336–7.

Chapter 10

1 The term 'Northern Union' was retained until 1922 when the ruling body of the breakaway game changed its name to 'Rugby Football League'. However, the latter name came into informal usage prior to that date.
2 'Tawd Vale', 'The Malaise of Rugby League', *The Rugby Leaguer*, 31 Jan. 1969, p. 3.
3 Frederick Wall, *Fifty Years of Football*, London, 1935, pp. 119–20.
4 Nicholson, *op. cit.*, p. 15.
5 Newspaper cutting dated Saturday, 5 Sept. 1896. We found it in a scrapbook compiled by H. H. Waller, one of the founders of the Northern Union. It is now the property of the Rugby League and kept at their headquarters in Leeds.
6 Newspaper cutting dated Wednesday, 28 Aug. 1895; from Waller, *op. cit.*
7 Keith Macklin, *The History of Rugby League Football*, London, 1962, p. 20.
8 *Yorkshire Post*, 25 Jan. 1896.
9 Macklin, *op. cit.*
10 The minutes from which these two examples were taken are available in pamphlet form at the headquarters of the Rugby League.
11 Macklin, *op. cit.*, p. 18.
12 *ibid.*, p. 23.
13 *ibid.*, p. 35.
14 *ibid.*, p. 32.
15 H. H. Almond, '*Football as a Moral Agent*', *op. cit.*, p. 910.
16 H. H. Almond, *The Field*, Oct. 1896; incl. in Waller, *op. cit.*
17 Taylor, in Dunning, *op. cit.*, p. 359.
18 'Stands Rugby Football Where It Did?' *Yorkshire Daily Post*, 22 April 1896.
19 Circular, dated 23 March 1896, in Waller, *op. cit.*
20 Newspaper cutting, dated 23 March 1896, in Waller, *op. cit.*
21 *Yorkshire Daily Post*, 22 April 1896.
22 *Bradford Observer*, 28 Aug. 1896.
23 Minutes of the Northern Union General Committee for 9 Aug. 1910.
24 These figures were published in *The Wakefield Express*, on 8 April 1893.
25 *ibid.*, pp. 24–5.
26 *loc. cit.*
27 W. J. Morgan and G. Nicholson, *Report on Rugby*, London, 1959, p. 78.
28 J. R. Jones, *op. cit.*, p. 21.
29 *The People*, 24 Sept. 1967.
30 *The People*, 9 Feb. 1969.
31 This statement only applies to Britain. It has spread abroad, most notably to Australia, France and New Zealand.
32 See, e.g., Colin-Welland, 'The Trouble with Rugby League . . . Live T.V.', *Sunday Times*, 7 May 1972.

33 The *Guardian*, 10 Sept. 1975. At the same time, the John Player Company backed the RFU's national knock-out competition to the tune of £100,000. The fact that it was willing to sponsor Rugby Union by such an amount—i.e. by more than four times the sum injected into Rugby League—is indicative of the greater crowd-drawing power, and therefore advertising potential, of the ostensibly amateur game.

Chapter 11

1 O. L. Owen, *op. cit.*, p. 98.
2 It has also spread internationally, principally to the 'white' dominions of the former British empire, i.e. Australia, New Zealand, South Africa and, to a lesser extent, Canada. In addition, it has spread to such diverse countries as France, Fiji, Rumania, Russia, Poland, Czechoslovakia, Yugoslavia, Italy, Germany, Holland, Argentina, the United States and Japan. Indeed, Michael Green estimates that there are now more Rugby clubs in the USA than in Wales and as many in Japan as in England ('Out of the Scrum and Into the Limelight', *Daily Telegraph Magazine*, 31 Jan. 1975, pp. 14–19).
3 *ibid.*, p. 17.
4 Questionnaires were sent to 630 players and officials and replies were received from 327, a response rate of 52 per cent.
5 *Public Schools Commission, First Report*, vol. I: Report, HMSO, London, 1968, p. 24.
6 It is worthy of note that, in 1925, the secretary and assistant secretary began to receive, on top of their salaries, remuneration in kind. Thus, for the former, a house adjoining Twickenham was purchased. For the latter, one was built on the ground itself. (Owen, *op. cit.*, p. 131.)
7 *Report of the Mallaby Committee*, Twickenham, Feb. 1974, pp. 8 and 9.
8 O. L. Owen, *op. cit.*, p. 277.
9 *ibid.*, p. 278.
10 The list of gate-taking clubs was supplied to us by J. S. Marsh, Hon. Secretary to the Association of Gate-Taking Clubs, founded in 1969. Except where specified otherwise, the information regarding ground capacities, gate-receipts, etc., was furnished by the secretaries of the respective clubs.
11 Titley and McWhirter, *op. cit.*, p. 175.
12 The *Observer*, 1 Sept. 1968.
13 The *Guardian*, 15 March 1972.
14 Green, *loc. cit.*
15 These figures were supplied by the secretaries of the clubs. We are grateful to them but must add that, in some cases, they appear to be a rough approximation.
16 Green, *loc. cit.*
17 O. L. Owen, *op. cit.*, p. 274.
18 *ibid.*, p. 281.
19 *Report of the Mallaby Committee*, p. 12.
20 Titley and McWhirter, *op. cit.*, p. 172.
21 *Guardian*, 5 Jan. 1974.
22 *Guardian*, 5 Sept. 1975.
23 Howard Marshall in H. B. T. Wakelam (ed.), *The Game Goes On*, London, 1954, p. 73.
24 *Sunday Telegraph*, 19 Nov. 1972.
25 *The Observer*, 23 Mar. 1969.
26 Wakelam, *op. cit.*, p. 154.
27 *ibid.*, p. 73.
28 *ibid.*, p. 160.

29 *ibid.*, p. 162.
30 *Daily Express*, 18 Nov. 1972.
31 Quoted by David Hunn in the *Observer Magazine*, 19 Jan. 1975.
32 Green, *op. cit.*, p. 17.
33 *Guardian*, 3 May 1972.
34 Hunn, *op. cit.*
35 *loc. cit.*
36 *The Observer*, 7 May 1972.
37 *The Guardian*, 7 Feb. 1973.
38 *Mallaby Report*, p. 51.
39 *Mallaby Report*, p. 40.
40 *The Sunday Times*, 20 April 1975.
41 *Guardian*, 12 July 1975.
42 Christopher Brasher, *Mexico 1968: A Diary of the XIXth Olympiad*, London, 1968, p. 4.

Conclusion

1 Kurt Weis, 'Aggression, Violence, and Sports', paper delivered at the International Congress of Physical Activity Sciences, July 1976, Quebec.
2 Similar considerations apply, of course, to Rugby League.
3 Ulick O'Connor, 'The Case for the Prosecution', *Sunday Times*, 12 February 1978.
4 For a discussion of this concept, see Norbert Elias and Eric Dunning, 'The Quest for Excitement in Leisure', *Society and Leisure*, 2 (1969), pp. 58–85; repr. in G. Lüschen (ed.), *The Cross-Cultural Analysis of Sport and Games*, Illinois, 1970.
5 This concept is discussed in Elias, *Was ist Soziologie?* pp. 72ff., 92ff.
6 Emile Durkheim, *The Division of Labour in Society*, New York, 1964, pp. 257ff.
7 Elias, *loc. cit.*
8 See, e.g., E. E. Evans-Pritchard, *The Nuer*, Oxford, 1940.
9 Durkheim, *op. cit.*, pp. 185ff.

Afterword

1 The 'figurational' or 'process-sociological' perspective was pioneered by the late Norbert Elias (1897–1990). The first systematic application of this perspective to the subject of sport can be found in N. Elias and E. Dunning (1986), *Quest for Excitement: Sport and Leisure in the Civilizing Process*. See also E. Dunning and C. Rojek, (eds), *Sport and Leisure in the Civilizing Process: Critique and Counter-Critique*; E. Dunning (1999) *Sport Matters: Sociological Studies of Sport, Violence and Civilization* (1999); and E. Dunning, D. Malcolm and I. Waddington (eds), *Sports Histories* (2004).
2 We had striven to keep our use of jargon to a minimum but Nicholson took particular exception to the sentence: 'At an attitudinal level, achievement-orientation is increasing, manifested in victory-striving as the ultimate short-term goal' (p.233). Most academics, we feel, especially sociologists and psychologists, would regard this as an example of technical language of an acceptable kind.
3 White came across these figures reproduced in *The Gloucester Citizen*, Wednesday April 5, 1893.
4 Personal communication.
5 For an insightful and original study of sport and globalization, see Joseph A. Maguire (1999), *Global Sport: Identities, Societies, Civilizations*, Cambridge, Polity.
6 Although in September 2002 the RFU announced further development plans to 'complete' the rebuilding of the stadium by building a new South Stand at an estimated cost of £80 million.

7 This is not true in the Irish Republic, of course. The Gaelic Athletic Association owns Croke Park in Dublin, the major venue for GAA sports.

8 For players up to the age of 16, Rugby Union sides are organized into yearly age groups. After this, and to bridge the gap between junior and adult rugby, players from 16 to 18 years of age play together in a 'Colts' side.

9 As recently as 2000, the historian, Adrian Smith, felt able to write that '. . . concern that the RFU and all the other ruling bodies had sold their souls to Rupert Murdoch obscured the fact that well over 95 percent of clubs in the British Isles remain wholly amateur' (Smith, 179, 2000). Such an assertion is simply not sociologically tenable. Most junior clubs in Britain ceased to be amateur in 1995, if not before. Many players are openly paid for training and playing, others are accorded generous travelling expenses. Free beer is often provided, too. The majority of players – if they are wise – continue to pay the club subscriptions which allow them to benefit from club accident insurance policies but 1st XV players seldom pay the traditional match fees. This means they are subsidized by lower team players, who still pay them. Kit is now provided – shirts, socks, shorts – and laundered by the club, free of charge. Physiotherapy is often subsidized by the club. Few clubs can survive on membership subscriptions and bar receipts alone, and many charge a small entrance fee and/ or for programmes. All rely heavily on individual, commercial and industrial sponsorships and advertising. Much of the money thus generated is expended on meeting club running costs, but it also goes towards attracting and keeping key players.

10 Wigan also took part in, and won, Rugby Union's annual Middlesex 7-a-side competition, also held at Twickenham.

11 Following similar negotiations in Australia, Rupert Murdoch's News International media group (which includes BSkyB) offered to inject £77 million (later raised to £87 million) into a restructured European Rugby League programme. Super League, as it was to be called, was to involve teams from Paris and London, and – although it was vehemently denied that News International had insisted on these – the enforced merger of a number of clubs. Also to be involved was a switch from 1996 onwards towards playing in the summer. Whilst the mergers were initially rejected, some moves towards them have since taken place.

12 Managerial ideologies have become dominant or 'hegemonic' in Britain since the 1980s even though they are not, for the most part, based on demonstrable knowledge.

13 In the summer of 1997 the top two divisions of the national League were reconstituted as the Allied Dunbar Premiership Leagues One and Two. The Jewson National League One became the new name for the old Courage League Division Three, and the Jewson National League Two (North and South) the equivalent of the old Division Four (North and South).

14 In March 1999, 'a disillusioned and embittered' Sir John Hall relinquished his 76% controlling interest in the Newcastle club. His total losses were thought to be in the region of £9 million. See Smith (1999): 150.

15 Warren's financial difficulties, stemming from his dispute with boxing promoter Don King, meant that he had to withdraw support from Bedford in 1999, causing many of the club's better players to leave in the close season.

16 *Sunday Telegraph*, October 3, 1997.

17 Bristol, too, was to experience difficulties. Relegated to the 2nd Division at the end of the 1997/98 season, in July 1998 they called in the official receiver. By August 15, however, they had a new owner, Malcolm Pearce, and declared themselves solvent again. In an effort to secure 1st Division status for the 1999/2000 season, Bristol initiated a failed buyout attempt of London Scottish. Although

Bristol were to regain Premiership status they were relegated to Division 1 for the 2003–4 season.

18 Bale and Maguire, (eds) (1994), pp. 1–21.

19 Dunning and Sheard (1979), p. 252)

20 *Ibid.*, p. 253.

21 Elias and Dunning (1986), pp. 191–204.

22 Dunning and Sheard (1979), p. 249.

23 When the FA Carling Premier League agreed to the televising of matches on BSkyB, the deal involved the rescheduling of some games to Sundays and Mondays. In a more severe example, Barry McGuigan attributed the loss of his World Featherweight title to his being forced to box in the heat of the Las Vegas sun in order to meet the requirements of American television.

24 Mintel Survey 1989 'Spectator Sports', *Leisure Intelligence*, Vol. 3.

25 According to *Injuries in Sport and Exercise* (1991) there are 59.3 injuries per 100 participants per four weeks in rugby. Next in the list is soccer with 39.3 injuries, followed by martial arts (36.3), hockey (24.8) and cricket (20.2).

26 B. Rigauer (1981); J.J. Sewart (1987, pp. 171–190); Dunning (1999, pp. 106–129).

27 See, I. Waddington, M. Roderick and G. Parker (1999).

28 C. Gratton (2000).

29 However, in September 2003, the RFU announced that it had paid off the final instalment of its £38 m four-year loan on the redevelopment of Twickenham. The final repayment of £19m ensured that Twickenham is now debt-free with net cash balances of £23m (*Guardian*, September 2, 2003). There remain the ambitious plans referred to in note 6.

30 The England tour to Australia in the summer of 1998 was a particularly clear example of this. With so many players withdrawing from the tour, England were forced to field what many considered to be almost a second team. As a result, they suffered their heaviest ever defeat, losing to the Australians, 76–0 (*Electronic Telegraph*, 7 June, 1998)

31 To give some idea of the actual figures involved, the three year sponsorship of Rugby Union's top two divisions, Premierships One and Two, cost Allied Dunbar £7.5 million From this pot of money, Premiership One clubs received £500,000 each in 1997/98.

32 The more players play, the more money they earn but the greater is the risk of injury or decline in performance through staleness. Their position in the power relations of the overall figuration is dependent on such variables as their ability, their athleticism, their age, the demand for their services and, together with their estimation of it, will obviously influence the degree of control they have over the decisions they take. The degree to which players are unified relative to the degrees of unification of other groups in the overall 'rugby figuration' is another important variable in this connection.

33 The *Guardian*, 5 December, 1996.

34 The *Guardian*, 5 May, 1998. See also Smith (1999, p. 150).

35 The *Guardian*, 22 March, 1999.

36 London Scottish withdrew from professional rugby and are now working their way back up the Leagues, playing in London League in 2004–05.

37 A recent survey of the doctors and physiotherapists employed by professional football clubs in England and Wales has indicated that the qualification standards and appointment procedures used are relatively poor. See, I. Waddington *et al.* (1999).

38 The Rhino or Gilbert 'Neoprene' headgear was approved by the RFU for the 1996/97 season and shoulder pads, made of soft, thin material, were allowed to be incorporated in an undergarment provided that it is no thicker than 1 centimetre

when uncompressed [Law 4, 1998]. Information supplied by Rex King *via* the RFU website, http://www.rfu.com.

39 Similarly, with the introduction of padded gloves, the hands of boxers were better protected and they were able to deliver harder punches more frequently, thus increasing the damage – including the brain damage – to their opponents (Sheard, 1992; 1997).

40 For a discussion of the similar problems faced by soccer referees, see S. Colwell (2000).

41 In the Netherlands, the main proponents of a figurational approach to the sociology of sport are Ruud Stokvis and Maarten Van Bottenburg; in France, it is Alain Garrigou of the University of Paris, X, Nanterre; in Canada, Kevin Young of the University of Calgary has endeavoured to introduce elements of figurational thinking into his work but Michael Atkinson of Memorial University is the most full-blown Canadian exponent of a figurational approach; in Brazil it is Ademir Gebara of the University of Campinas; in Germany, the main figurational sociologist of sport is Michael Krüger of the University of Münster, though Bero Rigauer has attempted to wed a figurational perspective with a Marxist one. In the Far East, the chief figures in this regard are Koichi Kiku and Akira Ohira of Japan and Kwang-Leong Han of South Korea.

42 Christopher Brookes, author of *English Cricket: the Game and its Players Through the Ages* (London, Weidenfeld and Nicolson, 1978) could perhaps be included as well. Although he barely acknowledges it, the book is based on a Leicester PhD thesis supervized by Eric Dunning.

43 For a lengthier discussion of this, see Dunning (1999) pp. 106–129.

44 Horne and Jary have used here the idea of a dichotomy between 'true violence' and 'mock fights'. Figurational sociologists think in this connection in terms of a continuum, that between 'serious violence' and 'mock' or 'play violence'.

45 As far as we are aware, the term 'sociology of sport' was first used by Heinz Risse, a student of Theodor Adorno, one of the founders of 'the Frankfurt School', in 1921. Risse wrote a book, entitled: *Soziologie des Sports*, Berlin, Reher.

46 In our view, Norbert Elias and Eric Dunning made a mistake in not engaging more with Marxist contributions to the sociology of sport in *Quest for Excitement*.

47 This will be done in *The Making of Football: A Sociological History of the Peoples' Game* on which Eric Dunning and Graham Curry are currently working. We envisage it as a kind of soccer equivalent to *Barbarians, Gentlemen and Players*.

48 Norbert Elias (1950), 'Studies in the Genesis of the Naval Profession', *British Journal of Sociology*, 1 (4): 291–309. René Moeller is currently engaged in reconstructing for publication the book on this subject which Elias planned but never completed.

Index

Page numbers in **bold** represent **figures**. Page numbers in *italics* represent *tables*.